TAMARA'S CHILD

TAMARA'S CHILD

a novel

❥

B K Mayo

Fiona,

*Thanks for a great
book design!
I hope you enjoy
the story.*

Bob Mayo
10/26/09

FIR VALLEY PRESS

Library of Congress Control Number: 2009905452

ISBN 978-0-9815884-7-6

Book design by Fiona Raven

First Printing January 2010
Printed in the United States of America

Published by Fir Valley Press
P.O. Box 337
Winchester, Oregon 97495

www.firvalleypress.com

For my daughters, LeeAnn and Shelley,
with love

Acknowledgments

I WANT TO THANK the early readers of this novel—Marilyn Jenkins, Maxine Mattox, Sunny May, Becky Maier, and Melva Stultz, among others—whose feedback not only provided encouragement but also brought about changes that made the story better. Sunny and Becky also for reviewing the medical aspects of the novel. And Marilyn for being an unflagging cheerleader for the novel and an advocate for its publication.

Thanks also to Carol Craig, whose editorial guidance was invaluable throughout the revision process for this novel. Likewise, a well-deserved nod of appreciation to Arlene Prunkl, whose proofreading corrections amounted to a final edit.

Finally, I owe a huge debt of gratitude to my wife, Karen, for her continual review of the manuscript as it progressed through its various stages of development, and for her never wavering support of me as a writer.

PART ONE

~

Tamara Ames

Spring–Fall, 1979

1 TAMARA HELD BACK her tears as she marched away from Angela's house. Behind her, Angela cowered on the front steps mouthing "I'm so sorry" repeatedly, while Angela's dad bellowed from inside, "I don't care! That girl is trash, and I won't have her trashing our daughter's life too!"

It wasn't until she was blocks away that Tamara broke down—slumped to the pavement behind the ARCO, shoulders shuddering, mucus streaming from her nose, her tissues buried somewhere in her backpack. She wiped her nose on the sleeve of her T-shirt. *Now what am I supposed to do?* She cradled her middle and sobbed uncontrollably.

She'd been naïve to think that the baby would change things for the better. That the baby—as she'd convinced herself after getting over the initial shock of her pregnancy—would be the bridge that reconnected the broken relationships in her life. How wrong she'd been! Had she really expected shallow waters to suddenly run deep? Withered flowers to bloom? That her messed-up life would be magically transformed into a fairy tale?

Yes, she'd set herself up for a great fall. Wishes come true only for those who have the power to make them come true. But what made it

all so unbearable now was the knowledge that it was those she loved—
and who were supposed to love her back—who had failed her the most.
Jimmy. Her mother. Angela. No, not Angela.

The look on Jimmy's face when she'd told him about the baby
should have told her all she needed to know. It was on the eve of her
sixteenth birthday. They'd gone to the Denny's by the freeway, not to
celebrate but because Jimmy was supposed to meet a guy at the Motel 6
next door, "to do some business," he'd said. They sat in a booth with a
window that looked out onto the street. While they were waiting for
their food to arrive, she gave him the news, her voice quavering with
each word. Jimmy jerked his head toward the window, but she could
see the dark look of annoyance reflecting off the glass. "Tamara," he
said to the window—maybe he could see her reflection in the glass
too—"can't you do anything right?" He got up and strode out of the
restaurant like a cowboy walking off into the sunset.

She'd put off telling her mother after that, her confidence in her
mother's reaction shaken even as her own commitment to bearing this
child and giving it all the love it deserved became the guiding principle
in her life. But she could only delay so long, because soon she would
begin to show.

So one afternoon upon arriving home from school, Tamara blurted
out the news to her mother and held her breath. Her mother was in
the laundry room folding clothes from a basket and stacking them on
the wobbly table next to the washing machine. "Land sakes, girl," she
said, going on with her work as if the revelation was as notable as a
weather report predicting rain. "Don't you think I know that?" She
pulled a pair of jeans out of the basket and shook out the legs. "You'll
have to move out when the baby comes, of course. Having a wee one
around the house wouldn't be good for my nerves."

Tamara had braced herself against the clothes dryer, feeling as
if she'd been stabbed through the heart. Could it really be that her
mother was so damaged by tragedy that she had truly lost her capacity for love?

Reeling from her mother's rejection, Tamara hadn't waited for the
baby to come before leaving the house. Six months into her pregnancy,

she moved in with her best friend, Angela Ramos, whose family lived in a rambling two-story house on West Broadway that seemed to get bigger, according to Mrs. Ramos, every time one of the kids moved out. Besides a younger brother, Angela had an older brother and an older sister, both of whom had already left home. Mr. Ramos was a long-haul trucker and was gone on a run the day Tamara came to the house with only the clothes she was wearing and a bulging backpack. "You sure Mr. Ramos won't mind me staying here for a while?" Tamara asked Angela's mom. Mrs. Ramos winked at her. "I'll take care of Mr. Ramos," she said with a suggestive dip of her shoulder.

Tamara dug through her backpack and came out with a wad of Kleenex. She blew her nose, hiccupped as she tried to stem the flow of tears.

Mr. Ramos, it turned out, was not so easily taken care of. He'd come home late the previous evening with a case of hemorrhoids and a disposition to match. When, this morning at breakfast, he'd found out that Tamara—whose belly by now had ballooned beyond conceal-ment—was living there, he'd ordered her out of the house, banished her from the premises as rudely as if she was a dog that had peed on the carpet. Mrs. Ramos had issued cries of protest but had made no move to intervene.

Tamara sniffled, squared her shoulders. At least she hadn't allowed Mr. Ramos the satisfaction of seeing her cry.

But now what? She hadn't a clue as to what her next move should be.

She peered up at the heavens. Dark clouds were piling up in the sky like heaps of soiled linen. It was going to be another cool, wet spring day. On the street in front of the ARCO, cars were beginning to clog the traffic lanes. The morning commute was in full swing.

A rattling sound caught Tamara's attention. She looked over to see a woman with a red-leather face and dirt-caked spikes of hair come around the corner of the gas station pushing a grocery cart. The cart was overflowing with junk—cans, bottles, wadded garments, a coffee pot with no lid. The woman wore several layers of smudged clothing that hung on her like rags on a stick. Tamara stiffened as the woman

hobbled past, reeking of garbage and stale beer. The woman thumped her
cart against a big metal trash bin, tipped up its lid, and leaned inside.

Tamara scrambled to her feet. She scurried around to the front of
the ARCO, her mind suddenly clear and her resolve set. She would
do whatever she had to do to survive—to see to it that her child was
taken care of and loved in a way that she was not. And to do that she
needed to get away from this town and the people in it. The city of
Eugene held nothing for her now except more heartache. She paused
at the street corner long enough to get her bearings, then, shouldering
her backpack, hurried off toward the freeway.

She was huffing when she finally got there, her legs rubbery, her
skin moist and prickly. She shrugged out of her backpack and let it slide
down her arm to the ground. She raked her fingers through her sweat-
dampened hair, swiped moisture from her eyes with the back of her
hand. On the other side of the railing, vehicles on the interstate whisked
by in both directions, trailing exhaust fumes like phantom tails.

Tamara didn't know where she was going—that didn't matter. What
mattered was that she was going there to make a new and better life for
herself and her child. Others may have turned their backs on her, but
she would never forsake the beautiful being growing inside her. She
hugged her swollen belly. "It's you and me, sweetie," she murmured.
"All we've got is each other." She drew a shuddering breath, beat back
a surge of self-doubt.

When, moments later, a big blue car came chugging up the onramp,
Tamara stood tall and thrust out her thumb.

2   "I CAN TAKE YOU as far as Fir Valley," the old lady said.
She was propped up on a fat cushion like a toddler on a
booster seat. Even so, her head barely stuck up above the rim of the
steering wheel that she clung to with liver-spotted hands as she guided
the big blue car down the freeway, staying in the cradle between two
trucks. "Know anyone there?"

Tamara gazed out the window at the wooded hills whizzing by in a green blur and pondered the old lady's question. She didn't think she knew anyone in Fir Valley, not at first anyway. Then she remembered— and along with the memory came an extra thump in her chest. "My stepbrother," she said, frowning at the foul aftertaste the words left in her mouth.

Tamara had never been to Gary's house. Didn't know his address. Had only heard her mother mention to someone that he lived in Fir Valley, "in the old part of town, down by the river."

The old lady's eyes lit up as if Tamara's assertion had ignited a bon-fire in her brain. "I had a stepbrother. When he died, my sister-in-law collected a tidy sum from the life insurance policy she'd purchased just months before. Ti—ming," she said, her voice rising on the first syllable of the word and falling on the last. "You know what they say about timing." And she prattled on about that and a whole lot more before they reached their destination.

The old lady dropped Tamara off in the parking lot of a motel on Main Street in downtown Fir Valley shortly after ten o'clock in the morning. The sky had brightened during the drive down from Eugene, but Tamara's mood had not. She was tired, hungry, and alone in some Podunk town whose buildings looked as forlorn as she felt and whose air was so sooty you could taste it. The source of the soot was unmistak-able—the great plumes of brown smoke roiling out of twin stacks that punctuated the skyline like giant exclamation points. The smoke settled like valley fog in the bowl of land in which the town sat. Only the big homes situated on the high ground above the city escaped the haze.

Tamara sighed, put the stacks and the motel to her back as she headed down the sidewalk along Main Street. Her legs felt weighted, as if filled with sand, so that each step required a focused effort. She plodded along cheerlessly past a succession of dreary storefronts—a second-hand clothing store, a Greyhound bus station with no bus in sight, a hole-in-the-wall café belching the odor of burnt grease from its open doorway. In the next block, several scruffy-looking men stood outside the entrance to the Fir Valley Rescue Mission smoking, their jittery movements indicating a need greater than nicotine. Tamara jaywalked to the other side of the street, earning a horn blast from a truck driver who apparently resented having to touch his brakes.

She flapped a hand at the exhaust fumes and trudged on, trying not to think about the burning in her belly. Her stomach was in constant turmoil these days whether she ate anything or not. And then there were those annoying eruptions down low in her abdomen, like bubbles bursting inside her—to say nothing of the ever-present pressure on her bladder.

Where Main Street crossed Central Avenue, there was a Texaco station on the corner with a mini-mart attached. Feeling the need to relieve herself, Tamara used the restroom inside the mini-mart and, on her way out, bought a bag of Cheetos and a pint of chocolate milk from the meager funds in her purse. She sat down on a bench outside the mini-mart to eat her two-course breakfast.

A car pulled up to the gas pumps. The woman driving rolled her window down and said something to the man wearing the star. The attendant nodded, grasped a pump nozzle. The woman swiveled around in her seat, reached over the seatback, and hoisted a baby from a car seat in the rear. The baby bounced up and down on its mother's lap, cooing happily.

Tamara looked away, stung suddenly by the bleakness of her circumstances. She had escaped Eugene, but now what? What did Fir Valley have to offer that Eugene didn't? The critical questions still remained: Where would she stay? How would she live? How could she take care of herself, much less her child? She needed a plan, but she didn't even know how to begin laying one out. For all the resources at her disposal, she might as well have been dumped naked on the moon.

She thought again about her stepbrother Gary. She hadn't seen him since his father had died the year before. Gary hadn't come to the funeral, had just shown up at his dad's house in Eugene a few days later.

"What do *you* want?" Tamara's mom had inquired as soon as he'd come through the front door. Tamara was sitting with her mother on the sofa in the living room. They were going through a box of papers looking for a life insurance policy Darryl had claimed to have but, as it turned out, didn't.

"Daddy promised me his guns," Gary had said.

"They're in the bedroom closet," Tamara's mother told him. "Get them and get out."

"Hey, little sister, you've grown up," Gary said to Tamara as he strutted past. The look he gave her had made her skin crawl.

She hadn't laid eyes on Gary since that day and was glad of it. But here she was in Fir Valley where he lived, and who else could she turn to? No one, she thought, and the realization hit her like a punch to the gut. Minutes later, she was still trying to catch her breath.

Mounted on the wall on the other side of the entrance to the minimart, sheltered by a Plexiglas hood, was a pay phone and, beneath it, a phone book dangling from a short cable. Tamara deliberated for a long while before finally getting up and going over to the phone book. With a wetted finger, she flicked through its pages looking for a listing under the name "Neaves, Gary." She shivered when she found the entry. She let the phone book slip from her grasp, turned, and called out to the man wearing the star. "Where's Cedar Street?"

"Down there," he called back, pointing like a cavalry scout down Central Avenue. "Toward the river."

Feeling sick to her stomach, Tamara sat back down on the bench to rethink her options.

EVEN IN THIS NEIGHBORHOOD of dilapidated homes, the house at 726 Cedar Street distinguished itself as especially shabby, with cracked and peeling exterior paint, curled roof shingles heavy with moss, dangling rain gutters, and a front porch that tilted like a ski slope toward the cracked walkway leading to it. Highlighting this eyesore, like an X drawn on a map at the site of some disaster, a big crosshatch of tape had been applied to the home's front-facing picture window, apparently to keep the fractured glass from falling out. Outside the window was a weed-infested scab of ground that served as a front yard. In the driveway stood a faded red pickup, butted against the rusted-out hull of another vehicle.

Tamara quickened her pace as she reached the walkway leading to Gary's house, because she knew that if she hesitated even in the slightest she'd find herself retreating from this place. The loose boards on the front steps squawked at her ascent. She crossed the porch and, fighting off an urge to back away, knocked on the splintered wooden frame of the screen door. When there was no response, she knocked again, this time harder.

Abruptly the inner door swung open, causing a drag on the outside air that snatched at her breath. And there he was, looking just as she'd remembered him—tall, angular, rough-hewn, with his blue jeans shiny from wear, his faded T-shirt rendered sleeveless, and his pointy cowboy boots scuffed she was sure more from deliberate contact than from normal use. His fiery red beard had grown out full and frizzy. His oily hair was slicked back on the sides, and his deep-set gray eyes looked out at her through the ripped screen without the slightest hint of recognition. Maybe it wasn't too late to turn and run. She was about to do just that when she observed a flicker in his otherwise lifeless gaze.

He cocked his head. "Little sister," he said, his face breaking out in that lopsided grin of his, "you done got yourself knocked up." He uttered the remark with a light-heartedness that disarmed her, as if he was merely commenting on a new pair of shoes she was wearing or a new hairstyle. She wasn't sure what she'd expected of him, knew only that a part of her was hoping he would simply slam the door in her face. Instead, he pressed the screen door open with his thick hand and, stepping aside, by this gesture if nothing else, invited her in.

She moved past him into the house, surprised to find her eyelids squeezing out tears. She was relieved to have a place to stay, but she also knew Gary. He was just like his dad: a little good wrapped around a lot of bad.

3   TAMARA SAT CROSS-LEGGED on the jiggly little bed in Gary's spare room, leafing through the *Parenting* magazine she'd lifted a few days earlier from the mini-mart and doing her best to ignore the clamor coming from the other side of the wall. Gary

and his buddies were at it again in the front room, behaving with all the couth of the braying jackasses they turned into whenever they were drinking, which was just about any time they were around. They'd started early today with their version of a poker party—part card game, part dirty-jokefest, part belching contest. They'd hauled the dinette table and chairs from the kitchen into the middle of the living room, driving Tamara into her bedroom even before the sun had gone down.

She tossed the magazine aside and flopped back onto the bed. It was more of a cot, really—a narrow, metal-framed platform with open springs that supported a thin, musty-smelling mattress topped with threadbare sheets and a lime-green coverlet dappled with cigarette burns. "It's where Jerome sleeps when he's too drunk to go home," Gary had informed her that first day. She had no idea then who Jerome was, but when her head hit the pillow that night, she'd easily detected the odor of his alcohol-induced sweat.

She stared up at a cluster of cobwebs dangling from the ceiling and let out a sigh. She'd been with Gary three weeks now, but her circumstances hadn't improved much. She had a roof over her head, but little else. And in some ways she felt more vulnerable than ever. There was something about Gary that gave her the creeps, like distant howls at midnight. And Gary's drinking buddies, Brian and Jerome, were always hanging around, like spare personalities.

Jerome was the worst. He was a colossal oaf who leered at her stupidly as if she was the prize at a carnival game booth. He had a megaphone voice and drove a big, noisy truck. He always laughed at Gary's dumb jokes and jumped when Gary told him to. He looked more like an oversized boy than a man, with his pudgy cheeks, flabby arms, and plump butt stuffed into a pair of jeans two sizes too small. Most of the time, Brian would go home early because his wife would call or because he needed to get some sleep before going off to work the night shift at the mill. But Jerome never seemed to have anywhere else to be. He would stay until Gary said, "Go home, Jerome," then, looking like a chastened child, he'd plunk down his beer can and leave. Tamara was better off staying in her room whenever Gary had company.

She groaned, rolled onto her side, the baby having decided it was time to do its tumbling act inside her. A regular little acrobat, this one—and she was the tumbling mat. She lay still and waited for the performance to end.

It wasn't only being around Gary and his friends that undermined Tamara's sense of well-being. It was the unsavoriness of the life she'd fallen into. During those first days at Gary's house she'd tried just to stay out of his way, which hadn't been difficult since Gary came and went from the house frequently, at all hours, with seemingly little, if any, notice of her presence. When he was home, he would spend most of his time slouched in a big, smelly armchair in the living room, chain-smoking and drinking beer. The TV would be on and blaring, but if he watched the screen at all it was with glimpses that ricocheted about like a deflected gunshot.

The one thing Gary never seemed to do at home was eat. "If you want something to eat," he'd told her, "you'll have to scrounge for it yourself. This ain't no bed and breakfast." That was just before he drove off in his truck to meet his friends for a meal at some local café.

While he was away, Tamara had gone into the kitchen and rummaged through his cupboards and his fridge. She'd found a couple of unlabeled food cans in one cabinet, a partial loaf of bread growing mold in another, and a refrigerator crammed with six-packs of Coors. She'd gone to bed that night with her stomach rumbling. Ever since, scrabbling for food had been her main preoccupation. She could go without eating for days at a time if she had to, but that wasn't good for the baby. Anybody with any sense knew that.

By her third day at Gary's, Tamara had already consumed every edible morsel in the house. To stave off hunger a while longer, she'd used what little money she had to buy milk, bread, and peanut butter from the mini-mart at Central and Main. And when that was gone, she'd resorted to other means to survive.

She sat up in bed, hung her head, feeling dragged down by life, as if her prospects were like a stone sinking beneath the surface of a pond.

Regardless of her situation, she hated having to steal. Stealing was one of those *Thou shalt nots* she'd learned about as a little girl attending church with her grandmother. But what was she supposed to do? Without money, pilfering was the only way she knew to get food and other necessities for herself and her baby, and the Texaco mini-mart had proven to be an easy target. The lone clerk on duty was usually behind the front counter, ringing up sales, restocking the cigarette shelf, or giving someone directions. While out for the walk that had become part of her daily routine, Tamara would make a point of stopping at the store. She'd use the bathroom in the back, then on her way out pinch a tube of toothpaste, a bottle of vitamins, or an Oscar Mayer snack pack, which she would quickly tuck up under the tail of her T-shirt.

But how long could she continue providing for herself in this way? At some point, she was bound to get caught. What would happen to her then—and to her baby? She shuddered as her mind flashed on jail scenes from the old movies she'd been watching on Gary's TV.

No, she couldn't go on living this way. But as much as she wanted to make a new plan for her life, she couldn't seem to come up with one. She'd tried to envision herself getting a job, her own apartment, daycare for the baby when it came. Then reality would set in: she was sixteen years old, as big as a blimp, and as prepared for employment as a Barbie doll.

But the longer she was with Gary, the more anxious she became to change her circumstances. Because during moments such as this, trapped inside the closet of her mind, she had the awful feeling that coming to live with Gary was like having checked into a hotel without the means to pay the bill at stay's end.

Tamara's stomach gurgled, reminding her just how long she'd been cooped up in this dreary room. She slid out of bed, got to her feet. She grabbed her hairbrush off the dresser and began raking it through the tangles in her hair. The antique dresser was the only other piece of furniture in the room. It had club feet, but one foot was missing and had been replaced by a brick not quite as thick as the foot. The dresser listed forward and to the side, as did the mirror mounted along its back edge. The mirror had lost most of its reflective capacity so that looking into it was like peering into a dense fog. Gazing into the mirror now, Tamara felt an urge to smash it.

She gave her hair a few more rough brushstrokes, then slapped the brush down on the dresser. On the other side of the wall, the merrymaking continued unabated. Gary and his devoted band of revelers were just getting warmed up.

Tamara pulled her shoes on over her swollen feet, tied the laces loosely. After a quick stop in the bathroom, she ventured down the hall toward the loud voices in the living room. The room was veiled in tobacco smoke so thick it resembled a steam bath. She held her breath while passing through. As she was going out the front door, someone behind her belched loudly.

It was dusk when Tamara rounded the corner at the end of the block and headed up Central Avenue, hunger pains, like lashes from a whip, driving her forward. Following a route that by now was like a familiar face to her, she crossed over the railroad tracks and entered the shabby Fir Valley business district. The buildings along the street were cloaked at this hour in varying shades of gray, as if all the color in the world had bled into the ground. An exception was the lighted Texaco sign at Central and Main, which shone red and white against the dying sky.

Tamara didn't need to go to the bathroom, but she stuck with her routine. She entered the mini-mart and went straight to the back where the restroom was located. A few minutes later, she came out and glanced casually about. The clerk was at the front counter, dealing with customers. A couple of other patrons milled about surveying the shelves. Tamara entered an unoccupied aisle.

Partway up the aisle, without coming to a stop, she reached out and with a light touch—as if merely checking for dust—palmed a couple sticks of beef jerky from an open bin. She was slipping the packages under her shirt when she heard a voice behind her boom, "You! Stop!"

The words hit her like a blow to the back that renders one breathless. She staggered forward. *Run!* screamed a voice in her head. But before she could engage her body in the endeavor, she was ensnared in a flurry of action. From behind her came a quick shuffling of feet, followed by the din of cans and bottles crashing to the floor. The ruckus paralyzed her momentarily. She recovered and was about to dash for the door when something—or someone—rammed into her from behind. The collision knocked her off her feet. Her vision blurred. She lurched sideways out of control. Flashes of color and light came rushing at her. Then her head met something solid and everything went dark.

4   WHEN SHE CAME TO, Tamara was lying on her back on the floor with some padding under her head. A man with a thick neck and a shoulder patch on his white shirt was kneeling next to her. He was pressing something cold against her forehead, which felt as if it had been split open with an axe. All around her on the tile floor, like rubble from an earthquake, were strewn packaged goods from the store shelves. Confused, she made a move to sit up. A flaming arrow of pain shot through her left rib cage.

"Stay down," the paramedic said. "You've taken quite a hit."

Tamara let her body sag back to the floor, prompted less by the man's words than by the dizziness she felt. From where she lay, she could see one end of the front counter. A man in a brown uniform, with a gun in a hip holster and a baton dangling from his belt, was standing mostly with his back to her, talking to the store clerk.

The paramedic lifted the cold pack and leaned in closer. Tamara felt a trickle of blood run down the side of her face. She glanced down and saw more blood dotting the floor and reddish smears on several packages. And everything went black again.

WHEN SHE ROUSED a second time, Tamara found herself strapped down on a gurney that was being loaded into the back of an ambulance. Some kind of mask was over her nose and mouth. The thick-necked paramedic climbed inside with her. The rear doors of the vehicle slammed shut.

As if coming from afar, a mournful drone repeated itself overhead. The cityscape visible through the back window of the ambulance pulsed with a red glow, so that Tamara imagined herself gazing into the interior of a beating heart. "My baby?" she uttered through the mask, her voice coming back at her weak and muffled. "Is my baby okay?"

"Ah, you've rejoined us," the paramedic said, and squeezed her hand. She squeezed back reflexively even as she felt herself drifting off again.

"ONE, TWO, THREE," someone said, and Tamara was lifted off the gurney and onto a chrome-framed bed, itself on wheels. At the head of the bed was a cramped arrangement of standing equipment—boxes with knobs and dials and tubes, one sprouting wires with clips at the end. And enclosing all this—the bed and machines—a ring of curtains. The thick-necked paramedic leaned over her and displayed his dimples. "You're in good hands," he said, and disappeared outside the curtains.

Tamara's mind felt numb. She glanced around, trying to make sense of her surroundings.

"How you doing, young lady?"

A woman in a baggy green smock appeared alongside the bed bearing a clipboard and a clinical gaze. She was thirtyish, brunette, busty, and pretty in spite of having on little makeup and wearing her hair clasped back at the temples like a kindergartener.

Tamara wasn't sure how she was doing. But feeling exposed in a way she didn't understand, she was reluctant to say so. "How do you think?"

The ER nurse hung the clipboard from a hook on the bed frame. "I'd say from the size of that lump on your noggin, you just might have a headache." She swept Tamara's hair away from her forehead and inspected the injury. "Do you hurt anywhere else?"

Tamara's ribs smarted every time she made the mistake of taking a deep breath. "No," she said.

"Good."

The nurse took Tamara's pulse and blood pressure and recorded the results on a form on the clipboard. "Are you up to answering some questions?"

"What kind of questions?"

"Your name and address for starters. It seems the paramedics didn't get much information from you before they dropped you off."

"I guess I wasn't in a talkin' mood," Tamara said. And she still wasn't. But figuring it best to play along for the time being, she agreed to answer the nurse's questions—and did, at least until they stopped making any sense.

"Who is president of the United States?"

"Who cares?"

A man with bushy eyebrows and a mop of sandy-blond hair, wearing rumpled scrubs and a stethoscope around his neck, pushed his way through the curtains. The nurse handed him the clipboard and stepped aside. The ER doctor glanced at the clipboard before hanging it back on the bed frame. "Well, I see nothing wrong with being apolitical," he said, as if pronouncing her worthy of his attention. He took a penlight from his shirt pocket and shined it in Tamara's eyes. Then he used it to examine her forehead. "Are you experiencing any nausea?"

"No," Tamara said.

"Dizziness?"

"Not anymore."

He pressed the flesh around her wound as if checking for cracks in her skull. "Well, you obviously took quite a wallop. Heads are pretty hard though," he said, as if that fact was a scientific breakthrough. "There's a small laceration we'll take care of. And there'll be plenty of swelling and bruising. But I think your head's gonna be just fine." He put his flashlight away. "Now, what about down here?" He placed a palm on Tamara's pronounced abdomen.

She flinched.

"Any pain here or down lower?"

"No," Tamara said stiffly, once again choosing not to acknowledge the stitch in her ribs.

Undeterred, the doctor put the listening ends of his stethoscope to his ears. He hiked up Tamara's T-shirt and touched the detection end of his instrument to her belly in several places, cocking his head as he listened. "How far along are you?"

The question flapped around in Tamara's mind like a moth seeking light. "About seven months, I think."

"Is that what your doctor says?"

Tamara remained silent. Anything she said would be a lie.

The doctor draped the stethoscope back around his neck. He took another look at the clipboard before addressing the nurse. "Clean the laceration and apply a butterfly bandage. I'll see if I can get Dr. Castle in for a consult, just to be on the safe side. I think he had a delivery tonight. If we're lucky, we can catch him before he leaves the hospital." He patted Tamara's arm. "Sit tight," he said, as if she had a choice.

The doctor retreated from the curtained enclosure, and the nurse went about following his instructions. She was bent over Tamara, dabbing her head wound with an antiseptic-smelling pad, when the curtains parted again and a uniformed officer stepped inside. Tamara wasn't sure, but she thought it was the cop from the store. Her stomach fluttered as her concern shifted from her health to how much trouble she was in.

The nurse glanced over her shoulder at the officer, and when she turned back around her face was glowing, as if one look at him was all the makeup she needed. "Deputy Willard," she said, "what brings you around?"

The deputy stood erect in an apparent effort to maintain an official presence. "I'd like to have a word with your patient. If that's all right with you."

"Almost done," the nurse said. She dropped the cleansing pad into a stainless steel pan and, after pressing an odd-looking bandage to Tamara's forehead, peeled off her skin-tight gloves. "I'll be right outside the curtains," she told Tamara. "If this officer gives you any trouble, scream." She winked. "That's what I always do." Her face was still aglow when she brushed past the deputy. He turned to watch her leave, his gaze lingering until the last, rounded part of her was out of sight.

When he turned back around, Deputy Willard was smiling sheepishly. With his tousled brown hair, strong jaw, and cleft chin, he was quite good-looking. But he was still a cop. Tamara didn't return his smile.

"I just need to ask you a couple of questions," the deputy said. He took a pen out of his shirt pocket and clicked the button on the end of it several times. In his other hand, he had a rectangular metal box with a form secured to the top of it by a clip. "Do you know the young man who knocked you down in the store?"

Tamara thought for a moment. She wasn't really sure what had happened in the store. She shook her head.

"Had you ever seen him before?"

Tamara told the officer what she remembered about what had occurred in the store, leaving out the part about her filching the jerky, which she figured he knew already anyway. But if he did, he didn't let on.

Deputy Willard listened and nodded, occasionally scribbling on his form. Then he said, "The kid who bowled you over apparently panicked when the store owner yelled at him. It's not the first time he's stolen from the store. He got away after running into you, but not before the clerk grabbed hold of his jacket. The kid slid out of it. The pockets were crammed with stuff. It's all on the surveillance tapes. We know who the kid is and we'll be picking him up." He clicked the end of his pen again. "You think you'll want to press assault charges?"

The question surprised Tamara. "Me?"

"The DA has the final say, of course. But you're the one who got run over and ended up in the hospital. Without your cooperation, I doubt the DA would pursue the matter."

"No," Tamara said without hesitation. "Whoever knocked me over ran because he was scared. He didn't mean to hurt me."

"Fair enough," the deputy said. "But why don't you think it over? See how you feel about it in a couple of days." He handed her a card with an embossed Douglas County Sheriff's Department seal on it above his name and several phone numbers. "Call me if you change your mind."

"I won't."

"If you do."

Tamara shrugged. "Yeah, sure." But she knew she wouldn't, and not because of any silly sentiment about "honor among thieves." It could just as easily have been her that the police were looking to arrest instead of some frightened kid.

The cop had hardly stepped away before an old guy with wire-rimmed glasses, a fringe of white hair rimming an otherwise slick head, and a stubbled chin, like patchy snow, appeared inside the curtains. He pulled up short, giving her a startled look, as if he'd seen a ghost. The guy was so ancient and tired-looking he resembled the walking dead himself. After a moment's hesitation, he came forward, drawing himself up all dignified-like in his long white jacket.

"I'm Dr. Castle," he said. "I'm an OB-GYN. Dr. Nolan wanted me to have a look at you."

Tamara clamped her legs together. "I don't need looked at." She wasn't exactly sure what an OB-GYN was, but she knew enough about that kind of doctor to know what it meant to be "looked at" by one.

"Dr. Nolan seems to think you do," Dr. Castle said.

Caught in the sterile wash of the overhead fluorescent lighting, within a ring of tentacled medical equipment, Tamara felt like a test specimen about to be probed for the sake of science. She wanted no part of it. "Screw Dr. Nolan," she said.

She sat up, groaning in response to a piercing pain in her side. Biting down hard, she swung her legs over the bed's chrome railing.

"Young lady—"

But Tamara's feet had already contacted the floor. She pawed her way out through the curtains and headed for the nearest exit.

5   ONCE OUTSIDE THE HOSPITAL, Tamara had no idea which way to go. She stood staring out across a dimly lit parking lot at the darker streets beyond and wondering how far it was to Gary's house, and in what direction. A voice behind her said, "Tamara, let me give you a ride home." Tamara cast a backward glance.

It was the ER nurse. She was cradling a bulky handbag in one arm and digging around in it with her free hand. Tamara eyed her with suspicion. "Why?"

The nurse gave the handbag a shake, burrowed around in it some more, and finally came out with a pink ball of fur to which a ring of keys was attached. "I'm done for the night," she said, "and was heading home myself. It's on my way."

"How do you know that?"

The nurse laughed. "Honey, any place in Fir Valley is on my way home."

IT WAS A QUIET RIDE from the hospital to Cedar Street, which suited Tamara just fine. She'd expected some sort of lecture from the nurse—*the body is a temple . . . blah, blah*—or at least a feeble attempt to engage in useless conversation. Most adults were ill at ease around teenagers, seeming to view them as aliens, as if adolescence was a part of their past that had been erased from their memory. But the nurse had paid silent attention to her driving, and Tamara had pretended to pay no attention to her.

"You'll need to tell me which house," the nurse said.

Cedar Street, outside the wash of the car's headlights, was a black velvet canvas with only an occasional smear of porch-light radiance. During walks around the neighborhood, Tamara had seen groups of kids using the few streetlights in the area for rock-throwing target practice. A cheer would go up each time a globe was shattered.

"Here," she said, pointing at a pickup truck with an exaggerated lift parked at the curb—Jerome's truck. Why was he still here?

The nurse pulled in behind the truck—she could just about have parked under it—and left the engine running. Tamara fumbled around in the dark, trying to locate the door handle.

"You gonna be all right?" the nurse said.

Tamara's fingers found the handle. She yanked on it.

"Tamara—" the nurse said.

Tamara jerked around. "What?"

"I wouldn't go back into that market if I were you."

"And why not?"

"You know why."

Tamara felt her face burning. Was there some oath all adults had to take? *I promise to meddle in the affairs of every teenager I encounter, no matter how uninformed I am about their situation.* "You need to mind your own business," she told the nurse. She shoved the car door open. When the dome light came on, the sudden brightness startled her, like unwelcome truth. "And—and—that deputy needs to learn to keep his mouth shut."

She got out of the car and blundered through the darkness toward Gary's house. Faint light seeping from the front window did little to dispel the enveloping gloom. Using her feet as feelers, she ascended the steps to the porch. The front door was unlocked. As she was entering the house, she heard the nurse's car sputter away from the curb.

The living room was deserted. The lamp on the table next to Gary's chair had been left on. The porcelain body of the lamp was in the shape of an upright rifle. The lamp's stained shade had bullet cartridges dangling like tassels from its lower rim so that the light passing through it was accompanied by fingers of shadow that crept across the room. Tamara slogged through the shadows and headed down the hallway, feeling battered in body and spirit, as if she was the lone survivor of a train wreck.

Her bedroom door was open. She switched on the light and wasn't surprised to find Jerome, fully clothed, flopped on the bed like a beached whale. His blowhole of a mouth was open and he was snoring heavily. She flicked off the light.

She retraced her steps to the living room and collapsed onto the couch, her left arm clasped like a wing against her sore ribs. Her whole body ached now, and her head was pounding as if it had become stuck inside a booming bass drum.

All of a sudden she began to shiver. Her limbs shook and her teeth chattered. She curled up in ball. She rubbed her arms and legs as if to combat a chill but received no relief. It wasn't the temperature making her shiver; the air in the room was uncomfortably close. She was shivering, she knew, out of fear—fear of being back inside this house.

She'd been afraid of Gary ever since she'd first laid eyes on him, which was shortly after her mother had married Darryl, and she and Tamara had moved in with him.

Darryl had two teenage sons who lived at home at the time, although Tamara hardly ever saw them. Rocky was a seventeen-year-old hoodlum who mostly hung out with his buddies. Dwight, a skinny, sullen boy of fifteen, spent most of his time barricaded in his room, wearing the headphones to a cassette player that might as well have been surgically implanted. It wasn't until Gary showed up at the house one night, unannounced and drunk, that Tamara had learned there was a third brother, several years older than Rocky.

Darryl was out that night, as usual—as was Rocky. Tamara's mother was in bed. Dwight had already disappeared into his room. Tamara was alone in the living room, sitting on the floor in front of the television set with a bowl of popcorn in her lap, when the front door of the house burst open and Gary charged in.

"Where is the sonofabitch?" he shouted. "I'm gonna whip his ass."

Tamara thought some crazy man had broken into the wrong home. She scrabbled away from him, upending the popcorn bowl and sending buttery kernels cascading across the carpet.

Gary blustered his way into the kitchen. Finding no one there, he stamped down the hall, hurling doors open with resounding violence. Moments later, he was back. "Who the hell are you?" he said, glaring at Tamara. "And who's that cunt in Dad's bed?"

Dwight came into the living room. "Leave her alone," he said with half-baked bravado.

Gary seized his little brother by the arm, slammed him against the wall. "Listen, faggot, don't tell me what to do." He pointed an angry finger at Dwight. "You tell that s.o.b. I'll be back to kick his ass." Then he stormed out of the house.

Tamara ran over to lock the door. "Who was that?"

Dwight came up, massaging his shoulder. "That was my brother Gary. I guess he's out of jail."

Tamara leaned back against the door. "Who was he looking for?"

"Dad."

"Why is he mad at your father?"

Dwight emitted a nervous twitter. "Because Dad refused to bail him out this time."

She stared at her stepbrother.

"What?"

"Are there any more brothers I need to know about?"

Dwight rolled his injured shoulder as if making sure it still worked. "Just Gary," he said, and returned to his room.

Lying, shivering, now on the crummy sofa in Gary's living room, her eyes blurred with tears, Tamara felt herself sinking in a pool of despair. Here she was, barely existing in the house of a man she didn't trust, yet with nowhere else to go. It was bad enough she'd put herself at risk by coming here. But she'd also jeopardized the welfare of her child.

And the nurse was right. She couldn't chance going back into that mini-mart—not after what had happened tonight. She'd get caught for sure.

So what was she to do?

The baby moved inside her. She embraced the movement. "No, I haven't forgotten about you," she said. Nor would she.

And so, once more, Tamara dug deep inside herself for the resolve that resided at the core of her being. Because truly there was only one thing to do. She had to find a way to protect her child. And in order to do that, she had to regain control of her life.

6   IT WAS AFTER TEN O'CLOCK when Dr. Castle left the hospital that night. Following the strange episode in the ER, he'd gone back to the maternity ward for one last check on Mrs. Halloran and her eight-pound baby boy. Satisfied that mother and child were doing well, he exchanged his lab coat for his suit jacket and shuffled out of the building. In the parking lot, he got into his Mercedes and sat quietly with his eyes closed for a time, stealing a moment of hush from an otherwise hectic day. But he couldn't afford

to linger. He had one more stop to make before going home, and just the thought of it burdened his soul.

He started the car, pulled out of the parking lot, and drove the two blocks south to Mill Street where he turned east toward the river. It was a familiar route and he piloted the car by rote along streets lined with mostly darkened buildings—businesses put to bed for the night. They didn't actually roll up the sidewalks in Fir Valley after dark, but except for the nocturnal activity swirling about the taverns and convenience stores, the wheels of commerce generally ground to a halt in the aftermath of day.

But doctoring, done right, was—like the ministry—a service that had no use for time clocks and inflexible social calendars. It was not a job, it was a commitment—a commitment of the self—a commitment whose fulfillment invited the weariness that seemed to be his constant companion of late.

It was the long days like today that made Dr. Castle feel his age, that made him wonder why at seventy-two he was still delivering babies and lecturing women on the benefits of proper prenatal care. He should have packed it in long ago, applied for social security and his AARP card, and lived the easy life. But he knew why he hadn't.

At first it had been the bad investments that kept him going. Tax shelters, his financial advisor had called them. Tax *scams* was more like it. He'd lost tens of thousands of dollars just like that. Then when Lily had passed away ten years ago, he'd all but lost his incentive to retire. His practice became his life. Even now it was what kept him going, what got him up every morning to face the world without his beloved wife.

So his tenure as Fir Valley's foremost (or was it just oldest?) OB-GYN continued—over forty years of doctoring, and all in the same community. Had Lily lived, things would have been different. By now they would have been traveling the country in a new Winnebago, enjoying their golden years. But it hadn't happened. And never would.

The doctor glumly steered the car across the bridge over the river— the dark, brooding expanse of water shifting implacably beneath him. It was, he knew, more than the lateness of the hour, his fatigue, and his own sense of loss that weighed on him. It was the utter hopelessness of his current mission. This wasn't the way life was supposed to be playing out, for him or for the Troustes.

With the river behind him, he slowed, swung his vehicle onto Pine Ridge Road, and began the tortuous ascent up the steep hillside. When the road finally crested, he veered left onto Summit Drive. Within minutes, he was passing through the broad gateway at the entrance to the Trouste estate. At the far end of the tree-lined drive, where it sat on the edge of the bluff overlooking the city, Trouste House loomed castle-like in his headlights.

Suddenly the sense of responsibility he felt for the current residents of this magnificent Victorian home seemed a greater load than he could bear. Had it all come down to this? One colossal failure to end his career? Fate sardonically giving him the finger?

He pulled to a stop at the base of the steps leading up to the main entrance. Outside lights illuminated the expansive portico and spilled over in jagged ovals onto the sprawling grounds surrounding the home. He got out, clutching his medical case, and labored up the steps to the tall double doors.

Normally it was Elena, the Troustes' aging housekeeper, who answered the bell. But he wasn't surprised when at this late hour Russell opened the door, his patently handsome face tinged ruddy less from his ongoing anxiety than from the alcohol he used to assuage it.

"Thank you for coming," Russell said. His bearing, usually that of the captain of a grand seagoing vessel, had taken on of late the slouchiness of a man down on his luck.

The doctor put a hand on his friend's shoulder and kept it there as they walked across the gleaming hardwood of the foyer and into the great room with its soaring ceiling and massive crystal chandelier. "Give me a few minutes alone with her," he said.

Leaving Russell poised in the middle of the room looking lost, the doctor ascended the sweeping staircase as briskly as his exhausted frame would allow. He plodded across the plush carpet of the upstairs hallway to the second room on the left. He pecked on the door with his arthritic knuckles but didn't wait for an answer before entering. Margaret would be expecting him.

Dr. Castle had been seeing Mrs. Trouste weekly for the past five months, first in his office and then, when he'd ordered her to bed in her second trimester, here at Trouste House. More recently, he'd been attending to her almost daily.

Margaret Trouste, at forty-two years of age, was making her sixth and, by all accounts, final attempt to bring a healthy child of her own into the world. Yet, given her history of failure in this regard, there was no reason to believe that this attempt would end other than tragically. Already the fetus showed signs of stress. It was only a matter of time, in spite of all the precautions that had been taken, before it too succumbed.

But this time there appeared to be more than one life hanging in the balance. "If she loses this baby, I think it will kill her," Russell had commented to him privately during a recent visit.

Dr. Castle knew his friend well enough not to dismiss this statement as mere melodrama. Margaret's physical condition was tenuous at best, but her mental state was easily as fragile. Margaret wanted this baby desperately, so desperately that she'd become pregnant by not telling her husband she'd begun to ovulate again but wasn't going back on the pill. Then she'd ignored his pleas to end the pregnancy while it was still safe to do so. Since that time, she'd been willing to lie flat on her back in bed for weeks on end in order to improve her chances of carrying the fetus to full term. She was willing, it seemed, to suffer any amount of discomfort, incur any expense, risk anything and everything, including her own life, to see this child safely into the world. And that alarmed Dr. Castle as much as it did Russell Trouste.

Brandon Castle's relationship with Fir Valley's most prominent family had always been more than professional. He'd been best friends growing up with Frank, Russell's father. He'd once dated Russell's mom. "I could have been your dad," he'd once jokingly told Russell. And after Frank's untimely death, the doctor had become a confidant to the younger Trouste, who'd been forced to step in and take over management of the family-owned lumber mill. When Russell married Margaret, the Castles' bond with the Troustes only strengthened, as Margaret Trouste became not only a fast friend but a stand-in for the daughter he and Lily never had.

It pained the doctor now to see Margaret suffering so. And it aggrieved him to know that her suffering was only going to get worse— and there was nothing he could do about it.

The doctor tried to put all this out of his mind as he made his way to Margaret's bedside. He greeted her with a smile. Margaret attempted a smile in return, but the gesture, as if fashioned of parched clay, broke off before reaching its intended shape.

Dr. Castle set his bag down on a chair next to the bed. He checked Margaret's pulse. Then he grasped her hand and squeezed gently.

"Now you squeeze," he said.

Hardly more potent than an infant's grasp, her grip seemed weaker even than the day before. And she looked paler, if that was possible. She was not resting well, he knew, or doing a good job keeping food down. But he made no comment on any of this, knowing that to recite the details of her continued decline would only cause his patient further distress.

He retrieved his stethoscope from his bag, put it to his ears, and listened to Margaret's heartbeat, and for its faint echo inside her womb.

"Elena braided my hair," she said, obviously striving to be cheery about something.

"Nice," he said. It seemed that almost daily more strands of gray were appearing in Margaret's long brown hair. Previously she'd fretted about not being able to get to the salon and have it tinted. But Dr. Castle had insisted that would be too risky. Now she was content just to have Elena brush it out each day and braid it now and again.

The doctor moved on to the business at hand. "Russell says you're spotting."

Margaret nodded, her eyes sparking with apprehension.

"A little bleeding we can deal with," he said with a reassuring smile.

Margaret didn't say anything, but her eyes continued to reflect her fear. She knew all the warning signs, and his attempts to pacify her would inevitably be met with a well-educated skepticism.

He pulled on a pair of exam gloves and began turning down the bedding that covered Margaret's lower torso. She responded automatically to the routine, drawing up her knees and spreading her legs. She turned her head to the side as he probed inside her.

When the doctor was finished with his exam, he stripped off his gloves and stuffed them into a plastic bag. He took two pill bottles from his case, opened them, and took one tablet out of each. "I want you to take these, and then I'll leave the bottles with Russell, along with instructions, to administer as needed."

"What are they?"

"One is a coagulant—for the spotting. The other is a mild sedative."

"The baby," Margaret responded. "Will they hurt the baby?" Again, a flash of fear—in her eyes and in her voice.

"They're both perfectly safe," the doctor assured her. From a pitcher on the dresser, he poured water into a cup. He helped her sit up just enough to swallow the pills, then eased her back onto the pillow.

"You really should be in the hospital," he said, giving voice to his true feelings. It wasn't the first time he'd made that assertion.

Margaret looked away. "Whatever happens, happens here."

The doctor sighed. "Rest then," he said. He hefted his medical bag and left the room.

Back downstairs, he found Russell in the library, slumped over in his easy chair with his eyes closed. He was breathing audibly. A tumbler with melting ice in it sat on the glass-topped table beside his chair. When the doctor set the two pill bottles down on the tabletop with an inadvertent clunk, Russell's eyes popped open. He straightened in his chair. "Sorry, Brandon," he said, blinking. "I didn't hear you come in. How is she?"

There was no sense sugarcoating it for Russell. He knew only too well what was happening. "The medication should help with the spotting," Dr. Castle said. "But it's only a stopgap measure. I'm afraid it won't be long now before—" He saw no reason to finish the sentence.

Russell didn't say anything, but his hands had suddenly become fists, and Dr. Castle knew that his friend's pain was as real as Margaret's, as was his sense of helplessness. Life was about to deliver the couple another cruel blow, and Russell Trouste, a man of considerable wealth and influence, was powerless to fend it off. It wasn't a circumstance that fitted him well.

The doctor remained standing, medical bag in hand, afraid that if he set it down he might not be able to pick it up again. He glanced around the room—at the unlit fireplace, at the half-empty bottle of Chivas Regal sitting on the bar, at the tome-laden bookshelves lining one wall, at the mosaic of family portraits decorating another. "Life is fraught with irony," he said.

Russell looked up at him with a bemused expression. "Isn't it a little late in the day to wax philosophical?"

The doctor shifted his bag to his other hand. "I suppose it is. I was just thinking about a young girl I saw at the hospital earlier this evening."

"Your answering service said you had a delivery."

"Afterward—in the ER." He told Russell about the girl he'd been called in to examine after she'd taken a nasty fall. "She's sixteen, pregnant, and obviously clueless. Yet she'll undoubtedly carry to full term in spite of her lack of prenatal care."

Russell sank deeper into the padding of his chair. "The irony isn't lost on me, Brandon. But it's under-appreciated."

"Sorry to have mentioned it then," the doctor said. "But it struck me so forcefully because—well—" He hesitated, wondering if he hadn't already said too much. But he couldn't seem to check himself. "—the girl reminded me so much of Margaret. A much younger Margaret, of course."

Russell didn't seem fazed by the observation. "I thought all pregnant women looked alike."

"To the untrained eye, perhaps," the doctor said.

The comment struck a chord and they laughed together for a brief, uncomfortable moment. Then Russell said, "Can I get you a drink, or have Elena fix you something to eat?"

"Thanks, but I need to be off." The doctor tightened his grip on his medical bag. "Just one other thing. I think Margaret should have a nurse with her full time now. I'll have one sent over. In the meantime, the pills on the table should help. The directions are on the labels."

Russell started to rise.

"Sit, please," the doctor told him. "I know my way out."

Russell dropped back into his chair without argument.

During his drive home, Dr. Castle concentrated his thoughts on the bed waiting for him, on the brief respite he hoped sleep would bring. For his every waking hour of late was filled with torment concerning his treatment of Margaret Trouste. There were limits to everything—even to doctoring. And in this case he was skidding, perhaps disastrously, toward those limits.

7   THE NEXT MORNING, after a night of impoverished sleep that included enough writhing to enable one to escape from a straitjacket, Dr. Castle left home later than usual for the three-mile drive to his office. It was already 9:20 when he pulled into his parking space outside the medical building on Springer Street he'd moved his practice into several years ago to be nearer the hospital. His first appointments were scheduled for nine o'clock. He knew that patients would be waiting in each of his three exam rooms. He also knew that Marion would already have taken vitals and deposited each patient's folder in the rack outside the respective exam room door. His nurse was very efficient in that regard, as she was in every aspect of her duties.

When he entered the office through the back door, Marion scrutinized him head to toe, as if searching for missing body parts. She knew about the long hours he was keeping and had warned him on more than one occasion that he needed to slow down. "You'll end up dead on the floor of cardiac arrest if you don't," she'd scolded. She was right. But what was he to do? There was a shortage of gynecologists in the area, as there was in most rural counties. Young doctors, especially specialists, were drawn to the bigger cities—to the bigger practices, where expenses could be shared and profits maximized.

In his private office, Dr. Castle hung up his suit jacket, pulled on his lab coat, and draped his stethoscope around his neck. Marion appeared beside him holding a cup of coffee. He took the cup, sipped from it, then set it down on his desk. "Have Doris call the ER at the hospital," he told the nurse. He went to the sink and began washing his hands.

"Oh?"

"Last night Dr. Nolan asked me to take a look at a sixteen-year-old girl who'd been brought into the ER after taking a fall. In her third trimester, I'd say, although she bolted before I could examine her." He snatched a paper towel from the dispenser. "Her name is Tamara Ames. She lives with her stepbrother, I think they said. Have Doris get his name and phone number." He tossed the used towel into the wastebasket. "I'd like to talk to him and see how the girl is doing."

"You want me to make the call?"

"No, I'll take this one." He indulged himself in a few more nips of coffee before heading down the hall.

Outside the first exam room, he pulled the patient's file out of the rack and read the name on the label. He opened the folder and glanced at the current vitals. Everything else in the file he knew all too well.

The patient's name was Tracy Saunders. Tracy was twenty-one years old, single, and six months pregnant with her third child. She had delivered her first baby at the age of seventeen, her second at nineteen— each fathered by a different man. She'd been married briefly to father number two. Her two children—a boy and a girl—lived with Tracy's parents, and had almost from the time they were born. The boy was fair complexioned. The girl was brown-skinned. Nobody was taking bets on the hue of baby number three.

"Good morning, Tracy," the doctor said as he entered the exam room. "How are we feeling today?"

Tracy smiled, showing her bad teeth. "Fine, Doc."

Nowadays, more and more of Dr. Castle's patients were like Tracy: young, poor, unmarried, and very fertile. Their bodies were strong and resilient, and that was to their advantage. But seldom did they take proper care of themselves. Many smoked, used drugs, and ate junk food almost exclusively. Most of them weren't nearly ready for marriage much less for the responsibilities of motherhood. As a result, they suffered because of their pregnancies—emotionally and economically—as did those around them, especially their children, who all too often ended up being raised by their grandparents or other relatives.

Four months before, when Tracy had come to him pregnant for the third time, Dr. Castle had not been happy with her. He'd put her on the pill after her first baby was born, and again after her second. But she'd been irresponsible in that regard as well. So there she was back in his office, receiving the news that indeed she was once more with child. She'd shrugged. "Maybe I'll just get an abortion."

The doctor had peered at her soberly over the rim of his glasses. "You've come to the wrong place for that, young lady."

Dr. Castle had long been a staunch opponent of abortion. He'd devoted his entire working life to bringing babies into the world, not killing them in the womb. His beliefs had been tested over the years, particularly as he'd witnessed the devastating effects of teenage pregnancy. Even so, he'd stuck to his guns on the issue in spite of the Supreme Court's decision in *Roe vs. Wade*. There were always other options to taking a human life.

One of those options—and a very good one in his judgment—was adoption. There were many couples who for various reasons were unable to have children of their own and who were more than willing to take an unwanted child into their home. A lot of these couples had trouble finding children, especially infants, to adopt. Many resorted to overseas adoption agencies with mixed results.

Over the years, Dr. Castle had worked quietly with an agency in Eugene that helped couples find children to adopt. It was a little known aspect of his practice. He was low-key about it. That was why he preferred working with an out-of-town agency. And he never pressured anyone about putting a child up for adoption. But he'd always felt he would be remiss in his position as a physician, and as an opponent of abortion, if he didn't at least make his patients—particularly the younger ones who seemed so unprepared for parenthood—aware of this option. Tracy Saunders was a case in point. Following Tracy's callous response to the revelation of unplanned pregnancy number three, Dr. Castle had referred her to the adoption agency in Eugene. She had consequently given up her notion of getting an abortion and was now leaning in the direction of adoption.

"Your chart looks good this morning," he told her. "Now let's have a listen for ourselves."

Tracy was already unbuttoning her blouse.

The doctor put his stethoscope to his ears, touched the end of it to her abdomen, and listened for that life-beat that never failed to stir his emotions.

He saw patients for the next two hours without taking a break. His twelve o'clock appointment canceled. By the time the lunch hour had arrived, which for the office staff was from one o'clock until two, the waiting room had been emptied and the gals were heading out to Carla's Coffee Cup. "Sure you don't want to come along?" Marion said as she lingered outside his office doorway. "We can call and cancel your takeout order."

"No, no," Dr. Castle said, waving her off. "Too much to do here."

The nurse tossed him a disappointed look and then disappeared from view.

The doctor stayed busy, slogging through the latest blizzard of lab reports, while he waited for the delivery boy from Blossoms—the hole-in-the-wall Chinese joint down the block—to put in an appearance.

Twenty minutes later, the delivery boy having come and gone, the doctor sat at his desk with an empty carton of kung pao chicken in front of him, alongside a half-empty container of fried rice. He pushed the cartons aside, wiped his mouth with a paper napkin. After a moment of hesitation, during which he questioned his motives for doing so, he picked up the receiver to the telephone on his desk and dialed the number Doris had given him earlier in the day. A male voice answered.

"Yeah," the voice said with unvarnished irritation.

"Is this Gary Neaves?"

"Who wants to know?"

"This is Dr. Castle. I understand you're Tamara Ames' stepbrother."

"So?"

"I saw Tamara at the hospital last night. I was called in by the ER physician to examine her because of her fall."

For the next several seconds there was nothing but a faint buzz in the line. Unnerved, Dr. Castle continued. "Tamara was, shall we say, a reluctant patient. I never really had a chance to assess her condition. According to what I was told, she apparently took quite a tumble. Sometimes the extent of one's injuries under the circumstances—that is, when a pregnancy is involved—is not immediately evident, particularly in regard to the fetus." He was rambling. He paused, took a slow breath. "I called to see how she was feeling today."

"Don't know, haven't seen her."

"Oh?" Dr. Castle glanced at his watch. It was 1:38 PM. "Is she home now?"

"Don't know, haven't seen her."

The doctor blinked hard. What was going on here? "Mr. Neaves, are you Tamara's guardian?"

"Nope."

"Do you know who is?"

"You'd have to ask her."

"But she lives with you?"

"You could say that."

Dr. Castle pinched the bridge of his nose. He wasn't getting anywhere with this fellow. To hell with it. It wasn't worth the effort. The girl was probably fine. Besides, if he couldn't get any cooperation from her or her brother, what was the point? He was about to bid Gary Neaves a none-too-fond farewell when an uneasiness about giving up so easily stopped him. Even if he could write off the two siblings as misfits, could he so easily write off the unborn child? "Do you know what Tamara's plans are for her baby?" he asked, knowing full well he was sticking his nose where it didn't belong. He didn't care.

"You'd have to ask—"

"Yes, yes," the doctor said with rising frustration. "But—"

"Look, Doc," Neaves said, his voice hard-edged, "I don't know what the hell she's gonna do with the kid. She's sixteen years old. I doubt she knows what she's gonna do with it."

Dr. Castle had heard this assertion before, about—and from—other prospective teenage mothers. They had no concept of what lay in store for them as parents and no insight as to how to go about planning for that eventuality. Here was another tragedy in the making. Another child was about to be brought into this world with almost no chance at having a decent life. He could be wrong. Some teenage moms surprised him with their resourcefulness and their strength of character, somehow managing to forge a respectable quality of life for themselves and their child. But that didn't happen often.

There was only one question he had left, and he put it forth more to salve his conscience than out of any hope that he could make a difference in this case. "Mr. Neaves," he said, "has Tamara ever mentioned the possibility of adoption to you?"

"She hasn't mentioned jack-shit to me."

And that should have been the end of it.

But it wasn't. Again, Dr. Castle couldn't bring himself to let go. In his mind, he saw the anxious look on Tamara's face as she rushed from the emergency room. Then, strangely, that image morphed into another—the visage of Margaret Trouste imprinted with fear. The doctor gripped the arm of his chair, feeling a sense of urgency that was uncalled for yet seemed real. "Do you think you could convince Tamara to come to my office for an exam?" he said. "She really ought to be under a doctor's care."

"That's none of my business," Neaves said.

The doctor pondered that statement for a moment. It was obvious the kind of fellow he was dealing with here. This guy cared only about himself and how things affected him. Armed with this understanding, Dr. Castle decided to take one last shot at reaching him.

"Well, Mr. Neaves," he said. "I realize all this may be none of my business either. But just in case Tamara might be considering adoption, I think you should know that there are some wonderful people out there eager to bring a child into their home." He spoke fast, trying to get to his point as quickly as possible. "Some of these people are willing to pay certain costs of prenatal care for the natural mother and, where appropriate, a referral fee to assisting parties."

"How much?" Neaves said.

Gotcha. The doctor went on, ignoring Neaves' question. "I'm not saying this is a valid reason for giving up a child, especially one that is wanted. But if adoption is being considered, then its financial aspect, particularly as it relates to the welfare of the mother and the child, ought to be discussed."

"How much of a referral fee?" Neaves repeated, this time with the insistency of a pounding gavel.

The doctor shifted uncomfortably in his chair, feeling the need to proceed with caution. He didn't want to lead this fellow on unnecessarily now that he had his attention. "That depends on the arrangement. It could be a few hundred dollars. Could be more. If you go through an agency, it's generally a modest sum. In a private adoption, it can be a more generous amount." Then he hastened to add, "But Mr. Neaves, I want to stress the fact that we need to know Tamara's wishes on this score before any further discussion of this nature can take place. If you can get her to come to my office, I'm willing to waive my fee for the initial exam. After that, we can probably get her some services through the county health department. So, do you think you can get her in?"

"No problem. When do you want her there?"

"Let me check the schedule."

The doctor went into the front office and consulted the appointment calendar. He picked up the receiver to Doris's telephone and punched the blinking button on the console. "We can fit her in at four o'clock this afternoon." He rattled off the address to his office. "Would that work for you?"

"She'll be there," Gary Neaves said, and Dr. Castle didn't doubt him for a second.

8   TAMARA ROUSED TO the sound of Gary's voice prodding her like an insistent finger jab. She shifted in the bed and squinted at where he stood in the doorway mouthing words the

meaning of which failed to penetrate the fog in her brain. She swallowed a taste in her mouth like sour milk, worked to blink eyelids that felt glued shut.

"What?" she said in a hoarse whisper, which was all the voice she had.

"Get up and make yourself presentable."

Tamara's gaze flitted about the room. She was in her own bed and was wondering how she'd gotten there. She puzzled over this for a moment before it came to her. When Jerome had left that morning, the revving of his truck engine was like a lion roaring in her ear. She'd awakened with a start. She remembered feeling woozy as she sat up on the couch. She'd thought she was going to be sick. She staggered into the bathroom and hung her head over the sink. When the urge to throw up passed, she tottered across the hall and crashed again in her own bed. Now Gary was telling her to get up, and she wasn't sure she wanted to.

"Why?" she asked.

"You're going to see someone."

Tamara felt a jolt of alarm, as if she'd been blindfolded and didn't know why. "Who am I gonna see?" She didn't know anyone in Fir Valley except Brian and Jerome, and she didn't want to see them.

"The doctor."

"What doctor?" She concentrated hard, trying to fill the gaps in her understanding.

Gary's face turned wooden. "Your baby needs checkin' on," he said in a voice not open to challenge. "We leave in ten minutes." His footsteps resounded like hammer strikes down the hall.

Tamara lay there scouring her mind for the substance behind her stepbrother's words. Why would he be taking her to see a doctor? What doctor? And how had Gary become involved? Yesterday he couldn't have cared less whether she lived or died. Why should he care now about her welfare, or that of her baby? She considered ignoring him and going back to sleep. She didn't trust Gary, and she didn't like doctors any more than she liked cops.

She rolled over in the bed and, as she did, experienced a twinge in her left side. The same shooting pain from last night. She took shallow breaths and waited for relief. Maybe I should see a doctor, she thought. If not for myself, then for my baby.

Moving cautiously now, she pushed herself up to a sitting position. Her head felt big and tight, as if inflated with compressed air. She dangled her legs over the edge of the bed, slowly got to her feet. She braced herself with a hand against the dresser. Her swollen belly rumbled and gurgled and churned.

When finally she felt up to it, she minced across the hall to the bathroom. One look in the mirror startled her. Her hair was matted straw. Her face was blotchy-white and bloated, like the bellies of the dead guppies she'd once seen floating on the surface of Nanna's fish tank. There were dark pouches, like used tea bags, under her eyes. The bandage on her forehead had come loose on one side and her wound was exposed—a golf-ball-sized knot with a smiley face of dried blood at its center. The skin around the knot had turned a yellow-tinged purple. She stuck the bandage back down and got into the shower. Over the sound of the running water, she heard Gary's fist tattooing the bathroom door. "Five minutes," he hollered. She was not inclined to hurry.

THEY RODE WITHOUT conversation under a clear, blue sky to a brown-stucco building on the west side of town just down the street from Fir Valley Community Hospital. Tamara still hadn't connected the dots between Gary and "the doctor," and this gap in her understanding of what was happening unnerved her like the *drip-drip-drip* from a faucet. Gary parked his truck in a PATIENTS ONLY space in front of the medical offices and pointed to some glass doors beneath a gabled overhang. "Number 108," he said.

Tamara eyed the remnant of blacktop between them and the glass doors. The strip of pavement, shimmering in the sunlight, resembled a rippling black river—a river she was being asked to cross without knowing anything about the land on the other side. Life was like that.

A series of dark rivers to cross. Sometimes the crossing was forced. Sometimes it was of your own choosing. But once across, there never seemed to be a way back to the other side.

She entered the building through the glass doors, passed through a foyer that was a jungle of potted plants strangely lacking in aroma, and made her way along a carpeted hallway, reading the posted office numbers as she went. She stopped short outside suite 108, her joints locking up at the sight of the plaque on the door: BRANDON CASTLE, OB-GYN.

How? What?

She shut her eyes, swallowed hard. There was no sense turning back. She was already across the river.

9   THE WAITING ROOM was ringed with armchairs, a number of which were occupied by women, some showing, some not, but all obviously older than Tamara. She glanced about self-consciously, expecting everyone to be staring at her. Just the opposite was true. The women all seemed to be diligently ignoring her presence by giving their attention to a book or magazine, or by absently gazing in any direction other than hers.

Tamara went over to a glass partition inset in one wall, put her face close to a half-moon opening in the glass, and gave her name to a grandmotherly woman sitting at a desk on the other side.

The woman greeted her with a rubber-stamp smile and a cheery "Hello." She slid a glass panel aside and handed Tamara a clipboard with some forms attached to it. A ballpoint pen dangled from a string fastened to the clipboard. "Bring the clipboard back to me when you're done filling out the forms."

Tamara took the clipboard and sat down, leaving an empty chair between herself and a woman whose belly was so big it looked as if she might pop a kid any second. The woman sat tilted sideways, a look of misery lurking beneath a sheen of perspiration on her face. Tamara pretended not to notice.

In a little alcove off to the side, there was a low bookcase filled with colorful books and, next to it, a box heaped with toys and stuffed animals. A woman was sitting on a fluffy yellow rug in front of the bookcase with a toddler on her lap. The toddler, a curly-headed boy, was flapping the pages of a book, pointing at pictures and saying unintelligible things. "That's right," the woman said in a tender voice, "*gir-affe.*"

Tamara felt a squeeze around her heart. This was the way her mother used to talk to her, during the happy times before the accident, when the world was full of sweetness and light. She was Mommy's little helper then—and Daddy's little angel—and her days were filled with playtime in the park, sundaes at Dairy Queen, hug-filled visits to Nanna's house, and a story at bedtime, always with a happy ending. Her mother's lap was as soft as a down pillow, her voice as soothing as a lullaby, and her love as constant as the sunrise.

Tamara bit the inside of her cheek and fought the urge to cry. Her mother was a different person today, and that wasn't going to change.

She seized the ballpoint pen and forced her attention onto the paperwork. The only thing that mattered now was the kind of mother she was going to be.

The first form was easy enough, basic personal information: name, address, phone number, date of birth, social security number. Tamara used Gary's address and phone number. She wrote "no" or "none" in response to the insurance and employment questions, listed her income as "zero," and signed and dated the form at the bottom.

The second form was more of a chore. It was a medical history, containing a list of questions about illnesses and diseases she might have had—from heart disease to gout, and a lot of "itis" ailments in between. She marked the "no" box on everything except tonsillitis. She remembered that "itis." That was the one time in her life she'd been really sick. With her throat swollen closed, she hadn't been able to swallow anything solid for days. Nanna took her to the emergency room at the hospital. The doctor stuck a Popsicle stick down her throat until she gagged, then he uttered the "t" word that had seemed so big to her then and that she'd never forgotten.

The next series of questions on the form, which related to her "natural" parents, were problematic, beginning with whether they were "living" or "deceased." Tamara hadn't seen her dad since she was six years old, and for all she knew, he was dead. Her mother, following Danny's accident, had withdrawn so far inside herself that she might as well have died. Tamara wrote "don't know" on most of the questions and went on to the last form.

Its first question puzzled her. "When did you have your last period?" Why did that matter now? She wrote, "Last November."

She knew that because she remembered with aching clarity the day she found out she was pregnant. It was just before Valentine's Day. She'd missed her December period but didn't want to accept the possibility of what that could mean. So she'd shrugged it off; her body was just playing tricks on her. When another month came and went without blood, she'd consulted the school nurse, who referred her to the county health department. At the county health clinic she peed into a jar that a lady in a pink smock had given her and was instructed to come back the next day. The next day, she was given confirmation of what by then she feared to be true.

She remembered walking out of the clinic and into a slanting rain. It was a blustery February day. The naked branches on the maple trees lining the sidewalk rocked fitfully in the wind. Pellets of cold rain stung her face, ran down cheeks already wet with tears. She stood there for some time, staring up at the leaden sky, not really caring about the rain and unable to stop the tears.

She'd cried a lot after that. She cried because Jimmy had already begun to withdraw from her. She cried because when she'd turned to her mother for help, she'd found out just how helpless her mother really was. She cried because, not yet sixteen, she was herself a child—a child who had no idea how to become a woman in nine months, much less a mother.

She told the school nurse the test had been negative. No one else but her best friend, Angela, knew the truth for a long time after that. "Are you going to get an abortion?" Angela asked her after school one day while they were waiting for their bus to arrive. All the school buses were running late and no one seemed to know why. Kids were milling about everywhere. There was a lot of confusion, and no one was paying attention to the two of them standing off by themselves.

Tamara remembered being shocked by the question. She hadn't wanted to get pregnant. She'd slept with Jimmy because he'd said he loved her and wanted to show her how much. When the seeds of his so-called love sprouted into something real and long-lasting, he'd easily turned away, discarding her like a bank robber disposing of tainted money because it couldn't be spent. It wasn't the first time she'd been so casually tossed aside, and probably wouldn't be the last.

But that day in the parking lot at school, confronted with Angela's question about abortion, Tamara knew for the first time her true feelings about her pregnancy. The enduring reality of her time with Jimmy was that something wonderful was happening to her body. A beautiful thing was flowering inside her. New life was forming. And, in time, there would be a child—her child—that she would love unconditionally, and be loved by in return. What could be more wonderful than that!

She put her face close to Angela's. "No," she said, her breast blazing with passion, "I'm not having an abortion. I'm having a baby."

"ALICIA," A VOICE said.

Startled from her reverie, Tamara looked up to find a tall redheaded woman in nurse's garb standing in an interior doorway.

The poor lady who looked due any minute struggled out of her chair. She wavered in place, found her balance, and waddled over to where the nurse waited.

Tamara scribbled some answers to the remaining questions on the last form, then took the clipboard over and handed it in through the opening in the glass partition. She was back in her seat, chewing on her fingernails, when she heard a voice call her name. The same redheaded nurse was standing in the same interior doorway with a brown folder in her hand.

Tamara stood up, hesitated, her thoughts in turmoil. She needed to do this for her baby's sake. But what she really wanted to do was run, just like she'd done the night before. But run where? To what?

She joined the nurse at the interior doorway, followed her down a hallway and into a small room whose most prominent feature was a narrow bed that had metal stirrups protruding from one end. She froze at the sight of the stirrups.

"What's wrong, honey?" the nurse asked.

Tamara couldn't take her eyes off the stirrups. And she couldn't speak.

The nurse rested a hand on her shoulder. "Haven't you had a pelvic exam before?"

Tamara managed to shake her head.

"Well, there's nothing to it, really," the nurse said. "This set-up just looks imposing." She led Tamara over to the bed. "Now have a seat while I get your vitals."

When the old doctor came in a few minutes later, Tamara was sitting on the bed naked from the waist down, clinging to a paper sheet draped over her exposed parts. She stiffened at the sight of him.

"Tammy, it's nice to see you again," he said.

"It's *Tamara.*"

The doctor bowed slightly at the waist. "I stand corrected." He turned aside, plucked some latex gloves out of a box on the counter.

The nurse came alongside. "Let's get you situated," she said, and prompted Tamara to lie back onto the bed.

Tamara's heart was slamming against the walls of her chest.

The nurse adjusted the sheet so that it hung loosely over Tamara's torso, then began positioning her legs—knees up and wide apart. Tamara shuddered as the nurse placed her feet in the cold, hard, metal stirrups.

"We're going to do a routine pelvic exam today," the doctor said. "We'll make it as quick and painless as possible."

Tamara peered over the sheet at him. She could feel the sweat popping out on her forehead. When he turned around to face her, he had a shiny, probe-like instrument in his hand.

Every muscle in her body tightened. *Oh, God, please don't let this hurt too much.*

Then the doctor lifted the sheet and touched her down there.

10   ONCE AGAIN DR. CASTLE marveled at the vitality of the young, female human body. His examination of the Ames girl had revealed that she and her baby were in remarkably good condition considering the absence of prenatal care. There was some inflammation in the vaginal tract that needed treating, and the fetus was undersized for its stage of development—due no doubt to a lack of proper nutrition. But all in all, the news was positive. He'd discovered no anatomical abnormalities that would signal a potential difficulty with delivery and had noted no signs of fetal distress related to the girl's recent accident. He would withhold further judgment until after an ultrasound was conducted, but based on what he'd seen so far, he was encouraged.

He placed the speculum in a sterilization chamber and pulled off his gloves. "You can get dressed now," he told the girl, who lay on the exam table moist-eyed and wan. "I'll come back in a few minutes and go over some things with you." He picked up her file and stepped into the hallway to write up his observations.

When he reentered the room a few minutes later, Tamara was sitting in a chair fully clothed, legs clamped together, knees drawn up to her belly. She glanced up at him with a sullen expression before letting her gaze fall to the floor. He leaned against the exam table as he browsed through the patient history forms in her file.

"Well," he said, snapping the file shut, "besides a minor yeast infection, you and your baby seem to be doing fine. I'd say, based on the date of your last period and my observations, you're due the third week of August, which puts you at thirty weeks. I'll give you a prescription for the infection. Marion will provide you with information about diet and exercise, and Doris will set up an appointment for an ultrasound. Do you know what that is?"

"Of course," Tamara said, her lips assuming a pouty fullness. "I'm not stupid."

The doctor smiled. "I didn't mean to imply you were. But I know that maternity is something new for you. Not all first-time mothers-to-be know these things."

The girl didn't say anything.

"That about covers it for today," the doctor said. He tapped a corner of the file folder against his palm. "I'd like to see you again in a couple of weeks. By then we'll have the results of the ultrasound, and the yeast infection should have started responding to the medication. Of course, if you experience any difficulties in the meantime, like unusual pain or bleeding, I want you to come in right away. Will you do that?"

Tamara gave a barely perceptible nod, her mouth resuming its natural line.

Dr. Castle regarded that expressive mouth, that circumspect face, the vulnerability it tried to mask, and feelings stirred in him he couldn't explain. He was taking an interest in this girl's welfare that went beyond the clinical. He cared about all his patients, but at the moment, he cared about this girl more. "Are you in school?"

The girl shook her head.

"Have you taken any parenting classes?"

She tucked her chin against her chest. "No."

"Would you like to?"

Her head snapped up. "I'd like to be done here so I can go home."

"To your brother's house?"

"What's it to you?"

"Is that where you plan to live after the baby is born?"

Tamara's gaze veered to the side. "Like I said—what's it to you?"

The doctor tugged on his earlobe. "Fair question." He ignored it anyway. The girl's situation was far more desperate than she realized. As a teenage mother-to-be, she was facing a gauntlet of harsh realities and hidden consequences, and she didn't have a clue. Without the support of a loving family, she and her baby stood little chance of surviving the crucible of teenage motherhood unscathed. He looked at her now with a mounting sense of compassion. "Tamara, I just want you to know what your options are."

There was a flicker of wariness in the girl's eyes. Her mouth twitched, but she remained mum.

"You can have this baby and care for it as best you can."

"Or?" she said, hurling the word at him as though it were a javelin meant to pierce his heart.

"You can consider giving it up for adoption."

The girl's countenance colored. She brought her feet to the floor. Her back bowed. "What I do with my child is none of your business."

The doctor pushed himself away from the exam table, stood alongside it. "You're right. I mention adoption only to make you aware that you have options—legal options—to bearing the burden of responsibility for a child by yourself, at your age."

"I know my options," the girl said in a huffy voice.

The doctor doubted this but let it pass. "Then you must know that there are many childless couples out there looking to adopt a newborn—well-established couples who would provide a child with a comfortable, loving home."

Tamara's face took on a closed look and she said no more.

"Think about it," he said. "Only you can decide what is best for yourself and your child."

∾

GARY ALREADY HAD the motor running when Tamara got back to the truck.

"Have a nice time?" he said as she climbed inside.

"Screw you."

Gary laughed and put the truck in gear.

When they got back to the house, Tamara shut herself up in her room. She'd had enough of stepbrothers and doctors and everyone else who pretended to be helpful but really just aimed to control her. She shucked her shoes and curled up on the bed with her clothes on.

A tremor of fury rippled through her body. The examination in the doctor's office had been humiliating—having to lie on her back naked with her feet in those cold metal stirrups and her legs wide open while the doctor probed her female essence. She'd expected it to hurt, but it had only shamed her.

She gave her head a brisk shake, trying to break free from the memory of it. The doctor had said her baby was okay, that was all that mattered. The baby came first, her feelings second.

Besides, what the doctor had said later had been more disturbing than the physical exam. Adoption? Did he think she wasn't good enough to have this baby and raise it on her own? Did he really think she would give her baby away to some "well-established" couple?

No way was she giving up her baby—not now, not ever. That doctor could go to hell. She snugged her arms around her middle. She would have this baby and care for it better than anyone else could, because that's what mothers do.

11

THAT EVENING, WHEN Dr. Castle went to the Trouste estate to check on Margaret, the results of his examination were mixed. The vaginal bleeding had subsided, but Margaret's blood pressure was up and the fetal heartbeat seemed fainter than it had the day before. For reasons unknown to the doctor, the fetus—repeating the pattern of Margaret's previous pregnancy—had begun to decline during its fifth month of gestation, prior to any chance of viability.

"How we doing, Doc?" Margaret's voice was scratchy and broken, like radio static. Still she offered a wisp of a smile. Despite the stress of her confinement and the constant worry about her child, she'd been a trooper throughout her latest ordeal.

"Fine," he assured her, knowing that to say otherwise would plunge her into a maelstrom of depression. She continued to refuse admission to the hospital, where she belonged, so he had no choice but to manage her care here as best he could. He patted her forearm. "You're doing just fine."

Outside the closed door to Margaret's room, the doctor conferred with the nurse he'd arranged to stay with her full time now that her condition was so tenuous. Beatrice Gates was, for all practical purposes, retired, although she was still relatively young, having just turned fifty-eight the previous month. She was a sturdy block of a woman, with the shoulders of a man and a handshake to match. But she had the face of an angel, the beatific effect of which was enhanced by a halo of platinum blond hair and an otherworldly gentleness when dealing with patients. She had worked in Dr. Castle's office for nearly twenty years before quitting to spend more time with her husband, a retired building contractor, and their three grandkids. But she continued to make herself available to the doctor on an as-needed basis. And this was a time during which she was sorely needed, not only for her obstetrical skills but also for her commitment to the confidentiality of the patient.

"Just make her as comfortable as you can," Dr. Castle instructed as the two of them huddled in the hallway. "And call me if there's a change."

"I will, Doctor," Beatrice said.

Downstairs in the library, Dr. Castle had another post-exam chat with Russell, only this time seated on the sofa across from Russell in his chair, both of them with a drink in hand. After an initial bout of labored silence, the doctor spoke up, reporting honestly of Margaret's perilous condition and that of her fetus. Russell responded with continued silence, but the stricken look on his face communicated his feelings well enough. The doctor didn't know what else to say, as no encouraging words came to mind and there was no point in going on about the obvious: Margaret was sure to lose this baby as she had lost the others, and probably sooner than later.

After sitting with his friend for what seemed an appropriate time, Dr. Castle set his drink down on the coffee table in front of him and pushed himself up from the sofa. "Tomorrow then," he said, and took his leave.

He arrived at his home on the west side a little after eight o'clock. He and Lily had bought the spacious Mediterranean-style house a few years before she died. Lily had loved its interior courtyard. When she was alive, the courtyard had been festooned with flowering plants in decorative pots. She'd taken great pleasure in nurturing her potted paradise and showing it off to their guests. Now the pots sprouted nothing but stubble and the courtyard seldom had a visitor.

After Lily passed away, Dr. Castle had planned to sell the house. It was much larger than he needed. He'd even spoken to a realtor about listing it but had never followed up. It just seemed too much trouble— getting it ready to sell, putting up with prospective buyers traipsing through, then all the paperwork when an offer came in. Instead, he'd simply closed off a good portion of the house. He hadn't been in some of the rooms in years. No one had except Mrs. Johnson, the lady who came in once a week to clean and do laundry.

As was his routine upon arriving home each evening, Dr. Castle entered his study and phoned his message service. He'd received only one call since leaving his office for the day—from Gary Neaves. The message: "Call me. We need to talk business."

Puzzled, the doctor plodded into the kitchen and poured himself a glass of tomato juice from an open can in the fridge. He sat down at the breakfast bar, sipped from his glass, and contemplated whether or not to call this Neaves fellow back. He was beginning to think it had been a mistake to contact the Ames girl's stepbrother, much less to have brought up the issue of adoption during that first telephone conversation. His ploy had worked—it had gotten Tamara in for a checkup. But what now? What *business* could he and the likes of Gary Neaves possibly have to talk about?

Before he could come to a determination in the matter, the doctor's thoughts drifted back to Margaret. Her baby was dying—was literally withering in the womb. And by all rights, he should have allowed it to abort naturally instead of giving Margaret drugs to prevent that from happening.

He drained the last of his tomato juice and clanked the glass down on the counter so hard he was surprised it didn't break. Despite all his medical skill and years of experience, he'd been powerless to help Margaret Trouste bring a healthy child into the world.

He remembered how excited she'd been that first time in his office, almost twenty years ago, when he'd told her she was going to have a baby. She couldn't wait to get home and give Russell the happy news. The doctor had felt truly honored to be presented with the opportunity to deliver a new generation of Trouste babies.

Alas, it was not to be. Within a few weeks of having learned she was pregnant, Margaret lost her baby. Her body simply expelled it as if it was foreign tissue.

Another unexplained early miscarriage occurred about eight months later while the Troustes were out to dinner with a city councilman and his wife. Partway through the meal, Margaret fell silent. Her face drained of color. The councilman's wife helped her to the ladies' room. She lost the baby there.

Two years after that, her third pregnancy came to an end early in the second trimester. During a routine examination, Dr. Castle had discovered a slight premature dilation of the cervix and as a precaution prescribed bed rest. Margaret complied and everything seemed fine: the cervix stayed closed and the fetus grew. The doctor checked on her regularly. Then one night at home, Russell awoke from a sound sleep to find his wife screaming and the bedding saturated with blood and fetal tissue.

Margaret was hospitalized. Dr. Castle ran tests—for infection, for blood abnormalities, for signs of toxemia. All the results came back negative. Later, when Margaret felt up to it, he had her come into his office for a thorough exam that included scoping the uterus. He was relieved to find nothing wrong, nothing he'd overlooked that would have caused her to miscarry. But he was also distressed to have found nothing on which to blame her repeated failure to carry a fetus to full term.

Sitting in the exam room that day, after the examination, Margaret had turned her head away. A sob racked her chest. "I'm such a failure as a woman," she said through a torrent of tears.

The doctor had been at a loss as to how to comfort her. "Now, now," he said. "Just give your body more time."

But more time hadn't been the answer. The following years had brought the Trouste family only more heartache when it came to their efforts to procreate, beginning with Margaret's fourth pregnancy, and her fourth miscarriage. The pregnancy had occurred shortly after her thirtieth birthday. The miscarriage occurred four months later, this time due to a clear case of *abruptio placenta*, apparently resulting from an abnormally short umbilical cord and a bout of hyperactivity on the part of the fetus.

That there seemed to be a reasonable explanation for the miscarriage, although a relief to Dr. Castle, was of no consolation to the Troustes. Margaret was especially devastated by the loss because she'd carried the baby so long that her hopes of success had soared. Following this disappointment, even she seemed to give up on the idea of having children.

Then came her thirty-fifth birthday and another reversal in her thinking, as she became motivated by the reality that her childbearing years were slipping away. She informed her husband that she was going to give her body one last chance to get it right.

Russell was dead set against her becoming pregnant again and had looked to Dr. Castle for an ally in the matter. "How much more tragedy can we handle, Brandon?" he'd said one day over drinks at the country club. Then he'd hung his head and stared at the ice floating in his glass.

Dr. Castle felt great empathy for his friend. He too had reservations about Margaret's intentions, since he considered each of her failed pregnancies failures of his own as well. But Margaret, as usual, was adamant. Over her husband's objections, although with his tacit assent—he had, after all, participated in the act that led to the fertilization of her egg—Margaret became pregnant one more time. And it seemed that finally her faith in her body had been justified.

Indeed, every stage of her pregnancy was normal going into the fifth month. There was no premature dilation of the cervix, no vaginal bleeding, no unmanageable pathologies. Mother's and baby's vitals remained within acceptable limits. The doctor had restricted Margaret's physical activities, but merely as a precaution. And more out of deference to her family's status than of necessity, he'd begun making house calls rather than asking Margaret to come to his office. As the fifth month progressed, she was doing so well that even Russell was starting to believe in his wife's ability to carry this child to full term.

Then on a regular visit to Trouste House, Dr. Castle noticed that Margaret was looking unusually pale. He checked her vitals. She seemed okay, but the baby's heartbeat wasn't as strong as it had been on his previous visit. He decided not to take any chances. He called an ambulance and had Margaret taken to the hospital.

At the hospital, he continued monitoring mother and baby over the next few days. The fetal heartbeat continued to weaken. The doctor was puzzled. He searched his brain and the literature for answers to this troubling development but was at a loss to explain it. Dr. Reid, a specialist from Eugene, was brought down to consult. Together the two doctors reviewed every aspect of the case, including the history of each of Margaret's previous pregnancies.

But the baby's condition continued to deteriorate, and the doctors remained stymied as to the cause of its decline. Eventually the fetal heartbeat weakened to the point of peril. The doctors had to do something. But they didn't know what course of action to take. If they delivered the baby—it was just twenty weeks along—the chances of its survival were extremely low, while the likelihood of birth defects— assuming it did survive—was extremely high. On the other hand, if they didn't go ahead with the delivery, the baby would surely die in the womb.

During this time of crisis for the fetus, Margaret was frantic. She couldn't bear the thought of losing her baby—not now, not when she could, as she expressed it, "almost reach out and cradle it in my arms." When Dr. Castle informed her of the dire state of affairs and the limited options, she responded by sinking her fingernails into his wrist. "Don't even think about taking this baby before its time." Then she burst into tears. Finally she had to be sedated.

So the doctors held off on any plans for delivery, and miraculously the fetus held on to its tenuous existence. But then Margaret's physical condition began to worsen. Her blood pressure rose to dangerous levels, and her heart began to show signs of arrhythmia. Now *her* life was being threatened by their inaction.

Russell, who'd practically lived at the hospital during this ordeal, told the doctors to set aside their concerns about the baby and do whatever they had to do to save Margaret. Over her objections, they performed an emergency Caesarean section.

They were too late to save the baby. Inexplicably, the umbilical cord had shriveled, losing its ability to transfer blood from the mother to the fetus. The doctors could find no reasonable explanation for this.

Margaret survived the operation, but Dr. Castle knew it was only the follow-up counseling and a prescription for an antidepressant that had preserved her sanity.

Over the months and years that followed, she and Russell had seemed to come to terms with their lack of offspring. Russell had kept busy running the mill. Margaret dabbled in charities, assisted now and then with social events at the country club, and little by little became more involved with church-related activities.

Upon turning forty, Margaret became perimenopausal. "A bit early for this, isn't it?" she'd commented to Dr. Castle during an office visit not long after that benchmark birthday. She was referring to the hot flashes and mood swings she'd begun experiencing, and the occasional lapses in her period.

"Not that uncommon," he'd assured her. "These are symptoms you might experience on and off for years before you stop menstruating altogether."

She'd shrugged. "Just as well to put this business behind me."

The doctor wasn't sure what "business" she was referring to, but took her to mean ovulation, without which of course there would be no future pregnancies.

But then, five months ago, just prior to her turning forty-two, Margaret had come into his office complaining of symptoms similar to morning sickness. "Probably the flu," she'd said. But a pelvic exam had shown otherwise.

Dr. Castle was shocked. He was even more disturbed by Margaret's response when informed of the pregnancy. "It's God's will," she'd said.

He wasn't so sure—then or now.

The doctor deposited his empty juice glass in the sink. He traipsed back to his study and sat down at his desk. There was no use going to bed. He wouldn't be able to sleep. He had to put his anxiety about Margaret out of his mind before he could accomplish that feat.

He rifled through the papers and magazines on his desk, picked up a copy of *JAMA* and scanned its table of contents. Nothing piqued his interest. He plopped the journal down on the desktop next to a notepad on which was scribbled Gary Neaves' name and phone number. He stared at the notepad for a time, then almost unconsciously picked up the receiver to his telephone and dialed the number. When Neaves answered, the doctor identified himself.

"A private adoption," Neaves said without preliminaries. "Let's go that route."

"Mr. Neaves—" The doctor was already wishing he hadn't made the call.

"You can call me Gary now that we're in business together."

Dr. Castle wrinkled his brow. What was this fellow talking about? "Mr. Neaves, I may have given you the wrong impression the last time we spoke. I don't normally arrange adoptions myself. I refer potential clients to an agency in Eugene."

"No agency, Doc. Strictly private. Tamara wants it that way."

The doctor's mind did a double take on Gary's words. *Tamara wants it?* He took off his glasses and rubbed his eyes. "Are you telling me that Tamara has decided to put the baby up for adoption?" When he'd spoken with her earlier in the day, the girl had seemed quite unreceptive to the idea.

"That's right. Looks like she has some sense after all."

The doctor quietly mulled the skepticism he harbored regarding what Gary Neaves was saying. How much of this was coming from Neaves and how much from his stepsister? It was possible Tamara had reassessed her options on the basis of what was best for the baby, but given her state of mind when she'd left his office, that seemed unlikely. Even so, there was no doubt in the doctor's mind that both she and her baby would be better off with adoption.

"Okay," he finally said, "let me think about it. As I said, I almost always go through an agency. But there are situations in which couples sometimes want more privacy than an agency affords."

"Yeah, that's what we want, Doc—privacy. Lots of privacy. And, Doc, make it a rich childless couple, one that can afford a fat referral fee. After all, this is going to be a great kid they're getting."

Dr. Castle cringed. What rock did this guy wriggle out from under? "I'll get back to you," he said reluctantly, and hung up the phone.

12   TAMARA LINED UP the cans on the shelf with the labels facing out. Peas. Corn. Hash. Pork and Beans. Three kinds of soup. In a different cabinet, she'd already stowed the peanut butter, saltine crackers, and a package of buttermilk pancake mix. She picked up a can of Vienna sausages and placed it on the shelf next to the beans.

Tamara didn't know what had happened to alter the course of things, but life at Gary's house had taken a sudden U-turn for the better. For one thing, there was plenty of food on hand. Besides milk and bread, there was fruit and cereal, lunchmeat and cheese, and enough canned goods to bloat the kitchen cabinets. Gary had started coming home every few days with a bulging grocery bag that he'd plunk down on the counter and rip open, letting goods tumble out. It would be up to Tamara to put stuff in the refrigerator and organize the cans on the shelves, which she did with the pleasure of knowing where her next meals were coming from.

And there were fewer stag parties to put up with at the house. Although Gary remained seemingly oblivious to her presence, as if she was a planet moving in a different orbit than his, he'd started staying home more, while his buddies visited less. He'd plant himself in his armchair in the living room, a cigarette dangling from between his lips, a can of Coors in hand. His gaze would settle, with the indifference of a man loosely marking time, on the blaring TV, or on the mute telephone sitting on the table next to his chair, or out the picture window facing the street where children too sick to go to school but not too sick to go out and play practiced life.

Tamara mostly stayed in her room when Gary was home. It wasn't like they had anything to chat about. And just being in the same room with him for long got her nerves to jumping.

She closed the door to the kitchen cabinet, wadded up the torn grocery bag and stuffed it into the trash can under the sink. She took an apple out of a bowl of fruit on the counter, washed it under the faucet, and took a bite, savoring its juicy sweetness.

Even with Gary hanging around like he was this afternoon, life was better for her now. She was getting plenty to eat—for herself and her baby. Her forehead was mending. Her ribs were no longer hurting. And best of all, she was beginning to think again in terms of the future.

Just this morning, she'd started making a list of things to do to better her situation. It wasn't a full-blown plan, but it was a beginning. Deep down, she was still uneasy about being with Gary, because—well, Gary was Gary. But at least her circumstances seemed less hopeless than they had just days before, and she had begun to feel less desperate about having no other place to go. It was as if she'd been traveling through a dark, narrow canyon that had suddenly opened up into a wide valley bathed in sunlight that illuminated a network of byways, all of which she was convinced would lead to someplace better.

As she headed back to her room, she carried with her a lightness of spirit she hadn't felt in a long time. She retrieved her "to do" list from the dresser and read through it, wondering what to add.

———

See about getting back into school.
Look into local childcare.
Take a parenting class.
Find out how to get a work permit.

———

People who might be able to help me:
the old doctor
the nurse from the hospital?
county health department

———

What else? she wondered. Then she had a thought that made her heart flutter. She picked up her pen and below the last entry on her list wrote, "Write to Angela."

On her way out of the house later that afternoon, Tamara was surprised to find Gary still camped in his chair in the living room, as if it had been only minutes since he'd brought home the groceries, instead of hours. She thought it odd, his hanging around the house so much lately, but said nothing. Just kept on walking toward the front door.

"Where you goin'?" Gary said in a sentry-like manner that stopped her cold.

She stood still, staring straight ahead. "For a walk."

"Where to?"

It would have been easy for her to say truthfully, "I'm going to the post office to mail a letter to a friend." But Tamara felt a prickling uneasiness about divulging her mission. "What does it matter?"

"It matters because I asked."

Tamara thought about saying something sassy, then thought again. She didn't want to piss Gary off now that things were going so well at his house.

"It's stuffy in the house," she said. "I need some fresh air."

Gary took a puff from his cigarette, exhausted a rush of smoke. "Fresh air is overrated."

Tamara waited for him to say something else. When he didn't, she continued on out the door.

The next afternoon, it was the same story. Only this time it really was the heat that drove her from the house—summer had clamped down on the valley like a grandma's hug. Tamara thought she'd walk down to the park along the river where it was sure to be cooler than in her bedroom. Again, before she could get out the door, Gary quizzed her like an overzealous dad, wanting to know where she was going and when she would be coming back. It was more than brotherly concern, she thought, more even than parental. It seemed to her like self-interest, although she had no idea what stake her stepbrother could possibly have in her whereabouts.

13   DR. CASTLE SAT slumped over his desk in his private office, cradling his head in his hands. It had been another long workday, extended beyond normal business hours by an unexpected delivery at the hospital. Mrs. Dooley's water had broken prematurely while she and her husband shopped for baby furniture in Eugene. Her labor had progressed rapidly during their drive back to Fir Valley. They'd barely made it to the hospital in time for Dr. Castle to deliver a healthy baby boy. The doctor's required presence at the hospital had caused a backlog at his office, where, upon returning, he'd moved from exam room to exam room, chatting with patients, probing vaginas, and listening to fetal heartbeats, until Marion had finally stopped putting file folders in the racks. It was seven o'clock before the last patient had gone home and the ladies had closed up shop for the day.

The doctor sagged back in his chair, feeling as though his body could melt into it. Every measure of his sentient being had been given to the day. There was nothing left to distinguish himself from the physical property of the chair. Nothing except . . . He sighed. Nothing except his obligation to Margaret Trouste.

The doctor had been checking on Margaret at Trouste House nearly every evening and consulting with Beatrice several times a day over the phone. With the help of the drugs he'd prescribed for her, Margaret's physical condition had remained stable even as the health of her fetus, as evidenced by its fading heartbeat, had continued to decline. But experience told him that Margaret's body couldn't hold out much longer against its predisposition to abort a withering fetus. Something had to be done to resolve the situation, but he didn't know what. So he'd continued to play this dangerous waiting game, with Margaret opposing any action that might result in the termination of her pregnancy, while his concern for her welfare shadowed his daily activities like the angel of death looming over a potential tragedy.

Confusing matters in the doctor's mind was the issue of the Ames girl and her baby. Her stepbrother had become a thorn in the doctor's side, calling the office almost daily, wanting to "finalize" their arrangement. "Tamara needs to know that her baby will be well cared for," Neaves had said, speaking the words with such affectation that it made the doctor want to puke. He knew that all the fellow cared about was himself and what he could get out of "the arrangement." The doctor had put him off as best he could, explaining that it took time for suitable adoptive parents to be identified and screened. The placement of a child was not as simple as adopting a puppy from the pound.

The reality was that the doctor had no prospective couple in mind—unless . . . If only Margaret would relent on the issue of adoption. She and Russell would be the perfect match for Tamara's baby.

But he knew that would never happen. "It just wouldn't be the same," Margaret had declared on more than one occasion, repeating herself with fiery-eyed fervor each time the subject of adoption had been broached by either Russell or himself.

The doctor let out an expressive groan. He pushed aside a stack of lab reports, picked up the receiver to the telephone, and dialed Trouste House. Elena answered. Shortly thereafter, Russell's voice came on the line.

"How's she doing this evening?" the doctor inquired.

"About the same, Beatrice says."

"Do you think I need to stop by?"

"You sound tired."

"Long day, long week."

"I think we'll be fine. I'll have Beatrice call you if anything develops."

Dr. Castle felt a little of the weight fall from his shoulders. "In that case, I think I'll go home, have a drink, and crash."

"I'll have one here."

The doctor thought to bid his friend goodnight, but he couldn't seem to get the words out. And the longer he remained mute, the more he felt compelled to speak what was truly on his mind. "Russell," he finally said, "let me ask you something."

"Sure."

"Do you really think Margaret will simply give up on life if—when—she loses this baby?"

Russell answered without hesitation. "I think she will."

The doctor thought so too, and he felt his pulse rate escalate as he prepared to follow up on that assumption. "But what if there was a way to keep that from happening?"

An airy whoosh sounded in Dr. Castle's ear that he recognized as a heavy exhalation contacting the mouthpiece on the other end of the line. There was a forlorn moment of silence, then Russell murmured, "You've already said there is little, if any, hope that she will carry this baby to full term."

"I spoke the truth."

"Then, if not in body at least in spirit, Margaret will surely die along with it."

The doctor's mind eddied around that eventuality, which was anathema to him, especially if there was a way for him to intervene, to thwart fate. "But what if there was something we could do to save her? Something—unconventional—that would keep her from going over the edge emotionally. Would you want to try it?"

Another vacant moment passed before Russell said, "I'm listening."

The doctor squeezed his eyelids shut and blurted out the essence of the plan that had formed in his mind over the last several days. It was a plan, he knew, born of desperation—of a blind desire to make things right for everyone involved. But if it worked, it would change the course of so many lives for the better. When he finished speaking, he waited breathlessly for his friend's response.

For the longest time nothing but dead air came out of the phone. Finally Russell said, "You believe such a thing can be accomplished?"

"I do," the doctor asserted, despite his own doubts about the viability of his proposed scheme. So many things would have to go right for it to succeed.

"And the girl would agree to it?"

"In essence, she already has. She told her brother she wants to give the baby up for adoption. That's all the agreement we need."

"But wouldn't we be breaking some law?"

"There's nothing illegal about private adoption."

"Yes, but the girl would think—"

"And she would be better off in the long run to think it. Look, Russell,

I know from experience that it's natural for any woman who gives up a child to later wish she hadn't. Maybe it takes a year, maybe ten years, maybe twenty. But eventually there is guilt; there is regret. It's human nature. These women become haunted for a lifetime by a decision they made when they were girls, even if they continue to believe it was the best thing for them and for their child. But this way there's no guilt. This way, Tamara Ames can never have regrets. We'd be doing her a favor. And we'd be saving Margaret in the process." The doctor felt the prickling heat of adrenaline coursing through him. "This is a win-win proposition."

Again a gaping hush—like the prayer-filled interval between the words, "Yes we have, your honor" and the reading of a verdict. Then Russell said, "Can I think about it?"

Dr. Castle's mouth had gone dry. His heart was racing. "Of course," he said. "But we'll need to make a decision soon. Margaret could miscarry any moment."

14 RUSSELL TROUSTE POURED himself a whiskey at the library bar and promptly downed it. He poured another. In no time, it too was gone. Finally, acknowledging his inability to quash his anxiety with alcohol, he left the library and went upstairs to his wife's room. Beatrice was seated in a chair at Margaret's bedside with an open magazine in her lap. She rose as he entered.

"She's resting now," the nurse whispered. "She woke briefly and asked for you. I was about to buzz you, but she fell back asleep."

Russell studied his wife's care-worn face, its pallor in stark contrast to the dark crescents under her eyes. Strands of hair clung to her cheeks in sweaty ringlets. "Take a break," he told the nurse. "Go down to the dining room and eat something. Elena has fixed a nice dinner and is complaining because there's no one to enjoy it."

"Have you had your supper, Mr. Trouste?"

"All I care to have."

"Yes, sir," Beatrice said, bestowing a compassionate smile on him before leaving.

Russell sat down in the chair beside his wife's bed and watched her sleep. Her breathing was thin and erratic, like the soughing of a fickle breeze. Now and again she would moan and stir in the bed—her eyes would flutter but remain closed. During one fitful episode, the sheet covering her swollen belly slipped off to the side. Russell reached over and pulled it back.

He still had trouble believing all this could be happening again. He'd been stunned that night, nearly five months ago, when Margaret had told him she was pregnant. She'd been having only occasional periods and they'd been having only occasional sex. When the blunt reality of what she was saying finally broke through to his startled psyche, he reacted without thinking. "Don't worry, darling," he said, lowering the book he'd been reading in bed to look at her. "We'll have it taken care of."

Margaret, dressed in a red velvet bathrobe that hung loosely over her silk nightgown, was sitting on a stool at her vanity, brushing her hair. Her back was to him. She looked at him in the mirror without turning around. "Taken care of?"

"Yes—you know—before it becomes a problem."

"No, I don't know." Margaret's eyes were big and round in the mirror—full of innocence, feigned or otherwise.

It seemed perfectly clear to Russell what had to be done. Margaret's previous pregnancies had all ended tragically. The last two had nearly killed her. It had taken years for her to recover, physically and emotionally. She was no longer a young woman with a resilient body. This pregnancy was a fluke and clearly had to be terminated before it did irreparable damage to her health.

Besides, if the truth were told, Russell was beyond wanting a family. He was forty-five years old and had lost his desire to procreate. Other people's kids got on his nerves with their voices like screeching tires and their pinball movements. He no longer wanted any of his own. He'd never admitted as much to Margaret. The change in his thinking in this matter had seemed irrelevant, since with each successive failed attempt, the possibility of their ever reproducing had become remote at best. But now the issue, in living color, was staring them in the face again, and his concern truly was not for himself.

"Our foremost consideration has to be your well-being, dear," he said in his business-meeting voice, wanting to avoid a fight.

Margaret apparently was itching for one. She threw her shoulders back. "And for that of our child."

He knew then that she'd already made up her mind—that she'd chained herself to a rekindled vision of motherhood—but he pressed her nonetheless. "Surely you can't seriously be considering allowing this pregnancy to continue long term."

She spun around on her stool and gave him a rapier look. "Surely you can't seriously be considering otherwise."

Russell tossed his book aside. "What could possibly make you want to do such a thing?"

"What could possibly make you think I wouldn't?" Margaret countered.

Russell didn't want to be cruel, but he obviously wasn't getting through to her. "Just look at our history as would-be parents."

"History is just that," Margaret said, once again showing him her back as she went on brushing her hair.

He threw up his hands in frustration. "How can you think this pregnancy will end any differently than the others?"

Margaret laid her brush down on the vanity. She tilted her head back, swept her flowing locks to the side, and began braiding them. "Because this time it's meant to be."

"Meant to be?"

"It's God's will."

"And what if this baby dies?"

"It won't," his wife said, her voice lush with assurance. She picked up an elastic band and secured the end of her braid.

Russell was puzzled by his wife's certitude. "And why not?"

Margaret leaned toward the mirror as if to show him her face more closely. The passion of a true believer shone in her eyes. "Because God never allows us to suffer more than we can bear. And for me, this baby dying would be unbearable." She rose and strode toward the bathroom, one end of the tie to her bathrobe dragging the ground.

"Darling, please reconsider," Russell pleaded.

But she had already closed the door.

Sitting alongside her mounded figure now, he noted that her breathing had changed, had evened out and deepened. For the time being—and only because of the drugs in her system—she was resting.

But he knew this restful state wouldn't last. It was only a temporary lull in her travail, a travail that would continue so long as Margaret remained determined to see this pregnancy through to the end. Yet she was unwavering, was apparently willing to do anything—to risk her life even—for this last chance to have a child of her own.

The awful truth was that the fetus she was carrying would almost certainly never see the light of day. And when it succumbed, he would lose Margaret along with it.

The thought of that happening filled Russell with a suffocating dread, so that he sensed in that moment what it must be like to be buried alive. He clawed at the air as he would the inside of a coffin lid slammed in his face. And he could hear Brandon's voice in his head saying, "But what if there was something we could do to save her?"

15   THE BUTTERY GLOW of daylight coming in through Tamara's bedroom window had hardened into darkness. She'd undressed and climbed into bed. But she was too keyed up to sleep. Joy ruled her emotions, sent her spirits soaring to new heights. And the object of that joy had a face now, and arms and legs, and a slowly emerging personality expressed through movement the way a dancer communicates with her audience.

She sat up in the bed and, for the hundredth time since Gary had brought her home from The Imaging Center, studied the printout of the sonogram the ultrasound technician had given her. The printout was black and white and grainy, but she could still make out her baby's lovely features—the full-moon roundness of her head, the fleshy folds of her eyelids, her peanut nose, her pursed mouth, and—pressed against one cheek—her little fist that looked like it was getting ready to throw a punch. Tamara giggled. *I knew it was a girl. Mothers can tell.*

Lost in the adoration of the image of the child in her womb, Tamara had paid no heed to the eruption of voices at the front of the house. Gary probably had company, although she hadn't seen much of Brian and Jerome lately. She hadn't seen much of anybody, not since Gary had started making such a fuss whenever she went somewhere, acting as if he was her guardian angel or something. That's why she'd been so surprised when he'd insisted she keep her appointment for the ultrasound.

She traced a fingertip along the telling lines and shadows on the sonogram printout and smiled. "I see you. I—"

The verbal exchange coming from the front of the house had grown in volume to the point of distraction. Tamara got up to shut her bedroom door, which she'd left cracked open for ventilation. She had a hand on it, was about to snap it closed, when a familiar voice resounded down the hall and penetrated her consciousness. She stood still and listened. Could it be?

She hurriedly pulled on her pants and, spurred by an unwelcome sense of longing, trod barefooted into the living room.

Gary was in a wide-legged stance at the open front door, his back to her, speaking in gravelly tones to someone outside. She came up behind him. The porch light was on. She peered over Gary's shoulder and caught a glimpse of the face on the other side of the screen door. Her knees went weak. She grabbed hold of the inner door for support.

The last time Tamara had seen Jimmy was two months ago at the high school in Eugene. She'd just boarded the school bus one afternoon when she spotted him through a window, driving into the parking lot in his little green truck. She'd felt a heart-palpitating urge to dash off the bus and run to him, but had resisted. She was better off leaving him alone. He had used her, and she didn't want to be used anymore.

They'd first met early in the school year at a music store in Valley

River Center. She'd been taken with his charm and boyish good looks. Jimmy was twenty-two years old but could pass for eighteen. He was tall and slender and disarmingly handsome. He had long blond hair that he kept pulled back in a ponytail. And he had a sexy goatee. He'd told her he was a music student at U of O, which wasn't true, although he had been at one time. They listened to cassette tapes together in the music store. Then Jimmy treated her to pizza at the food court.

He gave her a ride home from the mall that day, and before getting out of his truck, Tamara wrote her phone number on his hand. The next evening he called and invited her to a party. They went to other parties together after that, where almost everybody was older than Tamara, who wasn't yet sixteen.

Jimmy started picking her up after school, and she introduced him to the other high school kids. Before long, he was hanging out with her at lunchtime too at the strip mall where she and her friends went for lunch. She didn't realize at first what he was doing, or didn't want to know that he was selling pot and pills to the other kids. Angela said to her one day, "Jimmy better be careful or he'll get busted." Tamara told Jimmy what Angela had said. Jimmy had laughed. "The cops got better things to do," he said. "Besides, the school officials are too stupid to know what's going on."

Tamara should have realized that Jimmy was bad news, but by then she was hopelessly in love with him. By the time Angela had convinced her that she needed to get out of the relationship, she was pregnant and Jimmy was the one backing off. She cried for days after he'd walked out on her at Denny's. When she finally came out of her funk, she vowed that she was going to forget him.

But now as she caught sight of Jimmy's face through the screen door—even cast as it was in the harsh glow of the porch light, with moths and gnats flitting about it—it still looked beautiful to her, and the old feelings she had for him stirred within her like the vibrations of a spring morning.

Jimmy's eyes bloomed wide when he saw her. "Tamara," he said, his voice breathy with excitement, "I want to talk to you. Angela said you were here."

Tamara didn't understand at first, then she remembered her letter to Angela.

Jimmy pressed his face against the screen. "Tell your brother it's okay to let me in."

But Gary wouldn't budge, and Tamara wasn't sure she wanted to talk to Jimmy anyway. It was bad enough that seeing him had brought back the old feelings.

But then Jimmy started to cry, saying how much he loved her and wanted to be a father to her child. And she began to cry too, not because she believed what Jimmy was saying but because she longed for it to be true—had longed for it from the moment she'd found out she was pregnant. Despite her misgivings, she found herself edging toward the door.

Gary stayed between her and Jimmy. "Get the hell out of here, man," he growled.

Jimmy clenched his fists and stood his ground, but he was still crying. "I want to talk to Tamara."

"No, you don't," Gary said. "You want to walk away from here right now. And if you know what's good for you, you'll do just that."

"You can't keep me from seeing her," Jimmy shot back.

Tamara cringed. Jimmy didn't know Gary. "Go away," she told him, even as she felt herself being drawn to him by a force beyond her control.

"Not until we've talked."

But Gary would have none of it. He thrust the screen door open so abruptly that its wooden frame struck Jimmy flush on the forehead. Jimmy staggered back, looking dazed. Gary grabbed him by the throat, drove him against the porch railing and levered him backwards over it until his upper body was nearly parallel to the ground. "I told you to get lost."

Tamara screamed for Gary to stop. She clutched his shirt and tried to pull him back. But he pushed her away, and all she could do was watch helplessly as Jimmy struggled to free himself, his fingers groping at the hand clasping his throat, his eyes bulging in their sockets.

Finally Gary let loose of him and came back into the house. He locked the door and switched off the porch light.

Tamara ran over and squinted out the picture window, using her cupped hands to shield her eyes from the interior light. She could see a dark figure humped over, a hand clinging to the porch railing. Then the figure wheeled around and plunged down the steps, into the darkness.

Tamara remained at the window, crying but not really knowing why.

16   TAMARA LAY AWAKE that night tussling with the questions posed by Jimmy's visit. Would he come back for her? Had he really meant what he'd said about wanting to be a part of her life again, and the baby's? Or was that just another lie?

She shifted her heavy belly in the bed, trying without success to get comfortable. Even if Jimmy was telling the truth, should she actually consider taking him back? She still loved him, wanted him, trembled at the thought of being in his arms. But what about the baby? What kind of father could a drug dealer possibly be to her child? No, she had to let him go—again.

Instead of sleeping, she sobbed quietly in the dark, her heart raked by a rekindled sense of loss.

When light finally began seeping into her room, making shapes out of shadows, Tamara gave up on getting any rest. She sat up in bed with the covers wadded around her, her portable radio in hand. She extended its built-in antenna, aimed it at the window, and switched on the power. The radio had been a sixteenth-birthday present from Angela. Some birthday that had been. Tamara was pregnant, and Jimmy had just abandoned her. She was in no mood to celebrate, didn't even want the gift. But Angela had insisted, and as it turned out, it was the only birthday present she'd received.

At first the radio had worked fine in her room at Gary's house, and playing it—even softly so as not to peeve Gary—made her feel better, because the music crowded out the dark thoughts in her head, as if a musical note was fatter than a thought. But now the batteries were almost dead, and she had to crank the volume up all the way even to hear the faintest of melodic strains. She was fiddling with the radio's tuning dial, trying to find the rock station she liked, when she heard an unrelated sound.

She looked up and gasped.

Gary had opened her bedroom door and was standing in the doorway dressed in nothing but his dingy underwear. She recoiled, shuffled backwards in the bed, one hand impulsively tugging down the tail of her T-shirt, which had ridden up above her crotch, leaving her exposed—especially since her underpants, in addition to being stretched by all the weight she'd put on, were sheer from wear.

Gary eyed her with a look of amused curiosity, the way a child would view an exotic animal in a zoo: *Young female Homo sapien, seven-and-a-half months pregnant, in casual sleep attire.*

Tamara stared back, clench-jawed, letting him have his eyeful but daring him to take one step farther into the room. The tension was like a taut rope between them. Then Gary backed out of the doorway and the rope broke.

Tamara sprang from the bed and slammed the door. She grabbed her pants and yanked them on, stood in the middle of the room quivering with rage.

IT WAS EARLY AFTERNOON when Tamara awoke from her nap, more rested, but jittery. She was surprised to have gotten any sleep at all after the incident with Gary that morning. The nature of the intrusion had shaken her, caused the old feelings of vulnerability to resurface, raw and tender, like an exposed nerve on a broken tooth.

She got out of bed, put on her shoes, and after a stop in the bathroom, ventured down the hall to the front of the house. Gary was in the living room, sitting on his shabby throne, fully clothed now. A ragged cloud of cigarette smoke hung in the air above his head. He didn't say anything to her, just peered out into space with a hooded gaze, as if his brain was idling in neutral.

Tamara went into the kitchen. She poured some Corn Flakes and milk into a bowl, then took the bowl and a spoon back to her room.

Minutes later, her hunger attended to, she was passing through the living room again, angling this time for the front door, when Gary's voice came booming across the room, nearly knocking her off her feet. "Stay put."

She whirled on him, feeling the flames of her ire licking up inside her. "I'm not your prisoner."

Gary stared at her with eyes as cold and vacant as a polar sky.

She met his gaze, held it as long as she could. But it was no use. She could never out-*Gary* Gary. "You bastard!" She stomped back into her room and flung the door closed, her fury blocking out every sensation but hate.

17

"THE MAIN THING," Dr. Castle said, keeping his voice low so as not to be overheard, "is to maintain your anonymity." He and Russell sat across from one another in a back booth at Benevido's—the only Italian restaurant in town not counting pizza houses, and Dr. Castle definitely did not count pizza houses.

The doctor had been able to talk his friend into meeting him for dinner only after assuring him that his wife's condition was stable and that Beatrice would call the restaurant if that changed. Russell had hardly been out of the house for the past several weeks, and Dr. Castle could see that the strain of his being cooped up at home with nothing to do except worry about Margaret and make occasional phone calls to his managers at the mill was harder on him than were the long hours he normally put in at work.

By now the two men had already eaten dinner, both having chosen the scampi, which Dr. Castle thought was especially good this evening, although Russell had left most of his on his plate. A waiter had just cleared the table, lingering only long enough to empty a carafe of Chardonnay into their wineglasses. Dr. Castle gripped the stem of his glass as he continued speaking, dropping the volume of his voice another decibel or two just for good measure.

"You'll have no contact with either the girl or her brother," he told his friend. "And they'll have no knowledge of your identity. I'll continue to see the girl in my office until it's time for us to act. Since she's a minor and is living with her brother, it will be expected that I should have some contact with him also. But I'll keep that to a minimum. Only what is necessary to finalize the arrangement."

"To make the payoff, you mean," Russell said without muffling his voice.

Dr. Castle scanned the room for anyone who might have heard his friend's frank but injudicious remark and was relieved to see that the only other patrons within earshot were seemingly engrossed in their own conversation.

∾

RUSSELL TROUSTE WAS too preoccupied with his own thoughts to care who might have heard what he'd said. He stared numbly at the candle smoldering inside the frosted goblet sitting on the table next to a faux-crystal vase sprouting plastic flowers. The candle gushed an oily aroma. The smell didn't agree with his stomach. He'd eaten too little and drunk too much, and he was not particularly comfortable with the subject currently under discussion.

After much soul searching, Russell had agreed to go along with Brandon's plan to save Margaret. In the end, there didn't seem to be a more desirable option. Even so, he had reservations. He trusted Brandon, loved him like a favorite uncle. Yet he couldn't help but feel that by committing to such a stratagem as Brandon proposed he had made a pact with the devil.

He reached over and snuffed out the candle with spit-wetted fingers. A last gasp of unctuous smoke spiraled up. He pushed the goblet aside, seized his glass, and downed some more wine—along with his misgivings about the decision he'd made. If there was any chance his wife could be saved, he had to take it.

"There's only one thing you need to do," Brandon said in a barely audible voice.

Russell met his friend's gaze. "What's that?"

"A wire transfer."

"I thought you said this Neaves fellow wanted cash."

"He does," Brandon said. "And he'll have it. His sister will be the unwitting conduit for the initial payment. She's due for her next appointment on Wednesday. She'll be passing the money to her stepbrother in what she believes to be a packet of county health department forms. The rest will be paid after. I'll see to that myself. But the money for the girl"—he stabbed the tabletop with an index finger—"needs to go directly into a bank account in her name only. Otherwise, she'll never see a dime of it."

"The brother agreed?"

"I didn't give him an option," Brandon said. "Will that be a problem?"

Russell thought a moment. Cash was safer. Too many ways to trace a wire transfer. But it was doable. "Not really," he said. "I can use money from an offshore account only my CFO and I know about."

The doctor hitched his brow.

Russell shrugged. "Slush funds are a necessity of doing business these days."

18   TAMARA WAS DROWNING in the ocean of tobacco smoke Gary's living room had become. She coughed and snorted and flapped her magazine at the choking haze engulfing the room. She needed a gas mask. "I want to go for a walk," she said from her perch on the end of the couch farthest from Gary's chair. She hadn't been out of the house for nearly a week, not since the morning Gary had taken her to see the doctor again. Only this time, he'd

escorted her in and out of the office as if he was her personal bodyguard.

"Can I at least go down to the river? I'll stay in the park. Just for a little while. Please. I'll come straight back."

Gary didn't even give her the courtesy of a reply, just stubbed another cigarette butt into an already brimming ashtray, lit another death stick, and went back to watching some stupid kung-fu movie on TV.

Tamara flung her magazine at him. "You can't keep me cooped up in here forever." The magazine flopped to the floor like an injured bird near one of Gary's booted feet. She folded her arms across her chest and glared at him, determined to make her point but not wanting to press too hard for fear of how Gary might react.

She'd been under his thumb ever since that first morning he'd appeared in her bedroom doorway in his underwear. His early-morning bed checks had become routine after that. At first light, she'd hear his barefoot steps in the hallway outside her door, see the doorknob turn. Quickly she'd pull the sheet up around her and pretend to be asleep. The door would groan open. She would hear him breathing, feel the chill of his gaze. Moments later, the door would creak closed.

What he didn't know was what she gripped in her hand under the covers. After that first startling intrusion, she'd sneaked a butcher knife out of a drawer in the kitchen. She'd hid it under her mattress on the wall side within easy reach. Every morning when she heard Gary approaching, she'd grasp the knife and have it at the ready. She would use it too if she had to.

She peered at him now through the pall of smoke, barely able to cap her frustration. It wasn't really the tobacco smoke that irritated her so much as it was the knowledge that she had come under Gary's control, that—like a leashed dog—she lacked the freedom to come and go as she pleased. How could she have allowed that to happen? If only she had some other place to stay, she could sneak out some night while he was asleep and not come back. But if she merely took off for an hour or so without his say-so and then had to return . . . Shadows shifted in her mind. She shivered—she knew what Gary was capable of.

When the kung-fu movie ended and a romantic comedy came on, Gary muted the TV sound.

"Turn it up," Tamara said. "I want to hear."

Gary stuffed the TV remote control down between the cushion and the arm of his chair. He fished his Bic lighter out of the breast pocket of his shirt, sparked a bright yellow flame, and torched the end of another cigarette. He took a drag, exhaled a storm cloud of nicotine-laden vapors that drifted toward the sofa.

Tamara fanned her palms in front of her face. It was wasted effort.

Gary pushed himself up from his chair and shambled over to the taped-up picture window. The divorcee across the street was in her driveway washing her car in cut-offs and a tank top. He stood at the window looking out, now and again flicking ashes onto the windowsill. Then he turned away from the window, strode past Tamara on the sofa, and disappeared down the hall.

When she heard his bedroom door close, she went over and dug out the TV remote from the crevice into which it had been crammed. She turned the sound up just loud enough for her to hear.

Several minutes later, Gary's bedroom door creaked open. Bootless footsteps ranged down the hall, short of the living room. Another door closed. The shower came on with its distinctive shudder of pipes.

Tamara was turning the TV sound up some more when the telephone rang.

The only phone in the house was in the living room, sitting on the table next to Gary's chair. Tamara stared at it as it continued ringing. Gary had told her not to answer the phone if it rang when he wasn't around. "Nobody's callin' for you," he'd said. On the sixth ring, she answered it anyway.

It was Angela.

"Why haven't you called me?" Angela said. "Your mother's so funny. She said she didn't know your stepbrother's last name. But it's the same as hers. I have wonderful news."

Angela never said just one thing when she opened her mouth. Thoughts gushed out of her in breathy bursts, like air being let out of a balloon. Tamara trembled with excitement at the sound of her voice. "What news?"

"Amanda and Tommy got jobs at Mohler Lake Lodge," Angela said, "and I'm going to stay with them now that school is out. You have to come too. It's in the mountains not far from Fir Valley, Amanda says. They have a cabin by the lake. We can sleep on an air mattress on the floor and go swimming and pretend to be drowning. Amanda says they have some cute lifeguards. But don't tell Tommy she said that."

Tamara was repulsed by the notion of stuffing her bloated body into a bathing suit. But the prospect of being with Angela again—and out of Gary's house—sent her heart off on a joy ride. "You really think Amanda and Tommy would let me stay there?" She didn't know Angela's older sister very well and had seen Tommy only a time or two at Angela's house before the couple had married.

"Of course they'll let you stay. Amanda's my sister, isn't she? And you're like a sister. So that makes us all family. And we have Tommy outnumbered."

Tamara's mind leapfrogged ahead, goaded by the possibility of a reunion with her best friend and freedom from Gary. "I'm not sure how I'd get there. I guess I could hitchhike."

"No you won't. Amanda and Tommy have a car. We'll come get you."

Swept up in her friend's enthusiasm, Tamara had forgotten about Gary. She muted the TV and held the telephone receiver away from her ear for a few seconds. The water pipes had ceased to rattle. Was that the bathroom door groaning open?

She brought the mouthpiece to her lips, her hand cupped around it. "I have to go now," she said in a husky whisper. "I'll call you later."

"But you've got to come," Angela said, her voice so melodic it was as if she was singing the words. "We'll have so much—"

Tamara cradled the receiver and scurried back to the couch.

Gary appeared from the hallway with a towel wrapped around his waist. Pearls of water nested in the tight curls of hair on his chest, and his beard and tousled mane were shiny wet. He had the tip of his little finger stuck in his ear and was wiggling it around. His other hand held up the towel. "You talkin' to someone?" he said.

Tamara looked at him as if she didn't understand.

Gary plumbed his ear some more, then turned away.

"Where's Mohler Lake?" she called after him, immediately wishing she hadn't.

"Nowhere in your universe," Gary said. He let the towel fall from his waist. It trailed from his hand as he walked away, flashing butt cheeks as pale and spongy as pastry dough.

19 IT WAS SEVERAL days later, just when Tamara was beginning to wonder if she'd ever get out of the house again, that Gary loaded her into the cab of his pickup truck as if she was a piece of luggage and headed downtown by way of Central Avenue. He hadn't told her where they were going, and she hadn't asked. She was just glad to be outdoors—glad for a reminder that there *was* an outdoors. She rolled her window down, poked her head out to catch a breeze.

They crossed Main Street, then blew past 1st, where pedestrians in the crosswalk had to scramble out of their way. At 2nd Street, Gary turned right, careening around the corner as if it was a tight curve on a racetrack. He drove to the middle of the block, whipped into a parking space in front of Citizens National Bank. An electronic sign overhead flashed "11:47 AM."

"Out," Gary said.

The sign flashed "92 degrees."

Tamara worked the passenger door handle back and forth and leaned into the door, but it wouldn't budge. She banged her shoulder against it a couple of times without success and then nearly fell out of the truck when Gary jerked the door open from the outside.

He gripped her arm with the subtlety of a lobster claw and marched her inside the bank, straight to the New Accounts desk. He plunked down a hundred-dollar bill and said to the lady behind the desk, "She wants to open a savings account."

Tamara thought he'd gone off his rocker.

The New Accounts lady smiled at them with glossy pink lips. "Please have a seat," she said, and deftly palmed the hundred-dollar bill.

Still not sure what was happening, Tamara sat down in an arm-chair in front of the desk. Gary stood beside her, poised like a palace guard.

"Have you ever had an account with us before?" the New Accounts lady asked.

Tamara shook her head. She'd never had a bank account anywhere before—didn't know a sixteen-year-old could have one. Besides, bank accounts were for people who had money they didn't know what to do with. She'd never had that problem.

The New Accounts lady opened a drawer and pulled out a buff-colored form. "I'll just need to get a little information, and I'll need to see some ID."

Tamara gave the bank lady all the information she asked for and, after rifling through her purse, handed over her school ID card with the awful picture of her on it. The lady had her sign her name at the bottom of the form, next to the X. Then she gave Tamara a little booklet spread open to the first page. "This is your account number," she said, tapping a long red fingernail beside a hyphenated number at the top of the page. She pointed at the one-hundred-dollar entry on a line below. "This is your beginning balance." She gave Tamara another glossy-lipped smile. "Welcome to Citizens National Bank, where we consider all our customers family."

"What do I do with this?" Tamara asked, holding up the bankbook as she and Gary cruised back down Central Avenue.

Gary tossed her a peeved look, as if she'd broken a cardinal rule: *Thou shalt not ask stupid questions.*

When they got back to the house, Tamara went to her room and shut the door. The window was wide open but the air barely stirred, and the room seemed to be generating its own heat. Her only option to cool down was to shed clothes. Her T-shirt was already clingy with sweat. She raised it over her head. She wriggled out of her trousers as well. Wearing only her bra and panties, she sat down on the bed and huffed for a time, her rounded belly, like a medicine ball strapped to her waist, making it all the harder to breathe.

Still confused about the trip to the bank, she dug the little bankbook out of her purse, flipped to the first page and scrutinized the dollar entry. The bank lady had written her initials, *ES*, next to the amount. What could possibly have prompted Gary to deposit a hundred dollars into an account in her name? Was the money really hers?

She winced in response to a sudden jolt inside her abdomen. Her darling girl was becoming increasingly rambunctious these days, giving Tamara constant reminders—in the form of judo chops and kidney punches—that she needed to be giving more thought to the future. But with Gary's ever-tightening rein on her, it was becoming more difficult each day for her to see into the future.

When the fracas in her belly ended, Tamara tossed the bankbook aside and stretched out on the bed. The future. Yes, she needed to give more thought to the future. She couldn't let her dreams for a new and better life for herself and her child fade.

But what kind of future could there possibly be for her and her baby as long as she was under Gary's rule? The first thing she needed to do was to get away from Gary. But how? And go where?

She thought about the call from Angela. Her pulse did a hop, skip, and jump as she embraced the possibility of joining her friend at Mohler Lake. She could slip out of the house late one night and hitchhike to the lake. She frowned. Hitchhike in the dark? Maybe she could leave the house just before dawn, then hide someplace in town until the bank opened so she could get her money. The question repeated itself in her mind: Was it really her money?

Her head began to spin with conjecture. She squeezed her eyes closed and tried to pin a tail upon a certain course of action. But the only firm conclusion she could arrive at was that she needed to get away from Gary's house. The answers to the questions of how and when remained a dizzying blur.

She batted her eyes, inhaled a lungful of soggy air. It was too hot for clear thinking on this, or any, subject. She could feel sweat pooling in her armpits. Her pumpkin belly, with its stemlike outie navel, glistened with perspiration. Too hot—yes—too hot. Too hot to think. Too hot to feel. Too hot, in fact, to do anything at the moment except lie here semi-naked and pray that someone would show her the kindness of turning off the sauna.

TAMARA AWOKE IN tears. She had slept long enough to dream. The dream had been so real. In the dream she'd been with Angela back at school. They were sitting in Mrs. Dolan's English class, passing notes back and forth the way they always did. She unfolded the scrap of paper Angela had handed her. On it, in a familiar cursive, was written, "Not in this lifetime." She looked at Angela and they both laughed. A bell rang and the two of them bumped shoulders and laughed some more as they left the classroom and strolled down the hallway toward the locker they shared. As they neared the locker, they could hear plaintive crying coming from inside it. Angela continued laughing, but Tamara was startled by what she heard. She twisted the wheel on the combination lock one direction and then the other in a hurried effort to open the locker. In her haste, she got the combination wrong—the door wouldn't open. She tried again without success. The crying from inside the locker shrilled. Frantic, Tamara turned to Angela, who was laughing even harder now. "Open it!" she screamed. Angela reached up and spun the wheel a couple of times. The locker door popped open as if forced out from the inside. Angela reached into the metal vault, plucked out a bawling infant by one arm, and held it up. "It's broken," she said. Then she pulled a book out of the locker, shoved the baby back in, and closed the door. The baby continued to wail, and Angela continued to laugh.

Tamara was sobbing now as she came out of her dream, having been roused, she thought, by the clamor inside her head. But why could she still hear noise? Booming noise.

She swung her feet over the edge of the bed and sat up, feeling woozy. There was a flash of shadow across the floor. And another. She glanced toward the window. Through the glass, she could see Gary standing outside the house banging away with a hammer. He had the screen off the window, which he'd closed, and was pounding a nail into its wooden sash.

"What the hell are you doing?" she shouted.

Gary kept his head down and pounded away. He took another spike from his shirt pocket and started hammering it into the other side of the sash.

Tamara got up and blundered toward the window. "You sonofabitch! I'll break the fucking glass!"

Gary rapped the nail head one last time and walked away.

Tamara shrieked at him. She wheeled and started for the door, intending to confront him as he came back into the house. But she didn't make it out of the room. Instead, she fell onto the bed, overcome by the seeming hopelessness of her situation and the troubling nature of her dream.

She remembered that day in school last fall when Angela's baby wouldn't stop crying. It was a new kind of doll that all the girls in Child Development class—a class Tamara hadn't taken—had been assigned to carry around for a week, at school and at home. The baby had a battery-operated voice box inside that caused it to cry when laid down. One morning Angela's baby got stuck in the crying mode. It wouldn't stop wailing no matter what she did. Her Child Development class wasn't until the end of the school day. In order to attend her other classes without being disruptive, she'd left the crying baby in their locker until she could get it fixed. When her Child Development teacher found out what she'd done, she gave Angela an F on the assignment. "What else was I supposed to do?" Angela had said to Tamara at the time. Tamara had been flippant with her response: "How am I supposed to know? You're the mother." But she knew the teacher was right—Angela had failed to take proper care of her baby.

LATER THAT AFTERNOON at Gary's house, Tamara maintained a caustic silence as she watched her stepbrother install a clasp lock on the outside of her bedroom door. She didn't ask what he was doing, just glared at him with renewed loathing as he tightened the screws.

She lay in bed that night, barely able to breathe much less sleep. She squinted anxiously into the dark, sensing the bedroom walls closing in on her. She clutched wads of bedding and swore. Gary had gained the upper hand on her, and she had let it happen. But why was he so intent on keeping her penned up? She probed the dim corners of her mind, trying to imagine why, and the possibilities she spied made her go numb with fear.

20

"BUT WHY ISN'T the baby moving anymore?" Margaret wanted to know, the depth of her concern etched like a fright mask into the normally soft features of her face.

"He's sleeping," Dr. Castle said. "Just like you should be."

"But—"

The doctor shushed his patient. "The baby is fine. Stop fretting and rest."

Dr. Castle had already gone through the motions of checking on Margaret's baby, listening to its heartbeat, assessing its position in the womb, judging its size in relation to the length of its gestation. It was all pretense for the benefit of his patient. There was no longer a detectable heartbeat—the baby had all but died on the vine. His sole concern now had to be for Margaret. Only she couldn't know.

He stood back while Beatrice repositioned Margaret in the bed, making her as comfortable as possible. To that end, he would keep her medicated and continue to assure her all was well, even though he knew it was not. Soon her body would begin to reject the withered fetus, expel it as extraneous tissue. When that happened, it would be impossible to continue this charade of normalcy. The end would come quickly. He had to be prepared to act when it did.

The basic preparations for that moment had already been completed. With Beatrice's assistance, and that of the nearest medical supply outlet, Dr. Castle had transformed Margaret's bedroom into a makeshift delivery room, complete with the necessary support equipment and surgical tools. Since Russell would be assisting, Dr. Castle had gone over the procedures with him several times, including those having to do with emergency C-section, were that to become necessary. He would much rather have had Margaret in the hospital, but that wasn't an option given the nature of what was about to take place. He would just have to do his best under the circumstances and hope that nothing went wrong. If it did, Margaret could die. He'd told Russell that.

"If she doesn't get her baby, she's as good as dead anyway," Russell had stated with the grim certainty of a biblical prophet.

Beatrice's continued presence was problematic but, in Dr. Castle's view, unavoidable. Because Margaret's condition could become critical at any moment, it was imperative to have someone with extensive medical training with her at all times. Dr. Castle, who still had a practice to run, needed a stand-in, and Beatrice filled that role nicely. She stayed with Margaret continuously during the day and at night slept on a rollaway bed in the adjoining room—the intended future nursery. The only relief she got was when Dr. Castle came to the house or when Russell spelled her for brief periods.

The nurse was fully aware, of course, that Margaret and her child were in dire straits—that something had to be done, and soon. But as always, she deferred to the doctor's judgment in the matter and, as importantly, had reaffirmed her vow to keep in strictest confidence anything and everything she witnessed during her care of Mrs. Trouste.

"We need her for now," the doctor had acknowledged to Russell in private. Russell had agreed.

Dr. Castle lingered at Margaret's bedside, waiting for her to settle into a milder state of agitation before leaving. He had upped the dosage on her sedative several times over the past few weeks, while continuing to administer a coagulant as needed and, more recently, a labor inhibitor. Margaret slept most of the time now, although fitfully, crying out at times as if reliving some holocaust. And when she was awake, her constant expression was that of a woman clinging to a shred of hope that she might be delivered from an impending tragedy.

When his patient was sufficiently composed, Dr. Castle said goodnight to Beatrice and went downstairs to report to Russell.

Russell wasn't in the library. The French doors to the outside stood open. Balmy air wafted in through the opening. Dr. Castle set his medical bag down and stepped out onto the deck. Russell was standing at the railing, leaning against it, gazing down at a river valley that had faded to gray beneath a muted evening sky.

Dr. Castle positioned himself alongside his friend and remained quiet for a time. "It won't be long now," he finally said.

Russell kept his eyes aimed downward. "Is the girl ready?"

The doctor peered at the dim lower landscape. Barely visible through the gloom, the South Umpqua River snaked its way through the valley, a dark watery highway that on its path to the sea carried with it all manner of possibilities. "She'll have to be."

Russell glanced over at the doctor, his countenance displaying the debilitating effects of a succession of sleepless nights. "You say she's at eight months now?"

Dr. Castle nodded.

"Will it be safe for her? For the baby?"

"At eight months, there are risks," the doctor said. "But the risks are"—he searched for the right word—"manageable."

Russell returned his attention to the valley below. "So what do we do in the meantime?"

"I'll check on the girl in the morning," the doctor said, "to be sure we're set on that end. Then—" He glimpsed the far horizon where what was left of the day was hiding behind the mountain ridges to the west. "—we'll take it one day at a time."

"Sounds familiar," Russell said in a voice that seemed to come from a thousand miles away.

21

TAMARA AWOKE TO the whoosh of a toilet flushing, to water pipes chattering, to Gary confronting morning in his usual way, clamorously, as though his actions required sound effects to make them meaningful. She half opened her eyes. Timid light crept into the room from a drab outside world. He's up awfully early this morning, she thought, then cringed as Gary began clearing his throat in repeated guttural spasms that reminded her of choking death scenes from the movies. He spat—hopefully into the toilet and not the sink. She turned over in bed to face the wall, as if that would help erase Gary from her consciousness.

She thought about Angela. Had Angela gone to Mohler Lake? Was she there now? Tamara imagined her friend at a lakeshore bathed in golden sunlight. She was lolling on a plush beach towel, reading a romance novel while wriggling her toes in the sand, water gently lapping at the shore. Close by, from his perch atop a lifeguard stand, a bronzed Adonis with sun-bleached hair gazed down on her adoringly.

Darker thoughts blotted out the pleasant images. Tamara had promised to call her friend back but hadn't been able to follow through on that promise. Anytime Gary left the house now, he either locked her up in her room or stationed Jerome in the house as a guard. Even prisoners had more privileges.

Tamara expelled a breath that seemed to scorch her throat, as if her hatred for Gary was a blaze inside her that needed a vent. More than once recently, she'd been tempted to make good on her threat to smash her bedroom window and climb out. But she feared cutting herself on the glass or getting injured while dropping to the ground. She couldn't risk it. She had to play it safe for her baby's sake.

So she'd bided her time, because she could think of nothing else to do—could envision no yellow brick road to a brighter future. But as the days had passed, she'd begun to feel more cut off, more vulnerable, as if she was stranded alone on an island with Gary as her keeper. Each day on the island brought fewer options, less peace of mind, more threats to her well-being. Gary had taken control of her life, and where was the future in that?

He was dressed now. She could hear his boots punishing the hardwood floor. When the footfalls advanced up the hallway and approached her bedroom door, she hastened to cover herself, knowing what was coming next. There—the familiar metallic clatter of the clasp being thrown back.

She squeezed her eyelids shut, lay motionless, and listened sharply. The door yawned open, stood mute for several ticks of the clock in her head, then creaked closed. Metal clanked against the outside of the door.

Tamara's eyes shot open. Had she heard correctly? Had Gary re-secured the clasp on her door? It sure sounded like it. But why, if he was up and dressed, would he bother keeping her locked up? Surely he wasn't going somewhere this early? It wasn't yet fully light outside.

Gary's footsteps trailed down the hall toward the front of the house.

She rolled out of bed, bent over, and grabbed her trousers off the floor. She was perched on the edge of the bed, poking a foot into a frayed pant leg, when she heard a deep rumble outside that caused the window glass to rattle in its frame. She couldn't see the street from the window, but she knew what the noise was. Jerome's big truck had just pulled up in front of the house.

She stood up, tugged her pants up as far as they would go, which was only to that abdominal area below her belly that now served as a waistline. From the front of the house there came a sudden hammering of boots on the floor. Her bedroom door shuddered as another door (the front door?) thudded closed.

"What the hell?" She fumbled with her belt. It wasn't a belt exactly, rather a strip of braided hemp that she knotted under her belly.

The rumbling outside continued. Jerome had apparently left his truck running. Then the engine snarled and began to roar, and the windowpane complained in earnest. Gradually the roaring subsided, faded away to nothing.

Questioning what she thought she'd heard, Tamara tramped to the bedroom door, twisted the doorknob, and gave it a yank. The door cracked open and snagged. "Gary!" she yelled.

No response.

Had he really gone off with Jerome this early and left her trapped in her room? She gaveled on the door with her fist and hollered louder. She was greeted by a taunting silence.

"Asshole!"

She sat on the bed and wrestled her feet into her sneakers. Surely Gary wouldn't be gone long. She got her hairbrush off the dresser and swiped it through the snarls ringing her face. He and Jerome had probably gone out for breakfast. They'd better eat fast—already she was feeling the need to pee.

She tossed the brush onto the dresser and sat there waiting for the sound of the beast-engine to return. Fifteen minutes passed. She berated Gary in her mind. Twenty minutes. She got up and paced the limited floor space in the room, which was like trying to hold a parade in a bathtub. Thirty minutes went by. She flung herself down on the bed, cursing. Forty-five minutes elapsed and still the guys hadn't returned.

Finally, fed up with this stupid waiting game—and not sure how much longer she could hold her bladder—she got up and went over to the bedroom door. She'd seen her stepfather take a closet door off its hinges once. The door was warped and wouldn't close right. Tamara's mom had asked him to fix it. Instead, Darryl removed its hinges, yanked it out of its frame, and left it standing against the bedroom wall as a token of his displeasure at being expected to perform husbandly tasks.

But what the hell—if Darryl could unhinge a door, so could she. All she needed was the right tool. She got her nail clippers out of her purse and used them to try to loosen one of the hinge pins. The clippers snapped apart. They were definitely not going to get the job done.

There was a milk-encrusted bowl with a spoon in it sitting on the dresser. She took the spoon, wedged it under the head of a hinge pin and pried. The spoon handle bent into an L shape. The pin didn't move. It seemed frozen in place. She groaned in frustration and looked around for a better implement.

She eyed the brick that served as a makeshift fourth leg for the dresser. Overkill, she decided. Then she remembered the butcher knife. She kneeled on the bed and pulled it out from under the wall side of the mattress. The knife had a long, heavy blade and a sturdy wooden handle. Just the tool she needed.

She used the butt of the handle like a hammer, tapping repeatedly against one of the hinge pins. Then she jammed the cutting edge of the blade under the pin head and worked it up and down. The pin popped up.

Tamara stared at the loose pin, her heart aflutter. There was a sudden rush of sound in her ears, like a heaving wind. A voice spoke to her, saying, *This is your chance! Get away from this house while you can!*

Her hands shook as she loosened the other pins and removed them. She pried the door out of its frame, then tugged on it, fighting the resistance of the clasp on the non-hinge side. Straining to the sounds of screeching metal and popping wood, she was able to get the door open just enough to pass through. As she did, she caught sight of the big yellow-handled screwdriver Gary had rammed through the catch to secure the clasp.

She rushed into the bathroom and relieved herself.

Hurry! said the voice in her head.

She scudded back across the hall and slid through the makeshift passage into her room. She grabbed her backpack off the floor and began cramming her things into it.

Barely a minute later, she was in the living room, making for the front door, when an impulse hit her. She stopped, rocked in place, caught between competing urges like a game show contestant tempted by a bigger prize. Finally giving in to urge number two, she dropped her backpack to the floor and hastened back down the hallway.

In all her time with Gary, Tamara had never set foot inside his room. There'd been no reason to go in there and seemingly every reason to stay out. Now, as she crossed the threshold into his private domain, she was greeted by a nauseating stench reminiscent of the inside of a gym locker. She held her nose while scanning the room.

A double bed with churned-up covers was pushed against one wall. Next to the head of the bed was an upside-down wooden crate on which sat a chrome-plated hubcap, its cavity choked with cigarette butts and ash. Against an adjacent wall stood a beat-up chest with its drawers partially open and some undergarments dangling out like streamers. On top of the chest, seemingly rooted in its dusty surface, was a squat lamp with a torn shade. Alongside the lamp lay a wadded-up hand-kerchief, a dirty comb, and a ring of keys.

Tamara was stepping toward the dresser when she heard a rumbling noise coming from outside. She froze. The rumbling grew louder.

"No!"

She whirled, lunged for the door, and propelled herself down the hall. Why had she delayed leaving the house? Stupid! Stupid! Now it was too late. Now, all she could do was try to save herself from Gary's wrath.

Furious with herself, she shoved her way back into her room and began maneuvering the unhinged door back into its frame. She grumbled as she fought with it, jiggling it this way and that, trying to get the hinge parts fitted together. Time was running out. Gary would be clomping into the house any second now. At last the hinges clicked into place.

She had just inserted one of the hinge pins into its slot when she felt the bottom drop out of her stomach. She slumped against the door frame. Tears sprang to her eyes.

She had forgotten her backpack. She'd left it sitting on the floor in the living room, and she didn't have time to go out and get it and then get back into the bedroom and re-hang the door. But whichever task she left undone would get her caught. Gary would know she'd been out of her room, would see that she'd intended to run away, would . . . There was no telling what he would do.

A cry of self-pity escaped her lips and she began to sob.

She'd stood there crying for a time before realizing that, except for her own whimpering, the house was still silent. Outside, there was silence too. The vehicle she'd thought was Jerome's had apparently passed by.

"Thank you, God," she said, feeling an exhilarating rush of relief. She pulled the hinge pin out, yanked the door open, and wedged through the opening.

Her heart was pounding when, moments later, she bolted from the house on Cedar Street clutching her backpack and—in her trembling hand—the keys to Gary's truck.

22 DR. CASTLE MADE the first call from home, before leaving for the office. He let the phone ring a half-dozen times, disconnected and dialed again, letting it ring at least as many times before hanging up. No one was answering the telephone at Neaves' place. He checked his watch: 8:28 AM. The last time he'd spoken with Gary Neaves, which was only a few days ago, the doctor had instructed him to keep the girl close to home. "She ain't goin' nowhere," Neaves had assured him.

"Someone has gone somewhere," the doctor muttered to himself.

He drove to work with sunlight glaring off the hood of his car and the small-town streets filling up more with heat than with people. Summer had arrived full bore. Fine with him. Good weather to thaw out old bones.

Upon arriving at his office, Dr. Castle was met with the news that Mrs. Menenger's husband had called and reported that his wife had gone into labor. The doctor wasn't surprised. Mrs. Menenger wasn't due for another two weeks, but this would be her third child, and her third early delivery.

"Doris is canceling your afternoon appointments," Marion informed him. "Mr. Menenger will call before he takes his wife to the hospital."

The doctor accepted without comment the information conveyed by his nurse, along with the proffered cup of coffee, and retreated to his private office. He probably would have time to take care of his morning patients before going to the hospital. Even so, it looked as if it was going to be another grind-it-out day.

He donned his lab coat. Before proceeding to the first exam room, he used the phone on his desk to dial Neaves again. Again, he got no answer. He hung up, beginning to feel somewhat peeved at the fellow, although certainly there was no cause for alarm. Neaves had most likely just gone off shopping or whatever, taking the girl with him, and would soon return.

The doctor savored a few sips of his coffee. He'd catch Neaves later. In the meantime he had other, more pressing business to attend to. He picked up his stethoscope and headed out the door.

It turned out to be a full morning indeed, with none of his patients doing him the favor of phoning in a last-minute cancellation. Between patients, the doctor made a point of slipping back into his office and calling Neaves, each time unsuccessfully. He tried to remain detached as he listened to the repeated *brrr-*ing on the other end of the line. But his irritation at not being able to contact the fellow deepened with each successive attempt, finally developing into an open sore of frustration. At the end of one call, he slammed the receiver down in its cradle.

"Can I be of assistance?" Marion asked. She was standing in the doorway, her face an open book of concern.

"No. No," he said, shaking his head. "It's nothing."

But by early afternoon, when he had to leave for the hospital to see to Mrs. Menenger—still without having connected with Gary Neaves—Dr. Castle was beginning to have the sinking feeling that there might indeed be a problem with the girl.

23 THE FIRST THING Gary saw when he and Jerome pulled up in front of his house after a luckless morning of bird hunting was the rusted-out hull of the '66 Chevette parked up on blocks at the end of his driveway. The car had been there for the last four years, which was how long Gary had lived in the rundown clapboard rental. The Chevette, or what was left of it, actually belonged to Brian. Brian had lived with Gary in the house on Cedar Street for six months before he up and married tight-ass Brenda from the accounting office at the mill. When Brian moved out, he left the piece-of-junk Chevette, which wasn't running even then, sitting right where it was now. He was going to work on it, he'd said. Fix it up. Get it running. All he ever did was take parts off it. First the battery, then the radio, then the tires and wheels. Over the last four years, the thing had been cannibalized to the point where it hardly resembled a motor vehicle.

Gary was still staring at the useless heap of metal when Jerome said, "Hey, Gary, where's your truck?"

Gary looked at where his pickup was supposed to be. Odd he hadn't realized it was gone. "Damn." He shoved open the passenger door to Jerome's truck and hopped out.

"I can't stay," Jerome said. "I promised Momma I'd take her to the eye doctor."

Gary was already striding toward his house. Behind him, the big truck's engine bellowed like an angry bull as Jerome took off down the street.

Gary bounded up the steps, charged through the front door, clomped through the living room and down the hall to Tamara's room. The hasp lock he'd installed on her door was still secured by the screwdriver he'd used to fasten it. But the door angled in on the hinge side. He yanked the screwdriver out, flipped the hasp back, and kicked the door with the sole of his boot. It toppled back, bounced off the edge of the bed, and crashed to the floor.

"Damn! Damn! Damn!" he said as he viewed the unoccupied room. Then he rammed the heel of his boot through one of the panels on the downed door.

He stamped down the hall and into his own room. Nothing seemed to have been disturbed there. He stuck his head inside the closet and checked on his guns, remembering only then that he'd left his 12-gauge in the cab of Jerome's truck. His deer rifles were still in the closet, propped up against the wall. He backed out of the closet and stood looking around the room and wondering how it could have happened that both the girl and his truck were gone.

His eyes locked on the chest of drawers and the stuff scattered atop its dusty surface, and it hit him. "Fuck! Fuck! Fuck!" he said, slapping his empty pants pockets. He swung around and laid a right cross on the door frame, pulling the punch just enough to keep from busting his knuckles.

"The little bitch is gone," he told Brian over the phone. "Took my truck and skipped."

"No shit?" Brian said. He yawned audibly into the mouthpiece. "Where were you?"

Gary knew his pal had pulled green chain all night at the mill and probably had just gotten to bed. But it couldn't be helped. He needed his assistance and he needed it now. "I went bird huntin' for a couple hours this morning with Jerome. What the hell—I was goin' stir crazy babysittin' that cunt. Guess I left my keys. She was gone when I got back." He cursed again. "So, can you come over? I need some wheels, and Jerome's off playing Momma's Boy."

A bleary-eyed Brian Dodd was at Gary's place twenty minutes later, and right away the two of them went hunting for the girl. They tracked around Fir Valley in Brian's rattletrap F150—first in the old business district, then up and down the residential streets on the east side. After that, they crossed over the river and combed the west-side neighborhoods all the way out to Glenview Park. When they'd found no sign of the girl or the truck in town, Gary told Brian to hitch back across the river and head up Briar Creek Road toward Mohler Lake.

"What makes you think she'd go up that way?"

Gary flicked his tongue at the corner of his mouth as he formed a recollection. "She asked me once about the lake. Wanted to know where it was. I think maybe she knows someone there." He felt the nape of his neck prickle. "Maybe that Angela girl who kept callin' the house for a time."

Brian braked hard to avoid rear-ending a silver van that nearly came to a stop in front of them before turning into the driveway of a Chevron station. Gary stiff-armed the dashboard. "I don't think she'd make it all the way to the lake though," he said, eying the Chevron's pumps. "That heap of mine gets twelve miles a gallon on a good day, and it had less than a quarter tank last time I looked—and that was a week ago."

"She got money for gas?"

"Hell if I know. If she does, don't know where she got it." Then he remembered the bank account in Tamara's name with the hundred dollars in it. "Shit."

"What's the matter?" Brian said. "Leave your wallet spread open along with your keys?"

"Go to hell, Dodd."

24

TAMARA KNEW AS soon as the truck sputtered and lost power what was wrong. She'd been watching the needle on the gas gauge drift closer and closer to the red E. Finally it waggled like an accusing finger, took a last dip, hit bottom, and died.

Heading into the mountains low on gas had been a gamble, but not as big a one, she'd decided, as making a sitting duck of herself at the bank. She'd arrived at Citizens National Bank shortly after seven o'clock only to discover that it didn't open until nine. Two hours! What was she going to do for two hours?

She'd sat in the truck for fifteen minutes studying a road map she'd found in Gary's glove box, all the while glancing anxiously up and down the street, feeling like some rookie getaway driver. She started every time a vehicle came into view or a pedestrian strolled by. In the end, she'd concluded that the risk of Gary catching up with her wasn't worth a hundred dollars. The bank was surely the first place he'd think to look.

Tamara veered onto the gravel shoulder and let the truck coast to a stop. She was almost relieved to have run out of gas. She knew how to drive. Jimmy had taught her. But this road into the mountains was curvy and narrow, with a picket fence of trees close on one side and a sharp drop-off to a creek bed on the other. She hadn't had much practice driving on straight roads much less on a road whose path resembled a tangle of rubber bands. She felt fortunate to have made it this far without killing herself.

She got out of the truck and stood alongside it, her backpack slung over her shoulder, waiting for some uphill traffic to appear in hopes of bumming a ride the rest of the way to the lake. She didn't have to wait long. Within minutes of running out of gas, she was picked up by an old couple in a Mercury Cougar with a camp trailer in tow. They were on their way to Mohler Lake, they told her, for a family reunion that was being held at a campground on the other side of the lake from the lodge.

"They're expecting nearly a hundred people," the old woman said with a nostalgic lilt to her voice. Then she turned to her husband, who wasn't doing much better than Tamara had in negotiating the snaking roadway. "Keep it on the road, Herbert."

Tamara flinched every time the old man made a jerky course correction, which he did going into and coming out of every curve. The trailer would fishtail behind the Mercury, and the car would rock side to side as its driver fought for control. Tamara felt like cheering when they passed a sign that read MOHLER LAKE 1 MILE.

After engaging in a brief squabble as to which end of the loop around the lake provided the most direct access to their destination, the old couple decided to stop at the lodge and ask for directions. "What a beautiful setting," the old woman remarked as the lodge compound came into view.

Tamara agreed. It was like something you'd see on a picture-postcard. A cluster of rustic buildings set on a tree-studded knoll overlooking an expansive blue oval of water, and as a backdrop, forested hills soaring into an azure sky. She couldn't help but be uplifted—by the setting, by the sense of freedom she felt being away from Gary, by the newfound hope that her life had finally taken a turn for the better.

The old man brought the Mercury to a stop in the lodge parking lot. "Thanks for the lift," Tamara said as they all got out. "Hope you have a good time at your reunion."

The old woman smiled and waved. "This way," she said to her husband, and began dragging him across the parking lot toward the main lodge building.

In need of a bathroom, Tamara headed for a smaller building closer by, with gas pumps out front and a sign above the door that read, simply, STORE.

A bell jingled when she entered the building. In front of her were aisles that ran away from her toward the back of the store. Along each aisle were shelves of goods—foodstuffs, sundries, knickknacks—and some clothes racks with mostly T-shirts with logos on them. To her right was a service counter where several customers with goods in hand were waiting to be checked out.

She found a restroom in a back corner of the store. A sign on the door read TOILET: ONE SIZE FITS ALL.

When she came out of the restroom a few minutes later and returned to the front of the store, only one customer remained at the service counter. Tamara stepped up to the counter, thinking to inquire about the employees at the lodge, and was surprised to find that the person behind the counter ringing up sales on an antique-looking cash register was Angela's sister Amanda. There was no mistaking her for other than a Ramos. Like her younger sister, Amanda had inherited her dad's raven hair and Latin good looks—his family was from Mexico—and her mom's fair complexion and delicate features—she was a glassblower's daughter from New Hampshire. The combination of genes made for a unique beauty that always struck Tamara as doll-like. She even teased Angela about it, calling her a Mexican Barbie.

Tamara felt a giddy sense of pleasure now upon seeing a familiar face.

Amanda counted out change for the customer at the counter and, when he'd walked away, made eye contact with Tamara.

"Hi," Tamara said with a cheerful smile.

"Hello," Amanda said, looking at her but seeming not to know who she was. "Can I help you with something?"

Tamara felt her chest tighten. "I'm Angela's friend Tamara." The bell on the front door jingled.

Amanda gazed at her for a time before a look of recognition spread across her face. "Of course," she said. "*Tamara*. I remember you. Angela said you were going to have a baby." Her eyes grew round. "And it looks like it's going to be sooner than later."

"Is Angela here yet?" Tamara blurted nervously.

Amanda seemed puzzled by the question. "At the lake?" Then it apparently dawned on her what Tamara was talking about. "Oh, no," she said, shaking her head. "Dear Old Dad said 'adios' to that idea. He doesn't trust me and Tommy to look out for my little sister out here in the big cruel world." She put her hands on her hips. "He doesn't trust anybody to do anything."

A man wearing a Seattle Mariners' baseball cap walked up to the service counter and plunked down a couple of sodas and a bag of chips.

"Excuse me," Amanda said, and began punching keys on the cash register.

Tamara's mind lurched. Angela wasn't coming to the lake! *Oh, God—what now?* She'd run away from Gary, stealing his truck in the process, thinking she had another place to stay. But without Angela here . . . She pitched forward, feeling a sudden urge to heave. She braced a hand on the counter.

"Are you okay?" Amanda said.

The man in the baseball cap gave Tamara a sideways glance as he left with his goods.

She pressed a palm against her side. "Just the baby acting up."

Amanda gestured to a stool behind the counter. "You need to sit down?"

Tamara shook her head. "I'll be fine."

Amanda looked on with an expression of concern. Neither of them spoke for a time. Then Amanda said, "So what brings you up to the lake?"

Tamara didn't know what to say. She tried to think of an explanation for her presence there that didn't involve the truth, and when she couldn't, burst into tears.

Amanda reacted with blatant inaction, as if at a loss for what to do, which only prompted more tears from Tamara. Finally—apparently realizing something had to be done and there was no one else to do it—Amanda came around the counter and put her arms around Tamara. "Hey," she said, "whatever's the matter, it's going to be okay."

Tamara wiped her eyes with her shirtsleeve. "I need a place to stay for a while," she said. "Angela said she was coming to the lake and that we could both stay with you and Tommy. But now . . ." She shrugged, feeling utterly miserable.

Amanda pulled back and stood with her arms crossed in front of her, looking uneasy. The bell on the front door sounded again and several more customers trooped into the store.

Tamara lowered her backpack to the counter, zipped it open, pulled out some tissues, and blew her nose. She felt really foolish now. How stupid of her to think people she hardly knew would take her in as if she was a lost puppy in need of a home. "Well," she said, sniffing hard, "I'd better go and see about getting a ride back to town." She shouldered the burden of her embarrassment, along with her backpack, and turned to leave.

"Wait," Amanda said. She hesitated, seemingly uncertain as to a course of action. Then she ducked behind the counter and came up with a tightly coiled cord to which a key was attached. She dangled the key over the counter. "Cabin number six. Walk down the stone path toward the dock. Turn left at the boat rental office. Ours is the third cabin on that side. Tommy gets off work at two o'clock. He's a cook in the lodge dining room. I get off at three. But you come back here at noon and have lunch with me. We'll go over to the dining room and have Tommy fry us up some juicy burgers." She smiled. "That sound okay with you?"

Tamara swallowed the gunk in her throat. "Sounds great," she said, feeling the way she did when sliding into a warm bath.

Amanda's eyes narrowed. "By the way, how did you get up here?"

"Hitchhiked," Tamara said. But not wanting to get into the sticky details of her situation, she gave Amanda a quick wave. "See you in a bit."

Following Amanda's directions, Tamara found her and Tommy's cabin easily enough. It was an end-gabled box with weathered wooden siding, square windows, and a moss-covered shake roof as steep as a ski slope for experts only. She'd passed two other almost identical cottages on her way to theirs. The weary little structures reminded her of the story *The Three Little Pigs*. Surely there was a wolf lurking about somewhere ready to huff and puff and blow the houses down.

Inside, the cabin was hardly bigger than a motel room. To one side of the entrance door was a kitchenette. A well-worn sofa, the kind you'd see at the curb waiting for Goodwill pickup, hugged the opposite wall—with the meager floor space between being the extent of the living area. The rear of the cabin was all but filled by a double bed and a dresser. Through an interior doorway next to the dresser was a bathroom just big enough to contain a commode, a little sink, and a bushel-basket-sized curtained basin that served as a shower stall.

Tamara let her backpack fall to the floor. This was definitely intimate living conditions, even for just two people. What was Angela thinking when she'd invited her here? She sank onto the sofa and blew out a breath. This wasn't what she'd expected—but at least she was free of Gary.

But free to do what? Angela wasn't coming to the lake, and Tommy and Amanda couldn't possibly want her to stay with them, not in this Little Piggy house. She drew up her legs and lay down on the sofa.

So, what now? It was a question she seemed to be asking herself at every turn lately. She could stay here while Tommy and Amanda were at work and could look forward to a nap and a nice lunch. But what would she do after that? She sighed. Suddenly freedom didn't seem like the grand prize she'd thought it would be.

After lunch she'd have to move on. But to where? A cold ripple passed between her shoulder blades. Wherever she went, it wouldn't be back to Gary's house. She couldn't imagine going back to Eugene either. There was nothing there for her anymore. Her mind searched for other possibilities. It was still searching when she drifted off to sleep.

25   THEY FOUND GARY's pickup abandoned on the shoulder of Briar Creek Road about twenty miles out of town, just past Granite Ridge Campground, a good fifteen miles shy of Mohler Lake, keys dangling from the ignition.

Gary slid behind the wheel, turned the key to accessory, and stared at the needle on the gas gauge. It remained stuck on the red E. "Fuckin' serves her right," he said, slapping the rim of the steering wheel.

Brian was standing outside with a hand on the open driver's-side door. "Fuckin' aye," he said.

The pickup was parked askew, barely off the pavement, on a rising slope. Gary put the transmission in neutral and let the truck roll backwards, steering it away from the traffic lane while mindful of the drop-off at the edge of the gravel shoulder.

"Whoa!" he heard Brian shout. He could see him in the rearview mirror with arms thrown up. "Any farther and you're in the drink!"

A loaded logging truck blew past, headed downhill, kicking up a whirlwind of grit, its Jake brakes reporting like a throaty Gatling gun. Gary set the pickup's parking brake, cracked the windows a couple of inches, and got out, taking the keys with him.

They continued on toward Mohler Lake in Brian's truck, keeping an eye out for the girl and stopping whenever they came upon anyone who might have seen her. But there were few souls around. This stretch of mountain road was mostly uninhabited, winding through federal forestland with minimal services along the way. They checked out two National Forest campgrounds, the few scattered homes along the creek, one gas station, a boarded-up country store, and a trailer court. There was no sign of the girl, and they talked to no one who'd seen her—or who would admit to it anyway.

Gary spat in the dirt as they were getting back into the truck at the trailer court. "Someone fuckin' had to see her." The girl had lousy timing, running off when she did. Her little trick would have been a minor irritation except for one thing: Her absence at this point put in jeopardy his big payday. He stomped the floorboard with the heel of his boot. "She's gotta be up this road somewhere."

But by early afternoon, when they chugged into the compound at Mohler Lake Lodge, low on fuel and with Gary's muscles knotted in aggravation, they still hadn't scared up a clue as to the girl's whereabouts.

Brian pulled up to the gas pumps in front of the lodge store.

Gary thrust a twenty-dollar bill at him. "Get some in a can too. I don't want to have to siphon when we get back to my truck."

He got out and strode across the parking lot to the lodge. He'd been in the big log structure before, had eaten in the dining room a time or two while hunting in the vicinity. He'd never stayed in one of the lodge's guests rooms though. Too pricey for his blood.

He shoved open the heavy wooden door that accessed the lodge lobby and immediately began scouring the area with his eyes. A lard-ass with melon boobs and a butch haircut was working the front counter.

A number of lodge patrons were milling about, looking through post-card racks or at maps on the wall of the hiking trails around the lake. Others were kicked back in bulky armchairs positioned in a semicircle in front of an unlit stone fireplace. No Tamara.

Gary ignored the counter lady and started making the rounds of the patrons, asking if any of them had seen a pregnant girl meeting Tamara's description. He was greeted with a lot of headshakes and odd stares.

"Can I help you, sir?"

Gary swung around to find himself face to face with Lard-ass. "You got someone named Angela workin' here?"

"What is this about, sir?"

"About the question I just asked you."

The counter lady puffed her cheeks. "The answer to your question is *no*." Her arms went akimbo. "Now, is there anything else I can do for you?"

"Not at the moment," Gary said, resisting the urge to grab the bitch and toss her across the room.

Back outside, he found Brian's pickup in the parking lot with a shiny red metal can smelling of gas fumes sitting in the bed—but no Brian. He glanced around, swearing, then finally spotted his friend sitting at a picnic table set on the grassy slope leading down to the lakeshore. He headed in that direction.

Brian was hunched over the table, drinking a beer, eating a fruit pie, and ogling a stretch of sandy beach where two bikini-clad teenage girls lay soaking up rays from the midday sun. The girls were on their backs with their tops untied and hanging loose over their breasts. The smell of coconut oil wafted up from their bronzed bodies.

Gary kicked the bench seat supporting Brian's weight. Brian jerked upright, spilling beer down his front. "Jesus," he said, swiping at the foaming wetness.

Gary picked up an unopened beer that sat sweating on the picnic table alongside a packaged fruit pie. "Keep your mind on business." He popped open the beer and drained about half of it while getting an eyeful of the sun goddesses sprawled on the beach.

"I was just waiting for you," Brian muttered.

Gary clunked the beer can down on the table. "Take a look around the compound while you're waiting." He fingered a cigarette out of the packet in his shirt pocket and lit it. "Meet me back at the truck in fifteen minutes."

Brian got up and trundled off toward some cabins along the shore.

Gary ambled down a stone pathway, past the boat rental office, to a floating dock that jutted a hundred feet or so out into the water. A light breeze ruffled the surface of the lake. Lazy wavelets lapped against the side of the wooden dock as Gary stepped up onto its planked decking. A kid, maybe sixteen or seventeen, was at the far end of the dock, in one of the few rental boats not out on the lake. Gary let his boots announce his approach.

"You seen a young girl around here?" he asked the kid. "Very pregnant. Scraggly, shoulder-length brown hair. Round face. Pretty. Possibly wearing a tie-dyed T-shirt and baggy brown pants."

"No, sir," the boy said. He scraped up a piece of sandwich that had been ground into the floor of the boat and dropped it into a five-gallon bucket.

"You sure?"

"Yessir."

Gary sized up the kid. "What's your name?"

"Kurt."

"You live up here?"

The kid nodded. "My dad owns the boats."

Gary took a last drag off his cigarette and flicked it over the edge of the dock into the water where it landed with a soft hiss. Farther out, on the shimmering surface of the lake, small boats bobbed up and down, bristling with fishing rods and the appendages of the people to which they were attached. "Well, Kurt-whose-dad-owns-the-boats, if I give you ten dollars and a phone number, will you call the number if you do see a girl like I described?"

The boy shrugged. "Sure. Why not?"

Gary opened his wallet, sorted through the bills, pulled out a ten-spot.

"Looks like I should've asked for more," the boy said.

"Looks like." Gary put his wallet away. "Got a pencil?"

"I can get one."

"You do that."

When Gary was finished with his business at the dock, he returned to the parking lot. Brian was leaning against the bed of the truck.

"Anything?" Gary said. Brian shook his head.

They climbed back into the truck, this time with Gary at the wheel. Figuring it was probably a waste of time and gasoline—but also knowing they were out of good options—he swung the pickup onto the gravel lane that skirted the perimeter of the lake.

An hour and a half later, having circled the lake and cruised by every campsite, cottage, and picnic area they'd come to, with nothing to show for their efforts but a craw full of dust and an overheated engine, they were approaching the lodge again. By then Brian had crashed—just slumped over against the doorpost and started snoring like a drunk—and Gary could no longer contain his anger. He jammed on the brakes and brought the truck to a skidding halt on the shoulder of the road. "She's gotta be up here somewhere!"

"Wha . . . what?" Brian said, coming awake with a start.

Gary wrenched the steering wheel so hard the cab of the truck shook. "A person can't just disappear!"

The girl had to be at the lake. Where else could she be? Beyond the lake, Briar Creek Road trailed off into the hills for only a few miles before dead-ending at the base of Mt. Tillman. There was no reason for Tamara to have come up this road unless she was trying to get to the lake.

"She's got to be around here somewhere, and I need to fuckin' find her."

"And I need some fuckin' sleep," Brian complained.

Gary sat there with arms twitching, primed to rip the steering wheel off its post and beat someone with it. But there was no one around worth beating. And Brian was right. They'd done all they could for today. He needed to rescue his truck, and Brian needed to get home and get some shuteye before his next shift at the mill.

He pulled back onto the road and cruised past the lodge on his way back toward town. He was sure Tamara was at the lake. But she would just have to keep until tomorrow. Tomorrow he'd enlist Jerome's help. First thing in the morning, they'd come back up here. They'd do an all-out search for the girl. They'd find her even if they had to plow up every inch of the lodge grounds and toss every cabin and campsite around the lake. Then he'd take her back home and sit on her like a mother hen until the deal was done and he had the rest of his money.

He only hoped that in the meantime the doctor didn't call.

26   TWO MEN STOOD near the open tailgate of a dirt-encrusted GMC pickup parked on the shoulder of the logging road where it crested a high ridge in an area of heavily wooded hills east of town. Detective Hansen had had to call dispatch twice to get more explicit directions to the logging site. The hills around Fir Valley were networked with these narrow gravel roads used by the logging outfits to access the vast tracts of timber they owned or logged on contract. Once you got into the woods, the roads all looked alike and you needed the instincts of an Indian scout to find your way around.

Dan Hansen had yet to develop such instincts. He was an ex-motorcycle cop from Portland, who'd come to Fir Valley just eight months ago with his wife and two kids. His wife, a native of the area, had assured him there was less crime and more sunshine in this mostly rural region of southwestern Oregon. She'd been half right. He'd witnessed more blue sky since coming here, and that was nice. But, per capita, Douglas County seemed to have as many burglaries, rapes, and assaults as the metro areas to the north—and now this: a report of a body.

The glaring summer sun was well into its downward arc by the time Hansen pulled his cruiser in behind the pickup truck and addressed the two men standing there. "You guys report seeing a body?"

"We did," said the older of the two men, who looked old enough to be the other one's father. Both men were dressed the same: ankle-length trousers held up by suspenders, sweat-stained T-shirts, high-top work boots. Their faces were smeared with grime—the apparent result of repeated mopping with dirty handkerchiefs. Their hair, shiny from congealed sweat, showed the imprint of tightly clamped hats. Two yellow hardhats sat on the tailgate of the truck. In the bed of the truck were several chainsaws with the long bars used by tree fallers.

"Where is it?" Hansen asked, getting straight to the point.

"Down there," the older logger said. He pointed down the steep slope into a canyon where fallen trees, denuded of their limbs, lay strewn en masse like giant Pick-up Sticks. This was obviously a clear-cut operation. If there was a tree standing on the slope, it hadn't been left upright on purpose.

"We damn near dropped a big Doug fir on top of it," the logger said. He nodded at the younger man beside him. "Donny was limbing the tree when he spotted the body. Looks like the guy must have drove over the cliff."

"There's a vehicle down there?"

The older logger spat a gob of brown onto the ground. "Farther down the slope. In some heavy brush near the bottom of the ravine. Didn't see it until after we found the body. We been working this area for a week now and hadn't noticed the vehicle or the body. Should have smelled it."

"Anyone you know?" Hansen asked.

"We didn't take that close a look. Saw just enough of it to know it was human and wasn't going to get up and walk away."

"Just the two of you been working out here?"

The logger spat again. "There was a third for a time." He licked tobacco juice from the corner of his mouth. "But that's not him if that's what you're getting at. Donny here's my son-in-law. My son, Derrick, was with us the first few days. But he hasn't been out since. And he's present and accounted for. My wife and I had dinner with him and his wife last night." He shook his head. "This was to be our last day out here before they started yarding."

Hansen surveyed the sheer incline. Getting down into the ravine wouldn't be easy, and not just because of the abruptness of the slope. There wasn't a lot of undergrowth, but all the downed trees and limbs had created a maze of debris that would have to be maneuvered through, around, or over. It was amazing the terrain these guys could log. He stroked the back of his neck. "Guess I better go have a look. Can one of you come along and show me where the body is?"

"Donny will," Donny's father-in-law said. "He's got younger legs."

Hansen retrieved his evidence kit from the trunk of his cruiser. He was about to follow Donny over the embankment when another sheriff's unit came crunching up the road, its light bar glinting in the sunlight. Hansen held his ground at the edge of the precipice, happy to wait for a fellow officer. He always felt better confronting the dead in the company of others.

Deputy Willard emerged from his cruiser and stood alongside it, his thumbs hooked on his duty belt. "Going slidin' down a mountain, Dan? In a suit no less."

"That's right, Willie," Hansen said. "And you're going with me."

The deputy rocked back on his heels. "Now why would I want to do that?"

"Treasure hunt."

Willard combed his fingers through his hair. "I think I'd rather see you plunder this treasure by yourself." But when Hansen ventured down the hillside behind Donny, the deputy followed.

As Hansen had surmised, it was tough going with all the timber on the ground. They had to slog through piles of detached limbs and make their way around or over the downed logs. Donny wasn't having any trouble though. He scampered down the slope like a squirrel on holiday and was waiting for the officers near a recumbent Douglas fir close to six feet in diameter that stretched crossways in front of them for a hundred feet or more.

"Over here," he said, straddling the big log. He dropped to the other side.

Hansen followed him over the log.

"Damn!" he heard Willard say, and looked back. The crotch of Willard's pants had gotten snagged on the jagged stub of a torn-off branch. "If I get castrated," he said, "there's going to be a lot of disappointed ladies in town."

"I thought it was the ladies in town that wanted you castrated," Hansen shot back.

"Maybe one or two," Willard said, grinning. He hoisted himself over the stub like a gymnast doing a tricky pommel horse maneuver and slid down to the ground.

When Hansen turned back around, he saw Donny standing off to the side, pointing. "There," the young logger said.

Hansen peered in the indicated direction and saw a shoed foot sticking out of the brush. The rest of the body was screened from clear view, but its odor was pervasive at this range. With Willard at his shoulder now, he moved in closer, and the two of them tugged branches aside until the corpse was fully exposed.

The lifeless form lay on its side, torso and limbs contorted unnaturally, head cocked back beyond its normal range. The body was clad in jeans and a polo shirt, the tail of which rode up to expose black putrefaction of the skin on the lower back. A running shoe covered one foot, a dirty sock the other. The flesh on the face had been partially eaten away by maggots. There were dark blotches of encrusted blood in the scalp area. Long blond hair was swept back into a ponytail that had mostly come undone.

"Male Caucasian," Hansen said, leaning over the body as he inspected it. "Young adult, I'd say. Kind of hard to tell though."

"I'll second that," Willard said. He glanced up toward the crest of the ridge. "You think this guy was that bad a driver?"

Hansen shrugged. "Could have had help steering." He extracted a pair of vinyl gloves from his evidence kit and pulled them on. He checked the guy's pockets but wasn't surprised not to find a wallet or any ID. He looked over at Donny, who hadn't moved from his position about fifty feet away, and motioned him closer.

Donny inched down the slope, looking ready to turn heels at the drop of a hat.

"Sorry about this," the detective said, "but I'd like you to take a look at this guy and see if you recognize him."

"Do I have to?" Donny said. "Dead people creep me out. I didn't even look at my grandma at her funeral."

"I won't force you," Hansen said. "But it would be helpful to rule out anyone you know."

Grimacing, Donny edged closer to the body. He sidled a look at it, quickly shuffled back. "No one I know," he said. "Thank God."

Hansen was about to ask him about the vehicle when he heard Willard say, "Well, look what we have here." The detective moved over to where Willard stood pointing farther down the slope. About fifty yards downhill, near the bottom of the ravine, the rear end of a vehicle protruded like a misplaced headstone. A green pickup, one of those little foreign jobs, it looked like. And it hadn't fared much better than its driver in this recent misadventure.

"You want that I should get back up the hill and call for the ME and a hook?" Willard said. "Don't think we'll get much of a signal from down here in this hole."

"Go ahead," Hansen said. "And take Donny with you." The young logger was braced against the big downed fir tree with his head down. "I'm gonna stay down here and check out the area around the body and the vehicle. You get an official statement from the loggers. And when you're done with that, sweep the face of the slope between here and the road as best you can. There's so much brushwood on the ground now and the slope's been ripped to hell with all the felling these guys did that there's probably not much chance of finding anything, but I'd like you to look. And check for other tire tracks on the road." He flashed his fellow officer a sardonic smile. "Unless, of course, you've got something better to do until the ME arrives."

"Only if I get attacked by a nymph of the woods," Willard said with a hopeful gleam in his eyes.

"If you do, hold on to her," Hansen told him. "We could use an eyewitness."

27 WITH MORE RENTAL BOATS returning to the dock, chased off the lake by the chop that typically developed mid-afternoon because of a stiffening breeze across the water, Kurt Adberry got busier—and hotter. Sweat dripped off the end of his nose as he reached down to untangle a wad of fishing line snagged on a cleat in the bottom of the boat he was cleaning. It was amazing the trash people left in the boats. Not just discarded tackle, but cigarette butts, beer cans, lunch leftovers, fish heads. Some of the fishermen would cut up the smaller fish they caught to use for bait. They'd toss the leavings, mostly heads and guts, onto the floor of the boat, then step on them as they moved from side to side casting.

Once Kurt found a dead dog in a boat. A little brown ball of fur. His dad said he thought it was a Pekinese. Two guys had rented the boat for the afternoon and taken the dog with them onto the lake, along with a cooler full of beer. It was a hot summer day. All the rental boats were aluminum. The guys came back at the end of the day with sunburns and a mess of fish packed into their, by then, beerless cooler. Kurt asked them where their dog was. "We don't have a dog," one of the men said. The other man picked up the cooler and shoved it at Kurt. "Set this down at the end of the dock." Later, while cleaning out their boat, Kurt found the pooch wedged in the V of the bow with white foam gushing from its mouth.

"It must have been 140 degrees in the bottom of that boat today," Kurt's dad had said. "When the dog got thirsty, they probably gave it beer to drink."

"Why didn't they just dunk it in the water once in a while?" Kurt wanted to know.

"Drunks don't think about things like that," his dad said. "Remember that when you're old enough to drink."

Kurt had been fifteen at the time, and he knew kids his age even then who thought they were old enough to drink. He knew he wasn't. Not then and not now at the age of seventeen and a year away from high school graduation. Whenever he was at an unchaperoned party and someone offered him a beer, he'd wave them off. "No thanks,"

he'd say. "I knew a dog once that drank itself to death." He got a lot
of strange looks, but other kids stopped offering him booze, and that
was okay with him.

With his five-gallon bucket near to overflowing with debris, Kurt
stepped out of the boat he was cleaning and onto the dock. The wooden
planks creaked underfoot as, bucket in hand, he strolled toward the
shore. The afternoon was too hot and he'd been on the dock too long
to want to move any faster. How many times today had he made this
little jaunt with a brimming bucket?

He stepped off the shore end of the dock, proceeded up the path
alongside the boat rental office, and entered the Dumpster enclosure
behind it. A stench like the breath of a flesh-eating dragon permeated
the pen. Garbage halitosis, his dad called it. He threw back the lid to
the metal bin, upended the bucket over its gaping mouth. He rapped
the bottom of the bucket a couple of times.

When he let the Dumpster's lid drop back into place with a loud
clang, he heard what sounded like a muffled cry. Puzzled, he lifted the
lid again and peered inside. There was nothing in the container except
several days' worth of putrid trash that made his nostrils burn.

He closed the lid and glanced around, wondering what he'd heard.
He was about to head back to the dock when another noise caught his
attention—a scuffing sound.

The Dumpster was set on an asphalt slab inside a six-foot-high
wooden-slat fence. The back of the container hugged the fence line, but
there was a narrow gap on the far side, between the Dumpster and the
intersecting run of fencing. Kurt leaned over and inspected that slot.

"What the . . . ?"

A human figure huddled in the narrow space—knees drawn up,
shoulders hunched, arms entwined, hands fisted and tucked under a
bright red face streaming with sweat and tears.

28

"... YOUR HAND."

Tamara's eyes were stinging, her vision watery. She gazed up, blinking, and saw a face hovering above her, and an outstretched hand. The hand must have been right in front of her, yet it seemed far away, as if extended from the opposite end of a tunnel. She stared at the hand, confused, clinging to the edge of awareness.

"Give me your hand."

Tamara reached up. It seemed a great effort. Fingertips brushed against hers. Palms touched. All at once she was being pulled up and out of the crevice in which she'd become hopelessly stuck.

She clung to her rescuer for support. A man? A boy? A stick with arms and legs?

Bearing much of her weight, her rescuer led her out of the Dumpster enclosure and around to the front of a squat wooden building. They moved clumsily together, as if performing poorly in a three-legged race. Up some steps they went and into the building.

Her rescuer maneuvered her around a rack of upright paddles and along a wall where bloated orange vests hung from wooden dowels. A mustached man standing behind a counter looked on with a puzzled expression. They shuffled by him and continued on to a door at the rear of the building that her rescuer shoved open with his foot.

A welcome rush of cool air enveloped them as they went through the doorway and into a small room Tamara dimly perceived to be an office: filing cabinets along one wall, a desk heaped with paperwork, a chair on rollers. Her rescuer swiveled the chair around and eased her into it. A window air conditioner hiccupped and began to vibrate as its compressor kicked in.

"I'll be right back," her rescuer said.

Tamara sat there dazed, devouring big gulps of the cool air while trying to regain contact with her body and her mind. Her limbs were beginning to tingle with sensation, which was encouraging. But her first ordered thoughts were troubling. The sense of relief she felt at being rescued was already being pushed aside by the fear that had caused her to hide in that awful enclosure in the first place.

She had awakened from her nap in Tommy and Amanda's cabin in a sweat, her stomach churning. When she checked her watch, she'd discovered it was past noon. She was late for her lunch with Amanda. She sat up, rubbing her belly. "There, there, girl. We'll get you something to eat soon enough."

But she hadn't been able to fulfill that promise.

While walking up the stone path on her way back to the lodge store, she'd nearly run head on into Gary's friend Brian, who was strolling down the path not more than ten paces in front of her. He had his hands full of snacks and drinks and, fortunately for her, his eyes on something off to the side. They would have met face to face for sure had it not been for the fat man in the clingy-wet bathing suit lumbering up the slope in front of Tamara. As soon as she saw Brian, she ducked in behind the fat man and stuck close to his blubbery back. When Brian passed by, she darted in front of her human shield.

But once in front of the fat man, she didn't know what to do. She didn't dare continue on to the store and risk running into Gary, who was surely at the lake too, searching for her. And she couldn't turn around and go back the way she'd come, because Brian was there. Still she had to do something—otherwise she was sure to get caught. Gary would be furious with her for stealing his truck. And she knew what his fury looked like.

She stumbled to a stop. The fat man brushed past her. She stood there trembling, a dark mist enveloping her mind. She thought she might faint.

Out of the corner of her eye, she spied a gated enclosure off to the side and lurched toward it. She ducked into the enclosure and stayed there, afraid to come out even when it became insufferably warm inside the stinky pen. The first time someone came to dump trash, she hid from them by squeezing herself into the gap between the far side of the Dumpster and the wooden fence. But when she tried to get back out after they'd left, she found herself wedged in place as tightly as a cat stuck in a mouse hole. She would have been there yet, dying from heat stroke, if someone hadn't shown up and pulled her out.

That someone—*he's just a boy*—came back into the air conditioned room carrying a paper cup full of water. She gulped it down in an instant.

"More?"

She nodded.

The boy returned moments later with the cup refilled. She drained it again, then declined the offer of another refill.

"What were you doing behind the Dumpster?" the boy asked. "It's hotter than blazes in that enclosure."

Tamara didn't say anything, just let her jaw sag as she inhaled more of the deliciously cool air swirling around her face.

The boy looked at her with a pondering expression. Then his eyes sparked. "I know what you were doing behind that Dumpster." He stuffed a hand into one of his front pants pockets. "You were hiding—from a tall guy with a red beard."

Tamara almost fell off the chair. "What makes you think I was hiding from anyone?"

The boy yanked his hand out of his pocket with something in it. He unfolded a ten-dollar bill and held it out. Handwritten across the top of the bill was a number. A telephone number. Gary's telephone number!

Tamara gasped.

"Don't worry," the boy said. "I'm not going to call the guy." He handed her the bill. "Here. You can have it."

Tamara snatched the ten-dollar bill from his hand. "How do I know you didn't memorize the number?"

"You don't," the boy said, but there wasn't the slightest hint of taunting in his voice.

She looked him over, really seeing him for the first time. He was skinny, but not bad looking. He couldn't have been much older than she was. His face and arms were well tanned. He had short, sun-bleached brown hair and blue eyes that looked incapable of deceit. "What's your name?"

He told her.

"What's yours?"

She told him.

He was studying her now, body part by body part, as if assessing the condition of an accident victim. "So—think you're gonna need a doctor?"

Tamara cringed. "That's one thing I definitely don't need." In fact, she was feeling much better now that her body had done some cooling down.

She looked at her watch. Three-fifteen. Amanda would have gotten off work by now. She'd probably be at the cabin. Should Tamara go back there? Yes, she'd have to—she'd left her backpack there. Besides, she owed Amanda an explanation. And, more importantly, she needed a hiding place for the rest of the day, and time to rethink her options.

She stood up, fought for balance. Her legs were shakier than she thought.

Kurt put out his hand.

She waved him off, took a tentative step toward the door. Her legs quivered but kept her upright.

"Sure you don't want some help?"

"Thank you," she said. "You've helped enough."

"THERE YOU ARE," Amanda said. She took Tamara by the hand and pulled her inside the cabin. "I worried when you didn't come for lunch, and then you weren't here when I got home. Tommy said you'd show up, but I wasn't so sure."

Tamara glanced around. "Where is he?"

Amanda made a sour face. "Fishing. He goes out almost every day after work. Employees get free use of the boats." She wriggled her nose in a way that reminded Tamara of a rabbit. "So, where were you?"

Tamara had already made up her mind not to say anything to Amanda and Tommy about her time with Gary, her getaway that morning, and her recent close encounter with Brian. "I fell asleep on your sofa. Slept right through lunch. After that I took a walk to wake up." She pursed her lips apologetically. "Sorry to worry you."

"That's okay," Amanda said. "But you must be starving by now."

Before Tamara could respond, the entrance door to the cabin

burst open and Tommy lunged in carrying a fishing rod in one hand and a stringer of fish in the other. He held up the fish and grinned. "Dinner."

Amanda groaned. "I hope you like fish. Tommy loves trout. We eat it three times a week—grilled, fried, broiled, stewed. "

Tamara didn't say anything, but just the thought of consuming so much fish made her stomach ache.

"And why not?" Tommy said. He walked over and flopped his catch into the kitchen sink. "The lake is full of these beauties. We can't let them go to waste."

"But do we have to eat all of them ourselves?"

Tommy took off his baseball cap and tossed it in the direction of the bed. It came up short and landed upside down on the floor. "No, we don't." He sashayed over to the girls. "As a matter of fact, tonight we'll have some help devouring these." He smiled at Tamara. "In addition to present company."

Tamara looked at Amanda.

Amanda shrugged.

THE HEAD CROWNED.

"Breathe!" Mr. Menenger said, looking out of breath himself.

Mrs. Menenger forced air in and out of her mouth in audible bursts, as if imitating a bellows.

"Give us a big push now, Betty," Dr. Castle instructed.

Mrs. Menenger, whose face was already drenched in sweat from her efforts to expel the child from her womb, arched forward and complied. Her husband, sitting beside her bed in the delivery room at Fir Valley Community Hospital, cheered her on.

The baby's head popped out—free of the umbilical cord, Dr. Castle was glad to see. He reached down with his gloved hands and cradled it. "Almost there."

Mrs. Menenger sucked in what was left of the air in the room and bore down one last time, grunting loud and long.

A tiny shoulder showed itself. Dr. Castle supported the baby's head and waited patiently. Mrs. Menenger was very good at giving birth. She let out a cry as the baby's other shoulder broke free of the birth canal.

The baby slid out into Dr. Castle's hands: a fine looking boy who started wailing as soon as the doctor cleared his mouth. He laid the baby on the birthing cloth spread open between Mrs. Menenger's yawning legs and double-clamped the umbilical.

The beeper on his hip went off.

"Would you like me to finish up, doctor?" Nurse Faye said from behind her surgical mask. Nurse Alma was already occupied applying pressure on the fundus.

"Almost done." The doctor severed the umbilical, scooped up the baby, and held him out.

Nurse Faye swaddled the infant in a fresh cloth. Then she carried the bundle over and nestled it in the cradle of its mother's arms.

"He's beautiful," Mrs. Menenger said, her eyes gleaming with devotion.

"He looks like a third-baseman," her husband said.

"Don't start that, Franklin."

Dr. Castle skinned off his gloves. He pulled his mask down and came alongside his patient and her child in the bed. "Well done as usual, Betty." He winked at the father. "You too, Frank." Mr. Menenger beamed.

"Thank you, doctor," Mrs. Menenger said, but her eyes never left the child.

Nurse Faye had already taken the doctor's place at the foot of the bed in preparation for the expulsion of the afterbirth. "Page me if you need me," he told her.

In the prep area, he discarded his mask and gloves in one receptacle and his gown in another and quickly washed up. He glanced at the number showing in the window of his beeper and wasn't surprised to see that it was Russell Trouste's private number. He entered the nearest conference room and looked around for a phone.

Russell answered on the first ring. "Brandon, something's happened," he said, punctuating each word with urgency. "Margaret is having recurring pains. Beatrice thinks she's gone into labor." There was a pause filled with the sound of heavy breathing, then, "My God, what are we going to do? Things are happening too fast. Have you seen the girl today? Is she ready?"

"One thing at a time, Russell. Put Beatrice on the phone."

Dr. Castle conferred with Beatrice before being reconnected to Russell. "I'm sorry," he told his friend, "but I think you should call an ambulance immediately. Margaret has undoubtedly gone into labor. I—uh—" He broke off, feeling the barrenness that accompanies regret. "I haven't been able to make contact with the girl's brother today. No one is answering the phone at his house. Without the girl, there's no reason to keep Margaret at home." He sighed. "The hospital is the best place for her now."

"No!" Russell said. Then more softly, "No, no." There was agony embedded in his voice as he continued in the softer tone. "Can't you come over and take care of Margaret here? Give her more time. We're so close. So close . . ."

The doctor massaged a throbbing temple with his fingertips. It seemed clear to him what had to be done given the circumstances. But he could hardly blame Russell for thinking otherwise. After all, it was the doctor who'd given him reason to believe things could turn out differently.

"Russell, as your friend and Margaret's doctor, I advise you to call 9-1-1 at once. By the time I get there, she could be in great peril."

"Then for God's sake, Brandon, hurry!"

Twenty minutes later, having acceded—against his better judgment—to his friend's wishes, Dr. Castle was consulting with Beatrice outside the door to Margaret's room while an overwrought Russell waited downstairs. "How far apart are the contractions?" the doctor inquired.

"They're erratic," the nurse informed him, "coming anywhere from two to fifteen minutes apart and varying in intensity. It could be false labor."

"I doubt it."

The doctor pushed open the door to Margaret's room. Margaret lay curled up on her side in the bed, wincing. Rivulets of unkempt hair cascaded down her face and onto the pillow. She looked up at him through the hirsute veil, her eyes pleading. "Make it stop," she said. "It's too soon."

The doctor sat down in a chair beside her bed, reached over and brushed some of the errant locks away from her face. "It's not too soon."

When the pain subsided, Dr. Castle went to work, performing a brief but telling pelvic exam. Margaret's cervix had begun to dilate. She was definitely in labor.

Beatrice stayed with Margaret while the doctor went downstairs to talk to Russell, whom he found pacing the library floor. The doctor sat down on the sofa. Russell shambled over and dropped into his armchair, looking damaged in some elemental way.

Despair can do that to a man. How well the doctor knew. It takes its toll on you like a constant wind that erodes layer upon layer of topsoil until it has eaten down to rock and hardpan. Despair exposes the bones of a man's soul.

"Her time has come," he said.

Russell's body tensed. "But without the girl . . ." He looked around in an agitated manner, as if suddenly trapped by a cave-in. "Isn't there anything we can do?"

The doctor considered his options. Were there any good ones? "I can give her another, heavier dose of inhibitor. It might slow things down—forestall the process. But that's all it will do. And at this point, I don't think it's in Margaret's best interest to do so. Her body has gone through enough."

An expression of torment appeared on Russell's face. Tears trailed from the corners of his eyes. "I've lost her then."

Dr. Castle could think of no good response. He felt weary and defeated. His efforts to save Margaret had all been for naught. If only . . .

He stole a glance at his watch. It was five-fifteen. He'd made his last call to Neaves' house just before going to the hospital to deliver Mrs. Menenger's baby—about three o'clock. Maybe it was worth one last try.

"Can I use your phone?"

30 WHEN GARY NEAVES got home from Mohler Lake, he was hot, thirsty, and more than a little pissed off. He had his truck back, but not the girl. That put him in a bad position. He didn't like it. Not one bit.

He went into the kitchen and snagged a beer from the fridge. He took the beer into the living room, found some wrestling on TV, and sat down to watch it. The match ended with one of the wrestlers getting tossed out of the ring by his opponent. The next pair of gladiators climbed in through the ropes. Gary went back to the kitchen and got himself another beer.

When his second beer was gone, Gary returned for another, and while he was at it, made himself a bologna sandwich. He was back in front of the TV drinking his third beer since arriving home, eating his sandwich, and watching a guy in tights get body-slammed to the canvas repeatedly when the telephone rang.

"I've been trying to get ahold of you all day," an annoyed voice said the moment Gary answered.

Gary swore under his breath. "Yeah?" he said, deciding to play it cool.

"I wanted to check on the girl," the doctor said. "How is she?"

"Fine."

"Good. I'll be stopping by your place tonight. But don't tell Tamara. She's not to know."

Gary sat up in his chair. "Why you comin' here?"

"That will be apparent by the time I get there. Now, do you have those—"

"She's not here," Gary said, feeling his neck muscles tighten.

"What do you mean, she's not there? You just said she was fine."

Gary tossed what was left of his sandwich onto the table next to his chair, swiped his palm across the front of his shirt. "She is fine," he said, his sluggish mind working hard to come up with a plausible explanation for Tamara's absence. "She's visiting a friend up at Mohler Lake. Staying the night. I'll be pickin' her up—uh—in a couple of days."

"No you won't," the doctor said in a stern voice, as if talking to a child. "You'll get her back here immediately."

Gary resented the doctor's tone as much as he did this uppity prick telling him what to do. "Look, it's a full hour's drive up there on that goddamn twisted road. Plus an hour back. I just got home and I'm bitch-tired. I'll get her first thing in the morning. That ought to be—"

"You'll get her now!" the doctor bellowed.

Gary snarled back. "What the hell's the rush? She's not due for another month."

There was a pulse of silence before the doctor said in a quieter yet equally insistent manner, "I'll explain later. Now have the girl back tonight or—"

"Or what?"

"—or the deal is off."

Gary sprang to his feet, nearly yanking the telephone base off the table. He waved the receiver around in the air like a club, wanting to smash it against something—anything. And he would have too, except for the realization that by demolishing a telephone, he would also be destroying his chances of collecting the biggest paycheck of his life.

He kneaded the back of his neck, put the receiver to his ear. "All right—but—"

"Do you still have the pills I sent you?"

"Pills?"

"In the envelope I gave Tamara to give to you. Along with the—uh—health department forms, there were two small packets, each containing several pills. You said before that you got them."

"Oh, yeah, yeah—I got 'em." Gary was trying to remember what the hell he'd done with the packets. He'd only been interested in the envelope's other contents—the hundred-dollar bills. Eleven of them, all nice and crisp. He regretted having to use one of them to open that bank account for Tamara. He only half-listened now as the doctor prattled on, giving him some more stupid instructions.

"You got all that?" the doctor said. "It's critical that you do exactly as I've stated."

"Yeah, sure, I got it, but—" The line buzzed in his ear.

Gary banged the receiver down. Who did this guy think he was? And what the hell was the big rush with the girl?

The more Gary thought about the situation, the angrier he got. He stomped around the room swearing. On this asshole's say-so, he had to drive up to the lake tonight, find Tamara, and bring her back. Otherwise, he could kiss the rest of his money goodbye. That made no fucking sense. Especially after everything he'd done to protect his interest in the girl, including getting rid of that cry-baby boyfriend of hers. The kid just wouldn't stay away like he was told.

It was Jerome who'd spotted Jimmy's truck parked down the street that one afternoon, with Jimmy in it. "Look's like he's casing the place," he'd said.

Gary peered out the front window and saw who it was. "Stupid prick."

They'd waited until after dark that night to ambush the kid, sneaking down the back alley to come at him from behind, getting his attention by putting a pistol to his head. Then the three of them had gone for a ride into the hills, with Gary in Jimmy's pickup, telling him where to go, and Jerome following in his rig. Gary had meant only to rough him up and send him packing, but it felt so good hitting the guy he couldn't make himself stop.

"I don't think he's breathin' anymore," Jerome had said as he leaned over the kid where he was sprawled in the middle of the gravel road, blood streaming from his nose.

It was a dark night and the blood looked like oozing tar. Gary's chest was heaving from the exertion. "Shit. Help me get him back in his truck. And grab his wallet."

Jerome did as he was told. Gary got behind the wheel of Jimmy's truck, with Jimmy's rag-doll body slumped over next to him in the seat. They drove in tandem farther up the logging road until they came to a steep precipice. Gary aimed Jimmy's pickup toward the drop-off and stopped. He placed the vehicle's transmission in neutral, wiped down the steering wheel with the tail of his shirt, and got out. He stood just outside the glare of Jerome's headlights and motioned him forward. The bumper on Jerome's rig hit Jimmy's pickup high on the tailgate, but still with enough bite to do the trick.

"Give it a good shove," he told Jerome, and Jerome did.

Thinking about that night stoked the fire of Gary's wrath. When the living room could no longer hold his anger, he stalked throughout the house, throwing open every door, glaring into every room, searching behind every piece of furniture, as if Tamara would miraculously appear and he would be off the hook. But the girl wasn't there. He'd let her get away. And if he didn't have her back tonight, he'd be letting thousands of dollars slip through his fingers.

As he came blundering back into the living room, something inside him snapped. He grabbed the lamp off the table next to his chair and flung it at the wall. The lamp's base exploded, showering chunks of plaster onto the dingy green carpet. The shell casings attached to its shade tinkled dully as what was left of the lamp thudded to the floor.

The sight of the shattered lamp merely added to his fury. He turned and kicked a TV tray that was sitting in front of the sofa. The flimsy metal tray buckled and became disjointed from its legs. It sailed through the air, bounced off the windowsill, and clanked to the floor.

Gary roared and raised his fists in the air. He stood there shaking them at no one, except maybe God, and thinking that if he didn't get control of himself he would destroy the whole house, just like his old man used to do when he felt the need to satisfy his sweet tooth for violence.

The thought of his dad enraged, throwing things, hitting people—his mother, his brothers, him—sent a chill through Gary's veins. He dropped onto the sofa and stuck his head between his legs in a duck-and-cover mode.

After a few minutes of controlled breathing, he'd mostly quelled his rage. It was a technique he'd learned in counseling during his last stint in jail, not that he'd ever acknowledged that to the fag shrink who'd been brought in to fuck with his head for a half-hour every other Thursday. The judge in Gary's case had said that he was at risk of becoming a repeat violent offender and needed counseling. Bullshit. He just needed people to get off his back.

All he'd done to land himself in the pokey that time was to rough up the guy who was shagging his ex-girlfriend. Gary had been pumping gas at a truck stop in Rice Hill at the time. Tilly was a waitress in the restaurant there. She was a chubby little thing, but had a nice ass and an apartment of her own. Gary lived with her for three months, until she got a restraining order against him. Claimed he beat her up when he was drunk. Hell, he may have leaned on her a little when she wouldn't put out, but it was nothing excessive, and her going to the cops really ticked him off. But he hadn't wanted to break the restraining order, so he'd taken his anger out on the waitress's new boyfriend. Put him in the hospital with three broken ribs, enough stitches in his face to sew up a heart-transplant patient, and the prospects of some very costly dental work. After his conviction for assault and battery, Gary was lodged in the Douglas County Jail in Roseburg for six months. That was easy duty as far as he was concerned. Free room and board, an occasional hot shower, and his own private shrink.

With his head mostly clear, Gary sat up. He stared at the cracked picture window thinking about what the doctor had said and what he ought to do about it. It wasn't long before it came to him.

He went to his bedroom, pulled a tote bag out of the closet, and began stuffing it with clothes, some from the closet and some from his chest of drawers. From the bottom drawer of the chest, he extracted a wooden box. It contained his revolver, the envelope with the remainder of his advance payment, and—to his surprise—the two packets of pills.

He crammed the money and the pills in his pants pocket, and the revolver in his tote bag. In the bathroom, he gathered up some toiletries and bagged them as well. He took the tote out to his truck and tossed it into the cab. He made one last trip into the house and came out with his rolled-up sleeping bag and a six-pack of Coors.

It was quarter to six when he pulled out of his driveway and onto the street. He would drive back to Mohler Lake and look for the girl. But if he couldn't find her that evening, he wouldn't keep looking and he wouldn't bother coming back to the house, not for a while anyway. He'd hightail it out of the mountains and head for the freeway. He'd go—south. Yeah, south. He hadn't been to Reno in years. Reno sounded good.

He grinned. Fuck the doctor. And fuck the girl. He had his up-front money. A thousand bucks—or what was left of it. Push came to shove, he'd use it to take a little vacation from all this shit. It's not like the doctor could go to the cops.

He was chuckling to himself as he turned onto Briar Creek Road and aimed his truck toward the hills to the east.

---

31   LT. IVERSON BRANDISHED some paperwork at Detective Hansen. "Might want to take a look at this before you leave. ME's office just faxed it over."

Hansen's shift at the Fir Valley Sheriff's Substation was over, but he'd made the mistake of lingering in the front office while listening to Tom Riley, the duty officer, talk on the base radio with a deputy who'd responded to a report of a pickup truck overturned in a ditch out on Thorn Mountain Road. Several teenagers had been thrown from the bed of the truck as it skidded off the road and tumbled down an embankment. The officer was calling for an additional ambulance.

"Copy, Jay," Riley said. "We'll get another one rolling your way ASAP."

Hansen accepted the paperwork from his boss. "Thanks—I guess."

"Thank the ME," Iverson said, and walked away.

Hansen sat down in a chair by the duty desk and began flipping through the pages. It was a preliminary report on the body that had been found in the woods earlier that afternoon. He scanned its pertinent details: *White male. Late teens to early twenties. Five feet, ten inches tall. 160 pounds. Blond hair. Eye color indeterminate. No other distinguishing characteristics. Postmortem interval 10–14 days. Death probably caused by severe trauma to the head and body. External injuries consistent with those typically seen in beating victims. Fingerprints submitted. Blood work to follow. Autopsy pending.*

Several photos of the remains were attached but were of poor quality in fax version. Hansen glanced at them before handing the report to Sgt. Jessup, his replacement, who was standing nearby looking over the call log for the previous shift.

Jessup scanned the report and handed it back. "Looks like we got a killer on the loose."

"Don't reckon the fellow beat himself to death," Hansen said. He leaned forward and stretched his back. It had tightened up on him after he and Willard had finally made it off that mountainside. He needed a good backrub. His wife was great in that department. She had magic fingers.

"DB got a name?" Jessup said.

Hansen shook his head. "The truck we pulled out of the canyon along with this guy was registered to one Juan Ignacio Padilla of Woodburn, whose vitals, according to the DMV, don't match the ME's preliminary description of the victim." He reached over and dropped the ME's report in the circulation box for the other officers to read as they came on duty. "This guy was pretty messed up, but unless the ME was mistaken about ethnicity and was off on the age estimate by about thirty years, we're still looking to ID our guy. An evidence tech is going over the truck. Woodburn PD has been notified and will check out Padilla. But I suspect they'll find that he sold the truck to a young man who didn't bother getting it registered in his name because the tags were still good through October."

"Anything for me to do on this?"

Hansen smiled. There was always enough legwork to go around on a case like this. "Check the statewide missing persons reports for the last month. And the stolen vehicle reports for the same period. Also, if any prints come in tonight from the evidence tech, get them sent off right away to ISS, along with the ones the ME pulled off the body."

Jessup nodded.

The base radio had come to life again—a request for wants and warrants from a deputy who'd made a traffic stop on Ayers Road of a van with two passengers and six, or was it eight, dogs in it. The deputy was apparently having difficulty getting an accurate canine count because the dogs were crawling all over one another to bare their teeth at him through a partially open window. "I think the driver is drunk," the deputy was saying. "We need animal control out here."

Hansen chuckled as he visualized the scene. All in a day's work. He pushed his stiff body up from the chair. "One other thing," he said to his replacement. "Please solve all pending cases before I return in the morning."

"You got it," Jessup said, flashing a staunch thumbs-up.

Hansen headed down the hallway leading to the back entrance to the station house and the employee parking lot where his Jeep was parked. Lt. Iverson was standing in the alcove partway down the hall, cursing at the photocopy machine.

"Don't say it," the lieutenant warned as Hansen approached.

Hansen gave the lieutenant a Boy Scout salute and moved on to the rear door. He was looking forward to getting home to his wife and kids, and to that back massage.

32

TAMARA HELPED AMANDA clean up after dinner, although there wasn't much to do. Tommy had grilled the fish on the barbeque and they'd eaten off paper plates at a picnic table outside the cabin. Tamara was so hungry she'd been able to ignore the fact that she was eating fish, which she hadn't liked since she was a little girl and was served fish sticks every Friday in the school cafeteria that just the smell of made her feel like throwing up. But this fish didn't taste half bad, along with the rice and salad Amanda had prepared.

It was Kurt's presence at the table that had made Tamara squeamish. She was afraid he might say something about their meeting earlier in the day, or about his encounter with Gary. But he made no reference to any of that throughout dinner. He and Tommy mostly ignored the girls, taking turns telling fish stories like old men huddled in a smoky corner of some dingy backwoods café.

Amanda gathered the used paper plates and stuffed them into an already bulging garbage bag that stank of, among other things, fish innards and soggy tea bags. She turned the bag over to Tommy, who went off to toss it in the Dumpster behind the boat rental office. Kurt went with him.

She and Amanda carried the depleted serving bowls and glasses into the cabin. "He's cute, don't you think?" Amanda said.

"Who?"

"Don't be coy. You know who I'm talking about."

"If you mean Kurt," Tamara said, "you're wasting your breath." She clunked a glass down on the kitchen counter. "He's just a boy and I'm eight months pregnant."

"Angela said Jimmy was the father."

Just hearing Jimmy's name made Tamara's heart sink. He hadn't shown his face again since that one frantic night at Gary's house. So much for his devotion to her and the baby. "You know Jimmy?"

Amanda began rinsing out the serving bowls. "Not really. I saw him when he came to the house to take you and Angela to the movies or something. But he made an impression."

"Yeah," Tamara said. "Jimmy was cute too."

The guys had good timing, because just after she and Amanda had finished cleaning up and were stepping outside to escape the heat that had been trapped indoors, they came strolling back to the cabin.

"Madsen Falls," Tommy said.

"What about it?" Amanda said.

"Let's take a hike up to the falls."

Amanda turned to Tamara. "Want to?"

"I don't know," Tamara said. Something about the suggestion made her nervous. Then again, she'd been jumpy all afternoon, ever since nearly running into Gary's friend Brian.

"Come on," Tommy said. "It's an easy hike—less than a mile and not too steep."

"It is a pretty waterfall," Amanda said. "And the spray from it will cool us off."

Tamara wasn't thinking about the steepness of the trail, the beauty of the falls, or getting cool. She was thinking about Gary. Was he still at the lake, looking for her? Was he more likely to find her if she stayed at the cabin or if she went for a hike in the woods? She found herself looking at Kurt, as if he might have the answers to her questions. But he was staring at the ground.

"Won't it be dark soon?" she asked.

"We've got plenty of daylight left," Tommy said.

And Tamara thought, Then better to spend it hidden in the forest.

"A hike to a waterfall?" she said. "Sure. Why not?"

33   GARY STEERED HIS truck up the winding mountain road, flicking ashes out the window as he went. When his cigarette diminished to a stub, he lit another from the smoldering butt, and another from the dying end of that one.

Gary had started smoking when he was eleven, stealing cigarettes from his parents, both of whom smoked like chimneys. It was exciting at first, something illicit to do that made him feel manly and rebellious. Now he simply needed the nicotine to help him relax, to take his mind off all the shit life dished out on a daily basis to those who weren't born rich or pretty. He'd heard all the health warnings about cigarettes. But what the hell—you gotta die from something.

He coughed up some phlegm, spit it out the window. He wiped a trail of back-blown spittle from his cheek, cursed. He wasn't halfway to the lake and already he'd grown weary of the drive—the corkscrew curves, the strobe effect of broken sunlight on the road, the thinning air that made him feel short of breath no matter how deeply he filled his lungs.

He wished he'd gotten something else to eat before leaving town. The bologna sandwich had done little for him other than give him gas. He ripped open the top of the beer carton next to him on the bench seat, pulled out a Coors. At least it would take the edge off his appetite.

About five miles shy of the lake, he pulled over at a wide spot in the road and took a leak over the embankment onto some blackberry bushes, ignoring the hoots of the occupants of a passing van. Back in his truck, he popped open another beer. The lake was no more than ten minutes away. He was relieved—then again, he wasn't. It was going to be a bitch finding the girl, especially now that the sun was about to go down for the count. She could be anywhere up there—in a cabin on the lodge grounds, at an outlying campground, in one of the summer homes scattered around the lake, all down dead-end drives.

"What a fuckin' mess." He fired up the truck and pulled back onto the roadway.

Ten minutes later, with the turnoff to Mohler Lake Lodge in sight, he slowed and was about to begin his turn when he saw, a hundred yards or so ahead, several figures cross the road in front of him. It looked like two men and two women headed toward the lake. It could have been any two men and any two women, except that one of the women looked unnaturally heavy out front, and the way she moved was tantalizingly familiar. He came to a near stop and, clamping his eyes on the figure of interest, followed the group's progress away from the roadway and into the trees off to the right.

An invigorating heat coursed through his body, as if he was an ingot mold into which liquid gold was being poured. He took off again, keeping the truck aimed straight ahead, past the turnoff to the lodge. When he came to the spot where he thought the pedestrians had crossed, he pulled over and stopped. A walking path led into the trees on the lake side of the roadway. It was the continuation of a path on the opposite side of the road.

He pondered a course of action, knowing he needed to be quick about it. He didn't want to let the girl slip away again, if indeed it was her. But neither did he care to cause a ruckus by blowing into the lodge compound in his very recognizable rig and pinching her in front of a bunch of witnesses who might be stupid enough to try and stop him.

A roadside signpost told him there was a parking area ahead, on his left, at the trailhead to Madsen Falls. He gunned the engine, shot up the road, and veered into the lot. Within seconds, he was out of his truck and hoofing it down the walking path in hot pursuit of the four hikers. His luck was about to change. He could sense it.

34

AS DR. CASTLE had suspected, the additional dose of labor inhibitor he'd administered, at Russell's bidding, had a nominal effect on Margaret's troubled body. Her labor pains, although less frequent and intense, continued, as did the dilation of her cervix. She was going to give birth this night and there was nothing he could do to prevent that from happening. In the end, nature always prevails.

He sat alongside her bed waiting for the inevitable to occur, monitoring her minute by minute at this crucial time. It was all for the best that the birthing process had begun. Margaret had suffered enough.

She was between pains at the moment, her body tense nonetheless, poised for action, like a runner in starting blocks waiting for the gun to sound. Russell sat in a chair on the other side of the bed from the doctor, looking as frazzled as his wife. Each time Margaret writhed in pain, his body knotted in sympathy. Dr. Castle knew that his friend would be better off out of the room, but Russell had insisted on staying now that Beatrice was gone. The doctor was beginning to regret having sent her away.

"You're exhausted," he'd told her earlier in the evening. "You need some rest, and not just a catnap."

Beatrice had opened her mouth to protest.

The doctor cut her off with a raised palm. "I've already arranged for someone to replace you. She'll be here any minute now."

"Who?" Beatrice wanted to know.

"No one you know. She was referred by Dr. Reyes. Well qualified, I'm sure. It may not be the best timing, but what good would it do for you to stay here and then collapse from exhaustion when I need you most?" He patted her hand affectionately. "You've done me and the Troustes a great service. Now go home to your husband before he thinks you've abandoned him."

Beatrice didn't like being sent away just when things were coming to a head with Mrs. Trouste. But as usual, she acceded to the doctor's wishes.

"I am a bit tired," she admitted. She gathered up her things and shortly thereafter was shuttled home in a taxi.

Dr. Castle had indeed arranged for Beatrice's replacement. But he hadn't been totally truthful with her. The person taking her place was not a nurse and would not be coming to the house that night.

Margaret cried out. Russell leaned forward in his chair, hands outstretched, fingers flexing as if needing something to do. His wife doubled up and rolled onto her side with her back to him.

Dr. Castle motioned Russell toward the door. "She'll be in labor for a while yet," he said, leading his friend out into the hallway. "I want you to go and rest. It's going to be a long night. I'll buzz you when it's time."

"But the girl isn't back yet," Russell said in a plaintive tone.

"I'm sorry," the doctor said, aware of the emptiness of his apology. "But we have to let nature take its course. If we don't, there could be dire consequences."

Russell's face twisted. "But she's as good as dead anyway if she doesn't get her baby."

The doctor put a hand on his friend's shoulder. "Don't give up hope. There's still time. Neaves will call my service the minute he gets back with the girl. They know to call me here."

Russell was silent, somber.

"In the meantime," the doctor said, "you need to rest."

Russell stayed put, as if unable to comply.

"Go," the doctor said, and finally Russell turned and plodded down the hall.

Dr. Castle slipped back into Margaret's room. She was lying on her back now, clutching her mounded belly. She stared up at him with bloodshot eyes brimming with tears. "Is my baby going to die?"

The doctor caressed her forearm. "No, no. Everything is going to be all right."

But his words were more of a prayer than a statement. Margaret's hold on life had become so tenuous in recent days that only God could know the outcome of this night. And the doctor had only himself to blame. How could he have allowed Margaret to carry this withered fetus to such a point of peril? He'd tinkered with fate and, in so doing, had jeopardized her life.

God help her now if things didn't go as planned.

A cold hand gripped his heart.

God help us all if they do.

35

TAMARA CUPPED HER EARS in an effort to shut out the noise. It wasn't as though she hadn't heard the sounds of lovemaking before. But it had always been from the other side of a wall. This was different. As close as she was to Tommy and Amanda, with no barrier between, she might as well have been in bed with them.

The three of them had said their awkward goodnights shortly after ten o'clock. Tamara, hugely grateful to have been invited to spend the night, had shed only her shoes before sinking onto the sofa that Amanda had covered with a sheet for her. At the rear of the cabin, Tommy and Amanda had clumsily undressed in the dark.

It was only minutes later that Tamara had heard Amanda's whispered complaint, "Not with Tamara here."

But Amanda's verbal protest had turned out to be no more than paper-bag resistance, because before long she was writhing in the bed, moaning with pleasure as Tommy grunted out his efforts, the creaking bedsprings giving voice to his every thrust.

Tamara felt like a voyeur, and she didn't like the feeling. It made the whole thing seem dirty, her being a part of it—or at least feeling as if she was. She flattened her palms against her ears, trying to block out the sound. But she only succeeded in muffling it, and her ears only listened all the harder because some other part of her brain wanted to hear. So when Amanda began to cry, "Go for it, baby!" Tamara decided that she needed to do more than just plug her ears. She got up, groped the darkness for her shoes, and with them in hand retreated from the cabin.

She hobbled barefooted across the prickly gravel to the picnic table outside. It was a cloudless night. A three-quarter moon dropped bits of silver onto the quivering surface of the lake. The nearby trees cast jagged shadows all around. A stillness broken only by the distant call of peepers rode a gentle breeze off the water. She sat down at the table, dusted grit off the soles of her feet, and slipped her shoes on. She didn't know what else to do then except sit and wait.

It wasn't long before she was shivering. The night mountain air was much cooler than she'd expected. She rubbed her arms, wishing she'd thought to dig her sweatshirt out of her backpack. She wouldn't stay out long, she decided. Just long enough to allow Tommy and Amanda to finish, although she wasn't sure how long that would be.

She thought about the two of them in the cabin making love and remembered her conversation with Amanda earlier in the evening as they'd lagged behind the guys on their return trek from the falls. Tamara had wondered aloud what it was like to be married. Amanda was only two years older than Tamara and Angela. She and Tommy, who was a year older yet, had been a couple for almost two years when Amanda had graduated from high school the previous June. She'd stepped out of her cap and gown one day and into a wedding gown the next.

"Marriage is okay," Amanda had said.

The needle-strewn path they were following was growing darker by the second, as if the sun's light was on a dimmer switch being turned down.

"But are you happy?" Tamara wanted to know.

"It beats living at home," Amanda said. "I don't have to put up with my old man getting on me all the time for coming home late, or tolerate him sniffing my clothes to see if—or what—I've been smoking."

Tamara looked at her, curious. "But that's not why you got married, is it? Just to get away from your dad?"

"Of course not," Amanda said, lifting her chin defensively. "Tommy and I are in love."

Tamara was envious. "You're lucky then." She turned her face away. She'd been in love too, and see where it had gotten her.

She wriggled in place on the hard bench seat of the picnic table. She touched her cheeks, which were beginning to sting from the cold, and wondered how much longer she should wait before going back inside.

A sound off to the side, like gravel crunching underfoot, caught her attention. She jerked her head in that direction and gaped at the blackness looming there. Then her entire body spasmed as she realized that something was coming at her from the shadow of the trees.

But she realized too late what—who—it was. By the time she got her mouth open in the shape of a scream, Gary already had a meaty hand clamped over it. With his other hand, he pinned her right arm behind her back, pulled her to her feet, and began shoving her toward the darkness that had all but hidden his advance.

"You even think about biting me, little sister," he said, blowing his tobacco breath in her ear, "and I'll snap your arm like a twig."

36   THEY MOVED TOGETHER through the gloom, Gary in control, using Tamara's bent arm to steer her, all the while keeping his other hand cinched over her mouth. It was hard breathing only through her nose, and Tamara thought she might pass out for lack of air as Gary propelled her along the same path through

the woods that she'd hiked earlier with the others on their way to and from the trailhead to the falls. Except now the pathway was more like a dark tunnel.

"If I take my hand off your mouth," Gary said, "do you promise to be a good girl and not scream?"

She nodded, desperate for more air.

He removed his hand.

"Why are you doing this?" she blurted between gasps. It was as if she was being arrested for an unstated crime.

Gary ignored the question, forced her farther down the dim trail.

"You're hurting my arm," Tamara complained, and he finally loosened his hold, allowing her arm to drop down to a less severe angle. She immediately twisted her body around and tried to pull away. He yanked her back, cranked her arm up higher than before. She cried out from the pain. He clasped his hand over her mouth again.

Her muffled cries came out her nose, which began to run, making breathing all the more difficult. Tears pooled under her eyes, where Gary's broad hand dammed them up.

Tamara must have lost consciousness after that, because the next thing she knew Gary was manhandling her into the cab of his pickup. She huddled on the bench seat, cradling an arm that felt disjointed at the shoulder. "You sonofabitch," she said. "You broke my arm."

Gary climbed in behind the wheel. "You're lucky I didn't break your face. And your friends are lucky I didn't break down their fuckin' cabin door hours ago."

He started the truck's engine, switched on the headlights, and backed out of the parking space. They were approaching the paved road when he brought the truck to a sliding stop.

"Almost forgot," he said. He leaned back, reached into his pants pocket, and pulled something out. Tamara couldn't see what. She heard a tearing sound. Gary was doing something with his hands. He thrust an open palm toward her. "Take these."

She squinted down at the four lumps in his hand. Pills? "What for?"

"They'll make you feel better."

Tamara shrank away. "I don't want to feel better."

Gary stuck his hand under her nose. "Take 'em or I'll cram 'em down your throat."

Tamara felt something go soft inside her, as if she might lose control of her bowels. "How do I know you're not trying to poison me?"

Gary slapped her with his other hand. "Shut the fuck up and take the damn pills."

Tamara groaned. Her face was on fire, her mind muddled from the physical shock of the blow. Tears tumbled down her cheeks. She reached out and scooped up the tablets.

"In your mouth," Gary said.

She pinched a pill between two fingers and put it in her mouth.

"All of them."

Tamara glowered at him, her lips trembling. She opened her mouth and tossed in the remaining tablets.

"Now swallow."

She tipped her head back, waggled it as she tried to swallow. The pills clumped in her throat, gagging her. "I can't," she said, coughing up the words along with the pills. "My mouth is dry."

Gary reached around her in the seat and came up with a can that glistened in the moonlight slicing through the windshield. He pulled the tab on the can, and she caught a whiff of the alcoholic mist shooting out of it. "Here." He handed her the can.

She screwed up her face. "I hate that stuff." But she knew not to resist too forcefully, could feel the imprint of Gary's hand on her face. She took the beer and drank just enough to down the pills. "Yuck," she said, and pushed the can back at him.

"That's a good girl."

"Screw you," she muttered, bracing herself for another slap.

But Gary just laughed. "Not tonight." He chugged some beer before tossing the can out the window. "No time for fun," he said, and laughed some more.

He spun the tires pulling the truck onto Briar Creek Road.

Tamara scooted away from him as far as she could. The side of her face still flamed. Her arm was killing her. The sour taste of beer lingered in her mouth. She sagged against the passenger door and wished her stepbrother a horrible death.

37 "WHAT SHOULD I DO?" Russell said, looking lost.

Dr. Castle was positioning Margaret in the bed in preparation for the event that was about to occur. "Just what you've been doing." he said. What Russell had been doing for the last half-hour or so, since returning to Margaret's room, was sitting at his wife's side murmuring occasionally, "It's going to be all right, dear." It was all the help Dr. Castle hoped to need.

It was approaching midnight and Margaret's ongoing labor had brought her to the brink of the significant moment. It was time to put those contractions to good use. Past time, really. The doctor's last check of Margaret's vitals had startled him. Her blood pressure was elevated, her pulse erratic. The labor pains had taken an immense toll on her already debilitated body.

Margaret, responding to the doctor's instructive touch, scooted lower in the bed. She spread her legs, modesty having gone out the window, replaced by the instinct to survive.

Dr. Castle tucked one end of the birthing cloth under Margaret's buttocks. On a rolling table next to the bed were other cloths and instruments, most of which he hoped not to need during the birthing process. He lifted the sheet covering Margaret's torso and made one last check. Yes, the cervix was fully dilated. Her time indeed had come.

He nodded reassuringly at his patient. "It will all be over soon."

Margaret's face took on a panicked look that told him another contraction was coming. Limited by circumstances to using a systemic, the doctor had administered as much painkiller as he dared. He needed Margaret to be alert enough to follow his instructions. "Hang in there," he told her.

He glanced at Russell, whose face had turned the color of ash. "You too," he said, not wanting to address the fact that the hour was late and there'd been no word from Neaves about the girl.

Margaret groaned and began to shake. The doctor made a final adjustment in her positioning. "Don't forget to breathe."

Margaret gasped for air between agonized moans.

"Now, when I say *push*, you push," the doctor instructed. "And when I say *stop pushing*, you stop. That's all you have to do." He waited for the right moment. "Now push."

"Push, dear," Russell said.

Margaret's face flushed. Sweat beaded on her forehead as her upper body racked forward. The veins in her neck bulged like straws.

38

THE PICKUP'S HEADLIGHTS flitted wildly among the trees along the road, throwing and dissolving shadows in dizzying succession. Tamara stared out the windshield, her thoughts as clipped and jumbled as the scenery flashing by. What was going on here? What were those pills? Would they hurt her baby? Why was Gary doing this? And driving every question was the stomach-wrenching recognition that once again her stepbrother had gained the upper hand on her. What could he possibly want from her? She didn't know, and the fear of not knowing gripped her in a suffocating clench.

They met only a couple of other vehicles on the mountain road, and as they entered Fir Valley, the city streets at this late hour were as dark and silent as a broken promise.

When the truck jolted to a stop in Gary's driveway, Tamara didn't wait to be told what to do. She kicked open the pickup's sticky door and tramped into the house. The door to her room was missing. She found it soon enough, almost falling on her face as she stumbled over it. She shoved it aside. She was already settled in bed when Gary appeared as a silhouette in the doorway.

"You need to take a shower," he said.

"I don't feel like taking a shower." She was in no mood to do anything

Gary told her. He was the enemy. Worse—he was the devil. She would resist him.

"I don't care what you feel like doin'." His voice was flat, chillingly indifferent.

Tamara glared at him. "I suppose you're going to beat me up some more if I don't do what you say."

"If I have to."

She sat up, her hands knotted into fists, her mind swirling in the blood-redness of her rage. Why did it matter to Gary whether she went to bed clean or dirty? It had never mattered before. He just wanted to control her, bend her to his will, and she wasn't going to let him do that anymore. She was through being pushed around. "Go to—" she shouted. But the final word wouldn't come out—because she believed him. He would hurt her if she resisted. Maybe even hurt her baby.

She pounded her fists against her thighs and let out a shriek that left her throat raw. She got up, pushed past him into the bathroom.

She was crying as she undressed and climbed into the shower. She hated giving in to Gary. Hated him for forcing her to do things against her will. Hated how helpless it made her feel. But most of all, she hated being a prisoner in his house again. Why is he doing this? she repeated in her mind. But no answer came to her, and she was left clinging to the knowledge she'd brought with her the day she'd first arrived at Gary's house: he was not to be trusted.

She lifted her face, let the stinging spray sluice down her neck and over the tight skin of her bulbous belly.

She dried off, put her clothes back on—would leave them on as she went to bed. She cracked the bathroom door and listened. The house was quiet. She stuck her head out. The smell of tobacco smoke hung in the air, relentless as the scent of road-kill skunk. Faint light spilled down the hall from the direction of the living room. She crept across to her bedroom, not surprised to find that Gary had re-hung the door. She was too tired to care.

She crawled into bed, longing for sleep—for oblivion—for release from the fear and pain that seemed to plague her constantly of late, as if she was the victim of some mad voodooist bent on her destruction.

Her arm still ached, along with her back and swollen feet. And she'd begun to experience in the last half-hour or so rumblings in her belly that were different than anything she'd felt before.

She curled up on the bed and willed her body to relax. But no sooner had it begun to obey her than she felt a flare-up of the odd seismic activity down low. She sighed. Sleep would be difficult in spite of her fatigue.

39

DR. CASTLE REACHED OUT his gloved hands and received the lifeless form as it emerged from Margaret's womb, slick with blood and amnii. With the final effort at expulsion, his patient had passed out. Just as well. It was a wonder Russell hadn't done the same. To his credit, he'd hung in there to the end, giving his wife what encouragement he could muster.

Dr. Castle laid the shriven fetus on the birthing cloth, allowing the umbilical to trail loosely from Margaret's vagina. He shed his sullied gloves, tucked them into a plastic trash bag, and pulled on a fresh pair. He moved around to the side of the bed, placed an open hand on Margaret's abdomen, and began applying firm, consistent pressure on the fundus.

He glanced over at Russell, sitting there now as if in a trance. "When she rouses, talk to her," he told his friend. "Keep reassuring her that everything is all right. We need to keep her spirits up. As soon as I can, I'll give her something that will allow her to have a nice, long, well-deserved nap. After that, we'll face"—he hunched his shoulders—"whatever it is we have to face."

Twenty minutes later, with Margaret still only semi-conscious, the placenta was expelled from her body in one final contraction, not nearly as devastating as the ones that had come before. She sank back onto the bed, eyelids fluttering. Russell wiped her forehead with a damp cloth.

The doctor checked to see that all the connective tissue had emerged intact. When he was satisfied it had, he laid the placenta beside the silent fetus, with the umbilical still attached. He folded the birthing cloth around the mass of inert tissue and then slid the bundle into a second trash bag. He tied the end of the bag and set it on the floor near the door. Without pausing, he went about the task of cleaning up his patient, attending first to the blood trickling from her vagina. He was pleased to see that it was a modest flow.

When the cleanup work was done and the soiled clothes and linens bagged, he checked Margaret's vitals again. Her heart rate was still high, but it was stable, and that was a miracle in itself. Her blood pressure had dropped to an acceptable level. She was resting for the moment, but he needed her to rest more soundly and for an extended period of time. He took a syringe from his medical case and gave her an injection he was sure would do the trick.

Russell remained at his wife's bedside, gazing at her with an expression of grave concern.

"She'll be all right," Dr. Castle assured him. He disposed of the used syringe. "She'll be out for quite a while though, so don't get anxious."

Russell shook his head. "I'm just wondering what will happen when she wakes up." His shoulders slumped as if his body was a collapsing tent. "How can she possibly survive another loss like this?"

The doctor was doing his best to stay positive. "She'll get through this," he said, hoping he spoke the truth.

The telephone rang.

40

TAMARA HAD FALLEN ASLEEP, but it seemed as if no time at all had passed before she was awakened by another twinge, this time in her lower back. She grumbled, changed positions in the bed, and tried to go back to sleep. But whenever she drifted off, the annoying backache would return, prod her awake, then seconds later, mysteriously disappear.

She thrashed about in bed, groggily muttering her displeasure at the recurring interruptions. "Just let me sleep!" she pleaded, imagining herself being harassed by some mischievous sleep fairy. But this pattern of forced wakefulness continued, denying her the rest she craved.

Then things changed. The next wake-up call was more jolting than the previous ones. It was a cramp-like sensation that radiated from her back around to her belly. Her abdominal muscles seized up as if she had a charley horse in the pit of her stomach. The feeling came from deep within, like menstrual pain, lasted longer than the backaches had, and packed more punch.

On edge now, she stayed alert, waiting for the next cramp to come, any hope of sleep swept away by a rising tide of anxiety. When another pain occurred, more jarring than the last, she clasped her middle and rode it out, moaning—not so much from the hurt as the knowledge that something was wrong with her body. Very wrong.

41

RUSSELL TROUSTE WAS on his feet exulting in the good news of the girl's return. The telephone message from Gary Neaves, delivered to them through Dr. Castle's answering service, had been short and sweet: "We're back." It might as well have said, "Your wife has just been given a new lease on life."

Russell tripped about the room feeling like a sports fan at halftime eager for the game to resume, sure he was about to witness a bold second-half comeback. He glanced at his wife in her bed, sleeping heavily now because of the medication, and a dark thought undercut his joy. He turned to the doctor, who was at the dresser hunched over his medical bag. "It's not too late for her, is it Brandon? It's not too late for Margaret?"

Brandon smiled wearily. "No, Russell, it's not too late. As I said, she'll be out for a good long while. That will give me time to take care of things on the other end. But we must be patient. The exact timing of these events is not something one can control."

Russell felt like being anything but patient now that things were back on track with Margaret and the girl. But, once again, there was little for him to do except watch and wait. At least now there was an end in sight to Margaret's misery.

Buoyed by an ascendant sense of hope, he returned to his station at Margaret's bedside and resumed his vigil. His wife was going to have her baby after all, and he was going to have his wife around for years to come. What their life would be like from here on he couldn't know, although he sensed that things at Trouste House would never be the same.

As the night slowly drained away, Russell remained reflective, hopeful. At some point, Brandon—taking up a position on the opposite side of Margaret's bed—joined the watch. Both men had long since gone mute, the sound of Margaret's breathing providing background music for their silent symphony of thought.

Russell stayed alert for as long as he could. But with the passing minutes becoming passing hours, his rekindled optimism faded and was replaced by a dull lethargy. His eyelids grew heavy, drooped closed. A fatigue-induced fog descended on his brain.

Occasionally the fog would lift and he would open his eyes to witness Brandon standing over Margaret, taking her pulse or touching the end of his stethoscope to her chest before dropping back into his chair. Twice the doctor used the phone on the dresser to call Neaves.

"How's she doing, Brandon?" Russell had inquired after each call.

"Fine," the doctor had assured him.

"It's really going to happen then? Margaret's prayers are going to be answered?"

"God willing," Brandon said. And both men felt the irony of his remark.

42　　TAMARA STIFFENED AT the onset of another cramp. An unseen hand had grabbed hold of her insides and was squeezing them as if wringing out a sponge. A wave of nausea washed over her. She opened her mouth and sucked in air in desperate gasps.

Sweat oozed from her pores. She curled up around her belly in the bed, gritted her teeth, and groaned.

What the hell was going on down there? Was it the pills Gary had made her swallow? Had he poisoned her after all? But why? Why would he go to the trouble of dragging her back to town if all he wanted to do was make her sick enough to die—or, at least, wish she was dead? Was this his way of punishing her for running away?

Just when she thought she couldn't stand it any longer, the awful hurt in her belly went away as abruptly as water stops flowing from a closed tap. She was at once confused, relieved, and fearful of what would happen next.

She struggled out of bed and staggered down the hall into the living room. The only light in the room came from the television screen—a silvery, chaotic radiance that cast all objects within reach in varying shades of black and white, including Gary, who was sitting in his chair, a beer can in one hand, a lighted cigarette in the other.

"I think you'd better call the doctor," she told him.

Gary looked up at her, his face ghoulish in the aberrant light. "Having a little pain, are we?"

"It's bad, Gary," she said. "Please—call the doctor. I think something terrible is happening. I think—" She didn't really know what she thought. So she blurted out the first thing that entered her mind. "I think I'm dying."

Gary guffawed. "How far apart are the pains?"

"About ten minutes, I think." She peered into the dark hollows of his eye sockets. "Why, what's happening? What were those pills you gave me?"

"Relax," Gary said. "Nothing bad is happening." He belched. "You're just havin' a baby. Happens all the time. Now run on back to bed."

Tamara shook her head, confused. "But I can't be having a baby. It isn't time."

Gary licked his lower lip. "Oh, it's time all right, little sister. It's high time."

Tamara started to say something else but was distracted by a strange sensation between her legs. She looked down. Her pants were wet at the crotch. She felt fluid trickling down her legs. In her anxiety she must have wet her pants. She turned away and blundered back down the hall, arriving at her bed just as another pain stabbed her like a knife plunged into her belly.

43   GARY STUBBED HIS CIGARETTE in the ashtray perched on the arm of his chair, got up, and went into the kitchen to get another beer. He needed it to steel himself against the infernal wailing coming from Tamara's room.

Back in the living room, he tried to watch a movie on TV, a Western starring Henry Fonda. But he couldn't shut out the girl's complaints any more than he could ignore the plaintive yelping of an injured birddog. He turned up the volume on the TV. It didn't help. "Shit!" He clunked his beer can down on the side table.

He strode down the hall and stood in the doorway to Tamara's room, pushing against the darkness with his eyes. "Shut the fuck up!"

Tamara continued to bawl.

He switched on the overhead light. The girl lay on the bed, her body clenched like a fist. Her legs were bare. Her pants lay rumpled on the floor, dark streaks at the crotch and down the legs. She shifted in the bed to look at him. Her face was a misshapen mask lathered in sweat, her eyes those of a cornered feral cat.

"Call the doctor, you sonofabitch!" she hissed.

"Just keep it down," he said, shaking his head in frustration. "We don't need some neighbor hearin' you and callin' the police. And for your information, I've already called the doctor."

As instructed, Gary had called the doctor's answering service immediately after arriving home with Tamara. A little while later, the doctor had called back, wanting to know how she was doing.

"She's gone to bed," Gary told him, "but I don't think she's gettin' her forty winks. I've heard a lot of moanin' and groanin' coming from in there. What kinda pills did you say those were?"

"She's apparently gone into labor," was all the doctor had said. "Just monitor her pains. I'll call back later."

"You mean, she's havin' her baby tonight?" Gary wasn't sure he'd understood the doctor correctly.

"That's right."

Gary smiled. "Damn."

He was still smiling when he hung up the phone. Tamara was going to pop her kid that night and he was going to score some cool cash for his troubles. He went into the kitchen, got himself a beer from the fridge, and popped it open to celebrate.

But since then he'd had little reason to cheer, what with all the yowling coming from the girl's room.

"How far apart are the pains?" the doctor had wanted to know when he'd called the house a second time.

"About ten minutes," Gary said.

"Okay, I'll check back."

But that was over an hour ago and the doctor hadn't checked back. And in that time the muscles in Gary's shoulders and neck had tightened to the snapping point and there was throbbing at the base of his skull.

When Tamara finally quieted down, he flicked off her light and went back to the living room. But no sooner had he gotten comfortably reseated than she started up again, crying out as if old man death was dragging her off by the toes.

He charged back down the hall and into her room. He hammered the wall with his fist. "Didn't you hear me, bitch? I said, shut up!"

But Tamara continued keening, louder than ever. He stalked over to the bed, reached down, and clamped a hand over her mouth. She immediately bit his middle finger hard enough to make him yelp. He jerked his hand away and, barely checking the impulse to smash her face, stomped out of the room.

He blustered about the living room, shaking his finger and cursing. A drumbeat of fury resounded in his head. He went over to the side table, snatched up the receiver to the telephone, and dialed the number scribbled on the torn-off piece of paper bag lying there.

"Dr. Castle's answering service," a cheery voice said in his ear.

"This is Gary Neaves," he growled into the phone. "You tell Dr. Castle to get his sorry ass over here—and I mean *now*."

44   WHEN THE TELEPHONE RANG, Russell Trouste came awake with a jerk, realizing only then that he'd nodded off in his chair beside Margaret's bed.

Brandon was already up and reaching for the phone. "It's probably my service." He spoke a greeting into the receiver, then listened briefly. "Thank you," he said, and hung up.

Russell stretched his back and massaged the kinks in his neck.

Brandon remained standing at the dresser, taking drawn out breaths, as if trying to fortify himself for a challenging task. He removed the stethoscope from around his neck and tucked it inside his medical bag. "I need to be off," he said, painting a picture of fatigue with the indolence of his movement and the faintness of his speech. "Looks like I'm needed on the other end."

Russell was suddenly wide awake and on his feet, jolted alert by the realization that he was about to be left in charge of Margaret's care. He came around the bed. "What if she wakes up while you're gone?"

Brandon shook his head. "I don't think she will." He moved to the door with his medical case in hand, leaned down, and picked up the trash bag he'd placed there. "But if she does, just assure her everything is fine. Tell her the baby is in the next room with the nurse. If she frets or is skeptical, go next door and play the crying tape for a while before coming back into the room."

Russell was still apprehensive. He'd faced the hot coals of Margaret's willfulness before. He was afraid that alone with her, without Brandon's support, he'd lose his nerve and mess everything up. "What if that doesn't satisfy her? What if she insists on seeing the baby?"

"I really don't think she'll come to before I return," Brandon said. "But if that happens, and she questions you about the baby, tell her that the nurse will bring the baby in to her as soon as the doctor says it's okay to do so."

Russell gazed down at his wife in her bed, immersed for the moment in deep slumber, and considered the efficacy of such a strategy. Yes, that should work. If all else failed to mollify Margaret, he could always put the onus on her doctor.

He looked over to thank his friend, but Brandon was already out the door.

45

DR. CASTLE PARKED in front of a vacant lot in the 700 block of Cedar Street. The old home that had stood there had fallen down of its own accord and its debris had been removed. The owners were apparently not inclined to rebuild in that part of town. The doctor waited until he was sure no one was around before getting out of his car. It was a little after 3 AM when he approached Neaves' house on foot, silently applauding the dearth of streetlamps in the area.

"About fuckin' time," he heard Neaves say the moment he opened the front door. He stepped into a room lighted only by the fickle glow from a television set whose sound was turned up loud enough to shake the walls. Neaves was sprawled in an overstuffed chair angled toward the TV, his long legs jutting out in front of him like booted stilts.

The fellow was obviously drunk. The odor of beer permeated the room like the scent of cheap cologne, and the first, misshapen words out of Neaves' mouth had been as telling as a Breathalyzer. That could complicate things.

The doctor felt his grip on his bags tighten. This was the part of his plan that troubled him most. He hated having to rely on Gary Neaves, drunk or sober. He was an ill-mannered lout with a caveman mentality. But Dr. Castle knew he had no choice in the matter. To succeed in this endeavor, he had to insulate himself from what was about to happen here. That meant Neaves had to be a player in the game. At least the fellow had remembered to keep the porch light off, the door unlocked, and the shades drawn.

"What's that?" Neaves said, gesturing toward the trash bag dangling from the doctor's hand.

"My medical case."

"In the other hand."

The doctor scanned the room. A hallway led to the back of the house. A doorway to his right opened to a kitchen. He stepped into the kitchen, switched on the light, and set his medical case down on a scuffed Formica dining table. He lowered the trash bag to the floor and scooted it under the table with his foot. No sooner had he done so than he heard loud moaning coming from the back of the house.

Neaves appeared in the kitchen doorway clinging to a can of beer. "She's been goin' on like that for hours."

The doctor took off his suit jacket and hung it over the back of a chair. "Labor pains are no fun, Mr. Neaves." The labor-inducing drug had obviously done its job. He hoped the cervix ripener had worked as well—without any of its potentially devastating side effects. This had to be a vaginal delivery for his plan to work. He opened his medical case, reached in, and extracted a bottle of pills.

He turned to face Neaves, dreading the confrontation he knew was about to ensue. "Now," he said, feeling his gut tighten, "are you ready to deliver a baby?"

Neaves' head snapped back as if he'd been hit by a hard punch. "Me? What the hell you talkin' about?"

"It's time, Mr. Neaves, for you to earn your referral fee."

Neaves came at him from the doorway. "Wait a minute," he said, getting in the doctor's face, his breath like the stench from a broken sewer line. "This wasn't part of the deal. I don't know anything about deliverin' babies. That's your department."

The doctor's heartbeat was a runaway train, but he held his ground. "I told you earlier, Tamara must not know I was in the house."

"But you didn't say why."

"That will become evident soon enough."

Neaves stabbed him with his eyes. "Well, I don't like it."

The doctor's hand around the pill bottle was damp with sweat. He feigned indifference and pressed on. "You have nothing to be concerned about. I will be guiding you every step of the way. The birth process takes place by itself in nature every day without our assistance. You need only stand by and let it happen."

Neaves scowled. "Then why the hell do we need doctors in the delivery room?"

"In most cases, we don't," the doctor stated truthfully. "Only in those rare instances where something goes wrong do they serve a useful function. Ninety-nine per cent of all human births could be facilitated by a layman with a few basic instructions. And that's what's going to happen here tonight."

"Like hell it is," Neaves said. "I ain't deliverin' no baby." He sneered. "Especially not this one."

The doctor shrugged, deadpanning it in spite of his zooming heart rate. "Then we don't have a deal." He put his coat back on, picked up his medical case, and started to leave, hoping Neaves hadn't noticed he'd left the trash bag behind.

Neaves slung his beer can toward the kitchen sink. It missed the sink, skipped across the countertop, bounced off the wall and onto the floor, dispersing its remaining contents in a wide, foamy pattern. "All right, goddammit. But this fuckin' deal keeps changing every minute."

The doctor set his case back down, shed his coat. He swiped a sweaty palm on his pant leg. "It will all be over very soon," he said. "Then you'll have the rest of your money."

Neaves jutted his chin. "I want another five thousand."

The doctor regarded the fellow with disdain. He was in no position to argue with Neaves on this score though, and had in fact anticipated such a move. He puckered his brow, pretending to struggle with the issue in his mind. "Agreed," he finally said. "But no more."

"All in cash, within the next forty-eight hours."

"Done. Now, are you ready to proceed?"

Neaves blinked in apparent surprise at the quick acquiescence to his demands. "Yeah, sure," he said, the antagonism gone from his voice. "What do I have to do?"

The doctor uncapped the pill bottle. "First, I want you to give Tamara something for the pain." He shook out two capsules into his palm. "Then you need to round up some towels—preferably clean ones."

46 TAMARA COULDN'T UNDERSTAND why somebody wasn't helping her. Her body had turned on her the way a mad dog turns on its master. It was mauling her to death and no one seemed to care. Had the world around her gone deaf and dumb? She was having a baby, Gary had said. Liar! He'd poisoned her and was waiting for her guts to explode and splatter on the walls—modern art for him and his sicko friends.

Then, once again, there was only the pain.

Why isn't somebody helping me?

∼

GARY ENTERED TAMARA'S room carrying a glass of water and the pills from the doctor. He turned on the light. Tamara lay balled up on the bed, moaning. The bedding, having become dislodged from the mattress, trailed to the floor.

He moved to the head of the bed. "Listen up, girl. We got business to attend to."

Tamara started at the sound of his voice. She looked up, squinting at the light, and mumbled something unintelligible.

"Speak up if you got something to say."

"Get . . . doctor," she repeated in a feeble voice.

Gary chuckled nervously. "I am your doctor, little sister. Ain't that a kick in the balls." He bent over her. "You understand what I'm tellin' you? You're about to have a baby, and there's no one else here to help you. All you got is me. Understand?"

Tamara's eyes bulged. A tremor rippled down her body as if following a fault line.

He put his face closer to hers. "Do you understand?"

The girl nodded, but her eyes held the disbelieving look of an accident victim.

"Okay, then," Gary said, feeling out of joint himself. He took a heavy drag of air, trying to get more oxygen to his brain. "You're gonna have to do exactly what I say. First, I need you to take these pills. They'll help with the pain."

Tamara didn't hesitate this time. She snatched the pills from his hand, popped them in her mouth as if they were peanuts, and washed them down with a few quick sips of water from the glass. Then she curled up on the bed again.

Gary set the glass down on the dresser. He scrubbed his hands together as he worked to keep in mind the doctor's instructions. "Okay," he said, moving back to the bed. He cupped Tamara's bent legs with his hands. "I gotta take your panties off." He brought her knees upright, forcing her onto her back.

Tamara cried out and wrenched back over onto her side. He wasn't sure if she was reacting to his intent or to a recurrence of the pain. Then she clutched her gut and complained like a dying swan, so he let her be.

When her anguish passed, he rolled her onto her back and slid her panties off. She didn't resist. The last contraction had taken the starch out of her. "Now put your legs apart like you do for the doctor when he examines you."

A light seemed to go out in Tamara's eyes, which took on a flat, empty look. Fish eyes. Her head rotated slowly toward the wall. Her knees drifted apart.

Gary bent down and put his head between her legs. He couldn't believe what he saw. The girl's hole was nearly the size of the mouth of a canning jar. It was a disgusting sight. Nothing erotic about it. He jerked his head away. "Jesus," he said, and headed back to the kitchen to report to the doctor.

47 NOT LONG AFTER swallowing the pills, Tamara began
to feel a dulling of the senses that made the pain more
bearable but also caused her mind to drift off into a fog bank of vague
perception. Before long she was floating through a murky, slow-moving
world of fluid shapes, muffled voices, and blunted sensations. The
cramps continued to come and go, but now they were grenades explod-
ing in her belly instead of atom bombs.

When Gary came back into the room, he was carrying a bundle
of towels and dragging a chair from the kitchen. She watched him
from the edges of her eyes with the limited understanding of one who
enters a movie just as it is hurtling toward its climax. He dumped the
towels onto the foot of the bed, came up and stood beside her with
his hands on his hips.

～

GARY LOOKED DOWN at the girl and wagged his head. He couldn't
believe he was actually going to do this. What the hell was the doctor
thinking?

He bent down, rolled Tamara over, and repositioned her like before,
on her back, legs apart. She moaned softly in a singsong manner, the
way a crazy person would.

He spread out some towels between her legs. He pulled the chair up
next to the bed and sat down. "Breathe," he said. "In and out. Big breaths.
But don't do any pushing until I tell you." He glanced back at the open
doorway. He couldn't see the doctor. Was he there? He better be.

It wasn't long before another contraction gripped the girl. She cried
out, but not as loud as before—thank God. Gary clamped down on
her ankles to keep her from rolling over onto her side.

"Push," came a whisper from behind Gary.

"Okay, you can push now," Gary said.

Tamara looked bewildered.

Gary put a hand on her abdomen and pressed down, but not too
hard. "Push," he repeated.

The girl got the message. Her head racked forward and her face contorted with effort.

Torturous minutes passed, with more contractions and more grunting and groaning on Tamara's part. Gary was beginning to sweat almost as much as she was. Then, during one prolonged contraction, the baby started coming out. Gary's gut twitched. He reached down between Tamara's legs with a towel over his hand and supported the baby's head as it emerged.

"Push harder," murmured the disembodied voice.

"Push harder," Gary echoed.

Tamara arched her back and squealed.

This wet, slimy thing suddenly slid out from between her legs onto the towel in Gary's hands. He gaped at it, stunned by its abrupt appearance, as if he'd just witnessed a magician make a unicorn appear.

Then again came the voice from behind him, this time with piston-like insistence. "The umbilical—clamp it and cut it."

Gary laid the baby down on some towels. Beating back an urge to say "to hell with it" and walk away, he took hold of the fleshy cord that protruded from the baby's middle and trailed back into Tamara's womb. About six inches out from the baby's belly, he attached one of the clamps the doctor had given him, and a little below that, the second one. Using scissors, he snipped the cord in two at a point between the clamps as the doctor had instructed.

"Quickly," the voice outside said.

Gary scooped up the baby amid a tangle of towels and rushed out of the room.

48   IN THE HALLWAY outside Tamara's room, Dr. Castle eagerly received the bundle from Neaves. The doctor had attended to a thousand or more births in his time, but never had the silence between delivery and animation seemed like such a chasm to be crossed. Hurriedly he cleared the newborn's mouth with his finger,

turned it over, and patted its back. To his immense relief, the baby began to cry. The wheels of another life had begun to turn.

He took the bundle into the kitchen, eased it down onto the dining table, and peeled back the towels. It was a girl, as the sonogram had indicated. Margaret would be thrilled.

He did a quick head-to-toe inspection. By all visual signs, the baby looked healthy. Undersized, as would be expected with a pre-term birth, but fully formed, with consistent coloring. He checked the heartbeat, which was regular and strong. The respiration was a bit ragged, but not alarmingly so. He straightened up and took his first relaxed breaths in months.

Neaves appeared alongside him with a sloppy grin on his face and another beer in hand. "Looks like we hit pay dirt," he said, hoisting his can as if to make a toast.

The doctor ignored him. "Remember what comes next?"

Neaves looked around for an answer.

"The afterbirth," the doctor said. "Tamara will continue having contractions, although less acute ones, until the afterbirth comes out just like the baby did. Go back in, put more towels down, and wait for it."

"Christ!" Neaves said, and blustered off.

The doctor went back to work. He spread out a receiving blanket and transferred the baby to it. She fussed briefly, then quieted, as if understanding the value of being at peace with the world. He tied off the umbilical below the clamp—which he then removed—and applied antiseptic to the severed end of the cord. One more check of heartbeat and respiration. Still okay. That accomplished, he snugged the blanket around the infant and slid the bundle to the center of the table.

He was dabbing his brow with a handkerchief when Neaves, scowling, returned from Tamara's room with another towel-wrapped bundle. He thrust it into the doctor's arms.

Dr. Castle inhaled deeply, fended off for the moment the exhaustion he felt closing in on him. He took the new bundle to the kitchen counter, parted the towels, and examined the shiny-wet mass of tissue. Convinced that everything had been expelled from the girl that should have been expelled, he rewrapped the afterbirth in a towel and pushed it aside. The remaining towels he spread out on the counter.

Feeling a sudden heaviness of heart, he collected from under the table the trash bag he'd brought with him. He set the bag on the counter, opened it, withdrew the wrapped birthing cloth and its contents.

Neaves peered over his shoulder as he unwrapped the bundle. "What the fuck?"

The doctor regarded the pathetic product of Margaret's womb. "Like I said, Mr. Neaves, ninety-nine times out of a hundred nothing goes wrong. This is your one percent." He lifted one end of the birthing cloth and dumped the shriven fetus, still attached to its afterbirth, onto the waiting towels. He folded the towels loosely over the lifeless mass, picked up the bundle, and held it out to Neaves. "Now take this poor thing back to its mother."

"This is sick," Neaves said.

"This is business."

Neaves stood there, eyes smoldering. He jerked the bundle from the doctor's hands and clomped out of the room.

A few minutes later, having packed up his medical case and sanitized the kitchen, Dr. Castle walked to the front door, cradling the newborn in one arm. In his other hand he gripped his case and the trash bag containing the more recent afterbirth. A sullen Neaves sat in his chair attending to another beer.

"Remember," the doctor said, "the first call goes to my service. Make a stink about me not showing up. Then make the 9-1-1 call. When the paramedics get here, they'll take Tamara and the fetus to the hospital. You go too. I'll be there as soon as I can."

"What if the paramedics ask questions?"

"Answer them. Everything happened as it happened, except that the baby you delivered was dead. The 9-1-1 tape will support your version of things."

Neaves glowered at him, grumbling.

The doctor looked past him to the far corner of the room. "One other thing. You may want to pick up that broken lamp."

Neaves' shoulders twitched. "Don't you worry about my house-keeping, Doc. You just make sure I get my money, or you'll end up worse off than that fuckin' lamp."

"You'll get your money," the doctor said, and went out the door.

49

"THE BABY IS COMING!"

Gary felt foolish, yelling into the phone like a hysterical woman.

"Sir, you must remain calm," the 9-1-1 operator said. "Your sister needs your help."

Gary hoisted his beer can and took a pull. "Okay. What do you want me to do?"

"Is the baby coming out head first?"

"Uh—let me go see." He laid the receiver down, counted the throbs in his head until he was tired of counting, then picked it up again. "Yeah—head first."

"Good," the operator said. "The paramedics are on their way. In the meantime, go back in and put your hand underneath the baby's head. Don't pull, just let the baby come to you."

Gary clunked the phone onto the table. He flopped down in his chair and took another swig of beer. And another. Then, fed up with this silly game, he reached for the phone. "Lady," he said, "this baby has already popped. And it don't look good. It's all shriveled and messed up."

The 9-1-1 operator's voice came back an octave higher. "Sir, you need to clear the baby's airway. Open the baby's mouth. With your finger—"

"I already done that. Ain't nothing gonna help this kid."

"Do you know CPR?"

Gary cringed. "You say the paramedics are on their way?"

"That's right, sir. It should only be a matter of minutes. But in the meantime, you—"

Gary hung up the phone. Within seconds, it was ringing. He let it ring.

He stomped around the living room, cursing. A siren was screaming in the background now. As the wailing of the siren grew louder, Gary stomped harder. When the siren went silent, Gary stopped stomping.

He went over and raised the shade on the picture window. An ambulance had pulled to the curb in front of the house, setting the neighborhood ablaze with its red flashing lights. Two men jumped out of the cab of the ambulance and hurried around to the back.

Gary switched on the porch light, opened the front door. Moments later, the paramedics rushed up the sidewalk, carrying their life-saving props. They entered the house with an air of professionalism that announced their intent to take charge of the situation.

"In there," Gary said, pointing down the hallway.

The paramedics disappeared down the hall, and Gary went into the kitchen to get himself another beer. He was sitting in his chair having a pull when a sheriff's deputy sauntered in through the front door unannounced, followed by another one.

One of the paramedics came back into the living room.

"What do we got?" asked the first deputy, who was a head taller and fifty pounds heavier than anybody else in the room.

"Stillborn," the paramedic said.

"How's the mother?"

"In shock. We'll get her stabilized, then transport to Community Hospital."

"What about the baby?" Gary said.

The paramedic gave him a sideways glance. "We'll take it too."

"Okay," the tall deputy said. "We'll get a report here and touch bases with you later." The paramedic nodded and went out the front door. The shorter deputy, who had yet to say anything, headed down the hallway, his leather shoes squeaking with each step.

The tall deputy turned to Gary. "Tell me what happened."

Gary lit a cigarette. He didn't want to say too much, especially to the cops. Cops can blow up your words and twist them to their own purpose, like those clowns who make animal shapes out of balloons. He shrugged. "One minute she was screamin' for me to call the doctor. The next minute the baby was coming out."

"You called 9-1-1?"

"Yeah, right after I called the doctor's service."

"Wha'd you do then?"

"I did what the 9-1-1 lady told me to do."

"Which was?"

"You know, catch the baby when it came out and shit."

"But the baby never started breathing?"

Gary shook his head.

"You give it CPR?"

There they go again with that CPR crap. Gary knew CPR. When he'd worked at the mill before hurting his back—or pretending to, anyway—he'd been required to take first-aid training, including lessons in CPR. Chest compressions. Mouth-to-mouth. All that bullshit. But CPR wouldn't have helped that clump of flesh in there, not in a million years. "Go in there and look at that thing," he told the deputy, "then come back and ask me about CPR."

The paramedic who'd gone outside reappeared maneuvering a gurney in through the doorway. Its wheels clattered over the threshold. He aimed it toward the back of the house.

"Fair enough," the deputy said. He followed the paramedic down the hallway.

Almost immediately, the deputy returned. "I see what you mean," he said. He sat down on the sofa and began scribbling on a pad.

From then on it was smooth sailing, routine questions that Gary had no trouble answering, although he still didn't like it.

"You say she's your stepsister and she came to live with you—about six weeks ago?" the tall deputy said.

"That's right."

"Where are her parents?"

Gary blew a chain of smoke rings into the air. "Her mother lives in Eugene. I don't know nothing about her old man."

A paramedic backed out of the hallway, guiding one end of the gurney on which Tamara had been placed. She was covered to the shoulders with a sheet and strapped down in two places. Her eyes were closed. Her face was nearly as pale as the sheet. There was an oxygen mask over her nose and mouth. A tube ran from one of her arms to a fluid-filled bag hanging from a rod that projected up from the side of the gurney. The shorter deputy appeared on the other end of the rolling bed. Following him was the second paramedic, carrying a small bundle wrapped in Gary's towels.

The tall deputy stood. "I'll need the mother's address and phone number."

"I got it somewhere," Gary told him.

They watched the gurney being wheeled out the door.

"You going to the hospital?" the tall deputy asked.

Gary flicked ash off his cigarette into the ashtray. "Yeah. Sure."

The deputy fixed him with a stare. "You better come with us then."

"I'll manage on my own," Gary said.

Heat radiated from the deputy's gaze. Reluctantly, Gary dropped his can of beer into the paper bag of empties sitting by his chair. The can tipped sideways and began foaming out its remaining contents onto the other cans.

The deputy stared at him some more. They must teach that at the police academy. Fuck him. Let him stare all he wants. I ain't gettin' in no police car.

"All right," the deputy said, "but have some coffee first. We don't need another ambulance call tonight."

"Whatever you say."

The deputy nodded toward the far corner of the room. "By the way, what happened there?"

Gary glanced over at the debris from the shattered lamp. "Must have knocked it over rushing for the phone."

The deputy practiced his staring technique some more. "How 'bout you get me that address and phone number now," he said.

50   TAMARA DIDN'T UNDERSTAND what was happening. She'd fallen off the edge of the world into a dark pit of oblivion that wasn't sleep and wasn't death, only to rouse and find men in uniform loading her into the back of a red and white van that seemed vaguely familiar. *Why are they doing this again?*

She searched her mind for clues as to what was taking place, for what had taken place prior to this moment. She recalled Gary's face floating in the air above her, and in the background a murmurous voice, as if the room itself was speaking to her. And she remembered something else: She remembered the pain.

The pain had fallen upon her like a mugger, brutalizing her with repeated and increasingly vicious blows to her body. She could do nothing in response but cry out and hope to die before the next round of torture. But she didn't die, even when the final assault had occurred, bringing the ultimate agony that had caused her to sink into the dark pit. She had survived. But just barely, it seemed.

She had blacked out. She knew that now, the sensation of darkness lingering like a ringing in her ears. She also knew that, before the darkness had engulfed her, she had experienced a period of twilight—of hazy consciousness. It was during this time that she'd witnessed Gary hovering over her, had heard the whispering like wind in the trees, had perceived her own cries sounding as if they came from afar.

The van carrying her started to roll. Its rocking movement caused her to begin drifting off again. She fought against the blackness that wanted to engulf her. There was more she needed to remember. There had to be more.

She started over, from the beginning: First there was the pain. Then more and greater pain. Then there was the final agony as—as—as something came out of her.

"My baby," she heard herself say. "Where's my baby?"

"Lay quietly, young lady," a male voice answered.

And so Tamara lay quietly—gently rocking in the cradle of a new tomorrow.

51 DR. CASTLE HAD ALWAYS been generous with his time when it came to assisting the ER staff with cases in which his special expertise could benefit the patient. And although it wasn't his habit to show up in the emergency room in the middle of the night, the ER doctor seemed not in the least surprised to see him.

"Good of you to come in at this hour, Brandon," Dr. Graham said. "I'm told she may have been under your care."

Dr. Castle glanced through an opening in the ring of curtains surrounding the treatment station in which Tamara had been placed. "Yes, I've seen her a time or two. What's her condition?"

Graham motioned him aside. "She's stable at the moment thanks to the paramedics who brought her in. But she arrived only moments ago, so I've yet to examine her thoroughly." He pulled back a nearby curtain. "Looks like she delivered prematurely at home. A stillborn. I had them put the fetus in here."

Dr. Castle eyed the towel-wrapped bundle lying on a metal transfer cart. "May I assist?"

"Unless you need me," Graham said, "she's all yours. There was an injury accident on the freeway a short while ago. I've been told to expect several trauma patients. If you can take over here, that would be a great help."

"Of course."

"Much appreciated," Graham said, and hurried off.

Dr. Castle slipped inside the curtained station where Tamara Ames lay inert on a Stryker bed, eyes shuttered, face devoid of color. He took a deep breath and blew it out, trying to expel some of the anxiety that, like stomach gas, had accumulated inside him. Upon leaving Neaves' place, he'd hustled back to the Trouste estate, dropped off the baby with a fretting Russell, then sped across town to the hospital. He'd wanted, if at all possible, to attend to Tamara himself. And he certainly didn't want anyone taking too close a look at the dead fetus. As instructed, Neaves had put in another call to the doctor's answering service, which had in turn paged him. Dr. Castle's presence at the ER, or so he'd told the admitting clerk upon his arrival, was a direct result of that page.

His timing couldn't have been better, and Dr. Graham's eagerness to turn over Tamara's care to him was as predictable as spring rain.

He came alongside Tamara in the bed. The paramedics had started an IV drip for the infusion of fluids and medication, which was being continued. That was good, but there was much more to be done. He withdrew a pair of surgical gloves from a box on a nearby cart and slipped them on. He dared not delay treatment even for a moment. He was running on pure adrenaline now, and there was no telling how long that would last.

Within thirty minutes, the doctor had completed the examination and treatment of his patient, checked and bagged the fetus—attesting to its status as a stillbirth—and had seen to it that the girl was cleaned up by a nurse, dressed in a hospital gown, and provided with a fresh IV drip that included medication to allow her to continue resting comfortably.

Tamara had remained passive throughout his ministrations, stirring only briefly when he'd given her an injection of a local anesthesia. The tearing in the vaginal opening was not excessive but had required a couple of stitches to repair.

Already weary to the bone, Dr. Castle nevertheless took the time to write up a report on his treatment of Ms. Ames, along with orders for her follow-up care.

"Have her transferred to a general ward room," he told the ER nurse who'd been assisting him. "Not to maternity," he stressed. "I'll be back to check on her later in the day."

THE SUN WAS BEGINNING to backlight the hills defining the eastern horizon as Dr. Castle drove back to the Trouste estate. Almost there, he told himself, channeling the last remnants of his energy into the final phase of his plan.

He let himself in the front door of Trouste House and went directly up to Margaret's room. As he'd expected, she was still asleep, having yielded herself wholly to the sedative he'd administered following the trauma of the previous evening. He stepped into the adjoining room, which had been set up as a nursery using all the furnishings Margaret had acquired over the course of her previous pregnancies and then stored away.

"Oh, Brandon," Russell said, rising from a bentwood rocker, "I'm so glad you're back. The baby was crying and I didn't know what to do. She kept spitting out her bottle."

"Let's have a look," the doctor said. He bent over the baby's bassinette. She was fast asleep. The bottle of formula lay beside her, partially depleted. He took out his stethoscope, listened to her heart, checked her breathing. The baby was doing well. He told his friend so.

"That's great," Russell said. "But what am I going to do with her?" He tossed up his hands. "I can't take care of her. Margaret is in no condition to. And I can't ask Elena at her age to look after—"

The doctor clamped a hand on Russell's shoulder. "Everything is being taken care of," he said. "Help is on the way. I put in a call before I left the hospital."

Russell sank back into the rocking chair. "Thank goodness. I feel helpless here by myself."

"You're doing fine. Now just sit and relax while I attend to your wife."

Back in Margaret's room, the doctor checked her vitals as she slumbered. The numbers were as good as he had a right to expect. He sat down beside her bed to wait for their help to arrive.

Half an hour later, it did.

"Come in," Dr. Castle said, standing as Elena ushered the new girl into the room. "You must be Vera."

"Yes," the young woman said, wide-eyed and breathless. She gave him a fragile smile while stealing a glance at Mrs. Trouste in her bed.

"I'm Dr. Castle." He gestured toward the nursery. "The nervous father is in the other room with the baby." As the two of them headed that way, the doctor began to wonder if he'd made the right decision in bringing in someone so young and short on medical training to help Russell with Margaret and the baby. This girl, with her bobbed hair and angular body, looked hardly out of her teens, and she wasn't a nurse. She was, in fact, the niece of Mrs. Johnson, Dr. Castle's housekeeper, who'd asked for the doctor's help in getting her a job. Her husband— although she hardly looked old enough to have one—had recently been killed in an automobile accident. Having no other family on the West Coast, she'd come to live with her aunt. She supposedly had had some training as a nurse's assistant and had worked as a nanny for an attorney and his wife in Eugene. According to Mrs. Johnson, she was honest, hardworking, and desperate for a job and a place to live. The question now was, would she be able to handle the duties and responsibilities she was about to be given?

Shelving his reservations for the moment, Dr. Castle introduced the new girl to Russell, who stood and greeted her warmly, obviously pleased to see help of any kind arrive. "And this precious bundle is baby Trouste," the doctor said.

Vera leaned over the bassinette. "Hello, baby Trouste."

The doctor allowed her a few moments to ogle the baby, then continued speaking, more instructively now, wanting to get his business here concluded before he collapsed in a heap. "Because this pregnancy has taken a considerable toll on Mrs. Trouste, we will be bottle-feeding the baby. A supply of bottles and formula is available downstairs in the kitchen. I understand you've cared for an infant before."

Vera straightened. "Yes, sir." Her eyes darted about the room, taking in all the baby supplies that Russell had brought to the room and mostly stacked in piles.

"Good," Dr. Castle said. He went on asking questions and giving instructions until he'd covered all the essentials with the girl. She remained calm and attentive throughout their exchange, asking questions of her own that indicated a greater grasp of the situation than he'd perhaps given her credit for. He nodded in satisfaction before asking, "Is this arrangement acceptable to you?"

Vera smiled bravely. "Yes, sir."

"And you?" the doctor said to Russell, who'd reseated himself in the rocker.

Russell glanced up droopy-eyed. "Most certainly."

"Very well." The doctor turned back to Vera. "I'll be stopping by regularly to check on mother and baby. In between time, if you have any concerns about their welfare, call me at once—at my office or my home. Mr. Trouste has both numbers."

He checked on Margaret one last time before leaving the house. She continued to sleep, but her breathing had shallowed—she would be waking soon. He considered staying until she did. It didn't take much deliberation to decide against it. He'd already pushed himself to the brink and then some. Besides, there was more work to be done on the other end. What he needed now was rest.

52

TAMARA AWOKE FEELING as though she'd tumbled down a steep mountainside, her body having been bashed repeatedly against rugged terrain. She'd survived the plunge, but the punishment she'd suffered had altered her in a way she didn't fully comprehend.

She squinted up at a television set mounted high on the wall, its blank screen reflecting an image in miniature of the hospital room in which she lay. The image was indistinct, partially washed-out, like an overexposed photograph negative. She stared at the reflection, trying to recall the events that had caused her to be brought to this place, but her recollections were as vague as the image in the glass.

A young woman dressed in white pants and a rose-colored smock came into the room carrying a tray of food that she set down on a little table alongside the bed. Odors wafting from the tray made Tamara's stomach lurch. "I'm not hungry," she said.

The aide went over to a curtained wall and drew back the drapes. Shrill light sliced into the room, causing Tamara's eyes to water.

"Would you like me to show you how to turn the television on?" the aide asked. Without waiting for an answer, she switched it on by pushing a button on a control box hooked onto the side-rail of the bed.

Tamara licked her lips. They were dry and cracked. She swallowed. Her throat felt like sandpaper. "Can I please have some water?"

The aide brought over a pink plastic mug and held a straw to her lips while she drank. "I'll leave this here for you," the aide said. She set the mug down on the table next to the tray of food. "You really should eat something."

Tamara responded by depressing the "Volume Up" button on the TV's remote control and keeping it depressed until a mushroom cloud of sound blasted out of the television, sending the aide running for cover.

It was only after she was alone again that Tamara's thinking began to clear and she was able to rummage through her scant recollection of the night before, picking up fragments of hazily recalled events, like shards of broken glass, and fitting them together into a jagged pattern of remembrance. And it was only then that she realized what had changed: She was no longer pregnant, yet neither did she have a child.

She sat up and screamed, "My baby! Where's my baby!" And she continued screaming as hands and faces materialized around her, and voices shushed her, pleaded with her to calm down. But she wouldn't calm down—couldn't calm down—until they'd put the needle in her arm and all the light in the room had shrunk to a single dot that receded into the distance, taking her with it.

When she came awake again, a different tray of food lay untouched on the table by her bed. Someone had turned off the TV set. A voice was speaking to her, saying her name. She looked over at the man standing there.

"How're you feeling?" the old doctor said.

Tamara experienced a cold moment of panic.

"The nurse said you've been asking about your baby."

Tamara shuddered. Her heart was a storehouse of dread.

"Tamara," the doctor said, "do you know what happened last night?"

"Where's my baby?"

The doctor exhaled heavily. "I'm sorry," he said. "Your baby was stillborn."

"Stillborn?"

"Born dead."

Tamara felt the sound explode from her mouth before she heard it. It was the cry of a soul being cast into hell. And suddenly she was falling. Down, down, in an endless rush. The wind whooshed past her face and drowned out all other sound except for the cry. Down, down she plunged until she disappeared into a black hole of silence.

"GO AWAY," she told the doctor when he came back later in the day.

But the doctor stayed. He checked her pulse and listened to her heart. Then he spoke to her in a Grandpa Walton voice. "I want you to know this wasn't your fault. I don't know why, but for some reason the umbilical cord became compressed, and—"

Tamara squeezed her eyes shut, clamped her hands over her ears, tried unsuccessfully to close her mind to the awful image of her baby starving for food and oxygen. "Leave me alone," she said, sinking down in the bed. "Leave me alone . . . leave me alone . . ."

The doctor stood silently by, patient as death. When she quieted, he said, "Would you like me to have the hospital chaplain make arrangements for a service?"

Tamara blinked her eyes open, gazed up at him. "What kind of service?"

"A memorial service—for the baby."

"Memorial? For my . . . ?" She couldn't contemplate such a thing, couldn't make the logical leap. Things were coming at her too fast. She needed time to sort things out, separate the real from the imagined. She turned away from the doctor, curled up instinctively around her middle. But unlike only hours ago, there was no comfort in the gesture. She cradled an empty womb. That was real. She groaned. Tears welled in her eyes.

The doctor came around the bed. Through a blur of tears, Tamara saw him reach inside his jacket pocket and pull out a folded sheet of paper. "I'm sorry to have to bother you with this now," he said as he unfolded the paper. "But certain legalities must be fulfilled." He opened a drawer in a nearby cabinet, brought out a book. He leaned over her, held out the paper with the book underneath it, along with a pen. "I just need you to sign this form. It authorizes release of the—uh—remains to the crematorium. I'll take care of everything else."

Tamara let out a cry of frustration. She just wanted this man to go away. She snatched the pen from his hand, scribbled across the bottom of the form, and shoved the book and document back at him. "Now, get out!"

The doctor hesitated, seemed about to say something else as he stood there holding a Bible in one hand and the signed form in the other. Then he put the Bible back in the drawer and left.

And Tamara was alone. More alone than she had ever been.

53	IT WAS A MIRACLE. As God had promised, she had her child.

"She's beautiful," Margaret said, gazing in awe at the precious bundle cradled in her husband's arms. She sobbed softly, unable to hold back the tears of joy. "She's ours? She's really ours?"

"You did it, darling," Russell said.

Margaret felt a tug at her heartstrings. "Ohhh," she said, "where did you find that blanket?" She recognized the blanket Russell had wrapped the baby in. It was one she'd bought many years before, when she'd been pregnant for the first time. Within days of hearing the glorious news from the doctor, she'd gone out and purchased an extensive layette for the baby: diapers, bibs, nightgowns, jumpers, blankets, towels, a bassinette. Even a perambulator. Not one of those flimsy, wobbly-wheeled contraptions either—the ones that babies get strapped into and then fall out of when their mothers aren't looking— but a real baby carriage with thick upholstery, a canopy, balloon tires, and a spring-suspension ride so soft a baby might as well be floating on a cloud. "I didn't know we still had that blanket."

"I didn't either," Russell said. "I found it in a closet in one of the spare rooms, along with all kinds of baby stuff."

"That's nice," Margaret said, indulging in the dreaminess of the moment. The only reason she remembered the blanket was because she'd never seen another one like it. It was made of creamy-white velour and had pink and blue cherubs imprinted on it. The baby angels were all wearing diapers. It was the cutest thing. And now her little pink angel was snuggled inside it.

And what a beautiful angel she was! Her cheeks were the color of a rosy dawn. Her hair was wispy and flyaway. She had a button nose and—in slumber—eyelids that reflected pearls of light.

Margaret felt a sense of well-being course through her body, a fireside warmth spreading palliative and unrestrained. She reached up. "I want to hold her."

"Should you, dear? You're so weak."

"Just for a little while." She patted her tummy. "Lay her here, then sit beside me and make sure she doesn't fall off."

~

RUSSELL LOWERED THE CHILD onto the fleshy shelf that was Margaret's abdomen. He sat down in the chair beside the bed, marveling at the sudden difference in his wife's demeanor. The sparkle was back in her eyes, the animation in her voice. She was still weak and ghostly pale, but the bloom, he was sure, would soon return to her cheeks.

He looked on with satisfaction as Margaret fawned over the baby. Her suffering was finally over. She had her child and, along with it, a new lease on life. And he had his wife back. For him, the child was just part of the deal. The child was for Margaret.

And what about the young girl who'd given up the baby? She too would be better off, he'd convinced himself. She too had been given another chance—a chance to grow up in her own time, to blossom in the proper season without motherhood gripping her like an early frost. She too could make a new and happier life for herself. Then, someday, in a time of her own choosing, she could take on the fullness of maternity with the unabashed joy that it merits and with the wherewithal to give her child the kind of loving, caring home every child deserves—the kind of home he and Margaret could provide for this child.

Russell smiled as his wife let out frequent moans of pleasure in admiration for the supposed product of her womb. She brushed the baby's cheek with her fingertips, glided a palm across the soft spot on the baby's head. She folded back the blanket to expose the baby's hand, caressing the miniature fingers with a delicacy one might use to examine the petals of a rose. Then she strained forward and placed a kiss on the baby's temple.

Her head sagged back onto the pillow. Her eyelids drooped.

"Let me take the baby now," Russell said. "You need to rest."

Margaret didn't resist.

Russell scooped the baby up in his arms. It was an awkward feeling—holding a baby—like steering a car for the first time. He couldn't help but wonder as he looked upon this tiny human being what would come next. His only thought had been saving Margaret. The child was her salvation. But it was also a complication for their lives, one that would take some getting used to.

He took the baby back into the nursery where Vera was busy settling in. "I think my wife will sleep some more now," he said. He returned the child to the bassinette. "Maybe I'll lie down as well."

"You must be exhausted."

"It's been a long day—and then some."

"Rest as long as you like, Mr. Trouste," Vera said. "I'll watch over your wife and daughter."

Russell nodded, grateful. After satisfying himself that Margaret was resting comfortably, he trudged down the hall to his room, dragging his fatigue along with him like a ball and chain. He moved to his bed. When was the last time he'd even bothered folding back its spread? He looked down at his shoes. They seemed far away. He reached up to unbutton his shirt. Before his fingers could accomplish that task, he fell forward onto the bed.

54

AMANDA STONE SAT DOWN across from her husband at the picnic table outside their cabin, being careful not to lean too far over the table or let her hands stray from her lap. The tabletop was littered with Tommy's fishing lures, and she didn't want to snag herself on one of the barbed hooks. She looked at her husband and frowned. "I don't understand what could have happened to her."

It was almost dark and they still hadn't heard a word from Tamara. She'd vanished from the cabin—they weren't sure when—and had yet to reappear. Amanda didn't know whether to shrug it off or organize a search party. "Why would she leave without saying anything?"

Tommy picked up a funny-looking lure—it was speckled and had a fringe around it like a hula skirt. "Maybe Kurt knows something," he said. He fluffed the lure's skirt, cautiously avoiding the three-pronged hook underneath it.

Amanda shook her head. "I already talked to him. He hasn't seen her since we got back from the falls last night."

Tommy put the hula-skirt lure down and picked up a different one. "She must have gone back to town. Without Angela here, there was no reason for her to stay at the lake."

"Maybe," Amanda said, feeling slighted by the apparent snub. After all, she'd gone out of her way to be nice to Tamara even though she wasn't really *her* friend. She tossed her hair back over her shoulders to keep the ends away from the minefield of barbs. "She could at least have said goodbye."

"Maybe she didn't want to."

"Why on earth not?"

Tommy smirked. "Maybe she was embarrassed about last night."

Amanda kicked him under the table. "I told you to stop."

"Hey, don't blame me," Tommy said. "You're the one who makes all the noise."

"I can't help it," Amanda said. She got up and tramped into the cabin, where she pretended to sulk, but only for a little while.

55   THE NIGHT NURSE GAVE Tamara some pills to help her sleep. When she didn't sleep, the nurse gave her some more pills. Tamara dozed fitfully after that, coming in and out of

consciousness like a drowning person thrashing to the surface for air then sinking again. At one point, she came awake screaming, the one horrible image blazing in her mind—the face of her baby, mouth open in a scream of her own: "Help me, Mommy! Can't you see I'm dying?"

But it was too late for Tamara to help. She'd let her baby die just like she'd let her brother die. It was all her fault. Who else was there to blame?

"God," Tamara cried, "just let me die, why don't you? I'm dead already anyway."

IT WAS DAYLIGHT OUTSIDE when the nurse's aide came into the room with clothes for Tamara donated by the staff. "Your ride is here," she said. "Although I don't know why the all-fired hurry to send you home."

Tamara tried to dress herself. She didn't get very far. She had no strength and no will to summon any. Every effort at movement was like the painful reenactment of a calamity. She sat hunched forward in a chair beside the bed, staring at her bare feet.

The aide came back in and helped Tamara put her arms through the armholes of the T-shirt Tamara had managed to slip over her head. The aide held out a sock while Tamara wriggled her foot into it. Then the other sock. Then the shoes. The aide tied the shoes.

Tamara made a move to stand.

The aide put a hand on her shoulder. "Stay put for a minute." She left the room, returning moments later pushing a wheelchair. "Hospital regulations," she said.

Tamara didn't protest.

The aide helped her into the wheelchair, lifted her feet onto the foot supports. She pushed Tamara out of the room and down the hall toward the second-floor nurses' station.

Tamara wasn't sure if what was happening was real—that is, until she saw Gary standing at the counter with a mad-dog look of impatience on his face. "I'll take it from here," he said, and all but wrestled control of the wheelchair from the aide.

"Take care of yourself, honey," the aide called out as Gary man-handled the wheelchair into a waiting elevator.

Too late for that. Too late . . . too late.

56

DETECTIVE HANSEN STOOD in his boss's office at the Fir Valley Sheriff's Substation, waiting for the lieutenant to finish chewing.

Iverson didn't bother. "We got lucky," he said, shoving the words out through a mouthful of turkey on rye. "The kid had a record."

"Kid?" Hansen said.

The lieutenant wiped his mustard-stained fingers on a paper napkin before picking up a transmittal sheet and handing it across his desk, which at the moment was doubling as a lunch counter. "The DB from the logging site. ISS came up with a fingerprint match to those lifted from the wrecked pickup and the partials the ME got off the body."

Hansen took the communiqué from his boss and scanned it. According to the Oregon State Police Identification Services Section, the dead man had been positively identified as Albert James Stark, AKA Jimmy Stark, twenty-two years old. His last known address was in Eugene. He'd been arrested by Eugene PD when he was nineteen for posses-sion of an illegal substance—marijuana and methamphetamine. Was given probation and required to go through a drug diversion program. He was known to be a sometime student at the University of Oregon. No known occupation otherwise. In the past two years, he'd been cited several times for trespassing at various junior highs and high schools in the Eugene area.

"Why am I not surprised?" Hansen said, referring to the possible drug connection.

Iverson licked a fingertip. "Call Eugene PD and see if they can locate a next of kin. Also, we'd like anything they can dig up on Stark that might tell us why he came to Fir Valley."

Hansen blew air out his nose. "Apparently he came here to die."

The lieutenant gave him a don't-let-the-door-hit-you-on-the-way-out look.

Hansen didn't.

57

MARGARET ROCKED GENTLY back and forth with her daughter in her arms, feeling that sweet rush of joy that comes with the fulfillment of a deep longing, like honey in the veins. With each passing day, she was spending more time out of bed, worshipping at the altar of motherhood, and her favorite devotional was swaying in the rocker with her darling angel snugged against her breast.

The baby cooed. Margaret looked upon her with wonder. "She's so tiny and helpless," she said to her husband, who was sitting nearby, his face hidden behind the newspaper he was reading.

"That's why they call them infants," Russell said.

"Don't be patronizing, darling." Margaret brought the baby's hand to her mouth and kissed the fingers reverently. "Isn't she the sweetest thing you ever saw?"

Russell turned to a different page. "You're the sweetest thing I ever saw. But she runs a close second."

"Oh, Russell, it's so wonderful! We have our child!" Margaret's eyes moistened. She couldn't seem to stop crying in her happiness. One day, childless, she was lost in the wilds of her own personal gloom, and the next day she was a mother and her world was all sunshine and meadow.

Russell lowered his paper. "Have you thought more about what you'd like to name her?"

Margaret sniffed away a measure of her rising emotion. "Yes, I have. I've given it a lot of thought."

"And?"

"I want to call her Felicity, because she's the source of my happiness."

Russell smiled. "That's a beautiful name, dear—a beautiful name.

Now hand Felicity over to Vera so you and the child can get some rest."

"Do I have to?"

"Doctor's orders."

"Ooh-kay." Margaret clung to the child for one last, holy moment before giving her up to Vera, who'd been working nearby, folding freshly laundered baby clothes and diapers.

Russell came over and helped her out of the rocking chair. He guided her back into the adjoining room.

"I'm tired of resting," she complained. But as she climbed back into bed, Margaret could feel the gravitational pull of her weariness. She settled her head on the pillow, looked up at her husband and smiled. "God gave us a daughter."

Russell bent down and kissed her on the cheek. "Dr. Castle is a miracle worker."

58

TAMARA HAD HARDLY been out of bed since Gary had brought her home from the hospital. How many days had it been? Two, three, four? She didn't know and didn't care. And she wasn't inclined to get up now, except that Gary had told her to.

She lingered anyway, feeling no need to obey her stepbrother—or, for that matter, any urge to resist him. In fact, she felt very little of anything. When everything you care about has been taken from you, what is there left in life to look forward to or dread?

Gary didn't press her.

In time, she got up of her own accord, coercing her body into action the way one would force a rusty hinge to move. She took a warm shower and dressed, her every movement connecting with a soreness inside her that insinuated prior agony. Back in her room, standing at the dresser, she stuffed Kleenex into her bra to absorb the leakage from her nipples. Her breasts were painfully swollen, the wasted flow from them a cutting reminder of her loss.

She was lying on her bed, fully clothed, when Gary came to her room a second time.

IT WAS LATE MORNING when they set out from the house in Gary's pickup, Tamara shielding her eyes from the glint of sunlight off a landscape that seemed to be all metal and glass. Gary offered no explanation as to the purpose of this outing, or their destination, and Tamara didn't bother asking for any. What did it matter where they were going, or why?

At Mill Street, Gary turned east toward downtown, then stayed on Mill as it flowed through the old business district into another neighborhood of older homes. On the eastern edge of town, as the road was about to disappear into the wooded hills beyond the city limit, he angled onto a narrow gravel lane that passed through an archway. Lettering on the metal frame of the archway spelled out the words VALLEY MEMORIAL GARDENS.

Tamara felt a nudge to her numbed senses as she gazed out across a broad carpet of green grass that unfurled up a slope and into some trees. Set into the carpet were perfect rows of headstones and grave markers. Here and there, bouquets—some standing tall and proud, some with bowed heads—protruded from brass vases attached to the markers. In a clearing off to the side, a sculptured shepherd tended a small flock of sculptured sheep.

"Why are we coming here?" she asked, a cold apprehension seeping into the dead space inside her. Then she spotted Dr. Castle standing at the far end of the lane, and she knew why. She knew that life hadn't finished beating her down. She jammed her feet into the floorboard of the truck.

When they reached the cul-de-sac at the end of the lane, Gary pulled over and stopped. Dr. Castle, wearing a gray suit and a solemn expression, was standing next to a tall, slender man dressed in black. The two men were stationed at the entrance to a garden compound enclosed by a wrought-iron fence. Beyond the fence, in the center of the compound, stood a squat stone building. It looked like a bunker of some sort.

The old doctor stepped up to the truck and with some difficulty opened the passenger door.

"Out," Gary said.

Tamara's mind was busy building fences, boarding up windows, posting no-trespassing signs. It was a pointless exercise. You can't block out grief any more than you can plug a hole in a dam with your finger. She slid out of the truck onto the ground, feeling dazed.

"This is Mr. Renault," the doctor said in a voice that seemed to come from far away.

The man in black floated into view. He was carrying a small wooden box in the crook of one arm. "This way," he said, and led them into the garden compound.

They walked without speaking along a path lined with rose bushes in bloom. Tamara knew her feet were moving but couldn't feel them. The path bent around a fountain that had back-to-back angels as its centerpiece. Water sprayed up from around the base of the angels' flowing robes into a shallow pool with pebbles in it. Coins of various sizes and hues glistened among the pebbles.

On the other side of the fountain, the path ended at the arched entrance to the stone building. Mr. Renault pushed open a bulky wooden door and stepped aside for her and Dr. Castle to enter first.

Tamara had never been in a mausoleum before. It was cool inside and eerily quiet, like death itself. She flinched upon hearing the *bang!* of the bulky door being closed behind her.

The doctor put a hand on her shoulder and guided her through a tiled foyer, past a statue of the Virgin Mary, and into a dim open chamber. Center support columns ran along the length of the chamber, each flanked by benches. Except for the columns and benches, the chamber was empty, and it was this blatant emptiness that lent focus to the chamber's four polished marble walls.

The doctor coaxed her forward between two columns to a position in front of one of the shiny walls. "You'll be okay," he said, when she balked.

"How do you know?" she snapped, feeling disoriented as she stared up at the wall. It had horizontal rows of doorlike cutouts along its face, larger ones down low and smaller ones higher up. Above each cutout was a gold-plated marker with a name and dates etched into it.

Mr. Renault stepped forward and set his little wooden box on a shelf built into an indentation in the marble wall. The box had a glossy finish. A heart had been carved into its lid. On its front panel was affixed a shiny, engraved plate.

"Shall we pray," said Mr. Renault, and bowed his head.

Tamara kept her head unbowed and her eyes fixed on the little wooden box—on the metal plate on its front panel. She strained to read the inscription: "Baby Ames, 1979." Her body convulsed. Her heart stalled in her chest.

"Lord, we commend Baby Ames into your care," intoned Mr. Renault, "this child who never had the opportunity to behold the light of day here on earth, but who will nevertheless revel in the glory of heavenly light for all eternity. Be with this grieving mother and help her to accept your will in this matter."

Tamara had thought she was out of tears. Empty shells don't have feelings. But she found out otherwise. She found out that sorrow is a cup you can never completely drain. Her head drooped. She hugged herself and sobbed.

"We realize there are things in this life beyond our understanding," said the man in black. "But we also know that your plan for our lives is perfect and that someday, when at last we come face to face with your glory, we shall understand all things that remain a mystery to us now. The best we can do in the meantime is to accept what each day brings, and give thanks for our time here on earth—because we know that all life is precious, as precious as the first blossom of spring and even more fragile."

A fireball of grief exploded in Tamara's breast, and she found herself wheeling around and lurching toward the entrance door. But the strength was gone from her legs. Her knees buckled and she crumpled to the floor.

"Get away from me," she screamed as hands grasped her, tried to lift her up.

And when the hands released her, she dropped back to the floor and began crawling toward the exit, her cries echoing off the marble walls like a roundelay voiced by the residents of hell.

59 OTHER THAN RIDDING the kitchen sink of dirty dishes now and then, Amanda Stone never bothered to do much cleaning inside her and Tommy's cabin. Space to put anything was so limited it was impossible to keep the place from becoming cluttered. The clutter hid the dirt. What was the point of cleaning under the clutter?

Tommy's affinity for disorder didn't help. He cast off his clothes each night like a man scattering seed. His dirty socks would take root and grow before he'd ever pick them up. His fishing equipment littered the place like children's toys that were always underfoot. And when Amanda moved something of his—a rod or a fishnet—to a more suitable location, Tommy would grumble that she was always hiding his stuff. Life was easier all around if she just let heaping piles be.

It was no wonder, then, that it was nearly a week after Tamara had left the lake before Amanda found her backpack inside the cabin. And she only found it then because it was time to wash clothes and she couldn't locate all of Tommy's underwear. He had seven pairs of briefs and, counting the pair he had on, she could only account for six. She searched with her hand down in the crevice between the wall and the end of the couch and came up with a blue backpack.

"That's strange," she said, holding it up.

Tommy came out of the bathroom, bringing with him a putrid odor. Amanda forgot about the backpack for the moment. "What happened in there?" she said, pinching her nose.

"The damn toilet stopped up again, and I can't find the plunger. Don't we have a plunger?"

"We did, until you used it once too often as a rubber hammer."

"Oh," Tommy said, his expression that of a boy who'd been caught making muddy footprints on a newly mopped kitchen floor. Then he spied what Amanda held in her hand. "What's that?"

"It's Tamara's backpack."

"What's it doing here?"

"That's what I'd like to know."

Tommy shrugged. "Okay—well—I'm going over to the Adberry's to borrow a plunger."

Within ten minutes he was back with a plunger, and Kurt.

"Kurt thinks there may be a phone number where we can reach Tamara," Tommy said, and headed for the bathroom.

"Really," Amanda said. "And why didn't you tell us this before?"

"Before what?" Kurt said.

Amanda rolled her eyes. "Never mind. What's the number?"

Kurt scrunched his face. "God, it stinks in here."

Amanda walked over to the telephone mounted on the kitchen wall. "Just give me the number."

"Tommy said you found Tamara's backpack."

Amanda pointed to where it lay on the sofa. Kurt picked it up and began probing its various pouches.

Amanda frowned. "You have the number or not?"

Kurt withdrew a small leather purse from a side-zipper pocket. "Maybe." He opened the purse, sifted through its contents, pulled out a crinkled green wad. He spread the wad open and smoothed it out.

That's odd, Amanda thought as she peered at the ten-dollar bill in Kurt's hand. Then he began rattling off numbers, and she had to concentrate on dialing. She coiled the phone cord around her index finger and listened to the repeated ringing in the line. Finally a gruff voice answered. "Is Tamara there?" she asked more timidly than she'd meant to.

"Who wants to know?"

"Tell her it's Amanda."

"Tell her yourself," the gruff voice said. There was a loud clunk on the other end of the line, which remained open. "Tamara, telephone!" the gruff voice bellowed in the background.

Several minutes passed without Tamara coming to the phone. Amanda could hear Tommy in the bathroom, working the plunger and cursing. Kurt had retreated outside the front door, leaving it propped

open. Amanda kept the phone pressed to her ear but heard only static
in the line. Then the toilet flushed and Tommy reappeared, brandish-
ing the plunger like a sword.

"Once again he has slain the Turd Dragon," he announced, "sending
it back to Middle Earth, to the dark region of Septic, and along with
it the stench from its cruel maw."

"Actually, I think the stench has decided to hang around for a while,"
Kurt said from the doorway. He pumped the door open and closed
several times in a futile attempt to stir a breeze.

"Shush!" Amanda said. But the line went dead. She huffed. "Well—"
She tapped the switch hook to get another dial tone, then realized she
couldn't remember the number. She hollered toward the door. "Kurt,
what was that number again?"

Kurt came back inside, this time with the neck of his T-shirt pulled
up over his mouth and nose. He retrieved the ten-dollar bill from the
backpack and repeated the number to her. As Amanda redialed, she
resolved to be more assertive this time.

The gruff voice never gave her a chance. "Tamara ain't takin' calls.
Don't call back." And once more the line went dead.

"How rude!" Amanda said, glaring at the receiver a moment before
hanging up.

"What happened?" Tommy said. He flipped the plunger up into the
air and tried to catch it by the handle on its way down. He missed.

Amanda told the guys what happened with the call.

Tommy scooped the plunger up off the floor. "You think she's even
there?"

"I think so," Amanda said. "Otherwise, why would he have called
her to the phone?" The question searched for a place to land inside her
head. "Maybe she's sick or something."

Tommy laughed. "Yeah, like eight-months-pregnant-something.
God, I'd be sick too."

"What do you think, Kurt?" Amanda asked.

Kurt answered with a shrug, but the collapsed look on his face led
Amanda to believe he knew something about Tamara's situation that
he wasn't telling.

60　　GARY FOUND WHAT he was looking for at Andy's Guar-
anteed Used Cars out on Old Highway 99. The pickup
was five years old but looked brand new. It was a bright-red Ford F250
4x4. The salesman showing it was Andy's nephew, Denny. Gary had
seen him out on the lot before, dressed in his tan loafers and seersucker
sports jacket, schmoozing potential buyers. Doing the old bait and
switch. Gary feigned only a passing interest in the truck as Denny
made his pitch.

"It's only got thirty-two thousand miles on it," he said, wetting his
lips with his coffee-stained tongue. "And the heaviest thing it ever
hauled was groceries. The old guy who owned it was a friend of Uncle
Andy's. When he died last month his wife asked us to sell it for her.
Uncle is doing her a favor."

Favor, my ass, Gary thought, but let it go. He jerked his thumb at
his rig parked off to the side. "How much you give me in trade?"

Denny made a sucking sound with his lips pursed. "I don't know,"
he said, shaking his head. "That thing was knockin' so loud when you
drove in it sounded like a diesel. Was smokin' like one too. What is it,
early sixties?" He tilted his head. "I can see rust on it from here. And
your tires have about as much tread as a condom."

"The balance in cash—today," Gary said.

Denny snapped to attention. His eyes made pinball actions in their
sockets. "In that case, I'm sure we can work something out."

Ten minutes later the deal was done. Gary left Denny to do the
paperwork, while he went home to get the cash. The doctor had come
through with the rest of the money just like he'd said he would, a fist-
sized bundle of bills that changed hands in the hospital parking lot
the day after Tamara's baby was born. It had been burning a hole in
Gary's bottom dresser drawer ever since.

Inside the car lot office, Gary plunked down the cash payment for his
new truck. Denny counted it three times before finally deciding it was
all there. "Nice doing business with you," he said, extending a hand.

"The keys?" Gary said, not bothering to shake.

Gary was about to pull away from the lot in his new rig when the salesman flagged him down. He held up a red gas can. "This was in the bed of your trade-in. Want it?"

"Toss it in the back."

Gary was feeling downright high on life as he drove home and parked his shiny new truck in the driveway. He bounded into the house. Tamara was curled up on the couch watching television with the sound turned up too loud. "Shut that thing off," he told her, "and come outside and look at what I got."

Tamara kept her eyes glued to the TV screen. "I want to watch this movie."

"Watch it later. I wanna show you my new rig."

"I don't care about your new rig," Tamara said. She aimed the remote control at the TV and cranked the volume even higher.

Gary felt like ripping her arm off. Instead, he went over to the television set, reached behind it, and yanked its power cord out of the wall socket. The screen winked out and went silent.

Tamara jumped up from the couch and stamped down the hall. The door to her room slammed so hard it sounded like a rifle shot.

"Stupid bitch," Gary muttered. The girl was becoming a real pain in the ass these days. All she did was mope around the house and get in his way. When she wasn't crying, she was carping about something: *We're out of cereal. The toaster quit working. Can't you see I'm hurting?* He'd put up with her bullshit about as long as he was inclined to. If she didn't head out somewhere on her own pretty soon, he was going to throw her out. Here he was all happy about his new pickup, wanting to share something good with her, and she had to go and spoil it for him.

He blasted out the front door, climbed back into his new truck, and drove off toward more fertile ground.

61

"WE DRINK, YOU BUY?" Brian said, looking at Gary squinty eyed, as if he was sure he'd heard wrong.

Gary grinned. "Yep." He'd caught his friend just in time. Brian already had his work clothes on. Five minutes later and he'd have been out the door, knuckling under to The Man.

Brian pointed at him with both index fingers, double-barreled skepticism. "You're saying, we go out on the town, and I don't need to bring no cash?"

"That's what I'm sayin'."

Brian's face lit up as if he'd just won a big poker pot. He started unbuttoning his work shirt. "In that case, give me time to change clothes and call the mill. I'll drop my truck off at your place so Brenda won't know I didn't go to work."

"Call Jerome while you're at it," Gary said. "Have him meet us at the Red Owl." He nodded toward the front door. "I'll be waitin' outside."

When Brian came out of his house a few minutes later, more suitably clad, Gary was standing in the driveway leaning against the side of his new F250. Brian pulled up short. "Whose truck is this?"

"My new toy," Gary said, swelling his chest.

Brian circled the pickup, wowing in admiration. "How in hell did you swing a deal for this beauty? Your credit's as worthless as a toilet plunger in an outhouse."

"No problem," Gary said. "Everything down and nothing a month."

JEROME WAS ALREADY at the Red Owl Tavern when they got there, waiting for them in the parking lot. Gary honked as he wheeled into the lot.

"Damn," Jerome said, shambling up to Gary's new rig. "Wha'd you do, rob a bank?"

Gary chuckled as he led the way into the tavern. Robbery? Yeah. A bank? No—it was much better than that.

Music blared from a jukebox in the back of the joint. A blue haze hung over the few inhabitants who'd gotten a head start on them. Darlene, the barmaid, had seen them coming and already had the tap flowing. Gary straddled a stool at the long, polished bar, feeling like a cowboy glad to be back in the saddle. His buddies settled in alongside him. He pulled a roll of bills from his pocket, peeled off a couple of twenties and slapped them on the bar. "Keep 'em coming, darlin'. We got us some celebratin' to do."

Darlene clunked a foaming pitcher on the bar, along with three frosty mugs. "You keep payin', I'll keep playin'," she said, and proceeded to fill each mug until froth gushed over its rim.

"That's the spirit," Gary said. He lifted his mug and took a healthy pull. A satisfying warmth flowed down his throat and into his belly. And each pull after that stoked a fire deep inside him.

They left the Red Owl a little after seven and drove south of town to Willie's Bar and Grill. "I'm starvin'," Jerome said as they slid into a booth near the pool tables in the back.

Brian picked up one of the laminated menus wedged on end between the napkin holder and the rough-paneled wall. "We eat, you pay?" he said, looking at Gary for confirmation.

Gary nodded. "Damn straight."

They all ordered steaks and more beer. For dessert, they had a couple of rounds of tequila shooters with lime. After dinner they played pool and drank more beer, and the fire inside Gary burned ever brighter. He exulted in its glow, which made him feel loose and expansive, as if he was the undisputed champion of the world. But the heat from the fire also provoked a yearning in him that neither food nor drink could fulfill. He rammed his cue stick back into the rack and said, "Let's get down to some serious partying."

The Miller Lite clock on the wall said 11:15 when they tottered into the Busy Beaver. Brian stopped at the telephone in the lobby to call his wife, while Gary and Jerome went in search of a table. The place was dark inside except for the raised stage up front where, bathed in floodlight, two girls dressed in nothing but G-strings, cowboy boots, and cowboy hats were strutting their stuff for an adoring crowd.

The girls stomped their boots on the wooden stage and gyrated to the music booming out of the big speakers mounted on the walls. Guys were whistling and cheering and shifting in their chairs to get a better look at the bouncing bare breasts. Peering through a screen of tobacco smoke, Gary spotted some businessmen types vacating a table up front, next to the stage. He and Jerome swooped in and took their place, and Brian joined them moments later.

"I caught the waitress on my way in and ordered," Brian said.

Within minutes, the waitress was setting a pitcher of beer and three glasses on the table. Gary kept his eyes on the dancers and let someone else pour.

The girls continued to stomp and gyrate around the stage, and the guys in the place continued to hoot and holler. One of the girls, a blonde with heavy breasts and nipples as firm and red as pimentos, sidled over to their table, apparently to check out the newcomers. She stood above Gary, legs spread apart, shimmy-shaking her booty and smiling her fake smile while slinging her boobs around like bola balls.

Gary thumbed a twenty off his roll and held it out. The girl, still grinding her hips, moved up close enough for him to slip the twenty beneath her G-string. As soon as the bill left Gary's hand, she stepped back. She snatched the bill out with her quick fingers and held it up for all the other patrons to see the denomination. "All you cheapskates, take notice," she taunted.

A chorus of men booed. The buxom dancer leaned down to give Gary a kiss on the cheek. When she did, he reached up and put a hand on her breast. Instantly a big bruiser of a fellow was at the table, pulling Gary's hand back. The guy had come out of nowhere.

"No touching the merchandise," the bouncer said.

Gary yanked his hand out of the bouncer's grasp. "Go fuck yourself."

The bouncer didn't flinch. He gave Gary a backhanded smile. "You get one warning, pal, and that was it." He moved away, but not far, standing against the wall straddle-legged, arms folded across his chest—the prison-guard stance.

Gary tried to ignore him, but it was like trying to disregard a pistol pointed at his head. So he kept his hands to himself after that. And he drank not to feed the warmth inside him but in order to quell the riot of resentment he felt at being told what to do. He watched one of the dancers wrap her legs around a pole and slither down it. "What the hell good are they if you can't touch 'em?" he muttered.

A new set of girls came on dressed in fake animal skins—one in leopard and one in zebra. The leopard chased the zebra around the stage and finally cornered it—and *skinned* it. When the fake zebra skin fell to the floor, a big roar went up from the crowd as the girl beneath the hide was revealed in all her bare-breasted glory. Then the denuded zebra turned on the leopard and stripped off its skin. Another cheer went up.

But Gary didn't cheer. He sat there downing more beer and feeling an urge build inside him like pressure rising beneath a lava dome.

62   TAMARA CAME AWAKE with a jolt. The room was dark—too dark even for shadows. It was the dead of night, apparently a moonless one at that.

What had awakened her? Had she been having another nightmare? If so, she didn't remember it.

Voices.

She lifted her head from the pillow and listened.

The voices were loud, familiar. Gary and Brian were in the living room. But something was wrong. Their exchanges were sharp, high-impact, more like verbal blows than conversation. She tried to take in what they were saying, but could gather only disconnected scraps of speech. Brian's voice: " . . . crazy . . . can't . . . your sister . . ." Gary's voice: " . . . step-sister . . . my business . . ." Brian: " . . . you'll regret . . . drunk . . . had a baby . . ." Gary: " . . . out of my way . . ."

Tamara bolted upright in bed, breathing hard. She should have known it would come to this—Gary behaving just like his father. But one thing he may not have counted on: Tamara was not about to mimic her mother and meekly play the role of victim. She pulled back the edge of the mattress, found the handle to the butcher knife.

From the living room came a loud grunt, followed by a hiss, as if a tire had been punctured and was spewing air. Muffled footsteps in the hallway approached her bedroom door.

With the knife firmly in her grasp, Tamara wriggled backwards in bed until her backside pressed against the wall. She jerked the bed sheet up around her waist.

The bedroom door flew open, banged against its stop. A silhouetted figure lurched into the room.

"Get out!" she yelled.

The figure approached the bed, hovered over her. "Not till I get a little lovin'." Gary's voice was thick and husky.

Even in the gloom, Tamara could sense his nakedness, smell the alcohol on his breath and the acrid scent of his rampant body heat. "I have a knife," she warned, thrusting the butcher knife out in a threatening manner so that the point of it was aimed at his chest.

The next thing she knew, Gary had grabbed hold of her wrist and was twisting it so hard that she was crying out in pain. The knife fell from her hand and onto the floor. In desperation, she twisted her body around and kicked at him. The blows merely glanced off his sweat-lathered body. And when she swung her free arm around to hit him in the face, he caught the arm in a viselike grip. He forced her down against the mattress and sat on her legs.

She screamed as loudly as she could.

He slapped her.

Her head spun darkly, her ears buzzed, her eyes swam with tears. "You sonofabitch," she snarled.

Gary regripped her wrist, pinned both her arms above her head, and straddled her. He put his face close to hers. "You scream again and I'll kill you."

Tamara was too dazed to scream again. She struggled to stay conscious. Over Gary's shoulder she saw a dim figure appear in the doorway and wondered if it was real or a vision.

"Gary, don't," Brian said. He came forward and clamped a hand on Gary's shoulder.

As if spring-loaded, Gary's elbow immediately shot back, landing squarely on Brian's groin. Brian buckled at the waist, pitched sideways, and went down in a heap beside the dresser.

Gary reached down and pawed clumsily at Tamara's underpants.

"No! Stop!" She clawed at his chest, wishing she had longer fingernails.

He slapped her again, harder this time. She went limp, the force of the blow like a stun gun to her senses. Her eyes remained opened but unfocused. Her limbs twitched involuntarily. Aftershocks of raw sensation rippled through her body. She could sense Gary's hands undressing her now, pulling her legs apart, and she was powerless to stop him. *Oh, God, why are you letting this happen?*

Then Gary groaned. He slumped, slid off her, and dropped to the floor like dead weight.

She looked around, confused. Brian was standing by the bed with a brick in his hand. Behind him, without the brick under its one corner, the old dresser was near to toppling over.

Brian dropped the brick to the floor. He folded at the waist, braced his hands against his thighs. "Are you all right?" he said, wheezing out the words.

Tamara sat up, sobbing. No, she wasn't all right. But thanks to Brian, she'd been spared the final indignity Gary had intended.

"I think we both better get the hell out of here," Brian said. "When Gary comes to, he's gonna be really pissed." He straightened up. "Get dressed. I'll wait in the other room."

"Don't leave me here with him!"

Tamara scrambled out of bed, snatched her pants up off the floor. One of her shoes was wedged under Gary's bare buttock. She squealed as she worked to wrest it free. Clutching her clothes, she ran across the hall into the bathroom and closed the door behind her.

She dressed in a panic, afraid that Gary would revive any second and come after her again. But when she left the bathroom and started down the hall, she caught a glimpse through her bedroom doorway of his immobile figure—a humped inkblot—still on the floor.

A weak, fractured glow from the porch light trickled into the living room through the front window. Brian sat slumped over on the couch with his head in his hands. He looked up at her as she entered, his face carved out of shadow. "Where can I take you?"

Tamara tried to think but was at a loss. "I don't know." Her hands fluttered about her face seemingly with a mind of their own. "I don't know anybody around here."

"Well, you can't stay here."

"Can I go home with you?"

Brian winced. "No," he said sharply. Then in a softer tone: "I'm sorry, but my wife wouldn't understand. And neither would Gary." He ran his fingers through his hair. "How 'bout I take you to the Rescue Mission? They have a separate wing for women now, I hear. You can stay there until you figure out some other place to go."

Tamara stiffened. "I don't want to go to the Mission."

"Where else then?"

She opened her mouth, but couldn't come up with an answer.

Brian stood up. "The Mission then." He glanced around. "You got any other stuff, a bag or something?"

She shook her head.

Brian looked surprised, seemed about to say something else.

A loud groan echoed down the hall.

A picture formed in Tamara's mind of Gary's nude frame rising from the floor. She spun around and sprinted for the front door.

63

DETECTIVE HANSEN PULLED his cruiser to the curb in front of 726 Cedar Street. "Nice place," he said, scrutinizing the ramshackle home and barren grounds.

"Nice parking job too," Deputy Willard said.

A red pickup truck was parked askew in the driveway, its two front wheels resting on the lawn.

The officers got out and ambled over to the house. Hansen had brought Willard along as backup, not that he really needed any. He was just rescuing the deputy from one of the most dreaded assignments in all of law enforcement—a presentation at an elementary school assembly. That chore had been pawned off on a younger deputy still trying to prove his worth to the department.

They stepped up onto a sagging front porch. Hansen knocked on the tattered screen door. No answer. He knocked again, louder.

Willard moved over to a picture window marred by long, intersecting cracks that had been taped over with duct tape. He shielded his eyes from the reflected glare of the morning sun and peered inside.

"I'll check around back," Hansen said. "Just for grins, why don't you call in the plates on that truck."

"It does seem a bit upscale for the neighborhood."

Hansen headed around to the side of the house, accessing it through a gate in a tilting wooden fence that looked as if it could fall down any moment. When he returned to the front porch a few minutes later, Willard was just getting off the radio.

"Wha'd you say this guy's name was?" Willard asked.

Hansen pulled his notepad out of his pocket and glanced at the information he'd jotted down after reading the latest communiqué from Eugene PD regarding Jimmy Stark. "Neaves. First name, Gary."

"I got a red '74 Ford F250 4x4, same plate number, registered to a Philip Condon at an address in Winston."

Hansen slipped the notepad back into his pocket. "Well, let's see what Mr. Neaves has to say about that. The guy's either a heavy sleeper or he's passed out. He's sprawled on a bed in a back bedroom—in the buff."

"So now you're a Peeping Tom."

"Hey, I can't help it if the guy leaves his windows uncovered."

"I may have to tell your wife."

Willard was obviously enjoying himself. "Just try the door again," Hansen told him.

Willard was laughing as he unhooked his nightstick from his service belt and whacked it against the door frame several times. They waited a full minute but still got no response from inside the house.

Willard pulled the screen door open and thumped his stick against the solid inner door. They waited some more to no avail.

"Okay," Hansen said. "I'll go see if I can roust the guy."

"All right, *Tom*."

"And save the wisecracks."

The detective went back around to the side of the house and looked in through the bedroom window. The guy was still lying face down on the bed, dead to the world. There was no screen on the window. The detective knocked on the windowpane. The guy didn't move a muscle. Hansen rapped again, as hard as he dared, afraid of breaking the glass. The guy thrashed about in the bed, then went still again.

Hansen continued knocking. The windowpane rattled in its frame. Finally the guy lifted his head and looked toward the window. Hansen held his detective's badge against the glass. The guy blinked several times and, after a few moments of dopey-eyed staring, slowly cantilevered his legs over the edge of the bed. He sat up, head sagging, elbows resting on his knees. He was a mangy-looking dude with a thick, tossed red mane, a full, frizzy beard, and an excessive amount of body hair. Sitting there on the bed, bent over and naked, he reminded Hansen of a crouching lion.

When the guy continued just to sit there, Hansen knocked again. The guy glared at the window. Hansen motioned toward the front of the house.

After another long pause, the guy pushed himself up off the bed. He swayed like a man trying to steady himself on the deck of a pitching ship, then staggered out of the room.

Hansen returned to the front of the house. Willard was leaning against a porch support post with his arms folded across his chest.

"He's coming," Hansen said.

Willard smiled, made no comment.

They waited several more minutes. The guy didn't show.

Willard was reaching for his nightstick again when the inner door came partially open. A bearded face and bare upper torso appeared in the fissure.

"You Gary Neaves?" Willard asked.

The guy squinted at the daylight. "What's it to you?" he said in a gravelly voice.

"We're looking for Tamara Ames," Hansen said. "She live here?"

Neaves cleared his throat. "She don't *live* here. But she's been staying here for a while."

That statement jibed with the information Hansen had received from Eugene. The Eugene PD had done some legwork and concluded that Jimmy Stark may have come south to see an ex-girlfriend thought to be staying in Fir Valley with her stepbrother, one Gary Neaves, who resided at this address.

"Is she home now?" Hansen asked.

"I don't think so."

"You don't *think* so?" Willard said.

Neaves turned his head and hollered, "Tamara!" There was no response to his call. He faced the deputies again. "Like I said, I don't think so."

"Know where she is?" Hansen asked.

"I've been asleep."

"We noticed," Willard put in. "Long night?"

Neaves didn't answer.

Hansen glanced through the partially open doorway. "Mind if we come inside?"

"I told you," Neaves said, "she's not here. And, yes, I do mind."

"So now you're sure she's not here," Willard said, his voice ripe with sarcasm.

"That's right," Neaves shot back, glowering at the deputy.

"When did you last see her?" Hansen asked in a calm manner, trying to stay in control of the situation.

Neaves continued staring daggers at Willard, then finally gave his attention back to Hansen. "Yesterday afternoon. Some buddies and I went out for a drink. She was here when I left."

"What time was that?"

"Around three."

"And you got back when?"

"Sometime after midnight."

"She was gone when you got back?"

The guy rubbed his bloodshot eyes. "All I know is she ain't here now."

Hansen took a picture out of his shirt pocket and held it out. "Ever seen this guy before?"

Neaves angled his head and examined the photo. "Sure. That's Jimmy, Tamara's old boyfriend." He sneered. "The one who knocked her up."

Hansen felt his internal antennae go up. "Tamara's pregnant?"

Neaves shook his head. "Not anymore."

"Meaning?"

"Meaning just what I said."

Hansen let it go for the time being. "When was the last time you saw Jimmy?"

Neaves squeezed one eye shut, opened it again. "About three, four weeks ago. He came sniffin' around here. Wanted to talk to Tammy. Said he wanted to get back together with her." He snorted. "Just wanted to wet his dick again—that's what I think."

Hansen slipped the photo of Jimmy back into his pocket. "What did Tamara think?"

"She told him to get lost."

"And?"

"He did."

"Just left and never came back?" Willard said.

"That's right."

"Haven't seen him since?"

"Nope."

Hansen took a business card out of his wallet. "I'd appreciate your letting us know when Tamara does come home." He held the card out to Neaves.

Neaves took the card without looking at it. "That all?"

"This your truck out front?" Willard said.

"Whadda you care?" Neaves said.

Willard shrugged. "Nice truck—that's all."

Neaves was quiet for a moment. Then: "Bought it yesterday." And with that he slammed the door shut with enough force to knock paint chips loose from its frame.

"Sociable chap," Willard said.

"See the scratches on his chest?" Hansen said as the two of them walked back to the cruiser.

"Looked fresh to me," Willard said.

They were halfway back to the station house before either of them spoke again. "Tamara Ames," Willard said in a speculative tone of voice, as if dredging up a memory.

"What about her?"

"I know who she is." And the deputy proceeded to tell Hansen about the pregnant girl he'd interviewed in the emergency room at the hospital after she'd taken a tumble in a convenience store downtown. "I didn't make the connection at first. But I'm sure that was her name. And I seem to remember seeing another report several weeks later with her name on it. A couple of our graveyard guys responded to a 9-1-1 call. Premature birth at home. Stillborn, I think the report said."

"Easy enough to find out," Hansen said.

64

"ARE YOU OKAY, young lady?"

Who? What? Tamara squinted up through a screen of dew-dolloped leaves at . . . what? A face? Yes—one heavily powdered, framed in gray hair kinked like a Brillo pad, with deep creases at the corners of eyes magnified out of proportion by thick glasses. The eyes were peering down into the bushes as if trying to see into the bottom of a well. The woman the face belonged to was standing on the landing at the entrance to the Fir Valley Public Library. As the woman bobbed her head, the lenses of her glasses reflected darts of sunlight into Tamara's eyes.

Tamara felt like screaming at the woman: *No, I'm not okay! I lost my baby. My stepbrother tried to rape me. And I've just spent all night outside hiding in these damn bushes.* Instead, she pushed herself up off the cold, damp earth, fought her way out of the clingy shrubbery, and stalked away from the building.

"The library opens at ten o'clock," the woman said brightly.

Tamara reached the sidewalk along Mill Street and immediately crumpled against a postal drop box. Her joints ached. Her muscles were as stiff as chilled taffy. Her head felt clogged, as if packed with mud. She was caked head to toe in bark mulch, its sharp scent oozing from her like earth-sweat. It had been a long, terror-filled night spent exposed to the elements and potential predators, real and imagined, with the specter of recent events giving a face to her fears.

Brian had dropped her off at the Rescue Mission the night before as promised. But no way was she going inside that place. She knew exactly what would happen if she did. As soon as those in charge found out she was underage, they'd be obliged to call Children's Services. Then those do-gooders at CSD would be obliged to find an "appropriate placement" for her. Tamara was not about to let that happen. She'd already done her time in the system. She was not about to go back to that life. She'd been there, done that—thank you very much. Not again.

So she'd stood outside the entrance to the mission and watched the taillights of Brian's truck diminish to a pair of red snake eyes that slithered away into the night. Along Main Street, the storefronts and offices stood silent in the gloom, their blackened windows like empty eye sockets aimed uselessly at one another across the abandoned thoroughfare. The sidewalks along the street were vacant except for a couple of sprawled-out bums who'd gone to sleep outside the Greyhound bus station. It was too late even for the buses to be running.

Tamara scurried past the bums, feeling an anxiety vibrate inside her like the rumble of a distant train. She'd never been afraid of the dark. But now with her imagination taking control of her senses, she began to understand that childlike fear. She stumbled along Main Street, imagining a killer lurking in every shadow, a rapist waiting for her around every corner.

As she approached the Fir Valley Public Library at the intersection of Mill Street and Main, she felt feverish, spent, as if she'd just hiked across a great desert. She blundered toward the front entrance to the library. Just before reaching the concrete steps, she veered off into some shrubbery and collapsed onto the ground. That's where she'd spent the rest of the night, huddled like a frightened child hiding from the bogeyman.

Tamara backed away from the postal box, stood testing her legs. The storefronts along Main Street were awash in sunlight now, their

windows mirroring a bright world outside that was astir with pedestrians and vehicular traffic. It was an odd scene, or so it seemed, out
of character with the dark images of the night before.

She shook her head in an effort to dispel the dreariness inhabiting her soul. She needed to pull herself together, find a safe place to
stay, and she needed to do it sooner rather than later. With that goal
in mind—and one other, equally as urgent—she tottered off down
the sidewalk.

TAMARA HADN'T BEEN back to the Texaco mini-mart at Main and
Central since the night of the incident that had landed her in the hospital, but this was an emergency. The store was crawling with customers
when she got there. She made her way to the back. Damn! The bathroom was occupied. She paced outside its door. A man finally came
out, still zipping up. Tamara ducked inside and took care of business.
She kept her hands glued to her sides as she exited the store.

She was standing outside the mini-mart, trying to figure out her
next move, when a Hostess Bakery truck began backing up to the store
entrance, emitting a loud *beep, beep, beep*. The truck stopped, so did the
beeping. Moments later, its back door clattered and began rising on
tracks, exposing first some feet and legs and then the entire uniform-
clad body of the deliveryman, along with row upon row of wire shelves
lined with baked goods. Tamara gawked at the goodies with a longing
that must have shown like fireworks going off in her eyes.

The Hostess deliveryman was a lanky fellow, all arms and legs. He
had a long face and big flaps for ears. He looked to be about thirty.
Cursive stitching on the breast of his shirt spelled "Roy." He reached
into a wire basket sitting on the floor in the back of the truck and pulled
out a packaged pastry. "Here," he said, tossing it out to her.

A chocolate cupcake! Tamara ripped the package open, bit into it
eagerly. Cream filling oozed from the corners of her mouth. "Thanks," she
said, licking her lips. "But won't you get in trouble, giving stuff away?"

"Naw," Roy said. "The goods in this basket are outdated. What
we can't sell at the day-old store or push off on the shelters and senior
centers gets written off as spoilage." He hopped down from the truck

and offloaded a wheeled rack laden with fresh goods. "Eat as much of that old stuff as you want." He rolled his rack toward the entrance to the market.

Tamara took the deliveryman at his word. She finished downing the chocolate cupcake, then dipped into the basket for another treat. Within minutes, she'd polished off two Twinkies, a Suzy Q, a Sno Ball, and a package of Mini Muffins, and was beginning to enjoy a pleasant sugar high. By the time the deliveryman reemerged from the store, towing a mostly empty rack, she'd come up with a plan she hoped would get her away from Fir Valley.

"Where all do you go?" she asked.

Roy dumped a few items into the outdated-goods basket and loaded his rack into the truck. "Just about every market around here," he said with obvious pride. "As far south as Glendale, as far north as Yoncalla."

"How about east?"

"Not much commerce east of town, outside the store at Mohler Lake." He stepped up into the truck and began pulling the door down.

"You go there?" Tamara asked, the plan in her mind suddenly a roadmap with a destination.

Roy tilted his head sideways, peering under the door. "Where?"

"Mohler Lake."

"Oh," he said. "Tuesdays and Fridays only." He closed the door the rest of the way, with himself behind it.

Tamara scuttled around to the cab of the truck. Roy was already in the driver's seat, buckling up. She approached the partially open driver's window. "What's today?"

Roy rolled the window on down. "Friday," he said.

Tamara felt a warm rush of hope replace some of the chill inside her. "Can I ride along with you to Mohler Lake?"

Roy started the truck's engine. He shook his head. "Can't take passengers," he said. "Company rules."

Tamara climbed onto the truck's running board, stuck her head through the open window. "Please! I won't tell anyone," she said, her face only inches away from Roy's.

Roy gripped the steering wheel with both hands and stared straight ahead. "I'm sorry," he said, his tone matching his words. "But I can't take you. It's not allowed." He feathered the accelerator with a nervous foot.

Tamara clung to the truck—and her hopes. She searched for some alteration in Roy's bearing that might indicate a willingness to change his mind. Finally, seeing none, she dropped to the ground. Tears clouded her vision as she watched Roy put the truck in gear and pull away.

The truck hadn't traveled more than ten feet before it came to a jerky stop. Its engine went quiet. The driver's door swung open.

"Forgot some paperwork," Roy said. He got out of the truck, leaving the door ajar. He had a funny look on his face as he ambled past, like a little boy sneaking under the house to play with matches. "Now don't you even think about getting in my truck and hiding in the back of it while I'm in the store."

Which, of course, was exactly what she did.

65 TAMARA SIGHED WITH RELIEF when the bakery truck finally came to a stop in front of the store at Mohler Lake Lodge. She'd been sitting for hours on the ribbed floor of the truck's cargo bay—although by now the floor seemed more like a bed of nails—while Roy completed his deliveries in town and then made his way up to the lake. Her butt had long since gone numb. Her lower back had knotted up on her. A burning pain traveled like fire on a wire up and down her legs.

The mountain portion of the trip had been especially trying. Steered aggressively through the curves, the bakery truck had lurched endlessly side to side, tossing Tamara about like a carnival ride—the kind that always made her stomach roll. She was lucky not to have thrown up, especially considering she'd begun the journey just after consuming what amounted to about a pound of sugar.

Roy, as he had during the previous stops, pretended not to notice her presence as he passed through the cargo bay on his way to open the back door. It was a silly game he continued to play, but Tamara was happy to go along with it because it had brought her back to the lake. So, saying nothing—why shatter the pretense at this point?—she wriggled out from between the metal shelves, ducked into the cab of the truck, and bailed out via the driver's door.

She stood hunched over on the tarmac with a hand on the fender of the truck. Her head was swimming. Her stomach carried on as if it failed to recognize the stoppage of movement. And now that she'd arrived back at the lake, she couldn't help but wonder if she'd done the right thing in coming here. She'd acted on impulse. Had she acted foolishly? How could she possibly think that Amanda and Tommy would welcome her back after her little disappearing act? And what explanation could she offer them without opening herself up to questions she didn't want to answer?

She took deep breaths to calm her stomach and her nerves. Don't think about it, she told herself. Just face it as it comes.

She laughed a mocking laugh at her own puny attempt to pacify herself. *Face it as it comes.* Yeah, sure. That's what she'd been telling herself for so long now her life had taken on a kind of game-board destiny. Roll the dice and see what comes up. The problem was she kept landing on Chance. And all the Chance cards she drew ended up costing her dearly.

By the time Tamara felt composed enough to enter the lodge store, Roy was already inside with his cart of fresh goods. A Mr. Whipple lookalike was standing behind the service counter feeding a roll of tape into the cash register. She looked around for Amanda but spied only a couple of customers checking out the merchandise.

Mr. Whipple's double glanced up from his task. "Can I help you find something?"

"I was looking for Amanda," Tamara said, smiling uneasily.

"She's off today," the store clerk said. "Are you a friend?"

Tamara said she was.

"You might find her at her cabin."

"Thanks," Tamara said, feeling at once disappointed and

relieved—disappointed that she hadn't found Amanda, relieved that she didn't have to face her just yet.

Before leaving the store, she drifted down the baked goods aisle. Roy was stooped over, restocking the shelves. "Thank you," she whispered as she sidled by. Roy kept his head down and his attention focused on his work, but he was blushing so much that his face reminded Tamara of a candied apple.

Back outside, she headed down the pathway to the lakeshore, rehearsing in her head what she would tell Amanda when she got to the cabin. *I came back for my backpack. I need my purse—it has my ID in it. I'm sorry I didn't have a chance to say goodbye the other night . . .* Concentrating so intently on what to say, she was all the more surprised when she heard someone calling her name.

She glanced about, bewildered. Then she spotted Amanda waving at her from where she lay on a blanket spread out on the green that sloped down to the beach. She was wearing a red and white bikini, oversized sunglasses, and as Tamara discovered when she drew near, a lather of vanilla-scented suntan lotion. Tamara knelt down beside her.

Amanda sat up and gave her a greasy hug. "Tamara, we've been worried sick about you."

"Really?" Tamara said, having anticipated a greeting somewhere between cold shoulder and hissy fit.

Amanda pulled back and held her at arms length. "Of course we were. First you leave without saying a word. Then you refuse to take our calls—according to that brother of yours anyway. And then—" Her eyes widened. "Tamara, you've had your baby." Her surprised look instantly dissolved into an expression of pity. "Oh, sweetie, you must be devastated about Jimmy."

Tamara felt suddenly off balance, as if the earth had tilted a few degrees. "What about Jimmy?"

Amanda cupped a hand over her mouth. "Oh, Tamara, don't you know?" she said, uncovering her lips. "It was in the paper several days ago. Some loggers found his body in the hills."

"Body?"

Tamara felt her head lolling on her shoulders. "Body?" she repeated, her mind refusing to assign the obvious meaning to the word. But she got the message anyway, from that part of her brain that understood in the absence of reason. The expression on Amanda's face had said it all: *Here's another Chance card that is going to cost you dearly.*

She opened her mouth, tried to breath. She needed air, but her lungs didn't seem to know it. She looked at Amanda, who was floating in a mist now. She wondered why Amanda was leaning, why she had her arms outstretched as if to catch something. *Why can't I breathe?*

Then the mist thickened and blocked out all the light.

66

POOR KID, AMANDA thought as she lay in bed listening to the whimpering coming from across the room. Losing her baby like that. Then Jimmy getting killed—*awful*—and the police saying he was murdered—*awful, awful.* No wonder she's having nightmares.

This was Tamara's third night with her and Tommy, and it had unfurled the same as the previous two. Around eleven o'clock they'd turned out the lights and gone to bed blanketed only by moon shadows. After repeatedly fending off Tommy's groping advances, Amanda had finally managed to fall asleep. Then sometime after midnight she'd awakened to Tamara's agonized moans. By then, Tommy had sunk into manly slumber from which the roar of an avalanche wouldn't rouse him.

When the whimpering grew shrill—shriller even than the nights before—Amanda got out of bed and groped her way over to the couch. She stood over Tamara's twitching frame, unsure of what to do. Then Tamara cried out, sounding as if she was fighting for possession of her soul. Amanda reached down and shook her. "Tamara, wake up. It's okay."

Tamara's body quaked. Her eyelids flared open, revealing eyes drenched with dread.

"The same dream?" Amanda said.

Tamara nodded.

Amanda sat down on the couch and brushed clots of sweat-dampened hair away from Tamara's face. "You poor girl."

They were quiet for a time. In the brittle stillness, Tommy's breathing sounded like that of a hibernating bear.

"I'm afraid to close my eyes again," Tamara said.

"Would it help if I lay with you for a while?"

Tamara clutched her hand. "Would you?"

"Scoot over."

There was hardly enough room on the couch for one person, but somehow Tamara made a space for her, and the two of them lay cupped together like lovers, sharing the warmth of their bodies and that special comfort one can only experience through close physical contact with another person.

Amanda stayed awake long enough to feel Tamara's body go slack. Then she too relaxed and began drifting off. At one point she awakened to the pull of Tommy's voice. "Amanda, come back to bed," he was saying.

But Tamara seemed to be sleeping so peacefully that Amanda didn't want to disturb her by getting up. "Shut up and go back to sleep," she whispered into the dark.

Tommy mumbled something incoherent. The bed springs squawked in support of his complaint.

~

WHEN TAMARA AWOKE the next morning, having gotten her first real sleep in weeks, she was immediately hit with the scent of frying food. So thick and cloying was the aroma that, instead of quickening her taste buds, it made her stomach clench. She sat up squinting toward the sunlight flooding in through the kitchen window.

Amanda was standing in front of the stove with a spatula in her hand. Something was sizzling in a pan on the stovetop. Tamara glanced around the cabin. Tommy was nowhere in sight. "Who you cooking for?" she said.

Amanda flashed her a look of intent. "You need a good breakfast. You've eaten next to nothing since you got here."

Tamara grunted, got up from the sofa, and shuffled into the bathroom. It was true. She'd eaten very little since the morning she'd pigged out on Hostess sweets. Her body—like a bored lover—had simply lost interest in food.

By the time Tamara finished in the bathroom and got dressed, Amanda was done cooking. "Come to the table," she said.

"I'm not hungry," Tamara told her.

"Hungry or not, you need to eat something."

Tamara watched with dismay as Amanda scooped a large helping of scrambled eggs from a skillet onto a plate. She added a mound of fried potatoes, several sausage links, and toast. She handed Tamara the heaped plate. Tamara clapped a hand to her stomach. "I don't think I can—"

"Just try. Please."

Tamara didn't want to appear ungrateful. She took the plate, sat down at the table and waited while Amanda loaded a plate for herself—but not nearly as full.

"Dig in," Amanda said, bringing her food to the table and plopping down in a chair.

Tamara poked at the scrambled eggs with a fork, coming away with a morsel of yellow on the tines. She put it in her mouth and pushed it around with her tongue. "This is great," she said.

Amanda made a face. "No it isn't. I'm a lousy cook."

Tamara was suddenly in tears and didn't know why.

Amanda looked startled. She came around the table, helped Tamara out of her chair, and guided her back to the couch. "It's okay," she said, apparently blaming herself for Tamara's breakdown. "You don't have to eat my lousy cooking."

"It's not that," Tamara said. She didn't know what it was. She only knew that her life had spun out of control and she didn't know what to do about it.

Amanda sat down beside her on the sofa, put an arm around her, told her everything was going to be all right.

Tamara knew otherwise. "What am I going to do?" she said. "I've lost my baby. And I've lost Jimmy. Now I'll never have anyone to love me."

"That's not true."

"It is," Tamara insisted. "No one loves me—I have nowhere to go—I'm sixteen years old and my life is over."

"Your life is not over," Amanda insisted. "And you can stay here with me and Tommy as long as you like."

"But—"

"No buts," Amanda said.

Tamara sniffed, tried to smile, but the muscles in her face wouldn't cooperate, and that made her feel all the worse. She didn't even know how to smile anymore.

Amanda got her some tissues so she could blow her nose.

"Do I have to eat any more?" Tamara asked.

Amanda laughed. "No." She wriggled her nose. "Do I?"

They both laughed. But Tamara was still sick at heart, so she laughed and she cried.

Later, after calming down, she helped Amanda clean up in the kitchen. Amanda had made a dreadful mess. They were just finishing up when there came a knock at the cabin door.

Tamara froze, immediately thinking of Gary. She hadn't told Amanda about the assault or about her recently formed suspicions that Gary might have had something to do with Jimmy's death.

"Come in," Amanda hollered.

A scream rose in Tamara's throat. The door opened and Kurt appeared. The scream died away.

"Someone's been cooking," Kurt said, sniffing the air like a bloodhound.

Not wanting him to see that she was trembling, Tamara grabbed a towel and began drying the dishes that had been washed.

"You want the leftovers?" Amanda said. "We have lots of them."

"No thanks," Kurt said. "I ate already." Then he stood there with his hands in his pockets, like a boy at his first dance. "I came to talk to Tamara."

"Talk away," Tamara said, trying to sound breezy.

Kurt looked at Amanda as if seeking encouragement. She prompted him with a get-on-with-it motion of her hands. Finally he found his tongue again. "The lodge manager wants to know if you want a job."

Tamara almost dropped the plate in her hand. "Here? At the lake?"

"Uh, huh," Kurt said. "It wouldn't pay much, but it would come with room and board."

Tamara had to wait a moment for her mind to expand enough to make room for this astounding offer. She knew that, despite Amanda's declaration to the contrary, she couldn't stay with her and Tommy much longer, not without causing a terrible breach between the two of them. She'd almost decided that, like it or not, she'd have to go back to Eugene—to her mother's house. Her mother wouldn't balk at Tamara's coming home as long as she didn't bring a baby with her. But a chance to stay at the lake, at least for the rest of the summer, sounded wonderful. Maybe they could get Angela up here yet.

"Yes," she said. "I'd like a job." She didn't ask doing what, and Kurt didn't say.

67 RUSSELL TROUSTE SETTLED into his leather armchair in the quiet of the library at Trouste House, sipped his whiskey, and smiled. Life was good again. He'd been back at work full time for almost two weeks now and he could feel the sap flowing in his veins.

Today had been a very good day at the mill. In the morning, he and his timber manager had taken a helicopter tour of the Black Mountain tract, on which logging would soon begin: twenty-million board feet of mostly old-growth timber—enough to keep the mill going for several months. After lunch, he'd met with representatives of a Japanese building consortium looking to import American lumber. Considering the recent lull in the housing market in the U.S. and the resultant dip in lumber prices, the exploration of profitable overseas markets made good business sense.

He took another satisfying sip from his glass. Even things at home were settling into a comfortable routine. Having a baby around the house would take some getting used to, but in a way it made things easier for him because it kept Margaret occupied. And the young girl, Vera, was turning out to be quite a find. She was great with Felicity and seemed to know how to handle his wife better than he did. She wasn't afraid of hard work either, freely pitching in to give Elena a hand with the cooking and the cleaning.

A noise at the interior doorway caught his attention. Margaret swept into the room with Felicity in her arms. "It's time to kiss your daughter goodnight," she said, as if she were a dormitory matron enforcing house rules. She bent down and held the child out in front of him, while showing no willingness to let go.

That was fine with Russell. He still felt awkward holding the child. It was as if his arms were one mechanical part and the child another, and the two parts didn't fit together. He leaned forward and kissed Felicity lightly on the cheek.

She looked up at him without any recognition in her gaze, seeing him but obviously not comprehending. He was merely another fixture in her slowly widening world.

Margaret straightened, snuggled Felicity to her breast. "We're going to a birthday party tomorrow."

"Oh?"

"Loraine Dalton's daughter, Camille, is turning one year old."

"A birthday party for a one-year-old?"

"No, silly—for the mothers," Margaret said, and glided out of the room.

Russell was contemplating what mothers did at a birthday party for a one-year-old, when the telephone rang. He reached over the arm of his chair and plucked the receiver from its base.

"Can you talk?" Brandon said without preliminaries.

"Hold on." Russell got up and closed the interior door to the library. "What's up?" he said, seated again with the phone to his ear.

"I just got a call from our Mr. Neaves," Brandon said.

"And?"

"He wants more money."

Russell groaned. "Damn, Brandon, you assured me this guy wouldn't cause any trouble. Especially after we upped the payment once already."

"I guess I was wrong."

Russell rubbed his forehead. "Not your fault the guy is greedy," he said, doing his best to rein in his displeasure. "How much more does he want?"

"Another five thousand."

Russell deliberated on that for a moment, assessing it the way he would any other business deal. Considering how well things had turned out, Neaves' fee—including another five thousand—was a bargain. "He wants cash again, I suppose."

"You suppose correct."

Russell exhaled. "Okay. We'll give it to him. I'll have it for you tomorrow. But you tell him, that's all. No more."

"I'll tell him, but I don't know if he'll listen."

Russell Trouste was old school. He'd come up in a business world where a man's word was his bond and a handshake sealed an agreement. The thought of this guy coming back time and again, squeezing him for more money, rankled him. He swallowed the foul taste of bile in his mouth. "He'd better listen," he said, and hung up the phone.

When he picked up his drink from the side table, Russell found that his hand was shaking. He swirled the remaining liquid around in the glass and downed it. He got up to refill the glass, his wellspring of happiness displaced by a fomenting agitation.

68 TAMARA LIFTED THE LID to the washing machine, reached in, and grabbed a fistful of soggy towels that seemed ten times heavier than when she'd loaded them into the machine twenty minutes earlier. She hoisted the towels over the rim of the washer and dropped them into the wire basket on wheels. When that

washer was empty, she shoved the wire basket over to the next one, which had shut off as well, and began emptying it. A third washer, filled with linen, had just entered its first rinse cycle. Tamara had already learned to tell each cycle by the sound the washers made. If she had any doubts, the little lights on top of each machine kept her informed.

She rolled the heaped basket across the aisle to one of the dryers, swung open its door that had a window like a porthole, and began feeding the damp towels into its speckled metal belly. One of the other house-keeping girls came crashing through the swinging double doors into the laundry room pushing a big canvas bin brimming with dirties.

"Didn't want you to run out," Charlene said, way too perkily. She parked the bin behind the others that were lined up like a train of boxcars and left as abruptly as she'd entered.

Tamara blew a wisp of hair out of her face, wiped a droplet of sweat off the end of her nose. She stuffed the last of the wet towels into the dryer and shut the door. When she twisted a knob above the door, the big drum inside the dryer began to turn. Through the porthole she could see the towels tumbling end over end. Around and around they went, in an endless circle, like a dog chasing its tail.

Tamara's job at the lodge was pure drudgery. She was the newest member of the housekeeping crew, which meant that she was the new laundry girl, because that was where all the girls in housekeeping started. It was a job no one seemed to want, not for long anyway. The previous laundry girl had happily accepted a reassignment to room-cleaning duties, which was considered a promotion if for no other reason than it got you out of the lodge basement, where the laundry room was located.

Tamara didn't like the job either, not because it was in the basement but because all the bending and lifting made her back ache. But she was determined to stick with it, at least for now. It provided her with a place to stay and meals. Besides, the hours of physical exertion usu-ally left her too exhausted at the end of the day to think about all the bad things that had happened to her recently. And she'd been having fewer nightmares since she'd been working.

Even so, there were moments in a day or in the middle of the night when she'd find herself reliving a painful event as if no more time had passed since then than it took for a single breath. She'd be shuffling linen from the washers to a dryer and, for no reason she could think of, find herself doubled over in agony from the loss of her child. Or she would awaken in bed in the dark, stirred by a loud car in the parking lot or voices in the hallway outside her room, and sense Gary's nude body hovering over her. "Get out! I have a knife!" she would scream before orienting herself in time and place.

But having the job helped. It planted her feet in the present, helped her keep her head above the dark waters of her past. And every day that she didn't feel as though she was drowning in the past brought her one day closer to believing that she might actually have a future.

She stretched her back and glanced up at the clock on the wall, the face of which was imbedded in a wood carving in the shape of an owl. It was approaching eleven-thirty—as if the owl gave a hoot.

She sighed, went over and towed the next bin of dirties to the washing machines. Three more hours, give or take. Most days she was done by two-thirty or three o'clock in the afternoon, depending on when the last batch of soiled linen arrived. She'd eat a late lunch, then go up to her room and crash.

It wasn't much of a room—a cubbyhole on the second floor of the main lodge building, on the parking lot side. Tamara thought it might once have been a janitor's storage closet. It had built-in shelves and smelled of musty mops. A small fixed window on the outside wall had frosted glass that allowed in little light. There was no kitchen or bath. To relieve herself and for personal hygiene she used the public restrooms. The one down by the beach had a shower for swimmers and sunbathers to wash off the sand, the lotion, and the sweat—cold water only. She took quick showers wearing an old bathing suit Amanda had given her.

Her meals she ate in the lodge dining room, at a corner table by the kitchen, used mostly by the staff. Some evenings she didn't bother going down for dinner, she was so tired. She'd stay in bed until the next morning, getting up just in time to eat breakfast and make it down to the laundry by nine-thirty, by which time the bins of dirties would have begun arriving. This was now her daily routine, every day except Wednesday, her day off. Even the laundry girl got a day off.

When the next Wednesday rolled around, Tamara slept well into the morning. She awoke with a start, thinking she'd overslept and was late for work. She was up and dressed, swearing at the hands on her watch as she ran a brush through her hair, before realizing it was her day off. The realization made her spirits plummet: She would have to fill her day with something other than mindless labor.

She used the public restroom on the second floor, then went downstairs. She was too late for breakfast but didn't care—she wasn't hungry. She went outside, hoping to chase away the gloom that had already begun to darken her thoughts.

The sun hung dazzling in a cloudless sky, and the lodge grounds bustled with vacationers wanting to take advantage of the dwindling days of summer before school started again. On the grassy slope leading down to the lake, families had staked out their claim to picnic areas, marking them with big coolers, thermal jugs, and blankets spread out on the ground, so numerous as to form a patchwork like a giant quilt on the green. Down at the beach, pink-legged children in bathing suits splashed about in the shallows near the shore, while their parents lounged on colorful beach towels close at hand. Tamara heard the gleeful shrieks of the children and knew instantly that she didn't want to be alone and at loose ends today.

She glanced toward the lodge store. Amanda would be busy with customers all day. There wasn't any use in hanging around there. She released a heavy breath and headed down to the dock.

Kurt was in a rental boat tethered halfway down the dock, showing a man whose wife had yet to venture into the boat how to operate the outboard motor. The motor was running at a slow idle, its exhaust coughing up blue smoke.

Tamara felt some of the morning's tension drain from her as she listened to Kurt giving the man instructions. "Forward—neutral— reverse," he was saying. He moved the gearshift lever to each position in turn, eliciting a low clunk from the motor with each change of gear.

"Make sure to idle down before you switch gears, otherwise it'll die on you."

"Got it," the man said.

Kurt stepped out of the boat and helped the wife in. The boat rocked precariously when both the man and his wife shifted to the same side at the same time. They quickly realized their mistake and centered themselves before sitting on the bench seats, the wife in front and her husband in the rear, within easy reach of the motor's controls.

Kurt untied the rope securing the boat to the dock, coiled it into the bow of the boat. The man gripped the motor's control, switched the gearshift lever to reverse, and slowly throttled up. The boat began easing away from the dock. When it was far enough away, the man shifted the gear lever to forward. But he'd forgotten to power down. The motor gave a loud clunk and died. The man grimaced.

"It's okay," Kurt called. "Happens all the time. Just do what I showed you: move the gearshift to neutral and give a tug on the pull cord."

The motor started again on the second pull. With it idling, the man shifted into forward gear and, grinning now, throttled up. The boat rose at the bow and began skimming across the water, out toward the middle of the lake.

Kurt turned to Tamara. "Haven't seen much of you in the last couple of weeks."

"I've been sleeping a lot," she said, feeling suddenly self-conscious. "I'm not used to working so hard."

"Takes time," Kurt said.

They watched the boat with the man and his wife in it slowly diminish in size.

"I've been wanting to thank you for getting me the job."

Kurt let out a nervous laugh. "I didn't know whether you'd want to thank me or strangle me after you did it for a while. It's lousy work. That's why it was available." He picked up his trash bucket. "Besides," he said, moving down the dock to where another rental boat was tethered, "all I did was tell Dad about you. He's the one who talked to the manager of the lodge."

Tamara walked beside him. "Then thank him for me."

Kurt nodded. "I will." He climbed into the boat and started picking up trash from the bottom and dumping it into his bucket.

"Don't you ever get tired of cleaning boats?" she asked.

Kurt shrugged. "If I wasn't doing this, what else would I be doing?"

"I can think of a lot of things."

"Do they pay money and allow me to be on the lake?"

Tamara didn't have a ready answer to the question and was glad to have their conversation interrupted at this point by the noise of a bigger, private boat coming in off the lake. The boat's engine let out a deep rumble then quieted as its driver powered down, allowing the craft to glide up alongside the dock. A moment later, the dock shuddered in reaction to the boat's wake.

"Hey, Kurt," the boat's driver hollered.

"Mr. Westerly," Kurt hollered back. "How goes it?"

"Great. Limited out," Mr. Westerly said. "And now it's Miller time."

"Got that right," said one of the fishermen in the boat whose beer belly attested to his priorities.

"But thought you'd want to know," Mr. Westerly said, "you got a boat broken down out there. About a hundred yards out from Dingle Cove. Two old guys in it doing their best to get around using their oars. They were huffing pretty good. I told them just to drop anchor and that I'd let you know where they were. Would have towed them in, but they insisted on staying out. Said if they came back to the lodge, their wives would want to go shopping in town. Said they'd rather row."

Kurt waved. "Thanks, Mr. Westerly."

The boat's big engine growled as its skipper urged it ahead toward the boat ramp.

"Guess I better go tell Dad," Kurt said. He stepped up onto the dock. "Want to go?"

"Where?"

"Out on the lake with me to rescue those guys."

Tamara felt a bubble of gratitude expand inside her to the extent that she thought it might actually lift her off the dock. She wasn't going to have to face the day alone after all. She smiled for the first time since waking up that morning.

69

TAMARA CARRIED THE bulky orange life vests out of the boat rental office, while Kurt lugged a tool box and a can of gas. Back on the dock, Kurt loaded his gear into one of the rental boats, then gave her a hand getting in.

"Like this," he said, taking one of the vests and putting it on.

She donned hers. It sloshed on her shoulders.

"Needs to be snug," Kurt said. He reached over and cinched a strap on her vest.

"I can't breathe," she said, experiencing a moment of panic.

He loosened the strap. "Better?"

She expanded her chest, nodded.

Dingle Cove was on the opposite side of the lake from the lodge. It was approaching noon when they set out at a brisk clip across the water, the boat's motor wailing like a child throwing a tantrum. Tamara tilted her head back, filled her lungs with moist, tangy air. From her position in the bow of the boat, she had an unobstructed view of the far shore, where only a pale strand of beach separated the glistening bowl of water from the dense forest beyond. In the background, the mountain pinnacles looked like cardboard cutouts against the deep blue sky.

Tamara could remember only one other time when she'd been out in a boat. It was on a sixth-grade whale-watching trip out of Newport. The boat was much bigger than this metal tub. It had a bathroom and a snack bar. A voice on a loudspeaker lectured all the children about the migrating habits of the world's largest mammals. They didn't actually see any whales that day other than on a movie screen on the boat's lower deck. But she could still recall the sense of freedom she'd felt being on the ocean. It was so vast and open, so uncluttered by obstacles. So unlike life. Mohler Lake wasn't the ocean, but it seemed a lot bigger being out on it, and the farther removed they got from the shore, the more that feeling of freedom came back to her, like the loosening of a knot at her center.

She heard a knocking noise behind her and looked back. With his free hand, Kurt was pointing toward a larger boat passing off to their left. Then he moved his palm in a wavy horizontal line. Tamara didn't understand at first. Not until she saw the other boat's wake coming toward them, and Kurt was turning their boat into it.

The bow of the boat began skipping up and down, and she along with it. Every time the boat's underside clapped against a wave, a cool spray of water shot up over the railing and slapped her in the face. She snorted, wiped her nose and mouth on her shirtsleeve. Behind her, Kurt was laughing. She laughed too, and it was an odd feeling to laugh, but a good one.

They passed several other boats after that, and she got sprayed some more. By the time they were within sight of Dingle Cove, her front side was soaked and she was thinking that wearing a life vest had been a good idea in more ways than one.

"Looks like them over there," Kurt said, nodding toward a lone boat bobbing on the water off to their right. He pulled his boat alongside the stranded craft and cut the engine.

The two old guys in the rental boat didn't seem too concerned with their plight. "Hey, Joe," one of them said, "I think the Coast Guard has arrived."

"Sorry about the breakdown," Kurt said. "What seems to be the problem?"

"No problem, son," Joe said. "But we might need help finding Arnie's arm. It fell off after the fiftieth pull on the starter rope. Don't know what happened to it."

The two men must have rehearsed this routine, because Arnie had his right arm tucked inside his shirt, with the empty sleeve dangling. He reached with his other arm into the bottom of the boat. "Here it is," he said, pulling the hidden arm out from under the tail of the shirt. "Now if I can just get it reattached."

Joe was laughing, and Kurt and Tamara laughed too as Arnie pretended to reattach his arm.

"Had me worried there for a minute," Joe said. "I thought maybe we'd been chumming with your fingers all this time and didn't know it."

"Probably do better with my fingers than with that stink-bait you brought."

Kurt let the little drama play out, apparently not wanting to spoil the old guys' fun. "What I'd like to do," he finally said, "is to tie off stern to bow and bow to stern and shift you two into this boat. Then you can be on your way, and I can work on the dead motor."

"Fair enough," Arnie said. "We'll even leave you the oars."

"Thanks," Kurt said. "We might need them."

"Your helper here looks pretty strong," Joe said, winking at Tamara.

"Maybe I'll go with you guys," Tamara said, teasing.

Joe brightened. "Now that would be some catch to take home to the wife." And the two old men whooped it up good.

Kurt got busy tying off the two boats. He directed the transfer of the gear and bodies between them with the expertise of a dance choreographer. Arnie started the rescue boat motor without his arm falling off again, and the two old guys prepared to motor off. "Last chance to get out of rowing, young lady," Joe said.

Tamara sighed with mock concern. "I guess I'll just have to risk it."

"If you're not in by dark, we'll send out a search party."

"You do that."

Kurt was already engaged in checking out the dead motor when the old guys puttered away, but not in the direction of the lodge.

"Can you fix it?" Tamara asked.

"Don't know," Kurt said. "I was hoping it was just out of gas, but the tank is more than half full." He pulled the starter cord a couple times to no avail. He held the throttle full open and yanked on the cord a couple more times. "Not flooded."

Tamara sat there quietly observing as Kurt inspected the motor, the boat swaying gently beneath them. "There's gas in the line," he said at one point. "Whether it's getting to the carburetor is another question." He fished a screwdriver out of his toolbox and began removing the motor's housing.

"How do you know so much about boats and motors?"

"It's my life," Kurt said without the slightest hesitation.

Tamara felt a twinge of envy. Kurt was so sure of himself. Not in a cocky way, but in the way people have when they know exactly what they want out of life and go about achieving it. So, what was her life?

She slumped forward in response to a sudden ache in her breast. Her baby was to have been her life. But that too had been taken from her. Now her life was nothing more than a laundry cart full of soiled memories and useless motion. Was she destined to end up like her mother—lifeless, loveless—all but succumbing to the one great tragedy in her life?

"Ah ha!" Kurt said. "I don't know how that happened."

"What?" Tamara said, shaking off her moment of self-absorption.

"Fuel line got kinked just ahead of the carburetor. No gas was getting through." He dipped into his tool box for another tool and began making the necessary adjustments.

"That was it?" she said, watching him reattach the motor's housing.

"We'll see." He dropped his tools into the toolbox, snapped it closed. He gave a tug on the starter cord. And another. On the third pull, the motor started.

Tamara clapped and cheered.

The revving motor spewed a swirling column of smoke and fumes. Kurt throttled it down and left it idling while he hauled in the anchor.

"Guess we won't need the oars after all," he said, obviously pleased with himself.

With the anchor stowed, he motioned for Tamara to join him in the rear of the craft. She stood up and baby-stepped her way toward him, staying on a center line so as not to rock the boat. She sat down beside him on the rear bench seat.

"Put your hand here," he said, taking her hand and resting it on the motor's control handle. He wrapped his hand around hers, and she experienced an unexpected quickening, as if she'd been connected to an outside source of energy. The feeling was both delicious and troubling, like the last bite of the last candy bar.

"When you turn the throttle this way," Kurt said, "the motor powers up." His hand tightened around hers as he rotated the handle. The noise coming from the motor changed from a steady, low-pitched prattle to a banshee scream. He twisted the handle in the opposite direction. The motor quieted.

"The transmission is in neutral now." He pointed to the gearshift lever. "Slide it this way to go forward. The opposite way to go in reverse. Always with the motor idling."

Again he squeezed her hand that was on the throttle. "To steer the boat, you simply pivot the handle side to side the way you would the tiller on a rudder." He guided her hand through the range of steering motion. "Ready?"

Tamara wasn't at all sure that she was.

Kurt didn't give her a chance to decline. He moved to the front bench and sat down, facing her. "Now, with the motor idling, put the transmission in forward gear." She reached up and moved the gearshift lever the way he'd showed her. The engine bucked slightly and made a little clunking sound. "Now, power up."

She twisted the throttle. The boat began moving, but in a circular path.

"Straighten her out."

Tamara swiveled the control handle the way she thought she needed to in order to make the boat straighten out. Instead of straightening, the boat began moving in a tighter circle.

"Moving forward," Kurt instructed, "pivot the handle in the opposite direction you want to head."

Tamara reversed the action on the control, bringing the boat out of its tight arc. Then she played with the steering mechanism, aiming the craft first one way then another, until she got the hang of how it worked.

Kurt stretched his legs out in front of him. He raised an arm and circled his forefinger in the air. "Helmsman, ferry us home."

Tamara brought the boat around, headed it toward the lodge, and cautiously powered up. The boat pushed through the water at a deliberate pace. She smiled, feeling a rush of satisfaction. She was actually driving a boat. She was in control of something. It was a start.

70   DR. CASTLE TURNED THE KEY in the ignition and listened to his car's starter struggle to turn the engine over. He'd cranked it so many times in the last few minutes that the battery had all but died. The damned car was not going to start. He gaveled a fist down on the rim of the steering wheel and swore. "Forty-thousand-dollar piece of junk." He might as well have saved himself thirty thousand and bought a Volkswagen.

He got out of the Mercedes and flung the door closed. It had been another long day of doctoring, first seeing patients at his office and then making evening rounds at the hospital. It was after eight-thirty, and all he wanted to do was get home and crash. But now he would have to go back into the hospital and call AAA. No telling how long it would take to get someone out to look at the car.

He trudged across the dimly lit parking lot, his hunched frame casting an amorphous shadow that slunk among the parked cars like a ghost playing hide and seek. As he reached the driveway between the parking lot and the hospital, a red pickup came out of nowhere and pulled to a stop in front of him, blocking his path. Its passenger door sprang open and a big lug of a fellow tumbled out, leaving the door agape. A voice from inside the truck said, "Need a lift, Doc?"

It was Gary Neaves.

The doctor's legs went rubbery. He reeled backwards. "No, thanks," he said, working to regain his balance. "I'll manage." He turned to walk around the rear of the pickup and found his way obstructed by the big man who'd just exited the truck.

"He asked real nice, Doc," the hulking figure said. "I think you should go with him."

Dr. Castle's gut tightened. His face began to burn. He wheeled around and stepped up to the truck's open passenger door, but with no intention of getting in. "Look here, Neaves. What is this all about?"

Neaves ignored him. "Jerome," he said to the big man outside, "I think maybe the good doctor needs some assistance."

"I certainly do not."

But even before the words were out of his mouth, the doctor found himself in the grasp of two meaty arms that hoisted him up and deposited him into the cab of the truck as if he were a child being placed in a booster seat.

"This is outrageous," he said, aiming to get right back out of the truck. It was too late. The door had been closed and the pickup was rolling.

"Don't fret, Doc," Neaves said. "Jerome will have your car fixed in no time." His lips curled into a crooked smile. "Probably just a loose spark plug wire or something."

The doctor glared at him. "This is kidnapping, you know." He jabbed an accusing finger at Neaves, but his hand was shaking so he put it down.

Neaves laughed. "Whatever you say, Doc." He steered the truck out of the hospital parking lot and headed south.

"Listen here, Neaves—"

"Shut up, Doc," Neaves said, any trace of humor gone from his voice.

The doctor felt the blood drain from his face. Sweat trickled from his armpits.

Three blocks down, at the traffic signal, Neaves turned east onto Mill Street. Out of the corner of his eye, the doctor could see Neaves' stern visage in profile, illumined intermittently by a street lamp or by the headlights of an oncoming car, and each glimpse of it sent a dark sense of apprehension rushing through his mind.

Neither of them spoke as Neaves steered the truck through the freeway underpass and then over the river via the Mill Street Bridge. Just after leaving the bridge, he slowed and veered onto the narrow lane that angled down into Millsite Park. Partway down the lane, he cranked the steering wheel hard to the right.

The truck hit a curb, bucked violently going over it, and lurched down an embankment. The doctor's stomach was suddenly in his throat. His body flopped around like a test dummy, his arms outstretched, reaching for handholds that weren't there. The vehicle cut a path across a stretch of lawn before leveling off and coming to an abrupt stop in the gravel underneath the massive steel and concrete framework of the Mill Street Bridge.

Neaves switched off the truck's headlights and everything went black, inside the truck and out. In the instant before the lights went out, Dr. Castle thought he glimpsed several human forms scampering in different directions under the bridge. Then the cab of the truck filled with dust and he was bent over, coughing.

A dim figure appeared at the truck's partially open driver's window. "Hey mister," a young male voice said, "you buying or selling?"

"Beat it, pothead," Neaves said.

"Asshole," the kid muttered, and walked away.

The doctor's eyes were adjusting to the dearth of light, and now he could see several other murky figures assembling outside the truck. They huddled momentarily, then moving as a group, amoeba-like, vanished into the darkness.

Neaves remained quiet, facing straight ahead, his hands resting on the lower rim of the steering wheel.

Dr. Castle could feel his pulse thudding in his neck. His mouth was dry. There was a needling pain between his shoulder blades. "What do you want from me, Mr. Neaves?" he said in a subdued voice intended not to rile his abductor.

Neaves didn't say anything, but when his hands came off the steering wheel, the doctor recoiled.

There was a flare of light. Neaves lit a cigarette. Smoke filled the air space between them. "I figured we needed to have a little heart-to-heart about my pension," Neaves said.

The doctor feigned ignorance. "I don't know what you're talking about."

"I'm talkin' about a thousand dollars a month, every month."

The doctor clenched his jaw so hard his teeth hurt. "I told you before," he said, trying to project a calmness he didn't feel. "There will be no further payments."

"I think there will be," Neaves said with a derisive lilt to his voice. "Unless you want the cops to come knockin' on your door."

With the mention of the police, the doctor felt his mask of composure being ripped off to expose the ire that lay beneath. He lashed out. "And yours—" he said. "Are you prepared for that?"

Neaves flipped his cigarette out the window. The next instant he was shoulder to shoulder with the doctor, with a big hand clamped around the doctor's throat.

Dr. Castle was stunned, not only by the swiftness of the move but also by the overwhelming force behind it. His neck hurt like hell where Neaves' thumb and forefinger pressed into his flesh. He tried to speak—couldn't—could barely breathe.

"Don't ever threaten me, Doc," Neaves said in a whisper that seemed louder than a shout. "Now, like I said, a thousand dollars a month. That's what you'll see to it that I get paid, you piss-ant baby stealer. Or I'll personally break your fucking neck."

The doctor felt himself getting lightheaded, felt the pressure building inside his skull. He was sure the top of his head was going to blow off any moment.

Neaves released his grip. "Now get out," he growled.

Dr. Castle gasped for air. Lights flashed in his field of vision. He brought a hand to his throat, massaged it. "You're an asshole, Neaves," he heard himself say in a wheezy voice. He groped for the door handle.

"Yeah, and you're my money-bitch."

The doctor shoved the passenger door open. "Not anymore," he said, spitting out the words. He was a volcano of anger now and he erupted without thinking. "You'll not get another dime. I'll see to that." He slid out of the truck and onto the ground, his knees nearly buckling as his feet contacted the hard-packed gravel.

He held onto the door just long enough to gain his balance, then pivoted to slam it. Before the door left his hands, it came flying back at him, knocking him onto the ground. The hard landing jostled his senses, relieved him of what little breath remained in his lungs.

Confused, he gaped up and saw Neaves' booted feet projecting out the passenger doorway. The next thing he knew the guy was on top of him, slapping his face repeatedly—one side with the palm of his hand and the other side with the back of it. The doctor's eyeglasses flew off and went skittering across the gravel. He threw up his hands to ward off the stinging blows, but to little effect. The guy had seemingly gone mad.

Dr. Castle feared for his life, and the fear gave him strength he otherwise would not have had. Using a move reminiscent of his high school wrestling days, he whipped his legs, bucked his torso, and rolled to his right. Neaves, caught off guard and off balance, toppled left. The doctor kept rolling until he'd disengaged himself from his attacker. Then he scrabbled away, spikes of gravel biting into his palms and knees.

He didn't get far. Neaves had recovered quickly enough to get a handhold on his ankle. The doctor kicked the trapped leg as hard as he could. He couldn't break free. And all at once he was being dragged backwards across the serrated ground.

He walked on his hands in a backward wheelbarrow motion until his arms buckled and *bam!* his face slammed into the gravel. He felt his lip split open, tasted the warm, salty blood in his mouth. Disregarding the hurt, he twisted his body around and tried to kick Neaves with his free foot. But the guy merely brushed the foot aside. He got on top of the doctor again, pinning him to the ground, this time with both hands at his throat.

Dr. Castle flailed his arms and legs. It was a futile effort. He was overmatched. He tried to buck again with his lower body. When he did, Neaves hit him in the face with his fist.

The pain erupted white-hot in the doctor's brain. His entire body went flaccid, his arms flopping, useless, at his side. Neaves' powerful fingers encircled his neck, throttling him as effectively as a garrote. The doctor's incapacity to respond was total. He couldn't scream. He couldn't breathe. And he knew he couldn't stay conscious for long.

Lying there helpless, he felt his head grow bigger and bigger to the point where all it had left to do was explode. A funnel cloud of color and images swirled behind his eyes. There was a brilliant flash inside his brain, and from it streaked a million shards of light.

Then, mercifully, the pain left him. His body felt very light—free of the burden of gravity. In his mind, he saw Lily's face hovering above him—that beautiful face, so kind and reassuring as it smiled down at him. He wanted to reach up and touch that face, to cradle it. If only he could reach up and . . .

Vaguely Dr. Castle became aware of a smooth, cylindrical object under his right hand, and the touching of it brought him back from the brink of unconsciousness. He closed his fingers around the object, assessing its physical properties, and a strange clarity came over him. He adjusted the object in his hand. His thumb twitched purposefully. And in the shocking instant that followed, he could see, through his defective vision, one side of Neaves' face as it hung over him, glowing like a ghoulish jack-o-lantern, the one terrible eye filled with rage.

The doctor could move his forearm just enough. He brought it up so that his hand with the lit cigarette lighter in it rested against Neaves' side just above his belt.

The lighter did its work quickly. The cotton shirt began to smolder. Then it burst into flames.

Neaves looked down at his side, his eyes wide with amazement. He released his grip on the doctor's throat, lunged sideways, and began rolling across the ground trailing flames and smoke.

Dr. Castle's chest heaved as he panted and puffed. He rolled over and struggled to his knees. Neaves was writhing in the dirt about ten feet away. The doctor tried to stand, but he was too weak and dropped onto one knee, bracing himself with his hands.

Neaves was sitting up now, tearing off his shirt and swearing. "You're dead, you sonofabitch. Dead."

Releasing an anguished grunt, Dr. Castle pushed himself up off the ground and hobbled away. But in his confusion, he ran flush into the side-panel of the bed of Neaves' pickup. He clung to the side-panel, draped himself over it to keep from going down.

It was hopeless. He wasn't going to get away from this madman.

He couldn't even stand on his own, much less run, and already a shirt-less Neaves was on his feet and coming at him again. The man was going to kill him.

As the doctor continued gasping for air, he noticed that the air carried with it the distinct odor of gasoline. Impulsively he reached a hand down into the dark bed of the truck. There was nothing there but empty cargo space. He leaned farther into the bed, groped in a wider circle. His hand collided with a hard metal object. It had a round top and a handle.

Neaves was no more than a few steps away now, breathing hard and coming fast.

In desperation, the doctor grasped the handle of the metal object, lifted it out of the truck, and swung it around wildly in a sweeping arc.

The gas can hit Neaves flush across the bridge of the nose. He went down squealing, writhed in the gravel briefly, then passed out.

Dr. Castle stood trembling over Neaves' inert body. He peered down at the fellow, wanting to assess his condition without getting too close. Blood was streaming from a long gash across Neaves' nose, but he was still breathing. Then he moaned and began to stir.

The doctor stumbled back, nearly falling. He tossed the gas can aside and began groping his way out from under the bridge.

71   THE NEXT MORNING, Dr. Castle could hardly get out of bed. His body felt as if it had passed through a meat tenderizer. His nerves felt permanently jangled. He only vaguely recalled staggering out from under the Mill Street Bridge the night before and making his halting way back to the hospital parking lot. Thank God his car had started and he'd found a spare pair of eyeglasses, however outdated, in his glove box. How could he have allowed himself to get mixed up with the likes of that hooligan Neaves?

He managed to slip into a bathrobe and, moving gingerly, went into the kitchen to put on some water for tea. Hot tea was about the only thing that sounded palatable. His body was scraped and bruised on the outside. Inside it felt like mush.

He squinted at the clock on the stove. It was just after seven-thirty.

While the water was heating, he used the phone at the breakfast bar to call Marion at home and tell her to have Doris cancel all his appointments for the next two days. Today was Thursday; that would get him to the weekend. By Monday he should be doing well enough to go back to work.

Marion, who apparently assumed the doctor was suffering from fatigue, was all sympathy. "Don't worry about a thing," she said. "We'll have Dr. Reyes cover your emergencies. You just get some rest."

When the water was hot, Dr. Castle filled a mug and dunked a tea bag. He took the steaming tea into his bedroom and sipped it while perched on the edge of his bed. Then he set the cup down on the nightstand and fell back onto his pillow, quickly drifting off to sleep again.

He slept most of that day and the next day as well, getting out of bed only to eat a bowl of soup once and some oatmeal another time, and whenever he could no longer hold his bladder. By the second evening, he was feeling better—rested anyway—even though his body still ached from head to toe.

No longer in need of sleep, he propped himself up on a mound of pillows and read from a novel that had been sitting on his nightstand unopened for as long as he could remember. The story—a mystery involving the theft of priceless art—barely held his attention.

A few minutes before eleven, he put the book aside and turned on the television in the bedroom to watch the local news. The lead story was about the recovery of a body that had been discovered floating in the South Umpqua River, downstream from Millsite Park. The doctor was shocked when the reporter stated that the dead man had been identified as twenty-seven-year-old Gary Neaves of Fir Valley. A picture of Neaves flashed on the screen. The doctor stared at it in horror.

Unable to sleep now even if he'd wanted to, he spent the rest of that night and the following day dealing with competing urges. One minute he was convinced that he should get away from Fir Valley as quickly as possible—just get in his car and drive somewhere, anywhere. And the next minute, he was sure that the only sensible course of action was to turn himself in to the police. He hadn't meant to kill the guy. It was a classic case of self-defense.

But if he did go to the police, how could he explain what he'd been doing under the bridge with that scumbag in the first place? Would they believe he'd been the victim of an abduction and beating he hadn't reported until now? Not likely.

His ambivalence in the matter was deepened by several puzzling elements in the news report of Neaves' death. The last time he'd seen Gary Neaves, the fellow had been lying in the gravel near his truck, bleeding but alive. How had he ended up dead, in the river? Had he gotten to his feet and, staggering around in a daze, walked off the edge of a steep bank? Had the fall down the riverbank killed him? Had he drowned? And what about Gary's truck? There had been no mention of the truck. Surely it would have been found by the police.

Unable to convince himself of the rightness of a single course of action, the doctor acted on neither of his impulses, but instead kept to his bed and his regimen of tea and toilet.

By Sunday morning, he was heartened on a couple of accounts. His body was beginning to recover from the recent abuse it had taken, and no policeman had come knocking on his door. He donned his robe, went into the kitchen, and put on a pot of coffee. He was finally ready for some hard stuff.

With the coffee perking, he ventured onto the front porch and gathered up the newspapers that had accumulated there over the last several days. He dumped the papers onto the breakfast bar, sifted through them, and found the most current issue—the Sunday morning edition. He unfolded its front page. Just below the fold, under the headline "Investigation Continues into Death of Local Man," was a follow-up story on the death of Gary Neaves. Fear clutched at the doctor's throat as he sat down at the bar to read it.

When he finished the article, Dr. Castle laid the paper aside and took a deep, elating breath. According to this latest news report, Neaves' death was being investigated as an apparent homicide committed in the course of a drug deal gone bad. A sheriff's deputy had located Neaves' pickup truck abandoned on a logging road outside Canyonville, a small community to the south. Traces of marijuana had been found in a baggy discovered on the floorboard of the vehicle. That discovery, coupled with reports from various witnesses that the victim had been observed recently flashing big wads of cash around town despite having no known source of income, had fueled speculation regarding a possible drug connection. The investigation was continuing, but no suspects had yet been identified.

The coffeepot had finished perking. The doctor poured himself a cup and sipped from it while leisurely perusing the rest of the day's news.

When he arrived at his office the following morning, Dr. Castle was feeling better than he had in years. He'd had four uninterrupted days of rest, and Neaves' death, he'd decided, was an unexpected blessing.

72   DEPUTY RILEY WAS SITTING at the duty desk in the Fir Valley Sheriff's Substation, picking his teeth with the splintered end of a stir stick, when a gangly fellow with ears approaching the size of ping-pong paddles walked in through the front door, stepped up to the public access counter, and announced that he had a confession to make.

"About what?" Riley said, not bothering to get up. Hardly a shift went by without some nutcase coming into the office or calling on the telephone to confess to some misdeed. Sometimes the confessions were legitimate, although not very often and then almost always to minor infractions. But mostly the confessions were bogus, and for high-profile or invented crimes. Just the day before, a man had phoned in to confess that he, not Lee Harvey Oswald, had shot John F. Kennedy. Riley had recognized the guy's voice. He was a weirdo who lived in the rusted-out hull of a school bus parked out by Moyer's Pond. He was a regular contributor of phone-in confessions, although no one seemed to know how he accessed a telephone, since his less-than-humble abode wasn't connected to any services. Riley had inquired why he'd done it—killed JFK. "Jackie hired me," the fellow said. "I've been on the run ever since."

Riley didn't expect anything nearly as resourceful from the would-be confessor now standing on the other side of the counter looking as grim as a condemned killer facing a firing squad.

"I—I lied to one of your officers," the man said, his chin trembling.

"Oh?"

"He showed me a picture of a girl and asked me if I'd ever seen her. I told him I hadn't."

"But you had."

The fellow nodded, a hangdog look on his face.

Riley tossed his stir stick into the trashcan beside his desk. "You know the officer's name?"

"No, sir. If he said it, I don't remember."

"All right. Hang on a minute."

The deputy picked up the receiver to the inner-office phone and punched in an extension number. Hansen answered on the first ring. "Dan," Riley said, "wasn't Willard out the other day flashing around a photo of the Ames girl?"

"He was."

"In that case, there's a fellow up front you'll want to talk to."

~

"THIS THE GIRL you lied about not seeing?" Hansen said, holding up a picture of Tamara Ames for the man across the counter to view.

"That's her," the man said. "Am I in trouble?"

"We'll see," Hansen said, letting the guy stew in his own angst-ridden juices. He brought the fellow in through a side doorway and ushered him down the hall to one of the interview rooms. He gestured toward a slat-back chair on the far side of a small rectangular table. "Have a seat."

The contrite one sat.

Hansen took a seat opposite him. "What's your name?"

"Roy Severson."

Hansen leaned over the table and looked the fellow square in the eye. "Well now, Roy Severson, are you ready to tell the truth?"

"Yessir," Roy peeped, and proceeded to do just that.

Satisfied that the Hostess Bakery delivery driver had told him everything he knew about Tamara Ames and her possible whereabouts, Hansen let him off with a stern warning to never again lie to a public official, underscoring the admonition with a recitation of the penalty attached to such an offense.

"I can go then?" Roy said, apparently still unsure of his fate.

"You can go," Hansen said.

The fellow slunk out of the room.

The detective immediately went back to his office and got the manager of Mohler Lake Lodge on the phone. It was a productive call.

"She's living at the lodge," Hansen told his boss a few minutes later. "Working in the laundry room, although the manager wasn't sure for how much longer. Their summer season is winding down and they'll soon be cutting back on staff. Since she was only recently hired, she'll be among the first employees to be let go."

Iverson tipped back in his chair. "Then it looks like someone ought to get on up there and have a chat with the girl."

"Looks like," Hansen said, knowing who that someone was going to be.

IT WAS LATE AFTERNOON by the time the detective arrived at Mohler Lake, accompanied by a growing sense that this could well be the break he was looking for in his dual murder investigation. Ever since the second body had turned up, he'd put a much higher priority on locating Tamara Ames, who represented a direct link between the two murder victims. It was a good bet the girl knew something that would help move the investigation along—to say nothing of the fact that her disappearance was suspicious in and of itself.

Hansen parked his cruiser in a loading zone near the front entrance to the lodge and went inside. The lobby was deserted except for a Shelley Winters lookalike standing behind the registration counter glumly sorting through a stack of paperwork. The detective introduced himself.

"What can I do for you, detective?" the registration clerk said.

"Do you know where I might find Tamara Ames?"

The clerk glanced at her watch. "Try the dock."

Hansen felt a familiar prickling between his shoulder blades. Tamara Ames, he'd been told, worked in the laundry room. "Any particular reason you think she might be at the dock?"

The woman smiled coyly. "She seems to have taken a liking to boats."

"Ahhh," Hansen said, as if he knew exactly what the woman was talking about.

Back outside, he headed down to the lake along a stone path that bordered a grassy slope where scattered cliques of late-season lodgers lounged about on blankets or in Adirondack chairs, exposing themselves to the waning rays of a mid-September sun. Only a few hardy folks inhabited the beach area, and even fewer braved the water that nipped at the sandy shore.

Hansen followed the pathway around to a floating dock lined with small boats tugging gently at their mooring lines. All the boats appeared to be empty save one. In that one, tied out toward the end of the dock, sat two people facing each other.

A cool breeze spun off the lake, causing the detective's coattails to flap as he strolled the length of the dock. Upon approaching the occupied boat, he saw that the two people in it appeared to be teenagers—a boy and a girl. The girl's back was to the dock, with only her profile exposed to his view. The boy was sitting in the stern of the boat, facing the dock, with an open bag of pretzels between his legs. He looked over, expressionless, as Hansen neared.

Hansen, who preferred to dress in street clothes on the job, displayed his detective's badge. "I'm Detective Hansen with the Douglas County Sheriff's Office. I'm looking for Tamara Ames."

"What for?" the boy asked in a level voice.

The girl didn't turn around. It didn't matter. Hansen had seen enough of her profile to recognize her as the girl in the file photo. He put his badge away. "I'll tell her when I find her," he said, standing pat, allowing the weight of his official presence to settle on the young couple, content to let the action come to him, as he knew it eventually would.

A long moment of silence wound around itself. The dock creaked underfoot in response to a swell off the lake.

"So tell me," the girl finally said, still not bothering to face him.

"Miss Ames, can we talk privately?"

"This is private enough," the girl said.

Hansen glanced at the boy, whose expression remained placid even as his face—already darkly tanned—took on color. "Miss Ames," he said, "I'm investigating two homicides. I believe you knew both victims: Jimmy Stark and Gary Neaves."

73　　DESPITE HER SHOW OF CALM, Tamara felt as if the boat she was sitting in had sprung a leak and water was beginning to pool around her ankles. How had the cops found her? Nobody knew where she'd gone. Nobody but . . . A blast of heat shot up from her belly and turned her cheeks into smoldering coals. "You've wasted your time tracking me down."

"Maybe," the detective said. "Then again, maybe you know something useful to our investigation."

Tamara compressed her lips. "I don't see how."

"When was the last time you saw your stepbrother?"

Tamara gazed across the wrinkled surface of the water and sighed. She didn't want to think about Gary, or Jimmy, or anything that had happened before her return to the lake. The lake was her safe haven, her refuge from the past. She was just beginning to make a new life for herself here. She didn't want to go back, to reset the clock, to reopen a door that led only to her sorrow.

"Miss Ames," the detective said, "we can do this here or back at the sheriff's station in Fir Valley. Your choice."

Tamara jerked her head around and glowered at her interrogator, prepared to hate him, to defy him. What she saw surprised her. She'd envisioned a grim-faced hulk ready to do his best to intimidate her with gun and badge. What she found was an average-looking man in a brown suit, who could easily have been taken for a shoe salesman.

Her shoulders sagged. This man was going to take her back. He was going to make her remember. She felt a cold lump in the pit of her stomach. "Gary—" she said, and immediately unwanted images pressed against her mind. "Gary—last time I saw him was three or four weeks ago. He came home drunk one night and was—abusive."

"Abusive how?"

"How do you think?" she snapped.

Her response seemed to stop time, but only for a few ticks. Then the detective said, "What happened after that?"

Tamara stared at the bottom of the boat, chafing at the pointlessness of this interrogation. "I left his house and didn't go back," she said.

"You came up to the lake?"

"The next day. I—hitchhiked."

"Did you have any contact with Gary after that?"

"No."

"Do you know anything about his death?"

Tamara chewed on her lower lip as the truth bubbled up inside her. "Only that I wasn't broken up about it."

Kurt shuffled his feet. The boat quivered.

Tamara kept her eyes averted from him, wishing now that she'd taken the detective up on his offer of privacy.

The detective followed up with a few more questions about Gary, then turned his attention to Jimmy. Tamara hummed softly between responses, trying, like a child whistling in the dark, to distract herself from her true feelings.

"So you never saw Jimmy again after Gary ran him off that one night?"

She shook her head.

"You weren't surprised that he didn't come back?"

"*Hmmm* . . . not really. Gary scared him pretty good."

The detective went quiet then, and Tamara thought, *Okay, now go away and let me be.*

The detective said, "Tell me about the night your baby was born."

Tamara felt as if she'd been struck by lightning. She seemed to go deaf and blind for an instant. She struggled to get her next breath. When she tried to speak, her throat seemed melted closed. "Why do you want to know about that?" she finally managed to say. *And how do you even know about that night?*

The detective, as if reading her mind, answered both questions—the spoken and the unspoken. "A report was filed by one of our deputies regarding what occurred that night. But there are some things I don't understand."

Tamara jumped to her feet. "I don't want to talk about that night." Without thinking, she leaped out of the boat and onto the dock, leaving behind her a craft pitching chaotically with Kurt still in it, clinging to side railings. She brushed past the detective and rushed down the dock, her vision blurred by the tears now flooding her eyes. As she approached the shore end of the dock, she nearly bowled over Amanda.

"What's going on?" Amanda said, bracing herself to keep the two of them from tumbling off the dock and into the water.

"He's a cop," Tamara bawled, and sank into Amanda's arms.

"What does he want?"

But all Tamara could do was bury her face in Amanda's chest and sob.

"Miss Ames," the detective said as he came down the dock toward them. "I realize this is unpleasant for you. But we have two murders on our hands. You had contact with both victims just prior to their deaths. That makes you a material witness."

"But I don't know anything."

"Be that as it may, I have questions that need to be asked and answered, if not here, then in town."

"Come to the cabin," Amanda suggested. "You can talk there."

Tamara drew back just enough to make eye contact. "Will you stay with me?"

"Of course," Amanda said.

They looked to the officer for his consent.

"Lead the way," he said.

TEN MINUTES LATER, the three of them were seated around the dinette table in Amanda and Tommy's cabin, on the bleak verge of continuing a conversation Tamara was convinced served only to rip the scab off wounds that had hardly begun to heal. She'd gone into the bathroom and splashed water on her face, diluting the flow of tears she'd been unable to stem. She felt only slightly more composed when she came out and sat down across the table from the detective, who, to his credit, had waited patiently for her to calm down. Amanda had fixed her a cup of herbal tea, and sipping that helped. Still, she felt a smothering tightness in her chest as the detective again asked her about the night her baby was born.

She clasped hands with Amanda and began recounting that awful night's events. Out of self-defense—and because her recollection of that night was spotty anyway—she gave the barest of details, telling her story as if painting it using only broad brush strokes. Even so, her words captured the essence of what took place that night, and she soon found herself reliving the horror that was the loss of her child. And the grief poured out of her as if from a broken pitcher.

Amanda put an arm around her and held her while she finished the telling of her tale as best she could between sobs.

The detective, as he'd done throughout her commentary, scribbled notes on a little pad.

Tamara blew her nose on a tissue Amanda handed her. "Are we done now?" she said, praying that this ordeal was finally over.

The detective shifted in his chair. "Just one more question." He tapped the non-writing end of his pen against his notepad. "Do you know anything about Gary coming into some money?"

Tamara snuffled. "No. I don't know anything about any money."

The detective withdrew a sheet of paper from his inside jacket pocket and unfolded it. "What can you tell me about this?" he said, handing her the paper.

She was studying the paper, trying to decipher its meaning, when the door to the cabin burst open and Tommy swept in with a fishing rod in one hand and a tackle box in the other. He paused inside the doorway, ogling the trio seated around the table.

Amanda flapped a hand at him. "Go away."

"No way," Tommy said. "*Su casa, mi casa.*" He plopped his gear down on the floor, went to the refrigerator, took out a bottle of Pepsi, and twisted off its cap. He leaned back against the kitchen counter and sipped his soda while ignoring Amanda's frosty stare.

Tamara's nose was running. She dabbed at it with the wadded tissue as she examined the paper. It appeared to be some kind of accounting record. It had a "Citizens National Bank" letterhead. Her name was typed near the top, and there were some dates and numbers printed down the page. "What's this?" she said, puzzled by the numbers and the format, as well as the fact that her name was on the document.

Amanda was peering over her shoulder now, Tommy forgotten. "It's a bank statement."

A moment later, Tommy's head was hanging in the air next to Amanda's.

Tamara took another swipe at her nose with the tissue. "What does it mean?"

Tommy snatched the paper from her and gazed at it with fascination, as though he'd discovered a treasure map. "It means that you've been holding out on us, girl."

"Tamara," Amanda said, her voice ringing with amazement, "you have $20,000 in the bank?"

Tamara still didn't understand. "What are you talking about? I don't have $20,000." She groped around in her mind for something to hold onto, something that made sense. "Gary opened a savings account for me at a bank in Fir Valley a month or so ago. He put a hundred dollars in it."

Tommy slapped the bank statement down on the table in front of her. "But this piece of paper says there are 20,000 smackers in the account."

Tamara looked around helplessly. "How could that be?"

The detective sat back in his chair, folded his arms across his chest. "That's what I'd like to know."

Tamara shook her head. "I don't know." She didn't know what else to say.

"Could the money have been Gary's?" Amanda said. "The newspaper said he might have been involved with drugs. Maybe he was dealing and wanted to hide the profits by putting them into an account in Tamara's name."

"Good thinking," the detective said. "Could be that he sold something, all right."

"What else besides drugs?" Amanda said.

The detective fixed his gaze on Tamara. "I don't know." He shrugged. "A baby, perhaps?"

"A baby?" Amanda said.

"What baby?" Tommy wanted to know.

Then they were all staring at Tamara, who could only wonder why. "Not my baby," she said. "My baby was—"

"Yeah," Tommy said. "Who's going to pay $20,000 for a dead baby?"

74   AS SOON AS HE GOT BACK to his office at the Fir Valley substation, Detective Hansen called his wife to let her know he was going to be late for dinner—again. "I have some paperwork to do, then I'll be outta here."

"Get home when you can, sweetheart," she said. "We—and the microwave—will be waiting."

Hansen smiled as he hung up the phone. He hated missing another evening meal with Emily and the kids, but at least his wife was understanding about it, even if the kids weren't. Jason was six and Maggie eight. Although they knew he was a policeman, they didn't really grasp why he sometimes came home late from work or had to leave the house at odd hours when someone from the department called.

"Don't answer that," Maggie had taken to saying when the telephone rang. "Pretend you don't hear it." But the phone had to be answered, and sometimes that meant Daddy had to go off to work and catch the bad guys, because that was his job. The kids knew that much. They just didn't like it. What kids would?

Hansen tucked away his guilt on that score in the little compartment in his brain entitled "Sacrifices Required by the Job." Seated behind his desk, he angled his chair toward the pullout shelf on which sat his typewriter and commenced pecking at its keys, working up his notes on the Ames interview. He'd barely gotten started when his telephone jangled.

He answered and was surprised to hear Amanda Stone's voice come back at him from the other end of the line. He hadn't expected such a quick response to the business card he'd left on her dinette table with his name and number on it, "just in case Tamara remembers something else important."

"I don't know if this is important or not," Amanda said in a hesitant tone.

"Let me decide that," Hansen told her, and then listened with mounting interest as Ms. Stone informed him about a recurring nightmare Tamara had had following her return to the lodge.

"The dream was always the same," she said. "It was about the night her baby was born. In the dream, Tamara would hear the baby crying. Then someone would come and take it away."

Hansen pivoted his chair away from the typewriter. "Did she ever say who that someone was?"

"She didn't know. In her dream, it wasn't clear. You think it means anything?"

Hansen felt the part of his brain that did the heavy lifting kick into gear. "I don't know," he said. "But I'm glad you told me about it. And I want you to call me again if you think of anything else."

"Okay," Amanda said. "But don't tell Tamara. I don't think she'd like me calling you. She was really upset when she left here this afternoon."

"This will be our little secret," Hansen assured her.

He hung up the phone and sat there thinking about what he'd just been told. He'd never put much stock in dreams. Dreams were irrational, capricious, and generally unreliable. They were the playground of ghosts and gremlins. But this one was intriguing nonetheless. And even if there was nothing to it, he was still convinced of one thing: Tamara Ames and her baby were the connective tissue linking all the organic elements in these two murder cases. Her boyfriend, the father of her child, had been beaten to death not long after coming to see Tamara. Several weeks later, her stepbrother, who'd recently delivered her stillborn baby, had been killed after coming into and then—according to all accounts—squandering a large chunk of money. And more money had appeared in a bank account in Tamara's name—money she claimed to know nothing about.

That was a stroke of luck, finding her bankbook in Gary's house. That discovery had put him on the money trail. But where had all that money come from?

Hansen had already tried to trace the source of the $20,000. Tamara had been telling the truth about the origin of the savings account. The bank's records had verified that the account had been opened with one hundred dollars in cash that had been handed over by Gary Neaves. The new accounts rep remembered him and the confused-looking pregnant girl who'd come in with him and was able to ID both of them from photos—a mug shot of Neaves and a picture of Tamara taken from a high school yearbook. The balance of the money in the account—the $20,000—was another matter. The best information Hansen could get on that was that it was a wire transfer from a numbered account in a bank in the Bahamas, a fact that served only to fuel his curiosity. And the timing of the deposit, made the day after Tamara's baby had been delivered, was too coincidental to chalk up to chance. There seemed to be an obvious connection. Selling babies—although an abhorrent concept to Hansen, who revered his own kids—was a fact of life.

He settled back in his chair and conjectured for a moment. Suppose Tamara Ames, with her stepbrother's knowledge (or prompting), agrees to give up her baby for a fee of $20,000, plus whatever Neaves will get for his assistance in a surreptitious adoption. But before the baby is born, Jimmy—the baby's father—shows up. He doesn't want to give up the baby. Or, he wants to be cut in on the deal. In either case, he'd need to be removed from the equation. Hansen penciled in Neaves for that job: motive, opportunity, and a disposition to violence. His criminal record, which included several assault convictions dating back to his juvenile days, clearly showed that. Hansen would have preferred some physical evidence to tie Neaves to Jimmy's murder, but the search of his house and Jimmy's truck had been a bust. The evidence tech had lifted plenty of smudged prints from the truck, but none of them, because of their degraded state, could be conclusively matched to Neaves. Still, Hansen was convinced that Neaves was his guy in murder number one: he gets rid of the troublesome boyfriend and everything is back on track as far as the adoption is concerned.

But then another snag occurs. Tamara (did she have second thoughts about giving up her baby?) decides to split before the baby is born. Neaves has to go after her and bring her back. Tamara had filled the detective in on that bit of drama, and her story seemed to fit with everything else he'd learned.

Indeed, everything seemed to add up until the time the baby had come. The problem was the baby had been stillborn. Tommy Stone had already raised the $64,000 Question: Why would someone pay $20,000 for a dead baby? And why then kill Neaves? To keep him quiet? But why the need to keep him quiet if the deal had fallen through when the baby was born dead? Had Neaves put the squeeze on the prospective adopters anyway? Extorted money through threats of disclosure? But why pay him off and then kill him?

None of this last part made sense, because the baby had been born dead. It only made sense if there had been a live birth.

Hansen thought about what Amanda Stone had just told him. In her recurring dream, Tamara had heard the baby crying. Then someone had come and taken it away.

He sat up in his chair, picked up a pen, and on a lined, yellow pad wrote a note to himself: *Check again on report of baby's death.* He added: *Review death certificate; talk to doctor who signed it.*

Perhaps there was some substance to Tamara's nightmare after all.

B K Mayo

75 "WHAT YOU GONNA DO with the money?" Tommy asked for the umpteenth time that evening. It was all he and Amanda wanted to talk about as the three of them sat around the dinette table in the Stone's cabin, sharing a meal and what Tamara had hoped would be some pleasant banter.

She'd accepted their invitation to dinner because she'd wanted to banish from her mind the unwanted memories called up by that afternoon's visit from the sheriff's detective. But that didn't seem possible now, what with all this talk about "the money." If she'd known that was going to be the sole topic of conversation, she'd have stayed in her closet-of-a-room at the lodge. Although she didn't really want to be there either, alone with her thoughts.

"I told you," she said, clanking her fork against the edge of her plate, "I'm not doing anything with the money. It's not mine."

"How do you know?" Tommy said, just before delivering a haystack-sized portion of salad to his mouth.

"Because I've never had that much money in my life and never will."

"Maybe you inherited it," Amanda said. She and Tommy were playing a game called *Guess Where the Money Came From.* Tamara wasn't interested, but her friends persisted.

"Maybe you have a generous benefactor," Tommy put in.

"Sure," Tamara scoffed. "I have a millionaire boyfriend that I neglected to tell anyone about. And he likes to give money to teenage girls who get themselves knocked up."

"Salad?"

"What?"

"You want more salad?" Amanda held out a serving bowl containing limp lettuce and underripe tomato wedges.

Tamara pushed the bowl away. "I've had enough—of salad, and of talk about money."

"I'll have more," Tommy said.

Tamara picked at the food on her plate. Amanda had made a

chicken casserole for dinner. It smelled good, but Tamara couldn't seem to interest her taste buds in it. In truth, her friends weren't the only ones preoccupied with the knowledge of the hefty bank account in Tamara's name. She'd thought of little else since seeing the statement from Citizens National Bank. Where had all that money come from? And why? She had no idea—and having no idea troubled her, because everyone else was asking the same questions.

"Well, don't tell Kurt," Amanda said.

"Tell him what?"

"About your other boyfriend. He'd be jealous."

"What are you talking about?"

"Don't play dumb, Tamara. We know you and Kurt have a thing going."

Tamara squared her shoulders. "For your information, Kurt and I are just friends." But she knew that wasn't true. She hoped it wasn't true. She liked Kurt in a different way than she'd liked any other boy. She'd fallen hard for Jimmy because he was cute and he'd played her, paid her the attention she craved, while feeding her infatuation by pretending to be all the things he was not: caring, sensitive, understanding. Kurt wasn't like that. He was cute, sure, but he didn't even seem to know it. And there was nothing false about him. He was all the things Jimmy had only pretended to be. But whatever her relationship with Kurt, it was nobody's business but theirs. "Just friends," she repeated.

Amanda snickered. "Sure. That's why you sit together in one of those crummy little boats every afternoon making goo-goo eyes at each other."

"We don't make goo-goo eyes at each other—whatever that means."

"Then what do you do?"

"We just sit—and talk."

"About what?"

Tamara brought her chin up. "About anything other than money." She scooped a forkful of casserole, shoved it into her mouth, and spent the next few minutes chewing it to death.

76   DETECTIVE HANSEN DECIDED to show up at the doctor's office unannounced, opting for the element of surprise rather than the courtesy of advance notice.

"Is this a police matter or a medical matter?" the receptionist wanted to know.

"A police matter," Hansen said, putting away his badge. He could feel the stares of the women seated in the waiting room boring into his back. He raised his voice loud enough for them to hear his next words. "I promise to take only a few minutes of the doctor's time."

The receptionist brought him in through an interior doorway and ushered him into a room at the end of a short corridor that ran at a right angle away from a longer hallway, along which the examination rooms were located.

"Please have a seat," the receptionist said. "I'll tell the doctor you're here."

Hansen glanced around what was obviously the doctor's private office. To his right were wall-to-wall shelves jammed with medical texts. Along the adjacent wall, a sink with cabinets and counter space. In the far corner, a hat rack with a clothes bar underneath—a suit jacket suspended from the lone occupied hanger. Filling the rest of the room was a broad wooden desk with a padded armchair in its well. On the wall above the desk hung several framed medical degrees.

The detective eyed a straight-back chair situated at the near side of the desk and decided to stand. And the longer he stood there waiting for the doctor to appear, the more he wondered why he'd bothered coming here.

Already that morning he'd visited the county recorder's office in Roseburg, the county seat, where he'd checked on the death certificate for the Ames baby. Nothing was out of order. The baby had been declared dead at birth. Dr. Castle, a well-respected physician in Fir Valley—a "fixture," he'd been referred to by a helpful county clerk—had signed the certificate.

After leaving the county courthouse, the detective had stopped by the dispatch center for the local ambulance service. He talked with the two paramedics who'd responded to Neaves' 9-1-1 call on the night Tamara had given birth. They were both very clear about what they'd witnessed upon arriving at the house at 726 Cedar Street in Fir Valley. "DOA," one of the paramedics said as he helped his partner load an oxygen tank into the back of their rig. "Not a pretty sight," the partner added. Why Hansen hadn't dropped the issue then and there, he wasn't sure.

He still hadn't arrived at an answer to that question when Dr. Castle bustled into his office. He was an older gentleman, retirement age and then some, Hansen judged. He had a benevolent look about him, as if he might have been a monsignor instead of a physician. His lab coat hung on his slope-shouldered frame like a cassock, the stethoscope around his neck reminiscent of a cleric's stole. He went to the sink along the back wall and began washing his hands. "What can I do for you, Officer . . . ?"

"Hansen."

The doctor snatched a couple of paper towels out of a dispenser, dabbed at his hands, tossed the used towels into a wastebasket.

"First of all," the detective said, "thank you for seeing me without an appointment."

"It must be important," the doctor said. He sat down at his desk and motioned Hansen toward the straight-back chair.

Hansen didn't resist at this point. His feet were ready for a break. "You might have some information that could help us with a homicide investigation," he said, easing himself into the chair.

The doctor looked surprised. "Homicide?"

"Two homicides, really," Hansen said. "You've probably read about them in the local paper."

"Perhaps," the doctor said, squinting as if trying to recall. "Although I'm not much of a news hound."

Given the situation, Hansen decided not to waste his or the doctor's time with preliminaries. He took out the two photographs he'd brought with him and laid them on the doctor's desk. "Do you recognize either of these men?"

The doctor tipped forward in his chair, pushed his glasses up on his nose. His head moved back and forth between the two photos. "I don't recognize this fellow at all," he said, tapping a finger at the edge of Jimmy Stark's driver's license photo. "But this other one appears to be the brother of one of my patients."

"Which patient?"

The doctor sat back in his chair, laced his fingers together over his belt buckle. "A young lady named Tamara Ames."

"And you know the brother?"

"Not really. I spoke with him over the phone once or twice regarding Tamara's care—she lives with him, I understand. And I saw him a time or two in passing." The doctor cocked his head. "Why? Is he one of your suspects or one of your victims?"

"Yes," Hansen said.

The doctor looked puzzled for a moment, then shrugged as if dealing with conundrums was an everyday occurrence. "In any event, I don't know what more I can tell you about him."

"You had no other contact with him?"

"Not that I recall."

Hansen tucked the pictures away and considered whether to end the interview there. The doctor was believable enough, and he had great credibility. But Hansen still had questions with no answers, and until he did have answers, he needed to be a Doubting Thomas. "Dr. Castle," he said, "you signed the death certificate for Tamara Ames' stillborn child."

The doctor's eyes narrowed. "Hansen, you say?"

"That's right."

"Well, Officer Hansen, I fail to see how that would be relevant to your investigation."

"It might not be," Hansen admitted. "But, you see, Doctor, the other photo I showed you—the one you said you didn't recognize—was that of a young man named Jimmy Stark. Does that name mean anything to you?"

"Not at all," the doctor said.

"Jimmy Stark is our other murder victim. He was also the father of Tamara Ames' child."

"Oh, my," the doctor said. "And you think this Neaves fellow had something to do with his death?"

"Maybe."

The doctor shook his head. "Tragic," he said. "Nevertheless, I fail to see what this has to do with the stillbirth of Tamara's child."

Hansen stretched a leg out in front of him, trying to get comfortable on the hard chair. "As I said, it might not have anything to do with it. But since one of our homicide victims fathered Tamara's child and the other one delivered it, I think the circumstances surrounding the baby's unfortunate birth are a reasonable subject of inquiry."

The doctor gave him a measuring look. "What is it exactly, Officer Hansen, that you want to know?"

Hansen wondered that himself. Well, he wanted to know who killed Gary Neaves and why. He wanted to know where the $20,000 in Tamara Ames' bank account had come from. He wanted to know if there was any significance to Tamara's recurring nightmare. He wanted to know why Tamara and her lost child seemed to be at the center of every aspect of his investigation. But what could the doctor tell him that would help get to all this?

"Tell me about Tamara Ames' pregnancy," he finally said. "How did it happen that her baby was born dead?"

The doctor's expression took on an air of circumspection. He folded his arms across his chest. "You realize, of course, that I must maintain the confidentiality of my patient. I cannot divulge any specifics regarding my care of Miss Ames without her prior consent. But"—he dipped his head in a gesture of accommodation—"I can tell you this much without breaking any trust, since it is a matter of public record. A month or so before her unfortunate delivery, Miss Ames took a nasty spill—in a convenience store, I believe—and was transported by ambulance to the hospital. Such falls can cause a premature separation of the placenta from the wall of the uterus, or a propensity toward subsequent premature separation, which, if and when it occurs, causes the blood supply to the fetus to be interrupted or, at minimum, impeded—depending on the degree of separation. Either way, the viability of the fetus would be in jeopardy. That may very well have been what happened in this case, which would also account for the rapid premature delivery." He hitched his shoulders. "But there's no way for me to know for sure if this was indeed the cause of the demise of Tamara's child."

"But Tamara was a patient of yours, was she not? She was under your care?"

"Yes," the doctor said. "With her brother's prompting, I believe, she came into the office the day following the accident. I performed a pelvic exam, during which I found nothing that was cause for concern. She was given some dietary recommendations, as I recall, and we followed up with another checkup a few weeks later—again, no red flags. Miss Ames never complained of any symptoms that would have caused me to pursue any other course of action." He gazed at the detective with a compassionate light in his eyes. "Believe me, Officer Hansen, when I tell you that the subsequent stillbirth came as a complete surprise to me." He pushed himself up from his chair. "Now, if that's all, I must be getting back to my patients."

"Just one other thing," Hansen said, rising and standing between the doctor and the doorway.

"Please be brief."

"I understand that Gary Neaves called your answering service the night of the stillbirth to report that Tamara had gone into labor."

"Yes," the doctor said. "He called a couple of times, I believe, and the last time he was told to take her to the hospital. But the birth happened rapidly and there wasn't time."

"And your service called you?"

"It did, and I went to the hospital as soon as I was able to get away. But by then, it was all over. The baby was stillborn at home."

And then it clicked for Hansen, and he knew exactly what he wanted to know. "You went to the hospital *as soon as you were able to get away*," he said, feeding the doctor's exact words back to him. "You were otherwise occupied at the time your service called?"

The doctor's face darkened as if a cloud had passed over it. "I was— attending to another birth."

"But not at the hospital?"

"No." The doctor cleared his throat. "At the home of the patient. She preferred a home delivery. Some of my patients do."

Hansen glanced at the framed degrees on the wall, one of which was slightly askew. "I don't suppose you would care to divulge the name of this other patient?"

The doctor's expression turned glacial. "I don't see how that could possibly be—"

"I know," Hansen said, thrusting up a palm, "relevant to my investigation."

"Indeed," the doctor said, and swept out of the room.

77 IT TOOK DETECTIVE HANSEN less than twenty minutes from the time he left the doctor's office in Fir Valley to complete the short hop up the freeway to Roseburg and make his way back to the county courthouse. In the county recorder's office, the same accommodating clerk who'd assisted him earlier that morning helped him search the birth records for the day Tamara had given birth to her stillborn child, as well as for the preceding and following days. The records showed a number births in the county on those days, but only one in the local area that didn't take place at a hospital. That one—the delivery of a 5-pound, 8-ounce baby girl by Dr. Brandon Castle—occurred at the home of the parents: Margaret and Russell Trouste.

Hansen cringed when he saw the names. Even in his short time living and working in Fir Valley, he'd heard of the Troustes. He knew that the Trouste family owned Valley Lumber Company, the biggest employer in the county. They were also the biggest contributors to local charities, through the Trouste Family Foundation. Russell Trouste, CEO of Valley Lumber, was without question the most influential man in the county. Hardly anything of note happened in Fir Valley and the surrounding communities that didn't involve the Troustes, whether it was the dedication of a new public library or hospital wing built with grant money from their foundation, a charity auction with Mr. Trouste

as the celebrity auctioneer, or local buzz set off by the cyclical layoffs
and rehirings at the mill due to a fluctuating housing market. The
Trouste name and the family's long-standing influence were indelibly
imprinted on the community. There was a Trouste Street in Fir Valley,
a Trouste Elementary School, and a Trouste Community Park. The
town itself, which over a hundred years ago had sprung up around
the site of the original Valley Lumber Mill—the site now occupied by
Millsite Park—could rightly have been named Trousteville.

Hansen drove back to Fir Valley troubled by his thoughts. One
phrase kept flashing in his mind like a blinking freeway sign: CAUTION!
DANGER AHEAD! Was this a road he really wanted to travel down? He
certainly would have to do some serious deliberating before deciding
to go in the direction his investigation seemed to be leading him.

He also needed more information. Other than his familiarity with
the Trouste name and the lumber company's public affairs, he knew
very little about the Trouste family or their personal circumstances,
except that they lived in a big house on a hill overlooking downtown
Fir Valley and the river. This was definitely an information gap he
needed to bridge.

When he got back to the sheriff's substation in Fir Valley, he shut
himself up in his office. He sat down at his desk and dialed the number
for his most reliable informant regarding local matters.

"Mayor's office," said a cheery voice on the other end of the line.

"And a good day to you, Mother Holt," he said.

"Danny boy!"

Teri Holt, Dan Hansen's mother-in-law, had lived in Fir Valley all
her life. For the last twenty-five years, she'd been a secretary in the
mayor's office. Almost nothing happened in the town that she didn't
know something about. And if she didn't have first-hand knowledge
of a local occurrence, she could easily access someone who did.

Hansen exchanged pleasantries with his mother-in-law, then got
right to the point. "Mother Holt, didn't I hear you say once that Russell Trouste and his wife go to your church?"

"Margaret does," Teri Holt said. "We see Russell now and then, but
not nearly as much as we'd like."

"Do they have any kids?"

His mother-in-law issued a tonal snort into the phone. "Funny you should ask. They have a little girl, born a month or so ago. Word is they'd been trying for years without success to have a baby and had just about given up. The poor woman kept miscarrying. I understand she had to stay in bed during most of this latest pregnancy. Guess it was worth it. Why do you ask?"

"Now, you know I can't tell you that."

Teri Holt laughed. "I know—but that doesn't mean I can't ask. Besides, I always find out anyway."

"We'll see," Hansen said in a teasing manner. He thanked his mother-in-law for the information and bade her a good day.

He sat there, gripping the arms of his chair and thinking about what his next move should be. What his mother-in-law had told him only served to inflame his curiosity about the Troustes and their possible connection to Tamara Ames and her dead baby. Still, it seemed preposterous to think that Fir Valley's most acclaimed citizens could be involved in anything so sordid as he imagined might have taken place.

Again the sign flashed in his brain: CAUTION! DANGER AHEAD! Yes, he would have to proceed very carefully here. But he still had a job to do. He owed it to his investigation to follow up on all leads, regardless of where they might take him. But how best to go about it? He drummed his fingers on the chair arms. He needed to talk to Tamara Ames again, he decided. And he needed to have Willard do some unofficial—and very discreet—investigative work for him. What he didn't want to do was to precipitate a public scandal regarding the Trouste family on the basis of nothing but his as yet unfounded suspicions.

78   THE CLOSER THEY GOT to Fir Valley, the greater the effort it took for Tamara to breathe and the more she wished she hadn't agreed to meet with the detective again. It was only because Kurt had offered to drive her into town after getting home from school—and his parents had agreed to let him take the family car—that she'd consented to the meeting. It was a way to spend more time with Kurt away from prying eyes. But now as they approached the outskirts of town, the thought of having to face the detective's probing questions again made her feel like flinging the car door open and throwing herself out onto the road.

"Will you go in with me?" she said.

Kurt—who was obviously more comfortable driving a boat than a car—kept his eyes on the road and both hands on the steering wheel. "If you want me to," he said.

She moved closer to him on the bench seat. "I don't think I can do this by myself."

The sheriff's substation turned out to be an ordinary-looking, single-story stucco building located next to a strip mall on Main Street about a mile south of downtown. Except for the sheriff's cruisers parked alongside it and the SHERIFF'S STATION sign mounted over its front door, the building could easily have been mistaken for another retail outlet. Kurt pulled into one of the parking spaces in front marked VISITOR in white letters on the pavement.

"Can we just sit here for a minute?" Tamara said.

Kurt took her hand in his. "Sure. I don't think anyone's going to give us a parking ticket."

Kurt was still holding her hand ten minutes later when they entered the sheriff's station, stepped up to the counter, and informed the deputy sitting at a desk behind it that they were there to see Detective Hansen.

"Thanks for coming in," the detective said as he ushered them into his office. "You saved me another trip to the lake." He slid a couple of chairs from against the wall to in front of his desk. "Can I get you something to drink? Coffee? Soda? Water?"

Tamara shook her head.

"No thanks," Kurt said.

They all sat down then, with the detective behind a desk topped with several wire baskets of paperwork and—of greater interest to Tamara—a framed photograph. In the photograph, which was situated to the side at an angle that allowed both the detective and his guests to view it, Detective Hansen stood with his arm around a pretty woman, while two children—a boy and a girl—clung to his pant legs. Everyone in the picture was smiling.

Tamara experienced a pang of the antique sorrow that seemed to reside permanently under the surface of her skin, waiting for the slightest emotional scratch to expose it. She had once been part of a similar—and equally happy—family. She swallowed the knot in her throat, shifted her eyes from the photograph to the man in it. "I still don't see how I can help you."

The detective leaned forward, rested his forearms on the desk. "There are just some things I'm still trying to figure out. And the more information I have the better." The expression on his face softened. "I was hoping we could talk more about the night you lost your baby?"

Tamara felt a tightening around her heart. It was the last thing she wanted to talk more about. "Do we have to?"

"No," the detective said. "But it could help us find Jimmy's killer."

"What does losing my baby have to do with—" She bit her tongue. Tamara had her own suspicions about Jimmy's death. But that's all they were—suspicions. Besides, everything was so confused in her mind—the facts surrounding Jimmy's death, losing her baby, Gary's death, the money in the bank account in her name—she didn't know what *anything* had to do with *anything*. She sighed. "What do you want to know?"

"What I'd like you to do," the detective said, "is to think back on that night and then just tell me everything you remember."

Tamara shook her head. "I don't remember anything I haven't already told you."

"That's okay," the detective said. "Just tell me whatever comes to you. Gary found you at the lake," he prompted. "Then what happened?"

Reluctantly, Tamara closed her eyes and tried to make herself think back. What she saw in her mind was the wall she'd constructed to block out the memories of that night. She didn't want to tear down that wall. "I—I—" she said, her jaw muscles quivering.

"I know this is difficult, Miss Ames. But please try."

Tamara took a deep breath and tried again. She pulled a brick out of the wall holding back the unwelcome memories and peered behind it. She had been sitting at the picnic table outside Tommy and Amanda's cabin when Gary appeared out of the shadows. He'd clapped a hand over her mouth and dragged her away from the cabin. "I don't know how Gary found me," she said. Then she shuddered as the entire wall tumbled down and a torrent of chilling images rushed into her mind.

"Take your time," the detective said.

But Tamara didn't want to take her time. She wanted to get this over with. "He dragged me to his truck," she said, rapid-firing her words now, "and drove me back to—oh, yeah, first he made me swallow some pills. To make me feel better, he said. When we got back to his house, I was tired and wanted to go to bed, but he told me to take a shower first." She paused to breathe. "After that, I went to bed and slept for a while. Then the pain woke me up."

"Labor pain?"

Tamara nodded. "I didn't know what it was at the time. I just knew I was hurting."

"Did you tell Gary about the pain?"

"When it got bad, I did."

"What was his reaction?"

She snorted. "He told me to quit complaining and go back to bed. That I was just having a baby."

"What happened then?"

Tamara's only consolation in having to recount what happened that night was that her recollection of things after the pain got so bad was shrouded in a gauzy haze. "I'm sorry," she said, although she wasn't really sorry at all, "but I just don't remember much after that. Not until the next day, when I woke up in the hospital."

"You don't remember anyone else being at Gary's house that night?"

"Just Gary," she said. "Until the paramedics came. At one point earlier, I thought I heard another voice, whispering, but I didn't see anybody else."

"What about right after the baby was born? Did you look at it?"

Tamara felt her throat clog. "I—I don't remember."

"Did you hear it cry?"

She turned her face away. She didn't remember! Didn't want to remember! "I don't know."

"Yet," the detective said, pressing her, "for some time afterward you had nightmares in which you heard the baby crying?"

Tamara blinked away the tears forming in her eyes. How did he know that? Had she told him about the nightmares? She must have. "But that night," she said, feeling caught up in a whirlwind of confusion. "I really couldn't have heard the baby, could I, because—"

There was a breathless lull as the unfinished sentence hung in the air above them like poisonous gas that needed to be allowed to dissipate before anyone could inhale again.

Detective Hansen pulled a file folder out of a wire basket and laid it unopened on the desk. He placed his hands on top of it and left them there for a time, as if deciding what to do next. Finally, he opened the folder, brought out a photograph, and placed it on the desktop in front of Tamara. "Do you know this man?"

Tamara stared at the photograph. Concentrate, she told herself, trying to rid her mind of some of the anxiety that was crowding out logical thought. But the guy didn't look at all familiar. "No," she said. "Should I?"

The detective responded with a casual shrug. "Not really."

Tamara frowned. "I guess I haven't been very helpful?"

"On the contrary, you've been most helpful." The detective slipped the photograph back into the folder and closed it.

Tamara wasn't convinced. But at this point, she didn't really care. She just wanted to get out of there—after, that is, taking care of one other thing. "Do you have a ladies' room?"

～

KURT HADN'T SAID a word since the initial exchange of greetings. There hadn't been a reason to. But when Tamara left Detective Hansen's office to go to the bathroom, he spoke up. "I know who he is," he told the detective.

"Who?"

Kurt pointed at the closed file. "The man in the picture. That's Mr. Trouste. He owns the lumber mill."

"Ever met him?"

"Nah," Kurt said. "Only seen him on the news."

The detective returned the file folder to the wire basket. "Well, apparently you've seen more of him than Tamara has."

Kurt shrugged. "I guess so." Yet he couldn't help but wonder why the detective had shown Tamara Mr. Trouste's picture in the first place. He pondered the question a moment and concluded that there could be only one reason. "So, you think he was involved in the murders, or had something to do with Tamara losing her baby?"

"Who?"

"Mr. Trouste."

"Whoa," the detective said. He held up his palms. "I don't think anything of the kind."

Kurt didn't see how that could be. "But you must think he's connected somehow or you wouldn't have shown Tamara his picture."

The detective swiped an open hand across his temple. "Well, I probably shouldn't have." He was quiet for a moment, pensive in an agitated kind of way, the way Kurt's dad got when something was troubling him. He peered at Kurt across the desk. "Kurt, let me ask you something. You know Tamara as well as anyone does. Do you think it's possible that she had plans at some point to give her baby up for adoption?"

Kurt considered that possibility—but only briefly. He didn't know, and he didn't really care. "How could that matter now?"

"We're just talking theory here?"

Kurt hunched forward in his chair. "I don't think I want to talk that kind of theory."

"But you know about the money?"

Kurt admitted that he did. Tommy had told him.

"Well, it just so happens that the $20,000 was deposited into Tamara's bank account the day after she reportedly lost her baby. That's a very interesting coincidence, don't you think?"

Kurt thought about that too. He wasn't sure what the detective was getting at. Or maybe he was. "Are you saying that you think Tamara sold her baby to the highest bidder, then pretended to have delivered a dead one?"

The detective gave him a probing look. "You tell me. Is that possible?"

"No, it's not possible!" It was Tamara's voice, behind him.

Kurt jerked around, startled. Tamara stepped into the doorway, her fists clenched at her side. Her face was blotchy red. She glared at the detective—a look that could have scorched bare earth. "I should have known you'd try to pin something on me," she said. She whirled and charged from the room.

Kurt exchanged anguished looks with Detective Hansen, feeling that somehow this was his fault. He should have kept his mouth shut—should never have questioned the detective about Mr. Trouste. He got up and ran after Tamara. She was already out of the station house and down the block before he caught up with her. She was crying as she stumbled along the sidewalk in front of the strip mall next door. He put his hand on her forearm. "Let me take you home."

She jerked away and shambled on down the sidewalk. He followed her until she finally pulled up short and, appearing to wilt before his eyes, dropped onto the curb in front of a shop that had a big pair of scissors painted on its storefront window. Kurt sat down beside her, put his arm around her, held her while she cried some more.

"Damn him," she muttered, pounding her knees with her fists.

In time she quieted. "Stay here," he said. "I'll be right back."

He left the engine running as he coaxed Tamara into the front passenger's seat of his parents' Cutlass. She didn't say a word during the drive back to the lake, just sat there next to him radiating heat, but otherwise remaining as still and lifeless as a statue.

It was dusk when Kurt pulled the Cutlass into the driveway of the lakeside home he lived in with his mom and dad. Lights were on inside the house. Outside, a ghost moon ascended above the gabled rooftop. Against the gray slate of sky, bats could be seen swooping and soaring, silently gorging themselves on the host of winged insects that populated the evening air.

Kurt shut off the engine, set the parking brake. He didn't really know what to say or do at this point, so he said and did nothing, other than feel awkward and stupid for not doing or saying something. When Tamara made a move to get out of the car, he reached over and touched her shoulder. "What the detective said, I don't believe for a minute."

"But *he* does," Tamara said, her voice cracking with bitterness. She gave him a hard stare. "Just tell me one thing. Who was the man in the picture?"

Kurt hiked his shoulders. "Does it really matter?"

"It does to me!"

Kurt winced, feeling injured by her cutting tone. "If you really want to know," he said, "his name is Russell Trouste. His family owns Valley Lumber Company."

"Then he's rich?"

"I suppose so."

"Rich enough to pay $20,000 for a baby." It was not a question.

Kurt reached out to her again. She drew away. "Look, Tamara," he said, grasping nothing but air. "I know you didn't sell your baby."

But her eyes were wide with defiance. "No, I didn't." Her mouth bowed downward in a thin, angry frown. "But that doesn't mean somebody else didn't."

She flung the passenger door open, vaulted out of the car, and stalked away into the shadows, leaving Kurt sitting there wondering what she meant by the remark.

79   THE NEXT DAY, two events occurred that had Detective Hansen backpedaling in his investigation into the deaths of Jimmy Stark and Gary Neaves. The first event came in the form of a confession by a seventeen-year-old boy of complicity in Neaves' death. The boy had been brought into the sheriff's substation for questioning after his mother had called to report she'd found a wad of cash in her son's dresser drawer and a blood-spattered shirt stuffed in the back of

his bedroom closet. After two hours of tag-team questioning by Hansen and Lt. Iverson, the boy finally admitted that he and a friend had tangled with a man at Millsite Park the night of Neaves' death. The boy's name was Trey Adams. His friend was Donnie Pikes, also seventeen.

"I only hit him once," Trey proclaimed. "It was Donnie who did all the real damage."

The two deputies who went to pick up Pikes found out from his grandmother, with whom he'd been living for the past six months, that he hadn't been home for several days. "He might have gone back to California," she said when pressed as to his whereabouts. "His mother and stepdad live down there."

According to Trey Adams' account of the incident, the two boys, driving a car that belonged to Donnie's grandmother, had gone to Millsite Park just after sundown with a couple of girls to drink some beer and smoke a little pot. They'd parked down by the cove and stayed in the car, listening to the radio while they partied. A guy they knew came by and sold them a fresh stash of mary jane, and the party continued. After a couple of hours of necking and getting high, they decided to go get something to eat. But their car wouldn't start. Playing the radio so long without the engine running had run the battery down.

Leaving the girls in the car, the two boys started walking through the park, looking for someone who would give them a jumpstart. As they passed under the Mill Street Bridge, they came across a bare-chested man sitting in a pickup truck with the driver's door open, pressing a rag to his face. The man, as it turned out, was Gary Neaves. The boys asked Neaves if he had any jumper cables, and would he give them a jumpstart. He told them to "go take a flying fuck."

"Donnie has a bad temper," Trey Adams told his interrogators, "especially when he's been drinkin' and stuff. He grabbed the guy by the boot, yanked him out of the truck onto the ground, and gave him a stiff kick to the ribs."

But Neaves was meaner and tougher than Donnie had expected. He wrestled Donnie to the ground, got on top of him, and commenced to pummel him with his fists.

At that point, Trey, feeling inadequate to come to the defense of his friend with his own mere hands, looked around for help. He found it in the form of a softball-sized stone, which he used to smash Neaves soundly on the noggin. Stunned, Neaves fell over, moaning. Even so, he would have survived the blow, according to Trey, had not Donnie picked up the rock and made sure Neaves never got up. "I don't know how many times he hit him," the boy stated. "The guy hurt Donnie, and Donnie made him pay."

This version of Gary Neaves' demise jibed with the medical examiner's report, which stated that Neaves had received multiple blows to the cranium from a heavy object, causing splintering of the skull and the intrusion of bone fragments into the brain.

Before dumping Neaves' body in the river, where they also cast the bloody stone, the boys stripped him of his wallet in order to make identification more difficult. To their surprise, the wallet was fat with bills, including numerous large denomination ones.

"Donnie took most of the money," Trey said. "The big bills anyway."

The boys then checked out the truck, looking for more cash and some jumper cables. They found neither. But they did find the keys in the ignition. So they took the truck and drove it back to their car, telling the girls that it belonged to a friend. They delivered the girls home in the truck, then stopped at Trey's house just long enough to get some jumper cables out of the garage without his parents knowing it. Back at the park, they used the truck to jumpstart Donnie's grandmother's car. Then they drove both vehicles down to Canyonville, meaning to head up into the mountains to dump the truck.

"We were gonna run it off a cliff," Trey said.

But the truck ran out of gas just outside of town and they had to ditch it there, remembering only at the last minute to wipe it clean of fingerprints. It was found two days later by a sheriff's deputy.

Hansen stood with Lt. Iverson outside the interrogation room, shaking his head at the senselessness of it all. The kid had spilled his guts to the two of them and was now in the room alone with his mother, crying his eyes out.

"We'll put out a bulletin on Pikes," the lieutenant said. "When we get him in here, we'll see who he points the finger at."

"You can be sure he'll say that Adams did the heavy bashing," Hansen said.

"The girls may know something about that."

"Jessup and Riley are on their way to pick them up now."

Iverson nodded. "We were due for a break in this case."

"I suppose," Hansen said. He gazed through the one-way glass into the interrogation room. "It's just not what I expected."

"You mean, *Mom rats out her own son.*"

That wasn't what the detective meant at all. But he didn't want to explain himself. He didn't want to bring attention to the fact that his investigation into the death of Gary Neaves had been headed in an entirely different direction, because—right or wrong—he'd failed to mention to his boss his recently formed suspicions regarding the Trouste family's possible connection to the case. The caution sign had yet to stop flashing in his head—apparently for good reason.

"What does it matter?" Iverson said, going off on his own tangent. "You did your job. Besides, we take help where we can get it. If a frog jumps up on my shoulder and whispers a suspect's name to me, I'll follow up on it. If the guy is proven guilty, I consider it good detective work that I listened to the frog and didn't give him the boot just because he was slimy."

"Well, it looks like the frog came through for us this time."

"So be happy about it."

"I'm thrilled," Hansen said, without feeling the least bit enthused. He turned and walked back down the hall to his office.

He hadn't been there more than five minutes when Deputy Willard sauntered in and closed the door behind him. He was about to deliver the second piece of news that would have Hansen reassessing the scope of his murder investigation.

"I just got a call from my lady friend who works in the ER at the hospital," Willard said. "She checked the records for the blood types."

"And?"

"Tamara Ames' blood type is O-positive."

"Common," Hansen said, feeling another letdown coming on.

"The dead fetus that was brought in with her also had O-positive blood."

"I don't suppose they ran any other tests."

"No. And the remains were cremated a few days later."

"So there's no way at this point to prove the dead baby wasn't Tamara's."

Willard shook his head.

"Thanks," Hansen said. "I guess."

Willard puffed his chest. "Hey, you better appreciate it. I had to do some fancy dancing last night to get Marci to agree to look at those records on the sly."

Hansen pushed his chair back, propped his feet up on his desk. "Don't give me that crap, Willie. I know you well enough to know that the one thing you didn't do last night with Marci was dance."

Willard grinned. "Gentlemen don't kiss and tell," he said, and left the office.

Hansen sat there wondering where these latest developments left him in these two, now seemingly unrelated murder cases. He was still convinced of Neaves' complicity in the death of Jimmy Stark. But with Neaves dead, it seemed unlikely that could ever be proven. He could lean on Brian Dodd and Jerome Powers some more. He was sure Neaves' pals knew more about Stark's murder than they'd let on when he'd interviewed them earlier. But at this point, even if evidence of their involvement did surface, they could easily divert the blame for the killing onto Neaves, who was the one with the history of violence and the apparent motive.

And speaking of motive—or lack thereof—if Adams and Pikes did in Neaves, as now seemed apparent, what did that say about the detective's suspicions regarding Neaves' possible connection to Dr. Castle and the Troustes? The logic supporting his suspicions regarding a possible baby-swapping conspiracy had been based on the premise that the death of Gary Neaves was the culmination of a series of linked events—events that had been set in motion with the appearance of Tamara Ames in Fir Valley. Young Adams' confession corrupted that premise, and the news from Willard had all but run a stake into the heart of his conspiracy theory.

Still troubled by unexplained details—including the origin of the money in the bothersome bank account and the seeming interconnectedness of events on the night that Tamara lost her child and the Troustes gained theirs—but reconciled nevertheless as to what needed to be done, Hansen brought his feet to the floor. If Adams' story checked out, he would go ahead and close both murder investigations. He could always get them reopened again later if there were new developments that changed his thinking about either case.

80   RUSSELL TROUSTE WAS meeting in his office at the mill with Lance McKinney, the chief financial officer for Valley Lumber, when his intercom buzzed again. He jabbed the talk button, annoyed by the interruption. "Yes?"

"You have a call from Mrs. Trouste," his secretary's voice announced in an apologetic tone. "Would you like to take it, or shall I say you'll call her back?"

Russell glanced at his watch. It wasn't yet ten-thirty and this was already the third call he'd received from his wife this morning.

First she'd called to tell him there was a change in the date for the baby's christening. "Pastor Dalton will be out of town on the seventeenth," she'd informed him. "So we've moved it back to the twenty-fourth."

"Fine, dear."

"You think the dress is okay?"

He wasn't sure which dress Margaret was talking about. She'd bought three dresses for Felicity and kept changing her mind as to which one to have her wear for the service. "The dress is fine."

"She's napping now," Margaret said. "When she wakes up, I'll try it on her once more just to make sure."

The second call from his wife, twenty minutes later, was to tell him that the baby was awake and was obviously missing her daddy. Russell had no idea how a six-week-old baby communicated such things to the world, but he thanked Margaret for her thoughtfulness and got back to work.

Now, for the third time in the last hour and a half, in spite of his perturbation at the repeated interruptions, he found himself agreeing to take a call from his wife. "This shouldn't take but a minute," he told his CFO.

"No problem, boss."

"Hello, darling," Russell said into the phone.

"I know you're in a meeting, Russell, and I'm sorry," Margaret said. "But I wanted to catch you before you made any plans for lunch. You haven't, have you?"

"Nothing definite." In fact he'd planned to lunch with Lance and a couple of senior managers from the mill. They were going to Dooley's for hoagies. But, no matter. They could go another day.

"Debbie Moss from *The News-Review* just called," his wife said excitedly. "She's doing a story about Felicity for the newspaper. She'll be coming over to the house later this morning to talk to me and to see Felicity. She's bringing a staff photographer with her to take our picture. I want you to be in it. I thought we could have lunch here afterward. I've already told Elena."

Russell's neck and shoulder muscles bunched. Logically there was no reason to be alarmed about a reporter from the local newspaper doing a story on his daughter, even one accompanied by a photograph. All the same, he didn't welcome the needless exposure of their personal lives at this vulnerable time. He wondered how he could decline his wife's invitation to be included in the photo without hurting her feelings. "I didn't know the paper did stories about babies," he said, stalling for time to come up with a plausible excuse.

"Oh, darling," Margaret said, "this isn't just any baby."

81 TAMARA COULDN'T TAKE her eyes off the photograph. It was on the front page of the "Life" section of the newspaper. Tamara had shoved the newspaper aside as she'd sat down on the sofa in Tommy and Amanda's cabin. But the big color picture above the fold in the one section had caught her eye. She brought that part of the paper to her lap and studied the photograph with rising fascination.

In the picture, a beaming woman was holding an infant in her arms, while a man in a white shirt and tie stood next to her, looking oddly uncomfortable. In the background was a huge home that could only be described as a mansion. The photo's caption read, "Valley Lumber Company owner and CEO, Russell Trouste, with wife, Margaret, and daughter, Felicity, at the Trouste's hilltop estate in Fir Valley." A related article, under the headline "Fir Valley's Newest First Citizen," ran down the left side of the page for a column and a half and then was carried over to page five.

"What's so interesting in the paper?"

Tamara glanced toward the dinette table where Amanda sat penning a letter to her mother. But her attention was immediately pulled back to the photograph—to the figure of the infant nestled in the crook of the woman's arm. Could it be? A sense of longing tinged with dread coursed through her. Whatever the answer to her question, she was going to suffer.

"What *are* you looking at?"

Moments later, Amanda was shoulder to shoulder with Tamara on the couch. "Are these relatives of yours?" Amanda asked, pointing at the picture in the paper. "There seems to be a family resemblance between you and this woman."

And there it was—a voice given to a thought, however innocently. "No, I'm not related to her," Tamara said. "But I might be related to her baby."

Amanda rumpled her face. "What?"

Tamara didn't feel like explaining, didn't know if she could. Besides, it would all sound so preposterous to anyone else. She stood up, allowing the newspaper section to flutter to the floor, and left the cabin.

"Wait," she heard Amanda say. "I've got to put on some shoes."

Outside, iron-gray clouds hung over the lake like a lid on a pot, obscuring the surrounding mountain peaks and threatening to spill moisture. A stiff breeze had turned the surface of the lake into a murky chop. Tamara drifted down the slope toward the lake, stopping just short of the drop-off to its sandy shore.

Amanda came up alongside her, hugging her bare arms. "What's wrong, Tamara?"

Tamara gazed out across the churning water toward the headless hills in the distance and, above them, the collapsing sky. "The $20,000," she said. "I think I know where it came from."

Amanda took her by the hand and began pulling her back toward the cabin. "Talk to me, Tamara. Tell me everything—but inside. It's cold out here and it's going to rain any second."

They went back inside the cabin and sat, knees together, on the sofa while Tamara laid out her story piece by piece in an order she hoped would make sense and would allow Amanda to believe she hadn't gone crazy. And in the recounting of her time with Gary, Tamara was able to see prior events for what they were, as if she was a child peering behind the curtain at a puppet show.

"All that time," she said, "I couldn't understand what he was up to— letting me stay with him, taking me to see the doctor, putting money in the bank for me, and then keeping me locked up in his house." She shuddered, the sharp memories stinging her anew. "But now I know what that was all about. It's taken me a long time to figure it out, but— thanks to that detective—now I know." Her hands came together in a double fist. Tears flooded her eyes. "Gary wasn't being kind. He wasn't being a big brother looking out for his little sister. He was being cruel and scheming. He didn't care about me. All he wanted was my baby."

Amanda grasped her forearm. "Tamara, you've got to tell the police."

A bitter sob shook Tamara's frame. "It wouldn't do any good. They think I sold my baby."

Amanda's brow pinched. "What are you going to do?"

Tamara slid off the sofa and knelt down over the ruffled section of newspaper on the floor. She smoothed it out, brought her face close to it. A tear dropped from her right eye and splashed onto the photograph of Russell Trouste and his family, blurring the ink where it landed. Tamara reached out and touched a finger to the tear, smearing it across the page. And as she did, something flared in her heart—flashed like a meteor across the landscape of her inner self—and she knew what she was going to do.

"I'm going to get my baby back."

82

TAMARA LAY AWAKE in bed that night thinking about her baby. *My baby is alive!* she repeated in her mind, wanting to sweep away any doubt. Because as much as she wanted to believe, she couldn't seem to shake the fear that maybe she *was* going crazy. Maybe the truth was so painful that she'd built an elaborate fantasy to contradict it, starting with the photograph of Russell Trouste the detective had shown her, then adding so many fanciful details that the picture in the paper of the Trouste family seemed to reveal things that weren't really there. Was it possible that she just couldn't accept someone else experiencing the joy that should have been hers, the joy of having a child to love and who'd love her in return?

She sat upright in bed, her muscles jumping. *I have to know!*

She got up and dressed. It was nearly midnight when she left her cramped room at the lodge and hurried among wavering shadows through the compound to Tommy and Amanda's cabin.

"I have to see the baby," she said as soon as a sleepy-eyed Amanda opened the door. "Then I'll know for sure. Will you take me to town?"

Amanda's eyelids fluttered half open. "Tamara, it's the middle of the night."

"Tomorrow, I mean. It's your day off, right? And I should be done with work by noon."

"Oh." Amanda yawned. "Tomorrow? Yeah. Okay."

THE GIRLS WAITED UNTIL early afternoon before informing Tommy of their plans to do some shopping in town. He was scraping the grill in the lodge diner, getting ready for the late lunch crowd, although there hadn't been much of a lunch crowd lately—early or late.

"On whose money?" he wanted to know.

Tamara fidgeted on her stool at the counter. "I'll go to the bank and get all the money we need."

Tommy spun around, the wide blade in his hand dripping grease onto the floor. His eyes glimmered. "In that case, I'll take you guys to town myself. I'll get Marty to come in early. He's been complaining about not getting enough hours. Be ready in thirty minutes."

"He never wants to go to town," Amanda said as the girls strolled back to the cabin.

Tamara frowned. "Maybe we shouldn't go today. With Tommy along—well—it might get complicated."

"Nonsense," Amanda said. "I'll handle Tommy."

It was shortly after one o'clock when the three of them piled into Tommy and Amanda's beat-up Toyota Corolla and left the lake. Tommy drove the way he did everything, with bravado, taking the curves as fast as the roadway and his wife's nerves would allow. Amanda sat hunkered down in the front passenger's seat in edgy silence.

In the backseat, Tamara—having withdrawn into her own cavern of thought—was barely aware of the scenery flashing past. She couldn't keep her mind off the infant in the newspaper photo. Was it really her baby? How could she know for sure? And if it was her baby, how would she ever get it back? She massaged her temples as the questions echoed inside her head like a clanging gong.

"You guys sure are talkative today," Tommy said at one point.

Amanda harrumphed. "And you're complaining?"

It seemed like only minutes later when Tamara heard Tommy say, "What street's the bank on?" She looked around, surprised to see they were approaching the Fir Valley city limits. She scooted forward, stuck her head between the Toyota's front bucket seats, and gave him directions.

When the sign for the bank came into view, Tommy whipped into the first available parking space. "Who's got change for the meter?"

Amanda began rummaging through her purse.

Now that they'd arrived at the bank, it dawned on Tamara that she had no idea how to get money out of her account—or if indeed she could get money out of the account.

"Not to worry," Tommy said. "Money is my middle name." He hopped out of the car and led Tamara into the bank, leaving Amanda to feed the meter. At an island counter in the lobby, he began filling out a savings withdrawal slip. "How much money you want?"

Tamara chewed on a fingernail. "How much do we need?"

Tommy wrote in "$500." "That ought to get us through the day," he said with a chuckle. "Sign here."

Tamara signed her name, and after a brief wait in line, they were next up at the teller's window.

"How can I help you?" the teller said, greeting them with a smile.

Tommy handed over the withdrawal slip.

"Can I see some ID?"

Tamara dug around in her purse and found her old school ID card that had the awful picture of her on it.

"How do you want it?" the teller asked.

Tamara didn't understand.

"Twenties," Tommy piped in.

The teller counted out the bills in one-hundred-dollar stacks. Tamara had never handled that much cash before. She gathered up the bills with fumbling fingers and immediately handed the entire bundle over to Tommy. It made her too nervous even to carry.

The money apparently didn't make Tommy nervous. "All right!" he said as they got back into the car. He fanned out the bills in front of Amanda as though he were revealing a winning poker hand.

"Put that away," she said, pushing his hands down. "Somebody'll see it. There are people who hang out around banks just waiting for someone to come out with a wad of cash."

"Yeah, yeah—" Tommy folded up the bills and stuffed them into his front pants pocket. He patted the bulge. "I'm hungry. Let's go get something to eat."

"It's not your money," Amanda said, as if admonishing a child.

Tommy acted as if he hadn't heard her. "I feel like Mexican." He started the car and pulled back onto the street. He drove around downtown, obviously not knowing where he was going but pretending otherwise. Tamara didn't care. It gave her time to collect her thoughts.

They ended up at a TacoTime on Broad Street. It was mostly a take-out joint but had a few tables inside littered with food crumbs and splotches of something sticky. At the counter, Tommy ordered two tacos and a quesadilla for himself. Amanda wanted a vegetarian burrito. Tamara wasn't hungry.

They sat down at a table to wait for their order. "What's the plan?" Tommy said.

Tamara fired a look at Amanda. She was the one who'd said she would handle Tommy.

Amanda brushed some crumbs off the table with a napkin. "Tamara and I want to check out a mansion on the hill overlooking town that was featured in the newspaper. We want to get a closer look at it."

"I thought we were going shopping," Tommy said, drumming his forefingers against the edge of the table to some disjointed beat in his head.

"Later," Amanda told him.

Tommy shrugged. "Whatever." He struck a few more licks with his fingers, then ended his performance with a slap of his palm against the tabletop.

"Number 42," a man behind the counter called out.

FROM THE BACKSEAT, Tamara directed Tommy through the residential streets north of downtown onto the one she thought would take them to the high ground above the city. Before long, the road became steep and winding.

"You sure you know where this road goes?" Tommy said.

"Just drive," Amanda said.

They reached the top of the ridge, where the road forked. "Go left," Tamara instructed, hoping that was the right direction.

Tommy obeyed.

They were going along the crest of the ridge, the town far below them now, looking like a miniature village. Then the road strayed inland, weaving its way among a tangle of oak trees and conifers. Suddenly, through an opening in the trees that extended back to where the land dropped off to the river valley, a huge home came into view. Tamara's heart lurched. It was the house pictured in the newspaper, she was sure.

Apparently Amanda was too. "Stop!" the girls yelled in unison.

Tommy brought the car to a screeching stop in the middle of the road. Off to the left, leading away from the paved road was a gravel drive. A hundred feet or so down the drive, a wrought-iron gate spanned the gap between two bulky stone pillars, blocking access to the remainder of the tree-lined drive.

"We can't stay here," Tommy said, looking around anxiously. "We'll get rear-ended for sure."

Tamara pointed up the road to a turnout on the opposite side. "Park over there."

Tommy pulled up and did a U-turn onto the small island of gravel. "Now what?"

Something electric rippled through Tamara's frame. It was the same feeling she used to get as a little girl whenever her grandmother took her to church. She'd sit there in the sanctuary with its high, arched ceiling soaring above her like heaven itself, celestial light bleeding through the stained-glass windows, organ music filling the air like melodic thunder, staring at the lifelike statue of a woman—babe in arms—standing alongside the altar. What she felt, then and now, was awe bonded to fear. She had come to this place searching for truth, yet she feared the knowing. But she feared the not-knowing even more. *I have to know!*

She pushed her way out of the car and began striding down the driveway leading into the Trouste estate, hardly aware of Amanda walking beside her.

"You think they have guard dogs?" Amanda said as they approached the wrought-iron gate.

Tamara stepped up to the gate, grasped its metal bars, brought her face up close. What she saw on the other side took her breath away. The big house stood fortress-like on a knoll at the brink of the bluff. Encircling the home, like a castle moat, were colorful beds of flowers and shrubs. An emerald green lawn of oceanic proportions swept up the slope and flowed around the flower beds. A tree-lined lane cut a swath through the lawn before looping around a fountain situated in the center of a sweeping circular driveway at the base of the home. Wide steps led up from the driveway to the home's front door. The home itself—sprawling, angular, multi-level—blotted out a sizeable portion of sky.

Here, thought Tamara, was a place that could easily serve as the country estate of a king. But it was more than the grandeur of the place that struck her. There was something foreign about what she saw there, something unapproachable in her way of thinking. The stately drive, the immaculate grounds, the splendid home on the edge of the bluff—all existed in a world completely separate from her own, a world she knew she would never be allowed to enter, a world she had so little understanding of that she couldn't even conceive of what might go on there or what kind of people might inhabit it. And standing there at that moment, viewing that exotic setting through the metal uprights, she felt a hopelessness about the course of her life that left her insides hollow.

"Someone's coming," Amanda said.

Tamara struggled to settle her mind as she peered down the long drive. Sure enough, a vehicle had pulled away from the house and was moving in their direction. Instinctively she shrank back from the gate, stepped off to the side of the driveway, and slipped behind the trunk of a big oak tree, with Amanda huddling nearby.

As the vehicle approached, a mechanical noise sounded from behind one of the stone pillars and the iron gate rolled aside. Tamara couldn't control her curiosity. She peeked around the tree trunk. A gold Suburban shot through the gateway, its tires kicking up a wake of dust and gravel. She craned her neck to get a view of its driver.

"It's her!" she said, her next breaths coming in excited bursts. "And there's a baby carrier in the backseat! Did you see a baby in it? I think I did." The Suburban pulled up to the paved road, paused momentarily, then sped off toward town.

Tamara was suddenly running, running for her life it seemed, back to the paved road, back to the Toyota, where Tommy sat slumped behind the wheel, looking bored. "Follow that car!" She jerked open the back door and flung herself in.

Amanda hopped into the front passenger's seat.

"What car?" Tommy said, blinking as he glanced around. There was no car in sight.

"The one that just came out of that driveway and headed toward town," Tamara said. She flapped a hand in the open space between the bucket seats. "Go!"

"Okay, okay." Tommy fumbled with the ignition key, got the car started, and pulled onto the roadway.

"Faster!" Tamara ordered.

Tommy gunned the engine, and Tamara felt herself break out in a cold sweat.

83   THE TOYOTA CAREENED through a hairpin curve on the ridge road, its tires squealing like a frightened piglet. Tamara clung to the front-seat headrests, her eyes ticking back and forth between the sharp drop-off at the edge of the pavement and the snaking roadway ahead. In the front passenger's seat, Amanda had sunk down out of sight. Tommy had responded to Tamara's urging for haste by driving like a madman.

About halfway down the mountain, as they came out of another tight turn, Tamara spotted the rear end of the gold Suburban. Her fingers clawed into the headrests. Was her baby really in that car?

"Is that who we're chasing?" Tommy asked.

Tamara didn't respond, because at that moment Tommy didn't exist.

Her world had shrunk to include only the vehicle in front of them and a banner of light extending from it to a bubble around her heart. She sank her teeth into her upper lip.

"Is someone going to tell me what's going on?" Tommy said. "I thought we were going shopping."

The brake lights on the Suburban flared, and Tamara regained a broader view of the world around her. "Don't get so close that she knows she's being followed."

"Backing off," Tommy said. He rammed his foot down on the brake pedal, nearly sending the Toyota into a skid on the steep downhill grade. The rear end of the Suburban disappeared around the bend.

"Keep her in sight," Tamara instructed.

"Jesus—make up your mind."

They played peekaboo for a time with the vehicle ahead, Tommy alternately speeding up and slowing down to keep it in view without riding its tail. Finally the road flattened and uncurled. When they approached the four-way stop at Mill Street, Tamara told Tommy to pull over to the curb. "Let's see which way she goes."

The Suburban came to a rolling stop at the intersection, then turned west onto Mill Street. "Go!" Tamara said, but Tommy already had the Toyota lurching forward.

They followed Mrs. Trouste onto Mill Street and kept her in sight as she crossed the river and began cruising through the west side of town. "I wonder where she's going," Amanda said, sitting upright in her seat again. A blue road sign announced the turnoff to the hospital. A new office building was coming up on their left.

"I don't care where she's going," Tommy said. "I just want to know why we're following her."

Because I have to see the baby! Then another thought lodged itself like a dart in Tamara's brain. What would she do if she discovered that the baby really was hers? How could she possibly stand up to a family as rich and powerful as the Troustes? She suddenly felt weak and helpless. She breathed in deeply, trying to combat the feeling. She couldn't give up before even knowing what the stakes were. And she couldn't know that until she saw the baby.

The gold wagon on the road ahead began to slow. The entrance to the Westside Shopping Mall came into view on the right. The wagon's right turn signal began flashing.

"She's going into the shopping center," Amanda said excitedly.

The Suburban entered the driveway to the mall parking lot. Not waiting to be told what to do, Tommy followed the vehicle into the lot.

"Pull in over there," Tamara said, directing him toward some vacant parking spaces several rows back from where the Suburban had parked, but with a clear view of it.

Tommy blathered to himself as he steered the Toyota into one of the indicated spaces and killed the engine. His head jerked around. "Now will someone please—"

"Shush!" Tamara said. She poked her body as far as she could between the front seats and peered out the windshield, her skin prickling with a hot rush of expectation.

Tommy grumbled, slouched down in his seat, and fidgeted with the leather wrap on the steering wheel.

Tamara watched Mrs. Trouste get out of the Suburban and walk around to the rear of the vehicle. She was wearing high-heeled shoes and a mid-length, yellow print dress. Her brown hair cascaded down over a frilly collar. She opened the wagon's hatch door, slid out a baby carriage, let its wheels drop to the pavement.

Tamara inhaled sharply. "I knew there was a baby in the car!"

Mrs. Trouste rolled the baby carriage around to the back passenger's door, opened it, and leaned into the vehicle. After some delay, she came out hugging a baby-sized bundle of bedding to her breast.

Tamara gazed with longing at the bundle—at the infant she knew was inside the bedding but couldn't see. Her baby! She felt a sudden chill. Or was it? A vision of a little wooden box with a heart carved into its lid filled her mind. She braced herself against the seatback to keep from crumpling to the floorboard.

Across the parking lot, Mrs. Trouste bent down and placed the bundle in the carriage, taking her time tucking it in. She closed the vehicle's back door and began pushing the baby carriage toward the bank of glass doors at the front entrance to the mall.

Responding to a pull on her that seemed magnetic, Tamara pushed her door open and slid out of the car. Amanda followed suit.

"Where you going?" Tommy said.

"Shopping," Tamara said, and scurried toward the mall entrance. Here was a perfect opportunity to see the baby.

Amanda fell in step with her.

"What's your hurry?" Tommy said, catching up to the girls with a jogging gait. He walked along cheerily, his prior irritation seemingly forgotten.

Tamara plunged through the mall entrance doors, her eyes immediately darting about. "There she is," she said. About twenty paces ahead, Mrs. Trouste, walking erect, was guiding the baby carriage down the center of the mall's main corridor, her high heels clicking like a blind man's cane against the tile floor.

Tamara kept her eyes on the carriage. It was the biggest, fanciest baby buggy she'd ever seen. It had a gleaming chrome frame and big, spoked wheels. Its body was covered with maroon and white leather. Its canopy had fluffy baubles dangling from its rim. It was altogether a beautiful thing for hauling around a baby. But for all the carriage's appeal, Tamara was more interested in what was inside it.

"What are you guys looking at?" Tommy asked.

"Shoo, Tommy," Amanda said with a flap of her hand. "We have some serious shopping to do."

"What about me?"

"Go buy yourself a treat."

Tommy swaggered in place. "Okay by me. I got all the money. You want some, you'll have to beg."

But the girls were already walking away.

"On your knees," Tommy said.

They trailed along behind Mrs. Trouste as she steered the buggy on a meandering path through the mall, drifting from shop to shop seemingly with no intent other than to pass the time. The girls stayed far enough back so as not to raise her suspicions, stopping when she stopped—to peer in through a store window or to fiddle with the bedding in the carriage—and moving again when she did.

The longer this little tailing game played out, with no end in sight, the more anxious Tamara became to see inside the baby carriage. Finally, her muscles twitching with eagerness, she pulled up short. "I need a closer look," she whispered to Amanda.

"So do I," Amanda whispered back. They had by this time nearly reached the far end of the mall without as much as a peek at the baby.

Then suddenly they had their chance.

Upon approaching the entrance to Sadie's Fashions, Mrs. Trouste paused and stood gazing through the storefront window at something inside. Stepping closer to the window, she left the carriage in place behind her, her only contact with it being the fingertips of one hand that rested on its padded handle.

Seizing the opportunity, the girls immediately swooped in for a look. Tamara leaned over the rim of the buggy and peeked inside. She could barely see the baby's face for all the bedding around it. "Hi," she said, bending down closer. The baby blinked a couple of times, then looked up at her with Jimmy's eyes.

Tamara gasped.

Abruptly the baby carriage was drawn away. Mrs. Trouste, with both hands once again on the handle, stared at the girls with a look of dismay.

You have my baby! Tamara wanted to scream at her. But all she could get out was, "You—you—" She felt Amanda's arms encircle her waist and pull her aside.

"You have a beautiful baby," Amanda said to Mrs. Trouste.

"Thank you," Mrs. Trouste said stiffly, and propelled the carriage toward the opposite side of the corridor.

Tamara's eyes gushed tears as she watched the buggy being whisked away. "Did you see? Did you see? The baby looks just like—" But she couldn't continue.

"Oh, sweetie," Amanda said, drawing Tamara to her.

Tamara fell against Amanda and sobbed—out of relief, out of anger, out of frustration. Gary, the doctor, the Troustes had all betrayed her, had taken advantage of her innocence, her vulnerability, and she hated them for it. They had let her believe her baby was dead when all this time it was alive and well in the care of another woman—a rich woman who'd claimed the baby as her own. How could this nightmare have happened? How could anyone be so cruel as to steal someone else's baby? *Her* baby. The injustice of it gnawed at her insides, ate away layers of fear and doubt, so that what was left was raw rage and a single-mindedness she'd never known before. She gripped Amanda's shoulders. "I have to get my baby back."

"What's the matter with her?" Tommy said, choosing this moment to rejoin them. He had a bag from Croitzer's Sporting Goods in one hand and a half-eaten bearclaw in the other. "You guys run out of money?"

Amanda took hold of Tamara's forearm and began tugging her toward a side exit to the mall.

"No!" Tamara said, pulling away. "My baby!"

Amanda got between her and the diminishing figure of Mrs. Trouste. "Let's go to the car and talk."

"I don't want to talk," Tamara said, stepping around Amanda.

Amanda caught her arm at the elbow. "Help me, Tommy," she said, and moments later Tamara found herself being shuttled unwillingly by the two of them, out of the mall and into the parking lot.

"We can't let them get away with this!" she said. She could feel the tears burning her cheeks as the anger boiled out of her.

They circled around to the front of the mall where the Toyota was parked. "Who?" Tommy said. "Get away with what?"

"Just get her in the car," Amanda told him.

"Gary. Dr. Castle. The Troustes," Tamara yelled as she was being shoved into the backseat. "Stealing my baby!" The door slammed in her face.

Tommy slid in behind the wheel. "What's she talking about?"

Amanda didn't answer. She twisted around in her seat to face Tamara, her eyes filled with a mixture of sympathy and uncertainty.

"That woman," Tamara said, feeling the bitterness of a thousand past disappointments rolled into one, "has my baby."

Tommy's head snapped around. "What woman?"

"The woman with the baby carriage."

"Are you crazy?" Tommy said. Then he looked at her as if he was sure she was. "That can't be your baby. Your baby was"—he sputtered—"well, you know."

But Tamara didn't back down. She'd been terribly wronged, and there was only one way to make things right. "I *am* going to get my baby back," she said, expressing a resolve as deep and firmly set as the roots of the biggest tree on earth. She clamped her eyes on Tommy. "And you're going to help me."

Tommy sneered. "You gotta be kidding."

"I'm *not* kidding."

He waggled his head. "How can you sit there and say that you want to kidnap a baby?"

Tamara put her face close to his. "It's not kidnapping if it's your own baby."

"Who says it's your baby?"

Tamara felt something inside her snap. She could no longer abide the doubting, the resistance. "It is my baby!" she screamed.

Tommy turned away. "Girl, you have gone nuts." He inserted the car key in the ignition and started the engine.

Tamara launched herself through the opening between the front seats and began pummeling him with her fists. When he put his arms up to deflect her blows, she turned off the ignition and pulled out the key.

Amanda shrank back in her seat.

"Okay, okay!" Tommy said. "Just leave me out of this."

But Tamara was not going to be denied. She couldn't let Dr. Castle and the Troustes get away with this. And in order to stop them, she needed Tommy's help, and she needed it now. She clamped a hand on his shoulder. "If you help me, you can keep the five hundred dollars we got from the bank."

"No!" Tommy said, banging a fist against the dash. "This is insane!"

"And I'll give you another five thousand."

Tommy stopped banging. He turned to look at her, his eyes dancing. "You really think that's your baby?"

"I *know* it is," Tamara said. "And I want her back."

84

MARGARET TROUSTE NEVER tired of shopping, even if she ended up buying nothing. And her favorite place to shop locally was the new Westside Mall. The place was tiny compared to the sprawling shopping centers she frequented in Eugene and Portland, but it was a definite improvement over the cramped and aging shops in downtown Fir Valley that hardly anyone ever patronized anymore. She enjoyed the bustle of the new mall, its festive atmosphere—the colorful banners and piped-in music—and the foot traffic that on busy days flowed in and out of the contiguous shops like leaves caught up in a swirling breeze. She also enjoyed the attentiveness of the store clerks, most of whom recognized her, and the fact that while inspecting the wares of a particular store or just people-watching as she wandered the brightly lit mall interior, she almost always ran into an acquaintance she hadn't seen for a while. These unplanned reunions were particularly satisfying now that she had something new and exciting in her life to share with others.

So she was sorely disappointed this afternoon when, after spending a good deal of time cruising the mall with Felicity in her baby carriage, she'd crossed paths with no one of significance. The only people who'd made a point of fawning over her daughter were two teenage girls whose attention Margaret had neither invited nor appreciated. It was the one unpleasant aspect of mall shopping—the clusters of ill-mannered youth who seemed to have nothing better to do than rove the corridors offending others with their loud, unruly behavior. Although, in this case, she had to admit that the girls who'd made a fuss over Felicity were quite polite, if a bit forward. It was this boldness that had made her nervous. Like most young people these days, the girls were lacking in respect for the personal space of others.

"Thank you, Mrs. Trouste," the smiling clerk in Sadie's Fashions said as she handed over a shopping bag containing the mauve cashmere sweater Margaret had seen in the window but had resisted until the last minute. It was the only purchase she would make today. And now that she'd made it, she was anxious to get home and see how well it went with the black skirt she'd bought last week, and her silver serpentine necklace.

She exited Sadie's with the store clerk holding the door open for her to push the baby carriage through. Felicity hadn't made a sound for some time. Margaret paused outside the store to check on her, just to make sure she was still breathing. Her daughter was fast asleep, looking angelic in slumber, as always.

Margaret headed the baby carriage back toward the mall's main entrance, glancing about as she went in hopes of spying a familiar face but, regretfully, seeing none. She considered making one more loop around the mall but decided against it. She was tired and her feet were beginning to ache in these shoes. Besides, Felicity was bound to wake up soon and want to be fed. Margaret was inclined to go home and let Vera take care of that chore.

Minutes later, she was standing along with the baby carriage outside the canopied front entrance to the mall, looking around, trying to remember where she'd parked. She looked left, then right, then left again, relieved to spot her vehicle in the third row back.

Arriving at the Suburban, she wheeled the baby carriage between it and the car next to it, being careful not to bump against either vehicle and possibly scratch some paint. She rummaged through her purse for her keys, her eyes blurring. She was more tired than she realized.

She unlocked the Suburban's front door, opened it, and reached in and unlocked the back door on the same side. Then, in order to get the door open all the way, she nudged the baby carriage back a few feet. Only vaguely aware of scuffing sounds behind her, she leaned into the backseat of the Suburban to prepare the infant carrier for Felicity. The multiple straps on the carrier always confused her, but she succeeded with only a minor delay in getting them sorted and aligned so they wouldn't be in the way when she put the baby in place.

With that done, she pulled back and turned around to get Felicity. But when she bent over the baby carriage, arms outstretched, she found it empty.

She stared down into the buggy in disbelief. The baby wasn't there. But how could that be? Her mind swirled around the question. When it came to a stop a split second later, her disbelief became heart-pounding panic. She rifled through the bedding, finally yanking

it out and letting it trail to the ground, exposing the bare inside of
the carriage.

"Ohhh—" she whimpered. A searing pain shot through the middle
of her skull. She felt suddenly ill. She reared up, gasping for air. She
gaped at the space around her, not understanding what could have happened to the baby. Around the parking lot, people were walking away
from her in different directions, but all she could see was their backs.

She wheeled around and stuck her head into the backseat of the
Suburban, thinking that she must already have put the baby in the
vehicle and somehow forgotten. But the baby wasn't there either.

She began to tremble uncontrollably. In desperation, she lurched
back to the carriage, groped its innards as a blind person would. It was
still empty. Felicity was gone!

"My baby!" she screamed. "Someone took my baby!" Then she paced
in a tight circle between the two vehicles, crying and flailing her arms,
and screaming some more. "My baby! My baby!"

It was all she could think of to do or say.

85

DON'T LOOK BACK. *Don't look back.*
Tamara's heart beat wildly as, clutching the baby in her
arms, she wove her way between parked cars, dipping this way and
that to avoid clipping side-view mirrors. From close behind her came
the shuffling sound of Tommy and Amanda's footsteps. And in the
background, Mrs. Trouste was screaming words that, blessedly, were
being drowned out by a car's engine starting up nearby.

When they got to the Toyota, Tommy hustled around in front of
her and opened the back door. "Hurry!" he said.

Tamara tumbled into the backseat, the baby snugged against her
breasts. Seconds later, they were racing toward the exit from the
parking lot.

"Slow down!" Amanda shouted. "You'll get us all killed."

As if on cue, another vehicle appeared in front of them, and Tommy had to brake hard to keep from slamming into it. Tamara bent protectively over the child.

Tommy steered clear of the hazard and hit the gas again. When they reached the exit from the parking lot, the Toyota pitched through the uneven transition from driveway to street before settling onto the roadbed with a head-snapping jolt.

"I said, slow down!" Amanda shrieked, and punched Tommy's shoulder.

"All right," he said, drawing away as if expecting another blow, "I'm slowing down."

But Tamara couldn't slow down her heart, and all the yelling and jostling had awakened the baby, who began to fuss.

"It's okay," Tamara said in a soothing voice, rocking the baby the way she remembered doing her dolls when she was a little girl. The baby whimpered and acted like she was going to cry. Then she looked up at Tamara as if surprised to see a new face and quieted.

Tamara shifted the child onto her lap. She peeled away the blanket that had been wrapped around the baby as tightly as a mummy's casing. The baby immediately began thrusting her puny arms and legs. One of her booties had come off and was hanging by a toe. Tamara slipped it back over the baby's tiny heel. The bootie was soft and padded and pink, several shades darker than the frilly pink top and matching bottom the baby was dressed in.

Tamara rewrapped the baby's bare legs, more loosely than they had been, leaving the upper body free of the covering. The baby flapped an arm as if waving at her. She put out her index finger and let the baby grab hold of it. And when the baby did, an emotion Tamara had never felt before swept through her.

The emotion had a purity to it like something only God could have created. It was at once thrilling and humbling, and she ached with a longing that she knew had as its source this wonderful bundle in her lap. It was as if her heart had melted and poured itself into the child so that the child was an extension of herself that just happened to exist outside her body.

And she understood in that moment that she was a different person now, and would be forever. She was a mother. Her eyes fogged over and she felt lightheaded. *And I promise to be a better one to you than—*

"Where you want to go?" she heard Tommy say in an annoyed voice.

Tamara glanced out the window, blinking. They were headed east on Mill Street, approaching downtown. "Home," she told him. She wanted to take her baby home.

Tommy peered into the rearview mirror, and she could see the skepticism in his eyes, as if instead of *home*, she'd said *moon—take us to the moon.*

"What're you gonna do with a baby at the lodge?" he said. "Someone's bound to see it and be suspicious. God—" He shook his head. "This thing'll be all over the news in no time."

Tamara returned her attention to the baby. She gazed into those gem eyes, regarded that sweet, innocent face—and she trembled with hope and fear. "Just take us home. We'll figure out the rest when we get there."

86   AT THE FRINGE of her rational mind, Margaret Trouste felt a tapping on her shoulder. She whipped around.

"It's okay, lady," a man said. He had his arms up as if to guard against an attack. "We want to help you."

Margaret felt as if she were trapped inside a bubble. She peered through the watery skin of the bubble at an old man with horn-rimmed glasses askew on his nose and a few wispy hairs on his head. A frumpy, gray-haired woman stood beside him, looking startled.

"My baby!" Margaret cried. She rushed back to the baby carriage—the *empty* baby carriage. "They took my baby!"

"Who took your baby?" the old man said.

"Someone has to call the police," the gray-haired woman said.

The word *police* hit Margaret like a slap in the face. "My baby!" she repeated, feeling utterly bereft.

"I'll go inside and have someone call the authorities," the old man said, and took off at a hobbling gait toward the entrance to the mall.

Margaret watched him go, trying to make sense of things. One moment her baby was in the carriage, and the next instant she was gone. But gone where? She whirled around, gazing frantically in every direction. What had happened to her baby?

An image of her baby tucked safely inside the carriage came into her mind, then was immediately swept away by a rush of other images— swirling, kaleidoscopic snapshots of bloody miscarriages, solemn-faced doctors, a scarred and empty womb—all spinning on the pinwheel of her life. She felt her knees give way. She dropped to the pavement, landing hard. She tried to get up but wasn't sure which way that was. She reached out a hand. "I have to find my baby." Her fingernails scraped uselessly against the side of a vehicle.

She was still on the ground, sitting up now with her legs splayed out in front of her, her back propped against the side of her Suburban, when a brown sedan with a yellow stripe down the side and a light-bar on top pulled up and stopped nearby. The crowd that had gathered around her dispersed momentarily, then reformed around the sheriff's unit. A sheriff's deputy pushed his way through the ring of onlookers, rolled the baby carriage aside, and knelt down beside her.

"What happened, ma'am?"

Margaret gazed up at him, feeling befuddled, as if she was just coming out of deep anesthesia. She realized one of her legs was throbbing. She glanced down at it. She'd skinned a knee. Her dress was torn. The heel of one shoe was missing.

"That's Mrs. Trouste," someone in the crowd said. "Someone stole her baby."

The deputy faced the crowd. "Did anyone see what happened here?"

"We may have seen the getaway car," a man's voice said. He stepped forward, pulling a gray-haired woman by the arm. Margaret recognized him as the man who'd gone to call the police.

Murmurs reverberated through the crowd, but nobody else acknowledged seeing anything.

"Okay," the deputy said. "You two stay put. The rest of you, go on about your business."

Slowly those gathered around began peeling themselves away from the scene, some mumbling their displeasure at being sent away. The deputy turned back to Margaret. "Do you hurt anywhere? Do you think anything is broken?"

Margaret felt a resurgence of a deep-rooted agony, as if an unseen hand was twisting a knife embedded in her heart. "My baby," she said. But her strength was gone, and the words barely escaped her lips.

The deputy stood up and addressed the old couple, who'd remained huddled nearby. "Did you see who took her baby?"

"No," the old man said. "But we apparently drove in just after the abduction occurred, because as we were coming into the parking lot, we saw a car tearing out of here like a bat out of you-know-where."

"They almost ran into us," the gray-haired woman said, her eyes reflecting the fright she must have felt at the instant of the near-collision. "There were three people in the car. Two girls, it looked like, and a young man driving. They were in a faded blue Datsun."

"It was a Toyota," the old man said.

"Datsun," the woman insisted.

"You get a plate number?"

"Didn't get that," the old man said. "But I did see a decal in the back window that said *Garcia*—as in the fishing reel manufacturer."

"Thanks," the deputy said, "that should help."

"Did they have a baby with them?" Margaret murmured. She drew up her leg with the broken shoe and tried to push herself off the ground.

The deputy came over and put a hand on her shoulder. "Let us take care of this, Mrs. Trouste."

She crumpled back to the tarmac. "You don't understand," she said, bursting into tears again. "They took my baby."

The deputy went to his car and returned with a leather jacket that he draped over her, tucking it behind her shoulders. Then he walked back to the cruiser and sat in the front seat with the door open and one leg sticking out while he talked on the radio.

Margaret wept quietly as she listened to the deputy request medical assistance. She marveled at his calmness as he described the "suspect vehicle" and the "suspected kidnappers." "And have someone get ahold of Mr. Trouste," she heard him say. At the mention of her husband, a loud buzzing sounded in her head and she felt dizzy. What was she going to tell Russell?

An ambulance arrived within minutes of the deputy's call—red lights flashing, siren blaring. Two young men in uniform rushed to Margaret's side, obviously eager to attend to her. She didn't want to be attended to. "I want my husband," she said.

"He's on his way, ma'am," a baby-faced paramedic told her. "In the meantime, you really should let us check you over."

Reluctantly, Margaret allowed him to take her pulse and blood pressure. Then, ignoring his advice, she refused to be transported to the hospital. The paramedics hung around anyway, like kids in a schoolyard expecting a fight.

By the time Russell pulled up in his Lincoln, Margaret was standing next to her Suburban with her shoes in her hands, feeling somewhat composed but also feeling outside herself, the way she'd once felt after suffering a head concussion when her feet had gone out from under her on an icy sidewalk. Nothing around her seemed real. But the sight of her husband stepping out of his vehicle instantly brought the reality of her loss crashing down on her. She rushed over, threw herself into his arms, and collapsed there, allowing herself to slip into a welcoming stupor.

87   "SHUT THAT KID UP," Tommy barked. He shot an annoyed look into the backseat by way of the Toyota's rearview mirror.

"I'm trying," Tamara said.

She'd been trying for the last twenty minutes, ever since the baby had started fussing. But no matter what she did—singing, rocking, patting, hugging—the baby seemed only to get more agitated. Now she was yowling at the top of her lungs and Tamara didn't know what to do.

Amanda turned around and peered over the seatback. "She's probably hungry."

Tamara thought Amanda must be right, because when she put a finger in the baby's mouth, the baby quickly closed her lips around it and began sucking. But the sucking and the quiet that accompanied it lasted only a few seconds, then the baby was wailing again, all red-faced and teary-eyed. "How much longer 'til we get to the lodge?"

"Too much," Tommy said, grumbling as he steered the Toyota up the curvy mountain road. His riled expression flashed in the rearview mirror again. "Then what? You gonna give the kid a Pop-Tart and some potato chips?"

Tamara felt her stomach jump, like maybe she was getting car sick. She reached over and cranked a window down. What was she going to feed the baby? She hadn't thought about that. She offered the baby a different finger with the same result as before. "I'll get some milk at the lodge store."

Tommy let out a mocking laugh. "Babies don't drink milk. Everybody knows that. They drink formula."

"That's what I meant," Tamara said, feeling hot in the face. "Formula." Although she wasn't exactly sure what formula was.

"Out of a bottle," Tommy said.

"I'll get—"

Amanda's head popped up over the seatback, her eyes sparkling with inspiration. "Why don't you breastfeed the baby?" she said. "Then you won't have to mess with bottles or formula."

The suggestion confused Tamara. Her breasts had already dried up, although it had seemed like they never would stop leaking. But was it possible they would start flowing again if . . . ?

"Yeah, give the kid some tit," Tommy said. "Anything to shut it up. I can't even hear myself think."

Amanda poked him in the ribs. "You don't need to think. You just need to drive." She turned back to Tamara with an expectant look on her face.

"What?" Tamara said.

"Why not try it?"

"Try what?"

"You know. Give her your breast."

Tamara frowned. "I don't think anything will come out."

"How do you know 'til you've tried?"

"Hell," Tommy said. "I'll give the kid a tit if it will quiet it down."

Tamara thought they were both crazy at first. Then she thought, Why not? After all, it was a very motherly thing to do. "Block the rearview mirror," she told Amanda. "I don't want Tommy watching."

Amanda tweaked the mirror so that it aimed away from the backseat.

"Hey, I can't see behind me."

"Good," Amanda said. "Keep it that way."

Tamara reached back under her shirt and unclasped her bra. She pushed the loose cup up off her breast. She glanced up to make sure Tommy wasn't looking. Feeling a quiver of anticipation, she lifted the front of her shirt and brought the baby's face close to her bare nipple. The baby opened her mouth wide, wagged her head side to side, and latched onto Tamara's tit.

"Ow-w-w!" Tamara said. She pulled the baby's mouth away. "That hurts." She tugged her shirt down and rubbed her breast.

"What did you expect?" Tommy said, laughing.

Tamara didn't know what she'd expected. She just hadn't realized it would hurt enough to make her eyes water. And now the baby was crying again. "Shhh," she said, bouncing her gently up and down. "It'll be all right." But the baby continued to bawl.

And Tamara began to wonder if her baby would be all right. What did she know about taking care of an infant? She couldn't even keep one from crying. It wasn't as if she could stick it in a locker until she could get someone to turn off the crying mechanism.

All of a sudden she felt an odd sensation that caused her to sit up in the seat. "Oh," she said, holding the baby up.

"What?" Amanda said.

"The baby needs changing."

"Great," Tommy said.

Tamara's lap was sopping wet. She felt the blanket. The pee had soaked through.

"We sell disposable diapers at the lodge store," Amanda said.

But Tamara had stopped listening. Her mind had started making an inventory of all the things she would need to take care of her baby: formula, bottles, diapers, baby clothes, baby bedding, a baby bed, and a whole lot more things she probably didn't even know about—all the things that the Troustes, no doubt, already had in abundance. To say nothing of a fancy baby carriage.

Tamara bit her lip. Her eyes filled with tears. The bitter truth was, she had just taken the baby away from everything she hoped to give it.

"Is that an OSP cruiser?" Tommy said, his voice soaring toward falsetto. A dark sedan with a light-bar on top whizzed past them, going in the opposite direction. Tommy reset the rearview mirror. There was a fearful look in his eyes as he followed the path of the vehicle in the mirror. "Oh, my God—I think it is. And his brake lights just came on."

88

THE AMBULANCE MOVED with the flow of traffic down Mill Street, the driver having chosen not to use the siren on the way to the hospital, although Russell thought at one point he heard one wailing in the distance.

Russell had decided to go with his wife in the ambulance. Her collapse had shaken him, her limp body in his arms a grim reminder of the physical and emotional frailty that had been masked by the outward bloom Margaret had put on with the introduction of the child into her life. But now, unthinkably, someone had kidnapped the child. He felt a corrosive rage flow through him as he gazed down at his wife's recumbent frame strapped to the gurney. How? Why? Who—would have done such a thing to her?

From his position on the opposite side of the gurney from Russell, the attending paramedic was taking another blood pressure reading.

Margaret moaned. Her eyes fluttered open. She stared up at Russell, opened her mouth as if to speak, but no words came out.

"It's going to be all right," Russell said, squeezing her hand.

Margaret's eyelids flapped, fell closed again. Russell didn't know if it was his reassuring touch, the emotional depletion from her ordeal, or some tranquilizer being introduced into her veins through the IV drip that was keeping her quiet for the time being, but he was appreciative in any case for her release, however temporary, from the anguish that gripped her. She had suffered so much in recent months—and now this. He shook his head and sighed.

When the ambulance came to a stop outside the hospital's emergency entrance and its back doors swung open, Russell climbed out and stood aside while the paramedics off-loaded Margaret. Absorbed in his concern for his wife, he paid no attention to another vehicle that pulled in and parked alongside the ambulance.

"Mr. Trouste," a man's voice said.

Russell turned toward the voice and immediately stiffened. A sheriff's deputy was emerging from behind the wheel of a sheriff's unit.

"Sir," the deputy said as he approached, "the state police have in custody the people who took your baby. The baby appears to be unharmed."

It took Russell a few seconds to process this surprisingly swift reversal of fortune. "Thank God," he said, when the news finally sank in. He exhaled a breath, issuing along with it a silent prayer of gratitude. "Where is the child?"

"With an OSP officer out on Briar Creek Road," the deputy said. "An ambulance has been dispatched to the scene merely as a precaution. The paramedics will be transporting your daughter to the hospital as soon as she's transferred into their hands. But as I said, she appears to be fine."

"Thank you, officer," Russell said, reaching out to shake the man's hand.

The paramedics were rolling Margaret's gurney through the automatic double doors at the entrance to the ER. Russell turned to follow.

"Sir," the deputy said, "we'd like to have your daughter examined by a physician before releasing her to your custody."

"Yes, of course," Russell said over his shoulder. "I'll call our doctor right away." He broke into a jog.

"That'll be fine, sir."

Russell caught up with his wife's gurney in the ER lobby, where the paramedics had paused to allow another patient-laden stretcher to exit the treatment area. He gave his wife the good news about the baby. "She's perfectly safe," he assured her. "We'll have her back in no time."

Margaret burst into tears, but he knew they were tears of joy. "Get me off this thing," she said, and began pawing at the straps holding her down.

89

TAMARA PRESSED THE receiver against her ear and listened to the ringing on the other end of the line. Two rings. Three rings. Four. She kneaded the phone cord with her free hand, stretched it out, and let it recoil with a snap. Five rings. Six. She glanced over at the booking officer—a human boxcar hulking nearby with his legs spread apart, arms cinched across his chest. "One phone call," the officer had said out of the side of his mouth while stabbing a finger toward the phone on the wall. "Make it count." Tamara had still been wiping ink off her fingers. Seven rings. Eight. She chewed on the inside of her cheek.

"Hello."

Tamara's heart did a cartwheel in her chest. "Momma?"

"Tamara, is that you?"

"Yes, Momma."

"Where are you? You sound far away."

Tamara felt far away, separated from her old life by a million miles and a thousand years. "I'm in trouble, Momma."

"Trouble?"

Tamara worked to keep her voice flowing. "I'm in jail."

The ensuing silence lasted so long Tamara thought she might have lost the connection. "Momma?"

"I'm here."

Tamara gripped the receiver with both hands. "I said, I'm in jail. In Roseburg. The—something—County Jail."

"Douglas," the booking officer said.

"I'm in the Douglas County Jail, Momma—in Roseburg."

Again the silence taunted her, as if she'd gone deaf and was the only one in the world who didn't know it.

"Tamara, you should come home," her mother finally said. "Your grandmother will be worried about you."

Tamara slumped against the wall, feeling all the strength go out of her. "Momma, Grandma died three years ago."

"Oh," her mother said. "I forgot. Silly me." The line crackled like a bad radio signal. "What is it that you wanted, dear?"

Tamara drew a breath, let it out in fitful bursts. "Momma, can you come to Roseburg?"

"Roseburg? Oh, no, dear. That's much too far for me to travel in my condition."

Your condition? Tamara felt the old anger and hurt welling up inside her. She knew all too well about her mother's condition, acquired the day Danny had died, her mother wrapping herself in his loss like someone slipping into a self-induced coma. She swallowed. "Momma, I need your help."

"Honey, I don't know what help I could possibly give you."

"But, Momma—" Tamara was suddenly six years old again, crying out for the love and attention that had been so cruelly withdrawn from her. "Momma," she said in the desperate, whiny voice of the child within, "don't you even love me?"

"Of course, I do," her mother said in an insanely bright tone. "Come home, Tamara, and I'll fix you some spaghetti. You like spaghetti. I found this wonderful sauce in a jar. You don't have to add anything. Everything is right in the jar."

Tamara felt the tears sliding down her cheeks. Just down the hall from booking were the holding cells where Tommy and Amanda had already been taken. She'd seen them being guided into separate cells by broad-shouldered deputies. She'd heard the big metal doors clanking closed behind them.

A sob exploded from her chest and blasted out through her nostrils in a bubbly mist. "Momma, I can't come home. I'm in jail. They took my picture and my fingerprints. They're going to lock me in a cell unless a parent or guardian comes for me."

"Yes, honey. And you know if there was any way I could help you, I would."

Tamara doubled over at the waist, struck by a solid blow of reality: She and her mother had both been in jail for years, locked away from each other's love. She pawed at the wall for support, was finally able to lift her head. "I know, Momma." She brushed the tears from her eyes with the back of her hand. "I know."

"Think about what I said, Tamara, about the spaghetti."

"I will, Momma."

90   KURT SHOULD HAVE been doing homework—reading the next chapter in Civics or going over his Spanish vocabulary. Instead, he was sitting at his makeshift desk—a sheet of plywood supported by two stacks of cinder blocks—reading an article in the latest issue of *Field and Stream*, when there was a knock at his bedroom door. He glanced over. "Come in."

The door swung open and his dad appeared, a bankrupt look on his face. "Something I need to tell you. Something I just heard on the local news."

Tuning into the evening news was part of his dad's daily routine, like a hot shower and a tablespoon of bran. Sometimes Kurt watched the news with his parents, but mostly it was either boring or depressing—or both. Besides, he knew that if anything really interesting was reported his dad would repeat it to him later, usually starting his account with "You'll never guess what those crazy politicians are up to now." So Kurt wasn't surprised to find his dad at his door, ready to share a news story with him. But the expression on his face told Kurt that this story was about more than crazy politicians.

"It's about Tamara—and the Stones. And it's not good."

Kurt did a mental rewind of his dad's pronouncement and replayed it in his head, thinking he must have misheard something—or missed a transition. How did his dad get from "the local news" to "Tamara and the Stones"?

"They've been arrested," his dad said. His brow furrowed. "For allegedly kidnapping a baby."

"What?" Kurt said, frowning.

Kurt's dad went on to tell him everything he remembered from the TV report, including the identity of the baby and the fact that Tamara and the Stones were being lodged in the Douglas County Jail.

Kurt slumped over and held his head in his hands as he struggled to grasp what his dad had told him. Tamara and the Stones took the Trouste baby from its mother. That didn't make any sense. Or did it? His mind leaped back to the conversation he'd had with Tamara following their visit with Detective Hansen at the sheriff's station in Fir Valley. The detective had shown Tamara a picture of Mr. Trouste. What had Tamara remarked later, upon learning who Mr. Trouste was? That he was "rich enough to pay $20,000 for a baby." Did Tamara really believe . . . ?

He grimaced. "There might be a reason for what they did."

His dad nodded. "Usually is."

They were both quiet for a time, Kurt searching his mind and heart for what he should do—could do—to help Tamara. She was the first and only girl he'd ever really cared about. He always felt warm in her presence, the heat radiating from his belly out to his limbs so that his skin tingled. And each time they touched—brushed shoulders or held hands while hiking along a precarious stretch of the trail around the lake—he felt a pleasant vibration, like silent music, course through him. His muscles would go slack for an instant, his legs become undependable, and his sprinting heart would be the only organ in his body not in danger of shutting down.

He knew that bad things had happened to Tamara, although he was sure he didn't know the half of it. Yet somehow she had survived the tragedies in her life without taking on the lasting bitterness he'd seen in other people to whom life had been unkind. He admired her for that. It took courage for someone to keep getting up from life's smack-downs.

But this time, if the news report was true, she'd brought the grief down on her own head—and caused others pain as well.

Still, the thought of Tamara sitting alone and frightened in a jail cell sent shockwaves through him. She had messed up, and somehow gotten the Stones involved as well. But that didn't mean he should turn his back on her—or them. He felt his spine stiffen, his lungs expand, his spirit swell with determination. On the contrary, he had to make every effort to help them, if for no other reason than he was probably the only person in the world who had an inkling about why they'd done what they had.

He stood up so that his gaze was level with his dad's. "Can I borrow the car in the morning? And can I miss a class or two?"

"If it's important to you," his dad said.

Kurt set his jaw. "Yes, sir. It is."

91   TAMARA SAT ON THE bed in the holding cell hugging her knees to her chest. The bed was nothing more than a thin mattress atop a solid platform. Everything inside the cell was solid. Solid concrete floor. Solid block walls painted solid white. Solid stainless steel sink and stool. Solid metal door. And from the moment the door had come crashing closed—solid silence, broken only by an occasional whimper. She was alone in the cell, which told her that the whimpers were her own.

The phone call to her mother had shaken Tamara in a way she hadn't expected. It was no surprise that her mother had declined to come to her aid. But her mother's apparent lack of compassion for her troubles cut to the quick. How could her mother not care that she was in jail? Even after all this time, Tamara couldn't understand how a parent could lose the capacity to love her child.

In the metallic silence of the holding cell, she pressed her head against her knees and cried once again for the love she'd been deprived of at such a tender age.

~

TAMARA WAS SIX YEARS OLD when her mother stopped caring. Up until then, she'd lived a wonderfully contented life. Her mother was an elementary school teacher who gave up her career to stay home with her daughter and become, as it said on her favorite coffee mug, THE WORLD'S BEST MOM. Tamara's dad was a carpet layer, who had his own business and worked long hours to support his family.

When Tamara was three years old, her brother Danny was born. Danny was a sweet kid, curious, handsome, with a thoroughly agreeable disposition from the day he was brought home from the hospital. His parents and grandparents doted on him as they had on his sister before him, and Tamara loved him without reservation.

They were a complete family then, an American ideal: two vibrant kids, a stay-at-home mom, and a loving father who was also a good provider. As a little girl, Tamara had no reason to believe that life wouldn't continue to be as pleasant and manageable as a trip to the mall with Mommy, Nanna, and her little brother.

Then, in one horrifying instant, all that changed.

The day of the accident had begun like any other. Tamara's dad had gone off to work that morning after distributing plenty of kisses and hugs all around and promising to come home for lunch. Lunchtime was a special event in the Ames' household. Tamara's dad put in long days, sometimes leaving for work before the kids were awake and coming home late in the evening after they'd been tucked into bed. But he always made a point, if at all possible, to have lunch at home with his family.

Around noon most days, he'd chug into the driveway in his big white van, which was usually loaded with great rolls of carpet and padding that stuck out the back, beyond where the rear cargo doors had once been attached. He'd honk his horn to announce his arrival, and Tamara and Danny, after he was old enough, would go running out to meet him.

"Swing me," Tamara would plead, and her dad would oblige, and after several whirls that always made her stomach feel funny, he would deposit her into the back of the van on top of a carpet roll that she pretended was the back of a pony. Danny would be standing nearby with his little arms outstretched, none too patiently waiting his turn. Soon he too would be whirling around and around his gyrating dad. And he too would end up inside the van astride his very own steed, where he'd kick up his heels and shout for joy and do his best to ignore his mother's insistent voice calling him and his sister into the house to eat.

Then they'd all gather around the kitchen table for sandwiches and soup that Mom had prepared, or a special casserole hot out of the oven. And Jell-O for dessert, or ice cream and Oreos, or tapioca pudding. Right after which, with their parents' permission, the kids would rush out to the van for one last romp on the carpet rolls before Dad had to leave for work again. They'd jump and tumble and roll together, and ride the pretend ponies some more. And when they were tired, they would lie down in a groove between rolls and hide from one another and from their dad, who, when he came out of the house, always pretended not to know where his children were. Then he'd pull back a flap of carpet padding, and there would be Tamara, squirming and giggling, with Danny snuggled down in some crevice not far away, waiting to be discovered.

But on the day of the accident, they weren't discovered. For some reason, their dad left the house with uncommon haste, the keys on his belt jiggling fretfully as he jogged down the front steps and across the lawn. He got into his van and immediately started the engine. He backed out of the driveway and, after a jolting stop against the far curb, sped off down the street.

Tamara lay in her hiding place rigid with fear as the truck bounced along the uneven pavement. She didn't understand what was happening, knew only that the vehicle was moving and her dad wasn't looking for her. She was afraid to leave her niche, but also afraid not to, because she knew that things weren't as they were supposed to be. And the longer she remained undiscovered in the back of the speeding van, the more she sensed that something very bad was going to happen.

Finally, she pushed back a flap of padding, forced herself up to a sitting position, and looked around. The first thing she saw was Danny at the open end of the van, straddling a large roll of carpet where it projected out over the vehicle's rear bumper. His back was to her. His hair was standing on end and his shirt collar flapped frenetically in the blowback from the open doorway. She watched in horror as he bounced and weaved and wobbled, his little body being tossed about as though he were atop a bucking bronco.

"Danny!" she hollered, fear nearly choking off her words. "Get back in here!"

But Danny didn't hear—or didn't want to hear. He tossed up his arms and kicked up his legs and whooped excitedly as the truck continued rumbling down the road. With her heart hammering in her chest, Tamara scrambled toward him. Reaching the back of the van, she dropped onto her belly and scooted out on the big carpet roll where it hung out over the pavement. The street below was whizzing by at a dizzying pace. She kept her eyes on her brother as she inched her way toward him. When she thought she was close enough, she stretched out her arm to haul him in. Then the truck hit a dip, and Danny was gone.

Tamara screamed. Her father hit the brakes. But it was too late. Danny's head exploded on the pavement like a ripe melon.

In tears, Tamara crabbed her way backwards into the van. She ducked back under a flap of padding, wanting to hide there forever, convinced that surely she would be blamed for her brother's death.

But Tamara's dad blamed only himself. He cried out in anguish as he stood over Danny's broken body where it lay in the street; he cursed himself as it was carted away some time later by solemn paramedics; he writhed with remorse as the lid was closed on the little silver casket in which it finally was placed. One week after the funeral, he drove off from the house in his van and never returned.

Burdened by a terrible guilt, Tamara turned to her mother for emotional support. But it was as if her mother had left as well. Seemingly blind to the fact that she still had a daughter who loved and needed her, she shut herself up in her darkened bedroom and stayed there day and night, crying inconsolably over the loss of her only son.

Nanna stayed at the house with them. She looked after Tamara and tried to get Tamara's mother to rest or, at least, to eat or drink something. But Tamara's mom just sat there on her bed staring wild-eyed at the wall, crying, "Why? Why? Why?" She rocked back and forth, moaning like a fatally injured beast and clawing at her forearms until they were bloody. Within days, she was seriously dehydrated and clearly out of her head. Nanna called an ambulance and had her taken to the hospital. The doctors gave her nutrients intravenously and treated her for depression. She recovered physically. When she showed no signs of getting better emotionally, she was transferred to a mental hospital in Salem.

Tamara went to live with her grandparents. They were grief-stricken too, but they loved her and did their best to care for her, making sure that she got plenty of counseling and anything else she wanted. But what Tamara wanted was unattainable. The fabric of her happy life had been shredded beyond repair. The joy she'd once experienced being Mommy's little helper and Daddy's little angel was long gone. In its place was an ever-present emptiness—and her own nightly tears.

She survived the following months and years by, as much as possible, shutting out the hurt, along with just about every other emotion. She fell into a routine and stayed with it, wanting or expecting nothing more. There was school, time at home with Nanna, weekly visits to the counselor, and the occasional, frightening trip to see her mother at Fairview.

Then when Tamara was eight, her grandfather died of lung cancer. She hadn't seen much of him for quite a while before that because he'd been shut up in the spare room so much of the time. She would hear him at night, coughing and moaning, and would see him on the days he bathed. With Nanna's help, he would shuffle down the hall to the bathroom in pajamas that hung on him like scarecrow clothes, his face all sunken and pale. Then Nanna would help him undress and support him while he stepped into the tub of warm water she had run for him. While he soaked in the tub, Nanna would change his sheets and try to clean the stink from his room. One day when Nanna went to get him out of the water, she found that he wasn't breathing.

Tamara didn't go to the funeral. She stayed with a neighbor lady, who gave her a Popsicle and let her watch cartoons on TV, and told her that everything was okay because her grandpa had gone to a better place. Tamara wondered where that place was. She thought that she might like to go there too.

The following summer, her mother was released from the mental hospital and came to live with them at Nanna's house. "Now don't expect too much of her, at least at first," Nanna had cautioned. Secretly, Tamara's hopes had soared. Finally they would be a real family again. The love that had been withdrawn from her was about to be restored. But her hopes were instantly shattered when, greeted at the door by Tamara's open arms, her mother shrank away from being hugged by her own daughter.

Six months later, Nanna had her stroke. The stroke left her paralyzed on one side and, for all practical purposes, speechless. She was incapable of caring for herself, much less an emotional cripple and a nine-year-old granddaughter. Children's Services intervened.

For Tamara, there followed a series of stays in foster homes, while her mother and grandmother were relegated to different state-supported group homes. The family that Tamara had longed to see made whole was cruelly torn apart. In its place, she received revolving institutional care, which she learned came with a price. By the time she was twelve, Tamara had been groped and fondled by a string of pimply-faced foster brothers and overly affectionate foster dads.

Then a strange thing happened. Her mother remarried.

Darryl Neaves was a forty-four-year-old divorcé and part-time van driver for County Special Services, who could be very charming when he was sober. Three days a week, he did pickups and deliveries at group homes and assisted-living facilities in the area. Tamara's mother had become a regular on his bus, after having been prompted by her therapist to begin the process of reintegrating herself back into the community.

No one, least of all Tamara, expected that process to include marriage. It was only after she'd gone to live with her new family, including Darryl's teenage sons, that Tamara learned what had brought her mother and Darryl Neaves together. "Why do you let him do that to you?" she asked her mother one afternoon after school. She had come home just as her stepdad was leaving the house all red-faced and sweaty, with his shirttail hanging out. He winked at Tamara and hurried out to his van.

"It's what he wants," was all her mother had said.

But even then Tamara knew that her mother's submissiveness had nothing to do with Darryl's desires and everything to do with her own need to be punished. She'd been punishing herself—and, indirectly, her daughter—in various ways ever since Danny's death.

~

A SOUND LIKE A hammer striking metal resonated in Tamara's ears. She looked up, startled, realizing only as she saw the door to the holding cell slide open that what she'd heard was its heavy bolt being thrown back.

A uniformed guard appeared in the doorway. Short, stocky, female. All business. "Come with me, please," she said, managing to transform the polite request into a command with the sheer flatness of her voice.

"Where?"

"Processing," the guard said.

Tamara stiffened, her mind conjuring up an image of her naked body being strip-searched by hands eager to probe her private recesses. "Do I have a choice?"

The guard smiled, as if savoring the prospect of a confrontation. "You always have a choice."

Tamara glanced around her stark confines. She had a choice all right—between a hammer and a fist. She brought her feet to the floor, wriggled them into her shoes. Her shoelaces were missing. They'd been removed—along with her belt, watch, and earrings—during booking. She got up and walked to the cell door.

"That way," the guard said, pointing down the corridor, away from the booking station. Tamara moved in the indicated direction, with the guard so closely in step behind her that she could feel the woman's body heat.

Just past the bank of holding cells, another corridor led off to the right. "Down there," the guard said.

At the end of a short hallway they came to a door above which was lettering that spelled SHOWERS. The guard gestured toward the doorway. "Leave your clothes on the bench inside, where you will find a towel. You have four minutes to undress, shower, dress, and reappear outside this door."

"But—"

The guard looked at her watch. "Starting now."

Tamara bolted for the door. When she got out of the shower a couple of minutes later and began toweling off, she found that her clothes were gone. They'd been replaced by dark-blue cotton trousers cut more like pajamas, and a similarly hued, short-sleeved top that had no collar or significant shape.

"One minute," came the guard's indifferent voice from outside the door.

Tamara dabbed at her sopping hair with the towel—the shower spray had come out of a spout high overhead so that she hadn't been able to avoid getting her hair wet. She tossed the towel aside and donned the prison clothes. She looked around for her sneakers. Instead, she found a pair of vinyl sandals that looked—and felt, when she slipped her feet into them—two sizes too large. She stumbled out the door in the floppy shoes, feeling as though she was learning to walk all over again.

With the deputy once again breathing down her neck, she shuffled back to the central corridor. Several minutes later, after being shuttled through a maze of interlocking passageways, she found herself facing a broad metal door labeled ISOLATION. The word sounded in her head

like the fireworks screamers neighborhood kids set off on the Fourth
of July. She pulled up short. "Why're you putting me in here?"

The guard spoke some numbers into a microphone clipped to
the lapel of her shirt. The metal door buzzed. The guard pulled it
open. "You're a minor," she said. "We can't put you in with the general
population."

92   THE ELEVATOR DOOR clattered open, and Kurt stepped
out into the third-floor lobby of the Douglas County
Justice Building. It was his first visit to the imposing concrete and glass
structure in Roseburg that housed the Douglas County Jail in one
wing and the Circuit Court in another. And as he gazed about, trying
to get his bearings, he felt the oppressive presence of authority, like a
constant hand on his shoulder.

Ahead of him was a wide stairwell flanked by a railing that separated the lobby from open, interior space beyond. He peered over the
railing. The third-floor lobby was actually a balcony overlooking a
glass-enclosed atrium that soared from the building's ground level to
its fourth-floor ceiling. Tree-filtered sunlight spilled into the atrium,
no doubt raising the spirits of the potted plants decorating the lobby,
but doing nothing for the leaden feeling in Kurt's gut.

"They may not let you see her," his dad had cautioned earlier that
morning as Kurt had prepared to leave the house.

"I've got to try," Kurt had responded, the thought of doing nothing
long since banished from his mind.

He made a couple of sweeps around the perimeter of the lobby
without locating the visitor entrance to the jail. Then he caught sight
of a sign on the west wall that read CORRECTION DIVISION VISITOR
AREA. An arrow pointed the way.

He found the visitor entrance about halfway down a short corridor to his right. It was an ordinary-looking wooden door with a
little peek-a-boo window that had been papered over from the inside,

presumably to thwart prying eyes. A middle-aged woman in baggy slacks and a flowery-print blouse stood in the corridor not far from the closed door, hugging a red purse. She shrank back a few steps as Kurt approached.

He paused outside the door to read a notice posted on the wall, listing the jail visiting hours for that day: 9 AM to 11 AM. He looked at his watch. It was going on nine-thirty.

Feeling his pulse rate kick up a notch, he stepped up to the door with the intention of passing through. But for some reason, he couldn't make himself reach out and grasp the doorknob. He wanted to go in. Then again, maybe he didn't. Maybe it was the wrong thing to do after all. He wanted to help Tamara. But how would his coming here accomplish that? What if she didn't want to see him? What if his coming to visit her in jail would only make her feel worse than she undoubtedly already did? What if—

"They keep the door locked," the woman hugging the red purse said. She pointed to a white speaker box on the wall. "You have to push the button and talk to them."

"Oh," Kurt said, feeling more embarrassment now than anxiety. "Thanks." He pressed the speaker button.

A squawky woman's voice greeted him from the speaker box. "What can I do for you?"

"I'm here to see Tamara Ames," he said with as much self-assurance as he could muster.

"Are you on her visitor list?" the squawky voice wanted to know.

"Uh—I don't know," Kurt said, his confidence immediately undercut by the question.

"What's your name?"

He gave it.

"Spell the last name, please."

He did.

"One moment, please."

More than a moment passed. The voice came out of the box again: "I'm sorry, sir, but you are not on her visitor list. I cannot admit you."

In spite of his misgivings about having come here, Kurt bristled at the idea of being turned away at the door. "How can I get on her visitor list?"

"She must put you on," came the answer from the box.

Kurt frowned. "But how can I get her to put me on the list if I can't talk to her?"

There was a slight pause, then the box said, "I suggest you speak with her attorney about that."

"Who is her attorney?"

"They can tell you at the DA's office."

"Where's that?"

"One floor down and across the hall. In the court wing."

Kurt smothered an urge to complain. "Thank you."

"They hassle everybody," the woman with the red purse said. Her gaze flicked toward the ceiling.

Kurt glanced up and saw for the first time the video camera mounted high on the wall. The eyes of Lady Justice. They'd been watching him from the moment he'd entered the hallway. He sidled away from the door, feeling self-conscious and not knowing why.

He walked back to the lobby, his stomach flopping like a Mexican jumping bean. He descended the stairs to the next lower level and found himself in the center of a lobby almost identical to the one above. On his right was a set of tall, oak double doors that, according to a sign nearby, accessed the court wing. He was approaching the doors when one of them swung open and two men in suits stepped out. One of the men held the door open for him.

Kurt peered through the doorway. A uniformed officer was stationed just inside, the shiny badge on his chest as repellent as razorwire. Kurt stepped back. "Sorry," he said to the man holding the door, "I don't think this is where I really want to be."

With his thoughts a jumble now, he plunged down the stairs to the first floor lobby, exited the building, and made his way back to where he'd parked his parents' car. He sat in the Cutlass gripping the steering wheel and wrangling in his mind with the uncertainty that threatened to undermine his resolve. He wanted to help Tamara in the worst way, but he didn't know how to go about doing it, and not knowing made him feel powerless.

He gazed up at the hard-edged structure that was supposed to represent Justice. The windows in the jail wing were tiny slits that would admit little light and, he was sure, even less hope. The thought of Tamara being held captive behind those cruel walls sickened him. He wanted to turn himself into a wrecking ball so that he could smash down those walls and rescue her. He'd take her away to a place beyond the reach of the law or anyone else who wanted to harm her.

He choked the steering wheel and grunted in frustration. He wasn't a wrecking ball. He wasn't even a five-pound sledge.

But I have to help Tamara any way I can!

But how? How could he come to her aid?

He started the car and headed back to Fir Valley to find the one person he knew could answer that question.

93 OREGON STATE POLICE OFFICER Martin Rodgers steered his cruiser through another severe bend in the road, the cruiser's engine kicking into a lower gear to surmount the steep incline. "So, what's your angle, Dan?" Rodgers said. "You lookin' to get a private tour of the Trouste mansion?"

Detective Hansen smiled in response to Rodgers' query. Rodgers, who worked out of the OSP station in Roseburg, was the officer in charge of the Trouste baby kidnapping investigation. Hansen had worked with him on a previous Joint Task Force case and knew him to be a no-nonsense, by-the-book investigator who doggedly pursued the evidence on every case and had little time or sympathy for theories of a crime that couldn't be supported by the facts. So when Hansen had decided to ask if he could accompany Rodgers on this follow-up interview with Mrs. Trouste, he'd thought it best to tell the OSP officer

as little as possible about his motivation. Rodgers had agreed to let
Hansen tag along, but apparently that didn't mean he wasn't going to
press him about his intentions.

"Naw," Hansen said. "I can wait for it to show up on the next episode of *Showcase of Historic Homes in Douglas County.*"

"What then?" Rodgers inquired, displaying the persistency that
made him a good cop.

The detective decided he'd better level with his fellow officer—to a
degree. "The Ames girl," he said. "Her name keeps popping up."

Rodgers shot him a discerning look. "The two murders. I thought
those cases were closed."

"Yeah, but you never can tell." Hansen gave a casual shrug. "I might
learn something worth knowing."

Rodgers let the matter drop, and Hansen was glad of it. He was
skating on thin ice here, and he didn't want anyone else aware of it for
fear the *Clear the Ice!* warning would sound and he would be left on
the sidelines wishing he'd been more of a player in this latest round of
inquiry into what he still believed might be interrelated events. After
all, could Tamara Ames' involvement in the Trouste baby kidnapping
really have been mere coincidence?

"Just one thing," Rodgers said.

They'd reached the top of the ridge and were angling onto Summit Drive. The weather this morning had started out iffy and was
now showing its true intent as light rain began to patter against the
windshield.

"What's that?" Hansen said.

"When we get there, I do the talking."

Hansen sensed his legs being kicked out from under him. *Thin ice*,
he reminded himself. "Fair enough," he said.

Minutes later, they were being invited into the Trouste mansion by
a gray-haired woman wearing a white duster over a blue cotton dress.
"This way, please," the woman said, and led the way at a surprisingly
nimble gait. They followed her through a spacious vestibule, down a
side corridor, and into a darkly paneled room lined with bookshelves
and studio portraits. Across the room, in a leather armchair—the most

comfortable-looking component of an otherwise unoccupied grouping of furniture around an unlit fireplace—sat Russell Trouste.

"Gentlemen," Mr. Trouste said, rising from his chair. And to the old woman: "Elena, tell Mrs. Trouste the officers are here."

Rodgers stepped forward and shook hands with Mr. Trouste. "I'm Officer Rodgers. We spoke on the phone." He nodded toward Hansen. "This is Detective Hansen of the Douglas County Sheriff's Office. I hope this meeting isn't too much of an inconvenience for you, sir."

"Not for me," Mr. Trouste said. "I'm taking a few days off from work to be with my wife."

"How's she doing?"

Mr. Trouste gestured toward a sofa on the opposite side of a coffee table from his chair. "I'm afraid she's taking this very hard." He eased back down into his chair. "If we could make this meeting brief, gentlemen, it would be appreciated."

"Of course," Rodgers said as he and Hansen settled onto the sofa.

Rodgers had just finished briefing Mr. Trouste on the progress of his investigation when Mrs. Trouste shuffled into the room with her eyes downcast. She was wearing a lavender housedress and big, fuzzy slippers. Her face was pale, although perhaps not as pale as the color of her dress made it appear. There were dark patches under her eyes that resembled the eye black some football players wear.

The officers stood, and Mr. Trouste did too. His wife came over and nestled against him.

"These officers would like to ask you a few questions, dear," he said. "It shouldn't take long." He led her to a wing chair to his left, where she sat, head bowed, hands clasped together in her lap.

"Go ahead," Mr. Trouste said when they were all seated again.

Rodgers leaned forward on the sofa, elbows resting on his knees. "Thank you, Mrs. Trouste, for seeing us. I know this has been a terrible ordeal for you. We're only glad that it has ended well, with your daughter safe and her abductors behind bars. Our wish is to keep them there, and that's the reason for this visit. The more we know about what happened at the mall, the better case we'll be able to build against the individuals who took Felicity."

"I'll tell you what I can," Mrs. Trouste said, her voice small and timorous.

Rodgers pulled a pen and notepad from his shirt pocket. "Mrs. Trouste, had you ever seen any of the perpetrators before yesterday?"

"No," Mrs. Trouste said, keeping her head down as she spoke. "The first time I saw those two girls was in the mall when they came up to the baby carriage and made a fuss over Felicity, saying how pretty she was. I don't remember seeing the boy at all."

"Did you see any of them later in the mall while you were shopping?"

"No. Only the one time."

"Did you see them in the parking lot when you went back to your car?"

"No."

"So you didn't actually see them take Felicity from her carriage?"

Mrs. Trouste's head jerked up, her face suddenly full of color, and when she spoke again there was newfound strength in her voice—the edgy vitality of defensiveness. "As I've said before, *officer*, I was busy trying to get the car carrier ready for Felicity. The straps always get tangled." She paused, her eyes seeming to lose focus, and Hansen thought she must have been reliving those few critical moments she'd spent struggling with those jumbled straps—the moments during which she'd been inattentive to her child. "Then *someone*—" she said with bitterness in her voice, "—I didn't see who—just stole Felicity." She glared at Rodgers as if daring him to contradict her account of what had happened.

The OSP officer merely nodded. "I understand. Just a couple more questions."

Hansen, true to his word, remained silent while Rodgers proceeded with his questioning, deferent more than ever now to his witness and her obviously fragile state of mind. Mrs. Trouste, after the one bout of annoyance, settled into a more resigned, if not cooperative mode as she answered the officer's queries, each response confirming that she knew nothing more about what had happened the previous day at the mall other than the bare facts she'd already recounted.

If this disappointed Rodgers, he didn't let it show. "Thank you, Mrs. Trouste," he said when his last question had been asked and answered. "You've been very helpful." He stood. Hansen followed suit.

Mr. Trouste helped his wife up from her chair and escorted her to the door. He whispered something to her and kissed her on the cheek. When she'd disappeared down the hallway, he returned to where the two officers stood. "If that's all, gentlemen," he said dismissively.

"Yes, thank you," Rodgers said. "And as you've requested, sir, we'll keep you informed as to the progress of our investigation." With that, he turned to leave.

Hansen stayed in place, having decided on this moment to take the plunge into the icy waters of conjecture. "Mr. Trouste," he said, "if it's all right, I'd like to ask *you* a couple of questions."

Rodgers spun on his heels, a troubled look on his face. But he didn't intervene as Hansen thought he might.

Russell Trouste eyed the detective with polite disdain. "Of course," he said. But he remained standing, obviously intending that this impromptu inquiry be brief.

Hansen understood the situation and resolved to get to the point quickly. "Mr. Trouste, do *you* recall ever having any prior contact with any of the three alleged perpetrators?"

"Never," Mr. Trouste said, shaking his head emphatically.

"Did the name Tamara Ames mean anything to you before yesterday?"

"Why should it?"

"Did you know, sir, that Tamara Ames had been pregnant and had lost a child about the same time your daughter was born?" The detective locked eyes with Russell Trouste. "Stillborn, according to all accounts."

Mr. Trouste's gaze seemed to turn inward. His countenance softened, along with his voice. "No, I did not." He shook his head. "Very unfortunate." Then, as if only a scrap of compassion, like pocket change, was all he could afford to offer the needy, his back stiffened and his face assumed a look of scorn. "But that doesn't excuse—" He stopped himself.

Hansen didn't stop himself. "And were you aware, sir, that Tamara Ames—according to statements made by Tommy and Amanda Stone—has alleged that your daughter, Felicity, is in fact her child."

"That's preposterous."

Hansen felt a hand grip his shoulder from behind. "We're done here now," Officer Rodgers said in a firm voice.

Hansen ignored him. "Can you think of any reason, Mr. Trouste, why Tamara Ames would be making such a claim?"

Russell Trouste responded with stony defiance. "None whatsoever. The girl is obviously deluded."

"Thank you for your time, Mr. Trouste," Rodgers said. He stepped in front of Hansen and held out an open hand toward Russell Trouste, who stared at it for a time as if not understanding what it was for, then finally reached out and shook it.

Rodgers turned around and glowered at Hansen. "We're leaving now."

But Hansen had made his decision. It was now or never. "Just one more question," he said, sidestepping the OSP officer to face Russell Trouste again. "Mr. Trouste, does your company keep an overseas bank account?"

"I fail to see—"

Rodgers jumped between the two men again. "You don't have to answer that question, Mr. Trouste." He stiff-armed Hansen's chest and began shoving the detective backwards toward the door.

"Mr. Trouste," Hansen called out as he was being shunted away, "someone deposited $20,000 into a bank account in the name of Tamara Ames the day after her baby was born. Would you know anything about that?"

Rodgers pushed harder. "I'm sorry, Mr. Trouste," he said, his eyes firing flaming darts at Hansen. "Please disregard that question. It has no relevancy to our investigation."

Realizing that he had come to the end of his string, in more ways than one, Hansen allowed himself to be driven from the room and out of the house.

"What the hell was that all about?" Rodgers said, hunching his shoulders as they jogged down the front steps. The light rain from earlier had turned into a downpour blown sideways by the wind.

Hansen knew he owed his fellow officer an explanation. "There are just too many things—"

"No," Rodgers said, throwing up his hands. "I don't even want to know."

They splashed across the gleaming-wet driveway to the cruiser, got in, and slammed the doors against the weather. Rodgers started the car and pulled away, belatedly turning on the windshield wipers. "We'll have hell to pay for this," he grumbled.

He's right, Hansen thought. He combed his fingers through his soggy hair. What had gotten into him? If he'd wanted to play good cop/bad cop at the expense of Mr. Trouste, he should have clued Rodgers in on the plan. But that wouldn't have worked either, because the OSP officer would never have gone along with it, not when the target of the routine was the most prominent man in the county. Rodgers would have politely declined his request to accompany him on the interview. That would have left Hansen back at the station house cooling his heels, while Russell Trouste would have been off the hook.

But what if he was wrong? What if Russell Trouste really didn't know anything about Tamara Ames and her stillborn child?

Hansen's mouth went dry, and he felt the quickening of a latent desire. He turned to Rodgers. "Got a cigarette?"

"Don't smoke," Rodgers said testily.

Hansen swiped his fingertips across his lips. "Neither do I." Not for the last six years, anyway. He stared out the rain-pocked windshield without seeing anything beyond the glass. The sound of flapping wiper blades filled the empty space between him and Rodgers.

It wasn't until they were within a few blocks of arriving back at the sheriff's substation that another sound—the squawking of the car radio—broke through to Hansen's consciousness. The OSP officer snatched up the microphone. The call was from central dispatch. Neither man was surprised at the message: Detective Hansen was to report to Lieutenant Iverson at the Fir Valley Sheriff's Substation immediately.

Within seconds of the call, Rodgers was swinging the cruiser into the station parking lot. He pulled up alongside the building, leaving the engine running. "I got somewhere else to be," he said.

Hansen let out a nervous chuckle. "You don't want to come in and see the fireworks?"

Rodgers revved the engine. "I don't want to be anywhere in the vicinity."

94   HANSEN ENTERED THE substation through the rear entrance, for use by employees only. On his way down the hall, he paused in the doorway to the front office. Deputy Riley was sitting at the duty desk looking bored. There didn't seem to be a lynching party lurking about. The detective was about to head on down to his boss's office for the dressing-down he knew was in store for him, when Riley, spying him, spoke up.

"You got a visitor," the deputy said. He pointed toward the public lobby.

Hansen peered over the counter and was surprised to see Kurt Adberry, sitting alone and looking dejected. As soon as the kid spotted him, he hopped up and came rushing up to the counter. "Detective, can I talk to you? It's important."

"Sure," Hansen said. Then he remembered his prior engagement. "I just have one thing to do first. You can wait in my office." He admitted Kurt to the employee area and escorted him down to his office. "Have a seat," he told the kid. He took off his rain-soaked jacket and hung it over the back of his chair. "I'll be right back."

The lieutenant's office door was open. Hansen stepped through the doorway as reluctantly as a soldier exposing himself to enemy fire. Maybe he should have donned a flak jacket.

Iverson was sitting at his desk with his arms cinched across his broad chest. He fixed Hansen with a lethal stare. "I just got off the phone with the sheriff," he said in a barely controlled voice, "who just got off the phone with Russell Trouste." He paused to allow the weight of that news to land heavily on the detective's shoulders, which it did. "Dan, what the hell happened up there?"

Hansen knew he'd screwed up. He should have run all this by his boss first—his initial suspicions regarding the Troustes, set aside for a time and then rekindled by the recent desperate actions of Tamara Ames and the Stones, and his desire to follow up on those suspicions once he'd learned that Rodgers was going to interview Mrs. Trouste in her home. But it was too late now to make amends for that colossal oversight. The best he could do was to downplay the incident at the Trouste estate. He shrugged. "I just asked Mr. Trouste a few questions."

"Yes," Iverson said, scorching him with the heat from his gaze, "questions that implied you are putting some merit in Amanda Stone's claim that the Trouste baby really belongs to Tamara Ames. Questions that implied Mr. Trouste might have been involved in some farfetched baby-stealing scheme. Questions that—that"—the lieutenant's face flamed seemingly to the point of ignition—"that you had no business asking."

Hansen hung his head. "I'm sorry. I was out of line in not consulting you first. It won't happen again."

The lieutenant responded by slamming his fist down on his desk so hard that the file baskets on it hopped up and down and a pencil holder toppled over, spilling its contents onto the desktop. "Well, I just got my butt chewed out royally by the sheriff. And your sorry-ass words of contrition don't cut it."

Hansen was momentarily stunned silent. "Look, Lieutenant," he finally said. "I was just letting the facts lead me."

"Oh, were you?" the lieutenant shot back, his words dripping with sarcasm. "It just so happens that I've gone over the case files a time or two myself. And here are the facts as I see them: We have a busy obstetrician attending to two patients on the same day. We have a young girl who probably abused her body during her pregnancy and then took a serious tumble in a market, having a stillbirth. And we have the girl's brother—a fellow of questionable character, engaged in God knows

what kind of shenanigans—getting a payoff probably involving drugs,
part of which he apparently deposited into an account in his sister's
name." He shook his head disdainfully. "How could any of that possibly have led you to believe that Russell Trouste might somehow be
involved, other than as a victim of a kidnapping?"

"Tamara's baby is the key," Hansen said, hoping to make his point
before being blown out of the conversation by the force of his boss's ire.

The lieutenant's eyebrows shot up. "Really? And what happened
to the baby?" He stroked his chin and pretended to ponder the question. "Oh, yes—born dead, cremated, and given a proper interment."
His eyes bored into Hansen as if he were the bull's-eye on a shooting
range target. "Dan, the murder cases are closed. We've got confessions
from the two boys on Gary Neaves. You've said yourself that Neaves
undoubtedly did in Jimmy Stark before he got himself whacked. Now,
for God's sake—" He spread his arms, palms upturned, in a gesture of
supplication. "Let's put all this pointless conjecture about the Troustes
in the shit-can where it belongs."

Hansen mashed his lips together, holding his peace. "Yes, sir."

"And if you have any more urges to talk to Russell Trouste, see me
first."

Hansen nodded. "You can count on it."

"Good."

"Can I just say one thing?" the detective said. After all, the course
of action to follow under the circumstances seemed obvious to him.

The lieutenant groaned. "If you must."

"We can end all conjecture—pointless or otherwise—about the
Troustes' possible involvement in something nefarious by simply getting a court-ordered maternity test on the Trouste baby. If you talked
to the DA, I'm sure—"

"Court order?" the lieutenant said, his face breaking out in a deep-
furrowed scowl. "Maternity test?"

"Yes," Hansen said. "Test the baby against Mrs. Trouste and then
against Tamara Ames."

Iverson exploded, jumping to his feet so brusquely that his chair
blasted backwards into the wall, chipping the plaster. "You really haven't

been listening, have you?" he bellowed. He poked a forefinger at the detective as if aiming a pistol at a would-be assailant. "Dan, you are to have no more involvement in this investigation. And if you as much as whisper any more unfounded accusations against the Troustes, to me or anyone else, you will be suspended for insubordination. Is that understood?"

Hansen stumbled back, feeling as if he'd been struck by a hundred-mile-an-hour wind. He buttressed himself against the doorjamb. "Yes, sir," he said weakly.

"Good." The lieutenant waved his hand as if shooing a fly. "Now get out of my sight."

Hansen staggered away from his boss's office, struggling to understand how things had gone so wrong. Usually his instincts and his drive to get at the truth served him well. But in this case, they'd only landed him in hot water. He wasn't used to the dousing—or the heat.

He was surprised, and embarrassed, to realize that he was trembling. He rolled his shoulders. Shake it off, he told himself. This was just one little ass chewing. It wasn't his first and it definitely wouldn't be his last. Criticism—from within and without—came with the job, like shift work and phone calls at all hours of the night. In this case, it merely meant that his participation in this particular investigation had come to an end.

Hansen had forgotten about Kurt Adberry. The kid jumped up from his seat when Hansen entered his office.

"Sit," the detective said, and Kurt did. Hansen sank into the chair behind his desk, still feeling shell-shocked.

"Are you all right, sir?" the kid asked.

Hansen leaned back in his chair. "Yeah, sure." He took a deep breath, faked a tranquil expression. "What can I do for you?"

Kurt's gaze turned deadly sober. "Tell me what I can do to help Tamara."

Hansen regarded the kid for a long moment. In light of what had just occurred in his boss's office, he would have to be very careful here. He gestured toward the doorway. "Close the door."

The kid got up and closed the door.

"You really want to help Tamara?"

Kurt's eyes shone with youthful passion. "Yes, sir."

Hansen glanced over at the photo on his desktop of his wife and kids and experienced a familiar pull in his chest. "Good," he said, "because at this point you might be the only person who can."

95 TAMARA'S CELL IN Isolation varied little from the concrete and steel vault she'd been confined to in the booking area, and her first reaction upon being locked inside was the same—mindless panic. The white walls closed in on her so that she imagined herself trapped inside a refrigerator. *I'll suffocate and die in here*, she thought as she cried herself to sleep. But when morning came in the form of a blade of sunlight knifing through a small window high in the wall, she was still alive, and a breakfast of toast, oatmeal, and juice had appeared on a tray sitting on a metal shelf below a slot in the front wall she hadn't noticed before because it was covered with a flap.

She wasn't hungry. She wasn't thirsty. She wasn't anything. She was alive but felt dead inside. Her heart had been cut out of her chest. Her head had been opened up and suctioned out. There was nothing vital left inside her. And for the moment, this was a good thing because it meant that the mindless panic she'd experienced the night before had been replaced by a numbing mindlessness.

So the dawning of the new day didn't faze her. She didn't get up. She didn't move. She didn't do anything, because she didn't feel anything. And she didn't want to feel anything.

This numbness was a protective cloak that would stay wrapped around her for only so long. She knew this because she'd used the cloak before, many times, to shield herself from the pain that always followed a loss. And she was determined to use it this time for as long as she could. So she tried to lie perfectly still, the way a dead person would.

By the time the noon meal came sliding in through the slot in the wall, Tamara's stomach, which hadn't received as much as a corn chip in the last twenty-four hours, was gnawing on itself with painful results. She sat up and shakily brought the tray to her lap. She ate some of the potato soup. Nibbled on a soda cracker. Drank half a carton of milk. The food didn't taste good—or bad. Eating it was more like touching than tasting.

She set the tray aside and lay back on the mattress, wanting to slip back under her cloak of non-feeling. She sighed—it wasn't going to happen. Already she could sense a quickening at the center of her.

She tried to suppress it, tried to close the lid to the box that contained her heart and sit on it for as long as she could. But even before her intentions were fully formed, she felt a wrenching ache in her breast. Her chest heaved as the feelings of the night before came rushing back. Once again, her baby had been taken from her. Once again, she'd been stripped of her freedom. Once again, she'd had to confront her mother's inability to love her. Loss. Loss. Loss.

She curled up on the bed and cried out as loudly as she had the night before. But this time, the sobs that followed were dry sobs that expressed her pain but did nothing to cleanse it. Not because the pain wasn't real, but because she knew that the real hurt—the ultimate loss she would have to suffer—was yet to come.

96

THE LAW OFFICES of Crossfield and Brandt were located in a yellow house across the street from the Justice Building in Roseburg. Because the law firm had limited parking, Kurt, as advised, parked in the Justice lot and walked across to the yellow house.

"I'm here to see Martha Brandt," he told the law office receptionist. At least he thought she was the receptionist, because she was sitting at a desk in the front room of the house, looking harried.

"You must be Kurt," the woman said in a husky voice he recognized right off. "I'm Martha Brandt."

It was Detective Hansen who'd encouraged Kurt to contact Tamara's attorney. He'd made a few calls the previous afternoon while Kurt was still in his office and had obtained the name and phone number of the public defender who'd been assigned to Tamara's case. "Call her," Hansen had said, handing over a sheet of paper with the name and number scribbled on it. "I think she'll want to talk to you."

Kurt had taken the detective's advice. Upon leaving the sheriff's substation, he'd stopped at a pay phone outside the strip mall next door to make the call. He'd been so nervous that he'd dropped the first coin he tried to poke into the little slot on the face of the phone box. Finally completing the call, he was surprised when Ms. Brandt herself, rather than a secretary or a receptionist or whoever generally answered the phone in a law office, picked up on the first ring. He told the attorney who he was and she seemed interested in meeting with him. But she was tied up until the following afternoon.

Martha Brandt was blond, big-boned, and as Kurt found out when she stood up, a good four inches taller than he was. "Let's go to my office," she said, and headed down a hallway with strides longer than anything she could have achieved had she been wearing a skirt.

Kurt followed her into a back room that must have been a bedroom at one time but now resembled a storage locker. Boxes of books and file folders were stacked everywhere—on the floor, on an oak desk, atop file cabinets, on the windowsill—everywhere, that is, except on the empty shelves lining the walls.

"Don't touch anything," cautioned Ms. Brandt. "I don't want anything to get out of order." She paused just long enough for the absurdity of the remark to sink in, then laughed. But Kurt had already stuck his hands in his pockets for safekeeping.

The attorney shoved aside an overflowing box to make room for a battered wooden chair and gestured for him to sit. "We moved into this building only yesterday." She shot the gap between two tilting stacks and lowered herself into a swivel armchair behind the desk. "I have lots of putting away to do. Right after we hire a receptionist." She flicked her hair behind her ears the way women do when they want to keep it out of their face. "So tell me, Kurt, how long have you known Tamara?"

Kurt thought a moment. It seemed like a long time, but really it had been only a couple of months. He told her so.

"But apparently you've grown close to her in that time or you wouldn't be here."

"Yes, ma'am," he said, admitting what seemed to be obvious to so many others by now.

Ms. Brandt clicked her fingernails against the desktop. "Okay, Kurt, friend of Tamara's," she said, as if granting him a royal title, "let me tell you how it is with this case. I've been assigned to prepare Tamara's defense against some very serious charges. We won't know for sure until the arraignment, but I'd say we're looking at kidnapping, child endangerment, truancy, and whatever else the DA dreams up to make his case seem more substantial." She raised her eyebrows. "The problem is, Tamara won't talk to me."

Kurt felt something flutter in his chest "You've seen her?" He frowned. "I tried to see her, but they wouldn't let me in. Said I wasn't on her list."

"I saw her yesterday afternoon," Ms. Brandt said, "and again this morning." She shrugged. "Lot of good it did. She's not saying anything. The only details I'm getting about what happened, and possibly why, are from the DA's office or from the Stones' attorney, both of whom have their own agendas. The DA, of course, wants to hang all three defendants. And the Stones' attorney would like to shift all the blame for the incident onto Tamara, who, he says, misled his clients into believing that Felicity Trouste was really her child. Sooo"—she displayed upturned palms—"as it now stands, Tamara is being positioned to take the fall for everyone. I can't change that if she won't talk to me."

Kurt squirmed in his chair. "She's not much of a talker."

"So I gather," Ms. Brandt said. "That's why I was hoping you could tell me something that would help me get a handle on this case."

"I don't know what?"

"For starters, you could tell me why Tamara and the Stones kidnapped the Trouste baby."

Kurt felt his face grow hot.

Ms. Brandt stared at him as if she knew he had secrets to divulge. "Talk to me, Kurt."

Kurt hesitated, not sure what he was at liberty to say. But if Tamara wasn't going to speak in her own defense, then someone else had to speak up for her. And who else was there? So he came right out with it. "It has to do with Tamara's baby that died."

The attorney nodded. "Yes, I understand she gave birth to a stillborn a couple of months ago."

"Right."

"That would speak to her mental state. It would garner her some sympathy. Be a mitigating factor at sentencing. But it doesn't justify kidnapping a baby."

Kurt felt a moment of desperation, as if he was a cliff climber groping unsuccessfully for the next handhold. He reached farther out. "Would it help if it can be shown that Tamara really believed the Troustes' baby was hers?"

Ms. Brandt narrowed her eyes. "What are you getting at?"

With a nervous rush of speech, Kurt told the attorney everything he knew about the night Tamara lost her baby, the details of which he'd learned mostly from Tamara's conversations with others, and from Tommy and Amanda, who couldn't keep a secret if their lives depended on it. He told Ms. Brandt about Tamara's connection to Gary Neaves and Jimmy Stark, about Detective Hansen's investigation into their deaths, about Tamara's recurring nightmare, about the Troustes' baby being born the same night as Tamara's. And, of course, he told her about the $20,000 that had mysteriously appeared in Tamara's bank account the very next day.

The attorney's eyes were wide open now, flickering like dancing flames as she listened. "Are you telling me," she said after he'd run out of words, "that Detective Hansen might actually suspect that Tamara's baby was born alive and was then taken from her—with or without her consent—and that the Troustes might have had something to do with it?"

Kurt swallowed the peach-pit-sized lump in his throat. "Yes, ma'am," he said, hoping he hadn't misrepresented the facts in any way. "I think so. Although he never came right out and said it."

Ms. Brandt sat silently for a time seemingly lost in thought, and Kurt could sense the machinery of her mind whirring and grinding and stamping out analyses and conclusions. Then suddenly she was bending over her desk, reaching for a phone that was nearly buried by file folders. She lifted the receiver and dialed a number she apparently knew by heart. "Detective Hansen, please," she said into the mouthpiece—and a moment later—"Martha Brandt, attorney for Tamara Ames." She yanked open the center draw of the desk and pulled out a pen and a pad of paper. "Detective, this is Martha Brandt from the law offices of Crossfield and Brandt."

As he listened to Ms. Brandt's end of the conversation, Kurt could feel his heart throbbing in his chest the way it did when he played the stereo in his room with too much bass. He knew he'd put Detective Hansen on the spot by telling the attorney everything he had. He wondered how the detective would respond to her call.

"Thank you very much, detective," Ms. Brandt finally said, and hung up the phone.

"What did he say?" The throbbing in Kurt's chest had moved up into his head.

Ms. Brandt exhibited a wry smile. "He said that he could neither confirm nor deny anything."

"Is that good or bad?"

The attorney's smile broadened into a cheeky grin. "It's perfect." She slapped her pen down, seized the phone again, and dialed another number from her memory bank of phone listings. "I'd like to speak to Debbie Moss," she said to the person who answered. She covered the mouthpiece. "I just love having a cousin on staff at *The News-Review*."

A few seconds later, she uncovered the mouthpiece. "Debbie," she said brightly. "This is Martha. We need to meet . . . I'd rather not say on the phone. But trust me, you'll want to hear this . . . Tonight at seven—my place. We'll do Chinese . . . See you then."

Now Kurt was the one smiling.

Ms. Brandt cradled the receiver. "Okay," she said, rising from her chair, "let's go see Tamara."

97 IT TOOK ONLY A few minutes to walk across the street to the Justice Building and ride the elevator to the third floor. The thought of getting to see Tamara expanded Kurt's spirit. But as they headed down the hallway toward the visitor entrance to the jail, his elation was tempered by a resurgence of the anxiety he'd experienced during the previous day's failed attempt to enter.

The area outside the jail entrance door was deserted. Ms. Brandt stepped up to the speaker box on the wall and jabbed the call button with her index finger. A squawky male voice greeted them from the box.

"Martha Brandt to see Tamara Ames," the attorney announced with authority.

The door immediately buzzed.

"In," Ms. Brandt said with a nod, and Kurt ventured through the door.

He found himself in an open room, staring at a wall of wire-mesh-reinforced windows. At each window was a straight-back chair and, within reach of someone who might be sitting in the chair, a telephone. On the opposite side of the bank of windows were matching telephones and chairs. Kurt gazed at the visitor windows with a hushed sobriety as he envisioned what took place here: nervous relatives huddled in the chairs on the near side of the glass, speaking in solemn voices via telephone to stunned inmates seated on the other side, the silences between their words filled with sighs and anguished glances.

But none of the visiting stations were occupied at the moment. It was apparently not the prescribed hour for inmate-public contact.

Ms. Brandt turned to the lone window on the opposite wall, this one with an opening to pass things through. From behind the glass, where he sat at a large horseshoe desk cluttered with baskets of paperwork, video monitors, and electronic consoles, a broad-shouldered sheriff's deputy regarded them with a stern expression on his meaty face.

"And who is this with you, Ms. Brandt?" the deputy said.

"My co-counsel," Ms. Brandt replied without missing a beat.

The deputy groaned. "Give me a break."

Kurt slid in behind the attorney, appreciative of her towering physique.

"Give *me* a break, Deputy Teague," the attorney shot back. "We are here to see a juvenile being held in a facility for adult incarceration, under conditions unsuitable for all but the most dangerous of criminals. That is a big enough break for the state, I should imagine. In return, I expect a little latitude." She put her face close to the window. "Or shall we call the DA for his approval?"

The deputy waved her off. "All right, all right," he said, his voice conveying a note of abiding frustration, as if he'd tangled with Ms. Brandt in the past and had been rewarded for his efforts with nothing but heartburn and bad memories. He passed a clipboard through the slot in the window. "Sign the both of you in. Just don't make a habit of this."

"I wouldn't think of it," Ms. Brandt said.

Moments later, they were buzzed through a solid metal door into an inner hallway with bare, white walls and harsh overhead lighting. Off the hallway were several small rooms, each containing a table and a few straight-back chairs. Ms. Brandt chose a conference room to her liking.

"Are you sure it's okay for me to be here?" Kurt said as they sat down at the table. The décor of white walls and extreme lighting had been carried over into the conference rooms. A blinding radiance, like a prison-yard spotlight, glinted off the tabletop into Kurt's eyes. He angled his face away. "I mean—you're not going to get in any trouble, are you?"

"Nah," Ms. Brandt said, brushing off his concern. "This situation wouldn't even come up if Douglas County had its own juvenile detention facility. They know it isn't right keeping Tamara here."

It was eerily quiet as they waited, Kurt—in spite of Ms. Brandt's assurances—on edge. He flinched when a buzzing noise echoed down the hall. A door opened and closed with a loud, metallic clunk. Footsteps sounded in the hallway outside the conference room. "In there," a male voice said, and Kurt felt a rush of anticipation that nearly lifted him out of his chair.

~

WHEN TAMARA SAW KURT sitting at the conference table with the attorney, she staggered back stunned, feeling as if she'd walked into a door.

What was Kurt doing here? She was supposed to be meeting with her attorney—the third useless meeting in the last twenty-four hours. She'd wanted to skip this latest powwow but had been told that wasn't an option. Now she had to face not only the attorney's persistent questioning but also Kurt's certain disappointment in her. Her body sagged under the weight of failed expectations.

"Please have a seat," the attorney said.

Tamara glared at her, resentful of being ambushed like this. "Do I have to?"

"No," the attorney said. "You can stand if you like."

That seemed preferable to Tamara. She sidled along the wall, flattening her back against it. She crossed her arms, dipped her chin, and riveted her eyes to the floor. The deputy backed out into the hallway and closed the conference room door.

"How are they treating you?" the attorney said.

Tamara sniffed the stale air in the room. "I've been treated worse."

"Do you feel like talking to me this afternoon?"

Tamara clenched her jaw. "There's nothing to talk about." She knew the attorney was only trying to help her. At their initial meeting, Ms. Brandt had expressed a genuine concern for Tamara's plight and had displayed a fighting spirit that indicated her intentions to defend Tamara aggressively. All she needed, she'd said, was for Tamara to talk to her. Tell her what had happened at the mall and why.

But Tamara wasn't going to talk about what had happened—not then and not now. She *couldn't* talk about it. Talking about it would be like intentionally throwing herself in front of an oncoming train.

To Tamara's surprise, the attorney didn't press her this time. Instead, she turned to Kurt. "I'll be out in the hall." And without another word, she got up and left the room.

Tamara remained backed against the wall with her head down, her heart beating faster now that she and Kurt were alone. And in the long, quiet moment that followed, she could feel the silence pulsing in the room as if it had a heartbeat of its own.

Then Kurt said, "I wish you'd told me what you were going to do."

Something hard inside Tamara began to break apart, become dissolved by the softness of Kurt's voice—a voice devoid of condemnation. She glanced over at him, her emotions tangled. "I didn't know what we were going to do. We didn't plan it. It just happened. I—I—" She hunched her shoulders. "I just wanted to see the baby."

Neither of them spoke for a time. Then Kurt got up and came around the table to her. But he stayed back a few feet and kept his hands in his pockets. He looked at her, then dropped his gaze, as if maintaining eye contact was too painful. She knew the feeling.

"Can I bring you anything?" he said. "Ms. Brandt says you're allowed to have some personal items. Would you like some magazines or puzzles or something?"

Tamara shook her head.

"Can I call anyone for you?"

Tamara pressed her lips together as she recalled the recent conversation with her mother. "No. I've done all the calling I need to."

Kurt lifted his eyes, looked at her, holding his gaze this time. And she could see the caring in his eyes and it saddened her, because whatever their relationship was or might have become, it was part of her past now. Their time together would soon be reduced to cherished memories, like her recollections of a happy childhood. Her own actions had seen to that. She turned away, not wanting him to see the tears forming in her eyes.

"You really should talk to Ms. Brandt," Kurt said. "She wants to help you."

Tamara sighed. "It doesn't matter."

"What do you mean?"

"It doesn't matter what happens to me now."

"It matters to me," Kurt said, his voice suddenly resolute. "And I'm going to do everything I can to help you."

She whipped around to face him. "No. Go home. Forget about me."

"Tamara, I can't just—"

"Don't try to help me! And—and—" She had to end this now, for Kurt's sake as well as hers. "And don't come back to see me!" She stood there a moment longer, trembling, then turned and rushed out of the room.

~

KURT COULD HEAR Tamara's sandals slapping in double time against the soles of her feet as she retreated down the hall. A door buzzed, opened, and closed again with a heavy clank.

Ms. Brandt came back into the room, scrutinizing him as if looking for knife wounds. "Well, that obviously went well."

Kurt had been shaken by Tamara's outburst, but he tried not to show it. "It doesn't matter what she says, or doesn't say. We still have to help her."

"We will," Ms. Brandt said with a confidence he couldn't relate to.

98

"I'LL ONLY BE GONE a couple of hours," Russell Trouste said to his wife. He was facing the mirror in his dressing room, fumbling with the errant ends of his necktie in a futile attempt to craft a decent-looking knot. Margaret had always tied his tie for him. It had seemed so easy when he'd watched her do it, her nimble fingers manipulating the shiny band of silk into a perky Windsor. But with her current preoccupation with the baby, she had no time or inclination to be crafting knots for him. He made a final loop-and-tuck, then cinched the tie up under his chin with a frustrated jerk that nearly garroted him.

Margaret's reflection in the mirror grew bigger. She was dressed in a robe and slippers and had the baby, sheathed in a blanket, clamped to her breast. She poked her head up over his shoulder and flashed a fearful look. "But what if someone comes to get the baby again?"

Russell exhaled deliberately. It was the fourth morning after Felicity had been snatched from the parking lot at the shopping mall and then speedily recovered by the state police. Margaret had hardly put the child down since being reunited with her at the hospital, after Dr. Castle had checked her over and declared her to be "in mint condition." If his wife had been a kangaroo, she would have stowed the baby in her pouch and never let her out.

Russell understood Margaret's anxiety about the kidnapping and had stayed home from work those first three days to be with her. But this morning he needed to attend a nine o'clock meeting of the board of directors at the mill. He also needed to do something—anything—to get his mind off his own festering angst about the questions that had arisen in the wake of the kidnapping, specifically those broached by one overzealous sheriff's detective.

The episode with Detective Hansen three days earlier had shaken Russell to the core. The detective had obviously come to the house on a fishing expedition, his questions backed by nothing but raw suspicion. But even the hint of Russell's involvement in something as lurid as a baby-stealing scheme could lead to harmful speculation in the media. And if—God forbid—some evidence of the baby swap was somehow unearthed, he would be ruined. His business, his personal reputation, his marriage would all be in shambles. He could even go to jail!

He'd been on edge for the last three days, fearing the worst—every phone call sending icy tremors up his spine, every mention of the kidnapping on the news making his stomach knot. The strength drained from his body every time he replayed in his head the tape of Hansen's last question: "Mr. Trouste, someone deposited $20,000 into a bank account in the name of Tamara Ames the day after her baby was born. Would you know anything about that?" It was the threat represented by this kind of inquisitiveness that had kept Russell almost constantly wiping his brow for the last seventy-two hours.

Russell had done what he could to thwart Detective Hansen's reckless probing. His call to the sheriff immediately after Hansen's visit had had the desired effect of calling off the dogs for the time being. In addition, the sheriff had assured him that no details of the Stones' "ridiculous accusations" regarding Felicity's parentage would be divulged to the media by his or the DA's office. How the Stones' or Tamara Ames' legal defense team would use those claims, however, was still a matter of concern. It was this concern that had led Russell to consult his attorney regarding the need to prepare a strategy to combat any charges hurled at him in the press or in the courts, even as he continued to hope that his sphere of influence was wide enough to discourage some two-bit attorney from wanting to smear the Trouste name by bringing accusations that could not easily be substantiated.

But his fears of imminent ruin lingered and were, in fact, uppermost in his mind now as he looked into the mirror and met his wife's anguished gaze with a stolid expression of his own. "No one is coming to get the baby," he told her.

"How do you know?" Margaret said in a strained voice.

Russell turned to face her. "Because the people who took the baby are in jail. Besides, there are two armed guards stationed outside the entrance gate. No one will get onto the property without their say-so."

Margaret let out a fretful sigh, and he braced himself for further protests. But after a moment of electrically charged silence, she backed out of the dressing room. "You'll come home right after the meeting." It was more of a demand than a question.

Russell lifted his suit jacket from its caddy. "I should be home by eleven." He headed downstairs, with Margaret—still clutching the baby—at his heels. He paused at the front door, turned, and touched a hand to his wife's cheek. "There's nothing to worry about."

But Margaret's look remained troubled, and he knew there was nothing he could say that would alleviate her current distress. He considered phoning the office and having the board meeting rescheduled for a later date, but quickly concluded that whenever he left the house for the first time since the kidnapping, his wife would suffer the same dread that gripped her now. Besides, he needed to tune his mind to a different channel before his own anxieties got the best of him. "The baby is safe," he said, and exited the house.

Upon arriving at his office at the mill, Russell had just enough time to peruse the stack of phone messages on his desk and review the agenda for the board meeting before his secretary buzzed him and informed him it was time for the meeting to begin. He felt a sense of release wash over him as he strode down the hall to the boardroom, his personal concerns beginning to be nudged aside by considerations related to the workaday world in which he thrived.

The other board members were already seated around the big oval conference table, dressed up today with a colorful floral centerpiece, along with the usual sweating pitchers of water. Russell took his position in the chairman's seat and, after some perfunctory personal exchanges with several of those around the table, opened the meeting. Soon he was fully engrossed in a review of unit production numbers and projected market prices for lumber.

He had no idea how long the meeting had been going on when his secretary entered the boardroom and approached him. She leaned down and whispered in his ear, her breath laced with the aroma of chocolate. He glanced at his watch. It was 11:20. "I'll take it in my office," he told her, and excused himself from the meeting.

"What is it, dear?" he said moments later, speaking into his office phone.

"Come home, Russell," his wife said.

"I'll be finished here soon."

"Come home now!"

Russell grumbled to himself. "Okay, I'll be right there." More than a little piqued, he informed his secretary of his need to depart and, after hastily calling an end to the board meeting, left the mill.

When he arrived home, Russell found his wife upstairs in the nursery. She was sitting in the rocking chair with the child still clasped to her breast. Her cheeks were wet with tears. Mucus trailed from one of her nostrils. She had a glassy, faraway look in her eyes as she pitched forward and back in the chair at an accelerated pace.

"What's the matter?" he said brusquely, realizing in that moment that despite his desire to be sympathetic he was unhappy with the melodrama his home life had become.

Margaret's face took on a pinched expression that obscured every good and natural feature normally on display there. Her lips quivered, moved in ways that mimicked speech, but no sound came out of her mouth. She was too traumatized, it seemed, to speak, although he couldn't imagine why.

She continued rocking robotically in the chair, and as she did, there was an intermittent sound like the tearing of paper. Russell glanced down at the floor. Underneath one runner of the rocker was a section of newspaper being mangled little by little with each to-and-fro movement of the chair. He bent down, waited for the runner to rise, and with a quick jerk dislodged the paper from beneath it.

It was the front page of that day's edition of *The News-Review*, which normally wasn't delivered to the house until the afternoon. For some reason it had come early. He was about to toss the paper aside when its banner headline jumped out at him: KIDNAPPER CLAIMS TROUSTE BABY REALLY HERS.

"My God," he muttered as an avalanche of dread came crashing down on him. He stumbled back and dropped into a chair by the door. A barrage of messages assaulted his brain, all dark and portending catastrophe for him and his family. He sat bent over, taking slow, elongated breaths while struggling to fend off the feeling of impending doom.

When finally able to control his fear, he steadied the paper in his hands and read the article's lead paragraph: "The attorney for Tamara Ames, one of the teens arrested in the recent abduction of baby Felicity Trouste, asserted last night that her client had acted on the belief that the child was hers and had been stolen from her at birth. A District Attorney's Office spokesperson has discounted the statement made by Public Defender Martha Brandt. 'She isn't helping her client's case any by repeating such an outrageous claim,' Assistant DA Herbert Waller said. 'Her statement sounds more like an admission of guilt than anything.' Efforts to contact the Troustes for their reaction to Ms. Brandt's comments were unsuccessful."

Damn right, they were unsuccessful. Russell had referred all calls about the investigation into the kidnapping to his attorney. But why hadn't John contacted him about this new development? Then he remembered that his attorney was at a two-day law conference in Salem and wouldn't be back until tomorrow.

Russell skimmed the rest of the article, which went on to recount the essential facts regarding Felicity's abduction and subsequent return. Nowhere in the text was there a mention of Detective Hansen or the likelihood of a follow-up probe resulting from the inflammatory statements made by Tamara Ames' attorney. Nonetheless, it was obvious that with this claim by the Ames girl being published in the paper everything had changed. The question of Felicity's parentage was now a public affair that would have to be dealt with publicly.

Russell tilted his head back and took several more calming breaths, telling himself that for Margaret's sake—and for the sake of his own reputation and possibly his own freedom—he had to remain composed in the face of these new developments. Difficult days lay ahead, days in which he would have to do everything in his considerable power to dispel the cloud of suspicion that would inevitably materialize because of this news article.

He glanced over at his wife and the infant she clung to as if they were joined by an imaginary umbilical cord. This was his wife's child. And he could take solace in the knowledge that it would be very difficult for anyone to prove otherwise.

Short of the potentially damning results of maternity/paternity testing, there was no real evidence to undermine his and Margaret's claim to parenthood. Dr. Castle had covered his tracks well, leaving Detective Hansen grasping at the straws of coincidence and conjecture. And with that Neaves fellow conveniently out of the way, there was no one to contradict Dr. Castle's recounting of the events of the night of Felicity's birth, or the public record.

Even the threat of parental testing was a toothless bogeyman. Russell's attorney had assured him that it was extremely unlikely any judge would order such testing on the unsupported accusations of a kidnapper. And even if one did, the results could easily be challenged at trial, since HLA typing, the most accurate kind of testing available, was considered only 80 percent conclusive. So, in point of fact, it appeared that Russell had nothing to fear from Tamara Ames or her big-mouthed attorney—as long as he kept his cool.

Experiencing a restored sense of control over the situation, Russell felt his confidence reemerge like a phoenix from the ashes. He went over and knelt down in front of his wife. "Margaret," he said, gripping the rocker's arms. "Darling, stop for a minute and look at me."

Margaret continued lunging forward and back, her eyes still glazed and unfocused.

Slowly, as if easing a runaway team of horses to a halt, Russell used his strength to bring the rocking chair to a standstill. Margaret gazed about, seemingly confused by the lack of movement.

"It's going to be all right," he told her.

His wife looked at him as if seeing him for the first time since he'd entered the room. "Russell," she said, "you have to tell them it isn't true."

He caressed her knee. "We will, darling. We will."

99   WHEN KURT RETURNED to the county jail—this time on Saturday, so he didn't have to miss any school—he brought with him a copy of the front page of the previous day's *The News-Review*. Ms. Brandt had asked him to meet her in the third-floor lobby of the Justice Building at nine-thirty. Kurt arrived well before that. He passed the time waiting for her by pacing the lobby and conjecturing as to what would happen to Tamara now that it was publicly known she'd taken a baby from the Troustes that she believed to be her own. He hoped the news would help her. Surely the police would have to investigate. The truth was bound to come out. He didn't know what the truth was, but he didn't really care as long as it got Tamara out of jail.

Ms. Brandt arrived with a flurry of movement. She burst out of the elevator and swept across the lobby like a rogue wave. As she whisked by Kurt, she hooked an arm through one of his. "Let's go stir the pot some more," she said.

They followed the same procedure as before to get checked into one of the conference rooms inside the jail. While they waited for Tamara to be brought in, Ms. Brandt spoke to him about the purpose of their visit. "We need Tamara to talk to us. She's the only person who can attest to her state of mind at the time of the kidnapping—to her motivation. We need her to assert for the record her belief that the Trouste baby is really hers, and to tell us why she thinks that."

That sounded like a tall order to Kurt, but he wanted to remain positive. "And if we can get her to do that?"

"Then we'll have a basis for a defense. And I'll have reason to petition a judge to order a maternity test."

Kurt felt his pulse rise, along with his expectations. "You think a judge would do that?"

Ms. Brandt shrugged. "Doesn't really matter. We just need to keep the issue alive. Sow the seeds of doubt. Muddy the waters so that things won't seem so black and white to a jury if this thing goes to trial. Besides, the Troustes are the foremost family in the county. This story isn't going away by itself—and the DA knows it."

Kurt smiled. "You mean, he knows that Debbie Moss is your cousin."

Ms. Brandt winked at him. "That too."

There was a shuffling sound outside the doorway. They both looked over.

Tamara entered the room, keeping her head down as she slumped into a chair at the table without greeting either of them. She looked terrible. Her hair reminded Kurt of feathers on a molting bird. Her face was the color of cooked oatmeal. Her lips were swollen and cracked and rimmed with a red crust as if from excessive licking. And she seemed diminished in stature—not just thinner, but smaller, like really old people get as they fade toward death. Kurt thought, *We've got to get her out of this place!*

A period of silence slowly unraveled, and a pressure seemed to build inside the room like the atmosphere before a storm. Finally, Ms. Brandt spoke up. "Are we in the mood for sharing today?"

"I told you," Tamara said in a flat voice, "I have nothing to say."

"That's too bad," Ms. Brandt said, "because other people are saying a lot."

The attorney stood up, and Kurt felt stricken as he watched her leave. What if Tamara wouldn't talk to him either?

But as soon as the attorney was out the door, Tamara spoke up. "I told you not to come back," she said, yet there was no venom in her voice.

"I know," Kurt said, feeling more embarrassed than rebuked. "But I want to help you whether you want my help or not. So does Ms. Brandt."

Tamara didn't say anything, and it was her silence at that moment, her implied acquiescence, that emboldened Kurt to proceed. He brought the newspaper up from his lap, unfolded it, pushed it across the tabletop.

"What's this?"

"Just read what it says." He pointed to the lead article.

Tamara peered down at the paper, her eyes sweeping back and forth across the page.

Kurt went on talking, nervously, wanting to have his say while he still had the courage to speak. "Ms. Brandt thinks that, now that it's out in the open about your believing the Trouste baby is really yours, she might be able to get a judge to have the maternity of the baby tested. She just needs you to make a statement about—" He paused for fear he might use the wrong words, words that would alienate Tamara and cause her to pull away again. "—about why you took the baby and all. Then they'd just need to get a blood sample from you."

Tamara looked up from the paper, her eyes strangely vacant. "I want to talk to the attorney."

"Good," Kurt said, experiencing a rush of optimism.

He went to the door to get Ms. Brandt. Tamara was finally ready to talk—to help with her defense. But after Ms. Brandt came back into the room and they sat down at the table again, Kurt was shocked by what Tamara had to say.

"It's not true," she told the attorney. She held up the newspaper and stabbed it with her index finger. "Not true." She flung the paper aside.

She stared across the table, a look of desperation in her eyes, like that of a passenger the moment before a ship goes down. "The baby we took from Mrs. Trouste is not my baby." Her shoulders shuddered as she forced the next words out of her mouth. "My—baby—is—dead."

"Is that right?" Ms. Brandt said, all too dispassionately, Kurt thought, because he couldn't believe what he was hearing.

He gripped the edge of the table. "But what about the $20,000? It has to mean something. And what about that night?" He was trying desperately to reconcile the *then* with the *now*. "You thought you heard the baby crying. You told Amanda—"

"I was wrong!" Tamara cried. She jumped to her feet, red-faced and trembling. Tears gushed from her eyes. "I was wrong," she repeated. And there was such anguish in her voice that Kurt wanted to go to her and take her in his arms and comfort her. But he knew he couldn't. He knew that her pain was too deep for him to reach.

Tamara jerked around and staggered from the room.

Kurt turned to the attorney, feeling utterly deflated. "What do we do now?"

Ms. Brandt picked up her briefcase and rose from her chair. "We implement Plan B."

"You have a Plan B?"

"Of course I do. What kind of an attorney would I be if I didn't?"

100 KURT TOOK ANOTHER aimless turn around the landing outside the main entrance to Fir Valley High, his leg muscles snapping like rubber bands. This was the day he'd been looking forward to, and yet was dreading.

When he saw the sheriff's cruiser turn into the lane that looped in front the school, he bolted from the landing like a racehorse from a starting gate and sprinted down the steps, arriving at street level just as the cruiser came to a stop. He slid into the front passenger's seat, deposited his backpack on the floor. "Thanks for the lift."

"Least I could do," Detective Hansen said.

The detective completed the loop in front of the school and steered the cruiser back onto the street. At the four-way stop, he turned right. A road sign announced, FREEWAY I MILE. Beyond the sign, they followed the road through the S-curve that took them around the hillock on which squatted the city's water tower. The freeway overpass came into view.

"You know you'll only have a few minutes together," the detective said. He aimed the vehicle up the northbound ramp to the interstate and, accelerating to freeway speed, merged into the right-hand lane of traffic behind a tractor-trailer rig whose brake lights winked a couple of times, its driver apparently responding to the appearance of a sheriff's cruiser behind him.

"I know," Kurt said, his enthusiasm undimmed. "I just appreciate your making the arrangements."

"Martha Brandt actually deserves most of the thanks there," the detective said. "She seems to have a lot of pull with the DA's Office these days."

Kurt smiled at the mention of Tamara's attorney. He didn't really understand all the behind-the-scenes legal maneuvering that had taken place in Tamara's case over the last few weeks, but he was sure of one thing: Martha Brandt's Plan B had worked to perfection. And she hadn't wasted any time implementing it.

The day after Tamara's shocking admission in the jail conference room, Debbie Moss's follow-up article on the Trouste baby kidnapping had appeared on the front page of *The News-Review* under the headline "Teenage Kidnapper Recants Story." In the article, Tamara was said to have admitted that her baby "was born dead" and that she didn't know why she had thought otherwise at the time she and the Stones took the Trouste baby. A local psychiatrist, quoted in the article, thought he had the answer. According to the psychiatrist, Tamara, as the result of the loss of her child, had suffered a "psychosis" that caused her to believe that her baby had not really died but that someone—in this case the Troustes, who were merely a convenient target because they had an infant child—had stolen it. "The first stage of grief is denial," the psychiatrist was quoted as saying. "The mind can feed that denial in all kinds of creative ways. This is what Tamara Ames' mind apparently did."

Kurt remembered reading those words with a growing sense of doom. With a public acknowledgement of Tamara's guilt and the withdrawal of her accusations against the Troustes, Ms. Brandt seemed to be throwing in the towel. Or worse—she was fashioning the hangman's noose that would be slipped around Tamara's neck.

But Kurt's fears had turned out to be unjustified. The day following the publication of Tamara's retraction, the Trouste family, through their attorney, issued a press release that, although it condemned the kidnapping and Tamara's "blatantly false allegations," seemed to offer a ray of hope. The statement, which was printed in the newspaper and read on local radio and TV newscasts throughout the day, ended with this surprisingly charitable assertion: "The Troustes want to see justice done. But they are also well aware of the terrible circumstances that prefaced this crime, and they understand that sometimes justice needs to be tempered with mercy."

Kurt had puzzled all afternoon over the wording of this statement and what it meant for Tamara. Finally, he'd called Ms. Brandt for her take.

Ms. Brandt hadn't hesitated. "It means they'll support a plea bargain." There was a note of satisfaction in her voice that told Kurt Plan B was indeed advancing as it should.

They rode in silence for the next couple of miles. Detective Hansen stayed a safe distance behind the tractor-trailer, while its driver stayed within the speed limit. Kurt read the words painted on the back of the trailer, across its rear cargo doors: HOW AM I DRIVING? There was a phone number to call.

"There's just one other thing I'd like to say," the detective finally said.

"Shoot."

The officer glanced in Kurt's direction. "Things don't always turn out the way we would like them to."

Kurt thought about that for a moment. "Care to elaborate?"

The detective laughed. "Not really."

"That's okay," Kurt said. "I kinda know what you mean."

He was thinking about the plea bargain that had been worked out in Tamara's case. It had taken a single, brief meeting between Ms. Brandt, the DA, and the Troustes' attorney to hammer out the details. In return for the dismissal of all other charges, Tamara was allowed to plead "no contest" to something called "child endangerment." She was to serve nine months in juvenile detention, where she would undergo counseling. That would be followed by three years of probation. The Stones were allowed to plead out on similar charges, with similar consequences, time to be served in the county jail. "Considering the severity of the charges, it's an extremely generous settlement," Ms. Brandt had assured him. "The Troustes were obviously very eager to put this incident behind them."

"I guess so," Kurt had responded, even though the terms of the settlement vexed him, like nettles in his socks. It didn't seem right that Tamara should be confined for nine minutes, much less nine months. And since Douglas County had no lock-up facility for offending youth, she was going to be taken away to another county.

They got off the freeway at the City Center exit in Roseburg and traveled the mile or so through town to the Justice Building. Detective Hansen pulled into a parking lot on the jail side of the facility and parked in a space reserved for sheriff's vehicles. He pointed to a nondescript metal door at the end of a walkway leading to the first floor of the jail. "That's the door she'll come out."

Kurt looked at his watch. It was a quarter to two. Fifteen minutes. It was amazing how relative time was.

It had taken a week for a judge to sign off on the plea bargain agreement in Tamara's case. Each day that week, Kurt had gone to school and home again, enduring the long bus ride to and from Fir Valley with less patience than before. Evenings, he'd done his homework and his chores. And at night, he'd lain in bed and thought about Tamara and how much he missed being with her. And the longing that grew in him was like the billowing of a sail that, once filled to capacity, was destined to force movement or end up in tatters from the effort.

Kurt straightened in his seat. A sheriff's van had pulled into the parking lot. It rolled to a stop alongside the cruiser. The van's driver, a sheriff's deputy named Deana Merrick, to whom Kurt had previously been introduced, got out. She nodded in their direction as she ambled past. When she arrived at the metal door Detective Hansen had pointed out, she poked a finger at a speaker box mounted on the outside wall and mouthed some words. Moments later, she opened the door and disappeared inside the jail.

"It'll take a few minutes to do the paperwork," Detective Hansen said.

Kurt was trying to stay calm, but his heart had already broken into a gallop and he knew there was nothing he could do to rein it in. He hadn't seen Tamara since the day she'd recanted her accusations against the Troustes. She'd declined to add his name to her visitor list. He was hurt by this—by what he felt was Tamara's rejection of him. Then he found out from Ms. Brandt that there was only one name on Tamara's visitor list—her mother's. But her mother had never come to see her. After learning this, Kurt stopped feeling hurt and began inquiring about the possibility of his seeing Tamara outside the jail, on the day of her transfer.

At three minutes after two, the metal door swung open again and Tamara—escorted by Deputy Merrick—stepped out into the sunlight, using her cupped hand to shield her eyes. She was wearing blue jeans, a white blouse, and white sneakers. No handcuffs or leg irons. Her hair was neatly brushed and pinned back on the sides. She looked, Kurt thought with a sense of irony that threatened to cleave his heart, like any other teenage girl off to classes at the local high school. But she wasn't just any girl, not to him anyway, and her destination this day was not school. It was the juvenile detention facility in Medford, where she would be spending the next nine months in lock-up.

Kurt didn't wait to be told what to do next. He sprang from the cruiser and strode down the sidewalk toward the jail.

"You've got five minutes," Deputy Merrick said as the three of them came together. She moved past him to a position in front of the sheriff's van.

Kurt's eyes met Tamara's and suddenly all his rehearsals for this moment were as useless as tangled fishing line. "I—I—" But there was a logjam of words in his head. He stood there stupidly, not knowing what to say or do, worried even that action or words might corrupt the moment, as if his fate were balanced on a fulcrum and could be tipped one way or the other by the slightest breeze. He was relieved when Tamara finally made the first move.

She didn't hug him, but she came in close enough to lean against him and lay her head on his shoulder. And that made him feel real good, as if the breeze had blown him in the direction of hope.

"I'm sorry to have dragged you into this," she said, her voice as soft and tender as a lullaby.

"I wouldn't have missed it for the world," Kurt said, and he meant it.

Tamara lifted her head, looked at him with a shy smile. "You're not like any other boy I've ever known."

"You're not like any other girl."

Tamara let out a pinched laugh. "You better hope you don't ever meet another one like me."

Kurt grinned. "No chance of that." He took her hand, and— shoulders touching—they drifted unwillingly toward the van. "Can I come see you sometime?" he said.

"If you want to." She wrinkled her nose. "Though I don't know why you would."

"Ready when you are," Deputy Merrick called out. She slid the van's side door open, exposing two broad bench seats separated from the driver's compartment by a heavy wire mesh.

Kurt tensed at the sight of the wire. He swung Tamara around so that her back was to it. They leaned against one another, still holding hands. Then Tamara reached around and hugged him so tightly he thought his lungs might collapse. "I can't promise you anything," she whispered.

"I don't need promises," he said, reveling in the embrace.

Tamara released him, drew back a step. She looked into his eyes one last time, and he drank in her look, stored it away, like fat, for the lean times. Then, all too soon, she turned away, walked to the van, and climbed in through its open side door. Into the cage in which she was to be transported.

The deputy slid the door closed. Kurt cringed, feeling the bitterness of the moment overcome the sweet. The van's windows were tinted and he strained to see Tamara's face inside, her dim profile crosshatched by the mesh reinforcement in the glass.

Deputy Merrick moved around to the driver's side and climbed in behind the wheel.

Kurt felt a jolt of panic, sensing that he should have said more, done more, to let Tamara know the depth of his feelings for her.

The van shook as its engine started.

He lunged toward the side window, raised a palm, pressed it flat against the glass. "I'll come to visit," he said. *I promise.*

Tamara nodded, her mouth tight-lipped, like a crack in a rock.

The van began to move.

101 THE SHERIFF'S VAN moved past buildings, and cars on the street, and people walking on the sidewalks, singly and in pairs. It turned corners. It moved over a bridge and across a river. It turned another corner, and suddenly they were on the freeway going in a direction that could have been any direction, except that Tamara knew it was south because the afternoon sun was angling in the window on the right side. She gazed out the window on the left. Through flashes of tree branches and rooflines, she could see a stretch of the river they had crossed, the path of which they were following out of town.

She took a long breath and let it out slowly as she sorted through the cluster of emotions she was feeling at the moment. The thought of going to a juvenile detention facility for nine months didn't bother her. She'd suffered through stiffer sentences than that. Juvenile detention would be a piece of cake compared to some of the foster homes she'd lived in. But seeing Kurt had left her feeling vulnerable. The warmth she'd felt in his presence, the unconditional support he'd given her, the affection he'd shown, had ignited within her a sense of hope. But hope, she knew, was the most perilous of emotions.

The course of the river altered, bent toward the west. She caught a last glimpse of its rippling surface as it passed under the freeway. Which way was the water flowing? She couldn't tell, could only detect movement. All rivers eventually flowed to the sea, her science teacher had said, where they mixed with other waters of the world.

And the thought came to her that, like the intermingled waters of the ocean, her life was connected to other lives out there in ways and to an extent she couldn't fully fathom. It was a ponderous notion, and the bigness of it was such that she felt compelled to let it go for fear it would overwhelm her.

On the outskirts of town, they moved past an outdoor movie theater, its parking lot empty this time of day of everything except windswept debris, its giant white screen gleaming in the sunlight. Tamara kept her eyes on the screen as long as she could, as if expecting it magically to come to life with the sights and sounds of the make-believe world of the movies, where even the most tragic of circumstances can be transformed into a happy ending.

Abruptly the scenery out the window changed. They were moving through open country, with sheep-dotted meadows and tree-studded hills stretching all the way to the horizon, the only remaining evidence of civilization an occasional farmhouse perched on a knoll or a mobile home snugged against a wooded slope like a child tucked under her mother's arm. The river, twisting and tumbling its way through an exposed bed of rock, reappeared on the left side and then disappeared again, as if playing hide-and-seek with the highway travelers.

Tamara peered through the wire-mesh screen into the driver's compartment, at the checkered back of Deputy Merrick's head. "Will we be going through Fir Valley?"

The head bobbed. "Just beyond the next ridge."

Tamara sat up straighter on the bench seat and once again focused her attention out the window. They were approaching a long, steep grade leading to the summit of a mountain pass.

The van began to labor as they headed up the grade. On either side of them now were dark, far-reaching woods. The deputy steered the vehicle onto the paved shoulder of the road to allow faster-moving traffic to pass. The van was losing its struggle against the mountain. It seemed as if they would never reach the summit. Then, finally, they crested the ridge, headed downhill, and . . .

There it was, appearing like a pop-up in a children's book, the city of Fir Valley, awash in the glow of the afternoon sun. Even bathed in golden light, the town wasn't much to look at, just some drab buildings downtown and a tangle of ramshackle homes stretching from the river's edge up into the surrounding hills. Only one feature in the scene stood out as special: on a high bluff overlooking the city, towered a huge home—the Trouste mansion—where her child would grow up.

Tamara's heart clenched. She'd done the right thing, she was sure, in giving up the fight for her daughter. But the decision to do so had come only after an agonizing tug of war between the deepest yearning of her soul and her desire to do what was best for her child. And even now the pain of her loss cut so deep that it seemed the only way to make it stop was to die.

She brought her hands to her mouth, pressed her knuckles against her lips. *I did it for you, sweet one. I did it for you.*

"Might as well get comfortable," Deputy Merrick said. "We've got a good hour of nothing but blacktop ahead of us."

Tamara let her hands fall to her lap where they instinctively embraced her middle. She closed her eyes and tried to still her mind. Tried not to think about the baby—or the Troustes—or Kurt. She tried not to think about anything.

She concentrated instead on the hum of the tires on the road. The hum was constant and unbroken, like the rhythm of life itself. It vibrated up through the floorboard of the van and tickled her toes. It rose up, like warmth from a fire, through her feet to her calves, and on up through her thighs, relaxing her tight muscles. It ascended, steady and pervasive, through her stomach and her chest and into her head, where it went about displacing all negative and useless thought.

She sensed her mind drift off into a soothing mist. The hum—the constant, unbroken music of the road—was inside every fiber of her being now. It was as much a part of her as her own breath, and provided as much sustenance. And it was carrying her forward—forward—ever forward.

But forward to what?

A shudder rippled down her spine, and the realization came to her as beautiful and thorny as a rose: *I can't make my mother love me. I can't force my love on my child. I can only love myself and allow others to love me.* And she cried because of the terror and the joy such an understanding brought to her heart.

PART TWO

~

Felicity Trouste

Fall, 2000–Summer, 2006

1 MOTHER HAD TAUGHT ME as a young girl with curious fingers not to pluck the loose threads on my clothing lest the seams come undone. I was college-age and motherless before I learned that this lesson applied to life as well, only sometimes the plucking and the unraveling are beyond your control.

I had thought when Mom died during my sophomore year at Willamette that my life had come undone forever. It was Dad, Man of Compassion/Man of Steel, who kept me from flying apart at the seams. Eighteen months later, it would be Dad, Man of Deceit, who'd rip away the few remaining threads holding me together.

The unraveling began with his call on a Friday afternoon. I was sprawled like a rag doll on the sofa in my apartment in Salem, having barely survived another week of pre-med classes at the university, waiting for my brain to revive before doing anything as challenging as putting a frozen pizza in the microwave. When my cell phone rang, I ignored it, which wasn't easy since, like most girls, I had developed during adolescence a Pavlovian response to ringing telephones that fell just short of salivation. But this afternoon my head was stuffed with cotton and the only stimulus I was responding to was exhaustion.

Ten minutes later, Pavlov jingled his bell again, and again I resisted.

The third round of ringing ticked me off. I sat up and snatched the phone off the end table, wishing I had simply turned the damned thing off. "What!"

"Felicity?"

My mind reset itself. "Dad? Oh—sorry—I didn't mean to sound like an attack dog."

If he took offense at the currish greeting, Dad didn't let on. "I know it's last minute," he said, "but I'd like you to come home for the weekend."

"Oh?"

"There's someone I'd like you to meet."

I squinted across the room at the leaning tower of textbooks balanced on my study table. "Who?"

"An acquaintance of mine. She'll be joining us for dinner tomorrow evening."

A different ring tone sounded—the alarm bell inside my head. "She?"

"Yes, *she*. Why?"

Why? Because his wanting to introduce me to a *she* could only mean that Dad had a new lady in his life and that their relationship was more than casual. Mom had been gone a year and a half—snatched from us by breast cancer that had spread so quickly even the blessed trinity (mastectomy, chemotherapy, and radiation) couldn't save her. I knew Dad was lonely, and my being away at school didn't help. Had he found someone to fill the emotional void? Would this new woman make him happy? Another concern muscled its way into my thoughts. At the ripe age of twenty-one, was I ready for a new mom?

I clawed the carpet with my toes. "Does it have to be this weekend?"

"I'm afraid so," Dad said in a voice so somber there should have been a string quartet playing in the background.

I clasped my side, sure I'd felt a stitch come undone.

I DIDN'T WANT TO think about it, the same way I hadn't wanted to think about it for some time. That's why I'd avoided going home.

Too much space and time for reflection—like now, driving down the interstate on a Saturday afternoon with only a congealing cloud cover and the occasional lane closure for bridge work to keep my mind from inviting in unwanted thoughts. *Mom—how I miss you!*

Whenever I was at our family home in Fir Valley, I would feel Mom's absence more tangibly than I felt Dad's presence. I'd hug Dad and think of Mom's arms around me, her grasp as comforting as a rocking cradle, her lingering touch laced with the fragrance of lilacs in bloom. Dad's embraces were clumsy and brief. He reeked of cigar smoke much of the time and, lately, of expensive whiskey.

I cranked up the volume on the car stereo, hoping to blast away the painful memories.

On my visits home, Dad and I would sit at the dining table or by the fireplace in the library and engage in awkward chitchat. All the while I'd be thinking about the long talks I used to have with Mom, often late at night after I'd had a fight with my boyfriend or failed to get the lead role in a school play, or some such silly occurrence that seemed like life and death at the time. *Mom—I miss your sympathetic ear!*

I welcomed the first splashes of rain on my windshield, urging me to pay attention to my driving. I turned my wipers on, eager to meld my mind with their monotonous sweep.

Who was this new woman in my father's life anyway? And what gave her the right to think she could in any way replace my mom? And what if she was nothing but a gold digger? By local standards, Dad was a wealthy man, the owner of a lumber mill that had been in the family nearly a hundred years. Would he risk it all for some floozy itching to take him for all he was worth?

The rain came pelting down now, waves of fat droplets that popped against the windshield like broken strings of pearls. I gripped the steering wheel, stricken by a rekindled sense of longing, wanting more than anything to be able to turn back time, to know that Mom this very moment was waiting for me at home with eager arms and a love that never wavered. Mom had always called me her "little miracle," the child she'd so long yearned for but seemed destined not to have, until Heaven intervened.

I reached out a trembling hand and switched the wipers to "high." The roadway ahead had become a cyclone of mist. I peered through the mist at the winking brake lights, and my heart was raked by the knowledge that the best I could hope for was that the next Mrs. Russell Trouste would be worthy of the name.

2   I ARRIVED IN Fir Valley in the late afternoon, frazzled to the gills from nearly three hours of underwater driving and my efforts to cram my recollections of life with Mom back into the box I'd kept them in since her funeral. What progress I'd made was quickly undone when, crossing the South Umpqua River, I glanced up and spied the family home sitting castle-like atop a cloud as thick as cream of wheat. I knew there was a bluff behind the cloud, but the sight of Trouste House hanging in the air, like a vision, only added to my sense of nostalgia for the happiness I'd known there as a child. Were those feelings about to be trampled on by a new "woman of the house"?

A bittersweet brew of hope and fear bubbled up inside me.

I put the river behind me and entered the Old Mill District, whose blight of derelict homes was finally being addressed by a citizens' group, led by my father, intent on preserving the rich history of the area. It would take time and money to rescue some of these homes—the ones that hadn't already fallen down or been razed—from decades of neglect. But as my father was known to say when drumming up support for the restoration project, "We should never allow the past to become a rubbish heap, for if we do, we will surely find ourselves someday buried among the rubble."

Just prior to entering downtown, I swung left onto Pine Ridge Road and began my ascent toward higher ground. The town spread out below me in aerial-map fashion, old and new neighborhoods oddly interconnected, like slightly mismatched pieces of a puzzle—no piece more emblematic of this untidy confluence of present and past than the billowing stacks of the latest (and most high-tech) incarnation of Valley Lumber Company, rising into the sky like latter-day Towers of Babel.

At the top of the ridge, I veered onto Summit Drive and followed it along the forested lip of the bluff until I came to the private drive leading into the Trouste estate. My pulse quickened as I passed between the twin stone pillars guarding the entrance and proceeded up the tree-lined lane to our family home.

The view I encountered was like a postcard that since childhood I'd carried around in my head: the expansive green; the sweeping circular drive with a fountain as a centerpiece; the gaudy flower beds ringing the home like a giant Hawaiian lei; and the home itself—a grand Victorian with turrets, cupolas, balconies, and a wraparound veranda—situated on the rim of the bluff.

After Mom's passing, the house and grounds remained in pristine condition due to the cadre of groundskeepers, maintenance men, and house staff at Dad's disposal. But the postcard in my head had since bled color to the extent that it more closely resembled the early sepia photograph of the estate published by the local Chamber of Commerce in their *Guide to Historic Homes in Douglas County*. Now as I approached my childhood home, the two versions merged in my mind into one not-quite-overlapping image that gave me a case of double vision.

I parked my car in my regular bay in the garage and entered the house through a side door off the kitchen, so that not surprisingly the first person I encountered was Vera, the live-in housekeeper. Vera was much more than that, really. She'd been with the family for over twenty years—half her life, she'd pointed out to me recently—having served early on as my nanny and later, in matters too delicate for parental consultation, my occasional confidante.

When I came into the kitchen, Vera—looking matronly in her white apron and netted hair—was standing in front of the oven, checking on the doneness of a roast. I knew it was a roast because there's no smell in the world as tantalizing as one of Vera's pot roasts sizzling in the oven. Her face lit up when she saw me. "There you are," she said, "looking more like your mother every day."

She cringed at her, however innocent, reference to the dead. But I took no offense. All my life I'd been told that I favored my mother. "You have your mother's nose," someone would say. Or, "her eyes." Or, "her smile." And I was glad to look like my mother, because she was very pretty.

I kissed Vera on the cheek, ignoring the beads of perspiration that salted my lips. She immediately relaxed. "So Dad told you I was coming."

"He gave me fair warning," she said with a playful grin. She clanked the lid back down on the roasting pan and closed the oven door. "So I decided to make a pot roast." Her eyes sparkled with diamonds of delight. "Someone I know likes pot roast."

"Anyone I know?"

She yanked off her oven mittens and swatted me with them half-heartedly. "If you tell me you've become a vegetarian, I'll feed it to the dogs."

"Don't you dare!" And we laughed together like schoolgirls.

Vera went to the sink and started rinsing some utensils she'd used in her dinner preparations. I gazed out the kitchen window, which normally offered a panoramic view of the river valley below. Today it was a gray and formless basin. "Where's Dad?"

Vera knitted her brow. "I'm not sure. He's been prowling around the house all afternoon like a caged mountain lion. Something's got him going."

"Do you know who's joining us for dinner?" Vera, I figured, must know something about this mystery woman, something she could pass along to me—in strictest confidence, of course.

"Mr. McKinney," she said without looking up from her work. "And one other."

I wasn't surprised to hear that Lance McKinney would be joining us this evening. Lance had worked for my father for as long as I could remember. Dad probably felt the need for the support of a loyal foot soldier. But it was the "one other" I was interested in at the moment.

"And who might this *one other* be?" I said, feigning apathy as I watched for Vera's reaction out of the corner of my eye.

She shrugged. "Just someone your dad has met with a couple of times recently. I don't know anything about her, except that she's young and pretty."

As soon as the words were out of her mouth, her hand flew up to cover it. Water trailed down her forearm and dribbled onto the floor.

"Hmmm," I said, feeling my face flush. "Young and pretty?"

"Not that young," Vera said, trying to recover. "And not that pretty." But the cat had been let out of the bag and there was no getting it back in, and we both knew it.

I forced a smile for Vera's sake. "Well, I'd better go find Romeo."

3   I FOUND DAD in the library, standing next to a fireplace clogged with ashes. He was already dressed for the evening—gray slacks, a pale-blue dress shirt, a navy cardigan. His silver-gray hair was trimmed neatly on the sides and his chiseled chin had that polished look that told me it had met with a razor within the past half-hour. He was holding a tumbler with ice floating in a lucent brown liquid and was gazing at the darkly paneled wall where, among other framed family photographs, a studio portrait of him and Mom was hanging.

I knew that portrait well, because sitting on the dresser in the bedroom of my apartment—in a myrtlewood frame inlaid with seashells—was a smaller version of the same print. For weeks after Mom's death, that photograph had gone to bed with me.

Dad stirred from his reverie as I entered. "Felicity." There was pleasure in his voice, but his smile was like a setting sun, lacking intensity. "How was the trip down?" The words clung to his tongue for an instant before letting go.

I gave him a kiss and a hug and got a whiff of the whiskey on his breath. "Wet."

He held up his glass. "Can I get you a drink?"

"I'd like to get cleaned up first."

"Mmm," he said, nodding absentmindedly. His gaze returned to the photos on the wall then snapped back almost immediately toward me, and I could see that he was as jittery as a compass needle in a magnetic storm.

I gave him another peck on the cheek. "Build a fire," I said. "I want it unbearably warm in here when I return."

I traipsed upstairs to my room and stripped off my sweatshirt and jeans. I took a hot shower in the adjoining bath, hoping to wash away more than the day's accumulated grime. Dad wasn't the only one on edge. It was a big step for him to take, allowing another woman into his life. But it was also a bitter pill for me to swallow, watching him cozy up to someone other than Mom. I was toweling off in a fog of steam when a thin line of sound, high and unbroken, like the distant wailing of a child, pierced my thoughts. It took a while for me to realize that the sound was coming out of me. The full weight of what this evening was all about had come crashing down on me like bad news on Judgment Day. I crumpled to the bathroom floor in tears.

BY THE TIME I got myself together, dressed in something suitable to the occasion, and went back down to the library, Lance McKinney had arrived. He was sitting, drink in hand, on the sofa across the coffee table from where Dad was now ensconced in his padded leather armchair. A fire was crackling in the fireplace. Still the room felt cold to me.

Mr. McKinney clunked his drink down on the coffee table, stood, and greeted me with a polite hug. He was a handsome man with just enough gray in his wavy, black hair to be distinguished-looking. Lance was chief financial officer of Valley Lumber and probably would become its CEO when Dad stepped down.

"Lovely dress," Lance said as our upper bodies parted.

I smoothed down a wrinkle on its front. "Mom bought it for me for my eighteenth birthday. She loved lavender and—"

"Ready for that drink?" Dad interjected, rudely I thought.

Mildly miffed, I plopped down on the sofa. "A glass of Riesling would be nice," I said in an imperious tone I'd learned from Mother.

"Lance, would you do the honors?" Dad said.

Lance knew his way around the library bar well enough. Moments later, he was handing Dad a replenished glass and me a wine goblet filled nearly to the brim. He reseated himself on the sofa—an appropriate distance from me.

"Where's your wife tonight?" I asked.

He forced a laugh that came out more like a neigh. "Doing one of her ladies' nights out." He seized his drink and raised it to his lips. The ice in it clinked against his teeth. "I never ask for details."

Things got quiet after that, and I was wondering why. My dad and Mr. McKinney had always been great social conversationalists—a skill they'd acquired through years of entertaining important clients and local politicians. But this evening, they might as well have been bound and gagged, because all they did for the longest time was sit there mute, looking at one another—and at me—helplessly.

It was approaching seven o'clock and our other guest had yet to arrive. Finally, I spoke up. "We haven't had a cancellation, have we?"

Dad glanced over quizzically. Lance was studying his drink glass. "Our mystery guest?"

"No," Dad said, expelling the word in a dry, throaty voice that sounded like a dog choking on a chicken bone. He hopped up, suddenly the attentive server, and collected our glasses. "She'll be here."

He was at the bar pouring fresh drinks when our final guest arrived. I turned and looked at her as she was being ushered into the room by the new girl, Lydia. It was all I could do to keep from gasping.

Vera had told the truth. She was young and pretty. But there was something else about her that Vera had neglected to mention. This woman was a younger version of my mother—a mid-to-late-thirties model. She was shorter than Mom, a little stockier, and her hair was a lighter shade of brown. But her lucid green eyes, the rounded contours of her face, the way her nose tipped up at the end—was all Mom. It was eerie to say the least.

"Come in, Mrs. Adberry," said Dad, exhibiting a nervousness akin to that of an expectant father. "What can I get you to drink?"

Mrs., I thought. And I imagined the ad as it might have appeared

in the personals: *Young widow seeks the company of kindly, older gentle-*
man; money no object, as long as he has lots of it.

"Nothing, thank you," said Mrs. Adberry, displaying a demure smile
that could have been an expression of genuine modesty—or geisha
artifice. I reserved judgment.

I noted with interest, however, that her voice was nothing like my
mom's. Mom's voice was deep for a woman, husky. Mrs. Adberry's
was thin, reedy. Mom was a bassoon to Mrs. Adberry's clarinet. For
some reason, it made me feel better knowing that at least they didn't
sound alike.

"I hope I haven't held up dinner," she said. "I got off later than
planned."

"Not at all," Dad said, returning from the bar with drinks in hand.
He handed a whiskey to Lance, who was standing beside the sofa looking as if he'd just realized his zipper was undone. I accepted my glass
of wine and waited for Dad to offer formal introductions.

When he did, there was no handshaking, merely tight smiles and
nods all around. "Pleased to meet you, Mrs. Adberry," I said.

"Please call me Tamara. And tell your dad it's okay for him to do the
same." She winked at him. At least I thought it was a wink. It could
have been a nervous blink.

"Well, *Tamara*," Dad said, as if enunciating a newly learned foreign
phrase, "do sit down." He gestured toward a wing chair to his left. "Are
you sure I can't get you something to whet your appetite?"

Mrs. Adberry shook her head. "I'm fine, really."

We sat down in our designated places: Lance with me on the sofa—
to my left—Dad across from us in his easy chair, and a still smiling
Mrs. Adberry in the wing chair on my right. An uncomfortable interval
of silence followed, which the three of us with drinks attempted to
fill with frequent tipping of our glasses. Finally, Lance rescued us. "I
understand you live in the Coos Bay area," he said to Mrs. Adberry.

"That's right," she said, clasping her hands together in her lap. "My
husband bought a business there some years ago. Boat hull cleaning.
He loves boats and the water. And it's a nice community. But as long
as we've lived there, I'm still not used to the cold wind."

My mind went suddenly empty, then thoughts came crashing in like whitecaps pummeling a rocky shore. This woman was using the present tense when speaking about her husband. She was still married! What was going on here? Dad wouldn't have taken up with a married woman. And if she wasn't his new girlfriend, then who the hell was she?

"—a doctor," Mrs. Adberry was saying, and I realized that she'd been talking to me while I'd been talking to myself.

"I'm sorry?"

"Your dad tells me you're studying to become a doctor. That must be hard work."

I sat up straighter on the sofa and tried to focus on the topic at hand, while a litany of questions regarding this woman vied, like pop-up ads, for my attention. "I'm just finishing up my bachelor's degree this year. I'll be going to Oregon Health Sciences University next year to start the real grind."

Mrs. Adberry gave an approving nod. "Good for you. I'm sure your dad is very proud."

I glanced over at Dad. His lips were indeed curled up in the semblance of a smile, and his eyes glinted in apparent admiration. But I was guessing that it wasn't pride so much he was feeling at that moment as the effects of the whiskey he'd been drinking all afternoon. My head was already buzzing from the wine, to say nothing of the spin cycle of conjecture I was caught in regarding the true identity of this woman.

By the time dinner was announced—it was only minutes later but seemed like a lifetime—the conversation had bounced back and forth on a line between Mrs. Adberry and me, Dad and Lance deftly deflecting it whenever it headed in their direction. So we learned in the course of things that not only did Mrs. Adberry have a husband, she also had a son. His name was Brent. Brent was in junior high school, lived and breathed basketball, and hoped one day to play for the Ducks. We also learned that she was originally from Eugene. That she had worked as a waitress for a number of years before hurting her back. She didn't like seafood, and what a shame it was, because she lived on the coast and her husband cleaned fishing boats for a living.

At the same time, Mrs. Adberry learned more about me than I cared to tell. Every personal detail I divulged in her presence seemed somehow a betrayal of the many confidences I'd shared with Mom over the years. Finally I felt myself close up like a flower exposed to too much sunlight, and the small talk ground mercifully to a halt. Everyone, I think, was relieved when it was time to eat.

At dinner we all drank wine, including Tamara—by the second carafe we were all, grudgingly on my part, on a first-name basis. The free-flowing alcohol only made me more guarded, more wary—of the way the evening was playing out, of Dad's motives for insisting I come home for the weekend, of this woman at our table who reminded me of Mom but who was obviously not meant to take her place. When, during the main course, Dad offered me more wine, I turned my glass upside down, and a meal I should have relished remained mostly on my plate.

After dinner Dad and Lance drifted out onto the back deck to have their cigars. Tamara went into the guest bathroom—"to freshen up," she said. I made a beeline for the kitchen to face off with Vera.

"Okay," I said, going nose to nose with her, "who is this woman?"

Vera flashed me a bewildered look. "I honestly don't know."

"But doesn't she remind you of someone?" I remembered the old photographs in the family albums I'd always loved to browse through as a girl. I'd been fascinated by the changing styles in dress and hair, and by the youthful appearance of my parents and their friends.

Vera's eyes widened, the white surrounding her irises gleaming like polar caps. "Honey," she said, "she's like a ghost from the past."

4 MORE CONFUSED THAN EVER, I returned to the library. Tamara had arrived ahead of me. She was standing along the wall of family portraits staring up at the one of Mom and Dad. She turned and looked at me. Her face was mime white, with only a few Rorschach blotches of color in her cheeks. Her eyes were swimming in their sockets.

"Are you all right?" I asked.

She grimaced. "I'm not used to drinking so much. I'm a little sick."

I led her to the sofa and sat her down. I got a cloth from the bar cabinet, wet it, and had her hold it against her forehead.

"This is so silly," she said.

"It's not," I assured her, feeling a sudden kinship for someone who, only moments before, I had viewed with raw suspicion. "It's perfectly normal. I'm half crocked myself. I'm surprised I haven't thrown up."

I was sitting next to Tamara, holding her free hand, when the French doors leading from the library onto the back deck opened with a rush of tobacco-tinged air and Dad and Lance stepped inside. Dad took one look at us together on the sofa and froze in his tracks. Lance averted his eyes, as if guilty of something.

"It's all your fault," I said, addressing them both.

I expected an immediate protest, but they just stood there dumbly, like two wax museum figures unable even to blink.

"No, no," Tamara said. "I've always been a lightweight when it comes to alcohol." She removed the cloth from her forehead. "But I'm much better now." With obvious effort, she pushed herself up to a standing position, faltered briefly, then with a quick shuffle of her feet, found her balance. She smiled feebly. "It's been a wonderful evening, but I really must go."

"Surely you don't mean to drive back to Coos Bay tonight," I said, alarmed at the prospect of her traveling on that twisted road over the coastal mountains impaired and after dark. "We'll put you up here for the night, and you can get a fresh start in the morning." I looked at Dad for support. He remained stonily silent.

If Tamara felt snubbed, she didn't acknowledge it. "Nice of you to offer, but I've reserved a room at the Fir Valley Inn."

"At least let us call a cab for you."

"Really, that's not necessary. It's just down the hill. I'll be fine."

"But—" I said, but had no words to follow up with.

Tamara straightened her back, seeming to have regained her composure along with her balance. "Thank you for a wonderful evening,

Russell. It was good of you to have me over." She nodded at Lance. "A pleasure to have met you."

She gazed at me for a long moment, as if wanting to fix an image of my face in her mind, and in that moment something passed between us that I didn't understand. A message had been sent and received, but its meaning—having been encoded—was unclear to me. She gave me a quick, tight hug. "Goodbye," she said, and turned to leave.

As I watched her walk away, I felt a tug at my center, and I realized that I wasn't prepared for the suddenness of her departure. "I'll see you out," I said, and exhibiting more urgency than I'd intended, rushed to her side and hooked my arm through hers. Like two links in a chain, we moved together out of the library, down the hall, through the foyer—where Tamara reclaimed her purse and sweater—and out through the front double doors. Neither of us spoke, but it didn't seem to matter.

Outside, darkness had seeped into the valley and settled tarlike against the landscape. The crisp night air barely stirred, the storm having blown through and left behind an uncommon stillness. I'd neglected to turn on any exterior lights before leaving the house. We moved arm in arm down the front steps and across the driveway to Tamara's car with only the anemic glow from the curtained front windows lighting our way.

She opened the driver's door, got in, rolled the window down. She looked out at me, her lips forming an uncertain smile, like a barely drawn bow. "I know you're wondering who I am and why I was invited here tonight."

I opened my mouth to speak, but the questions inside me were too big and cumbersome to get out. I was suddenly a little girl again, with a little girl's vague understanding of the world.

"Your father will have to tell you that," she said.

We studied one another's shadowy faces for a time without speaking. My mind seemed to be floating in space. I didn't know if it was due to the alcohol I'd consumed or because of the confusion I felt about meeting this woman who was unknown to me yet seemed so familiar.

She turned the key in the ignition and the car's engine roared to life. "He loves you very much," she said over the roar. Before I could respond, she put the car in gear and pulled away.

She completed the circle in the driveway and headed down the lane. Her brake lights flashed as she reached the front gate and then, a moment later, disappeared.

I stood there peering down the empty drive, wondering once again what this evening was all about. Why had Dad gone to the trouble of bringing this woman and me together? And why the family resemblance? Was she a lost relative? Did I have an older sister I didn't know about? Had Dad engaged in some dalliance that, now that Mother was gone, he was ready to own up to?

I gazed up at the night sky, raked clean by the quick-moving storm. It was an unsullied canopy above the earth, a window to the far-flung constellations of our universe. I regarded the multitude of lights shimmering down on me and remembered something I'd read somewhere in a book or magazine. The author had said that by the time the light from some stars reached the earth, the stars themselves had already expired. Suddenly the air seemed unbearably cold, and I felt terribly alone. I stood there a moment longer, hugging myself, then turned and walked back to the house.

I met Lance in the foyer, struggling to pull on his overcoat. I gave him an assist. "Bailing out too, are you?"

He tugged at the collar of his coat. "I'm afraid Mrs. Adberry isn't the only one who drank too much." He gave me a polite kiss on the cheek before tottering out the front door.

I'd sobered up considerably as a result of my dip into the chilly evening air, and as I trod back down the hallway, I resolved to give Dad the third degree about Tamara Adberry. It was time for him to fess up to—whatever he needed to fess up to. But when I returned to the library, I found him slouched down in his chair, apparently asleep. Responding to a surge of frustration, I flounced over to the bar and, none too quietly, began tidying up.

Moments later, I heard Dad's voice, weak and raspy, like deathbed speech. "Lydia will do that tomorrow."

I tossed a coaster onto the bar, came around, and sat down across from him on the sofa. "I thought you were asleep."

"No such luck." He gazed over at me, and there was an ancient sadness in his eyes, as if he'd just witnessed the desecration of an ancestral grave.

"What's wrong, Dad?"

He didn't speak for a time. Finally the corners of his mouth ticked up in a rueful smile. "You know about my heart murmur?"

"Yes."

"It's worse."

"Oh?" I felt something come loose inside me. Unseen fingers were plucking at the threads holding me together.

"Doc Bradford thinks it's time I got a new heart valve—and the sooner, the better."

I leaned forward and hugged my middle like a kid with a bellyache. As a pre-med student, I understood the seriousness of open-heart surgery. I knew that sometimes there are complications, things go wrong, patients go under anesthesia and never come out. "Is surgery really necessary?" I said, realizing too late the whininess in my voice.

A look of resignation invaded the craggy features of Dad's face. "Apparently it's either that or, according to the medical experts anyway, face the likelihood of a massive coronary in the near future. Either way, I don't like my prospects. So I'll be stepping down as CEO at the mill and turning the reins of the company over to Lance."

I pressed my open palms against my sides. Stitches, it seemed, were popping all over my body. "Dad," I said, wanting to make sure I'd survived the worst of it, "is that why you had me come down this weekend? To tell me about your heart?"

He hesitated. "Yes," he finally said, but with an utter lack of conviction.

That's when I lost it, when some part of me broke open, and what came out, along with a rush of irritation, was the same question I'd had all evening—the question no one seemed to want to address, least of all Dad. I slapped my thighs. "Then who the hell is Tamara Adberry? And why was she here tonight?"

That primal sadness reappeared in Dad's eyes. "That, my dear," he said in a voice that barely pierced the air between us, "is also a matter of the heart. But it's one I'm afraid will have to wait until tomorrow to be addressed. We're both too tired and too much under the influence to delve into it tonight." He reached out a hand toward me. "Now help me up and point me toward a bed."

I didn't know if I could stand up myself, I felt so undone by the evening's events. I stared at Dad's hand, at his fingers twitching, and suppressed an urge to lash out at him for putting me off, for leaving me dangling over the edge of an emotional precipice by nothing but a finger hold. But he was right. We were both too exhausted.

I reached across the coffee table, grasped Dad's hand, and we pulled each other up. I came around the table. He cupped my face with his palms and kissed me on both cheeks.

"Tomorrow," he said. "I promise. Tomorrow I will tell all." A curtain seemed to come down over his eyes. "And even then will be too soon."

5   THE NEXT MORNING, I parted the curtains in my bedroom window just enough to glimpse the sky. It was a gray fist of clouds.

Feeling a morning-after wretchedness, I shrouded myself in one of Mom's flannel bathrobes and dragged myself downstairs to the dining nook. Dad was already sitting at the table, looking like the ghost of Trouste House past: pale-faced, unshaven, a wing of hair sticking out above one ear, eyes sunken in their sockets. He grunted a greeting and took a sip of black coffee from a mug with a logo that declared TIMBER IS KING.

"I see you slept well," I said. I poured myself a cup of coffee, splashed in some cream, and took a seat across from him. We sipped our brew and listened to the wind clawing at the windowpanes.

Lydia served us a breakfast of Spanish omelets, rye toast, and strawberries, which we ate in an unspoken pact of silence. The ambient noise was accompanied only by the tinkling of our dinnerware, while residual emotion from the absence of table talk accumulated like flood waters behind a dam. Lydia poured me another cup of coffee and withdrew, carrying our empty plates.

"I didn't know silence could be so painful," I said, adding cream to my cup.

"Sometimes it's breaking the silence that's painful," Dad responded, his voice dripping with melancholy.

I clunked my cup down in its saucer. "Stop it now. You're scaring me." My throat constricted as I spoke. "What's going on here?"

Dad didn't answer, just sat there with his elbows propped on the table, his grizzled chin resting on nested hands. His eyes were bloodshot, and I could see torment building in them like a thundercloud. I realized then that whatever Dad had on his mind, it was tearing him up inside and that it would be better for him to drag it out into the open where it could be exposed for what it was, rather than to keep it hidden away to be feared for what it might be.

"Just tell me what it is you need to say," I pleaded.

Dad took a deep breath and expelled it with such force I thought his whole body might deflate. "Felicity," he said, "you know how much I love you."

Somewhere at the edge of my mind I saw a lone bird flying across an empty sky, a sky so lacking in content that it seemed in danger of collapsing in on itself. The bird was looking around for somewhere to land. But at that moment, the whole world was nothing but that empty sky. I had no idea where this image came from or what it meant. I blinked a time or two and it was gone, replaced by my dad's face, disfigured now by an expression of anguish.

"And your mother," he said. "No one could have loved you more."

"I was her little miracle," I said, not really understanding the moment but feeling pulled into it by some undercurrent of emotion.

"You were," my father said. "But in a way—" His jaw trembled. He looked down at the table. "—you weren't *our* miracle."

"Not *your* miracle?" I said, then sat dumbfounded while the question hung in the air between us, as dispossessed as that lone bird my mind had so recently conjured up.

"Do you understand what it is I'm trying to tell you?" Dad said, shifting his gaze back to me—but only fleetingly. I think he was hoping to get *it* said without actually having to say it.

I responded with open-mouthed silence, because truly I didn't understand. Maybe I just didn't want to understand. I barely heard his next words, they were spoken so softly. And once again he was looking away—out the window, across the valley, across the universe.

"You—were—not—actually—born—to us," he said. "We—adopted you at birth. Tamara—Tamara Adberry—" But he'd gone as far as he could go. Tears flooded his eyes and streamed down his cheeks. His chin dropped to his chest, which began to heave.

I was crying too, but I wasn't sure why. I'd heard the words Dad had spoken and had understood them. But I hadn't really believed them. In fact, they made no sense to me at all.

"Can't be," I said, sitting upright in my chair. I blew my nose into my table napkin. I chugged some air and felt calmer, clearer—ready to apply some Logic 101 to this illogical situation. "I couldn't be adopted," I asserted with rock-hard certainty. "If I'd been adopted, I would have known. Besides, Mother couldn't have kept such a thing from me. She couldn't even keep my surprise birthday party a secret."

Dad nodded pathetically.

I shook my napkin at him. "Then how could she possibly have kept this from me while she was alive? Tell me that."

Dad looked pained. "It wasn't her secret to tell," he said in a croaky voice that broke off into jagged shards of sound.

I scoffed at that remark. That my father, one of the most reasonable men I'd ever known, would utter such an absurdity angered me.

I shot up from my chair, knocking it over backwards, and charged away from the table. I stalked down the hallway and into the library. I went straight to the wall of family portraits and ripped the picture of Mom and Dad off the wall. Welling with indignation, I hauled the likeness of my parents back to the dining nook, where Dad remained seated in stunned silence.

"Look at this," I said, holding the portrait next to my face.

Dad kept his head turned away.

I yelled at him. "Look at this picture!"

Slowly he turned toward me.

"I have this woman's face," I said, pleading for him to understand the implausibility of what he was asking me to believe.

His lips pinched together in an expression of woe.

"This woman is my mother!" I pointed an accusatory finger at him. "And you are my dad!"

He fixed his gaze on me, but his eyes were like dying embers, no longer capable of giving warmth—or any other emotion, except perhaps pity.

I stood there quaking, mentally plugging the leaks in the dike of my own disbelief.

That bird flew by again in the empty sky.

I let the portrait drop from my hand and rushed away from the sound of breaking glass, the sting of fresh tears in my eyes.

6   "FELICITY, PLEASE—" Dad called after me as, nearly blinded by my tears, I ran from the dining nook and blundered down the hall. "Please understand."

But I didn't understand. How could I? My father had just professed his and my mother's undying love for me and then proceeded to rip my heart out. "We adopted you at birth," he'd informed me. He might as well have said, "You're not who you think you are. Your whole life has been a lie."

I stumbled up the stairs, which seemed to dip and sway beneath me, cringing at the sound of my father's voice pleading for the one thing I was incapable of doing. Understand? Smash someone's world apart and then ask them to understand? One moment I'd known who I was, and the next instant that reality had been shattered and replaced by a black hole that was my past.

I fled to my room. I was frantically gathering up my things when a wave of nausea doubled me over. Were these really my things? Was this really my room? Did I even know whose house I'd lived in for the past twenty-one years? I rushed into the bathroom and threw up in the sink, not bothering to rinse the frothy slime off the glistening porcelain.

I lurched back into the bedroom, feeling lost. Everything around me seemed foreign now. Whose bed was this? Whose dresser? Whose panic-stricken eyes stared back at me from the dresser mirror?

As if escaping a burning building, I left everything except my wallet and keys and ran from the house. No one tried to stop me. Dad didn't dare. Poor Lydia, who must have witnessed at least some of my histrionics, kept to her chores. Sunday was Vera's day off. I leaped into my car and drove away.

It wasn't until I'd arrived back at my apartment in Salem that I realized I was still clothed in my mother's flannel robe and a pair of her fuzzy slippers. I shed the robe, kicked off the slippers, and flung myself naked onto my bed, where I flailed my arms and legs and screamed like an apoplectic child.

During the days that followed, I lived in the murky world of uncertainty. Having been stripped of my identity, I questioned the reality of everything else as well. I went to bed at night wondering if the sun would rise come morning. I arose each day skeptical of my surroundings, of the solidity of the walls, of the firmness of the floors, of the authenticity of the view out my bedroom window. I stumbled through each day's activities staring anxiously about as if expecting any moment the bottom to drop out of the physical universe the way it had been blown out of my personal world.

"I can't have been adopted," I cried at night when I should have been asleep. "I'm a Trouste. I look like a Trouste. I think like a Trouste. I act like a Trouste." Then again, Russell Trouste's voice would sound in my ears, at once pitiful and terrifying: "We adopted you at birth. Tamara—Tamara Adberry—"

"No!" I would scream and slam my face into my pillow.

At the university and in my personal life, I lost confidence in myself and my abilities. I felt like a fraud. None of my prior accomplishments mattered. Honor student. Cheerleader. Homecoming queen. Soccer team captain. Member, Governor's Youth Leadership Council. None of that was real, because none of that had happened to me. It had all happened to the person I only thought I was.

I shied away from my classmates, including the biotechie who wanted desperately to be my boyfriend. I felt unworthy of the companionship. I had nothing to offer, and to pretend otherwise served only to perpetuate the lie my life had become.

I tried to study but my mind simply glanced off the pages of my textbooks like feebly thrown punches. The research I'd accumulated for my paper "The Role of Stress-induced Analgesia in Antebellum Surgery" seemed full of foreign words and phrases the meaning of which eluded me. I began staring blankly in response to questions put to me in class by my professors.

"Felicity, are you having a bad day?"

A bad day? A bad day is when you twist your ankle coming up the steps of the science building. A bad day is when your boyfriend calls and cancels your date for the evening, and you hear female voices giggling in the background. A bad day is when you lose your makeup kit—in your purse. I wasn't having a bad day. I was having a crisis of ego-shattering proportions. I was grappling with questions so profound that even the slightest of complications, much less being informed by the man you've called Father all your life that "we adopted you at birth," could send my mind hurtling to the edge and beyond. And when that question—"Are you having a bad day?"—was put to me, innocently enough, I burst into tears and fled the classroom amidst the shocked stares of twenty-plus classmates and an equally astonished professor of biochemistry.

One night during this time of crisis, I huddled on the sofa in my apartment, hugging a blanket around me to combat the shivers I was experiencing. (For I had long since plummeted into a deep freeze of depression.) When the telephone rang, I let it go to voice mail. But the caller persisted with repeated calls. Finally, with a muttered curse, I tossed off the blanket and reached for the phone. I snuffled hard before answering—I'd been crying but didn't want the caller to know.

It was Vera, phoning from Sacred Heart Medical Center in Eugene. My dad had come through his open-heart surgery in good shape and was resting comfortably in the recovery room, she said. Mr. McKinney had already visited him. And Pastor Martin had stayed at the hospital during the entire operation. "You should come see him, Felicity. Or, at least, call him. He's suffering."

"And don't you think I'm suffering?" I said, assuming—correctly, as it turned out—that by now Vera had been made aware of my true parentage.

"I think your ego is suffering," she said.

"What do you know about my ego?"

"Enough."

"But I'm not even who I thought I was," I whined, wallowing in the muck of self-pity.

"Who did you think you were?"

"A Trouste."

"And how did that make you feel, being a Trouste?"

"Confident. Secure. Special. I felt like I could accomplish anything, because that's what Troustes do—they get things done."

"You're still a Trouste," Vera said.

I felt my lips arc into a pout. "In name only."

Vera was having none of it. "See here, Felicity—your father and mother gave you more than just a name. They gave you values. It's those values that make you who you are, not the name."

I discharged a high-pitched "ha!" in protest. "Then how come I feel like I've just had my legs cut off? Like I'll never be able to walk again on my own, much less run. How come all of a sudden I feel"—I searched for the right word—"worthless?"

Vera laughed. She actually laughed. "You'll get over it. You'll get over it as soon as you realize that you're still the same person you always were, and that what makes you that person—your intellect, your sensitivity, your sense of humor—no one can take away, not even if they change your name to—to—Felicity Fudd."

"Felicity Fudd?"

"Yes. Daughter of Elmer Fudd."

I shook my head at the inanity of what she was saying. This was not a cartoon character we were talking about here. This was my life. "You don't understand," I said indignantly.

"Will you come see your dad?"

"My *dad?*" An explosion of anger went off inside my brain, blasting much of the hurt and self-pity there to smithereens. My body rocked on waves of resentment. "He's *not* my dad," I said, my voice quavering from the awful truth.

7

VERA WAS RIGHT, of course—at least about one thing. In the ways that counted most, I was still the same person. All I had to do was accept myself as I was and not dwell on how I came to be this way. But I found this self-acceptance more difficult than embracing the idea of the immaculate conception of Christ. At least God had a plan that made sense.

And so I struggled through the weeks and months that followed like the lost child I'd become, fearful because I'd been cut off from the path behind me and terrified because there lay no clear road ahead. My nights were punctuated with tears and my days weighted with a longing for the old reality—a reality that was palpable at times and at other times seemed to be no more than a trick of my confused imagination. My personal life and my schoolwork continued to suffer.

With the suggestion—insistence really—of my biochemistry professor, I entered counseling with the school psychologist, a service free to every emotionally screwed-up Willamette student regardless of status. The sessions were excruciating excavations of my inner self, intended to unearth an answer to the crucial question, "Could I simply be *me*—whoever that was—moment to moment, without regard for who I thought I was yesterday or who I'd expected to become tomorrow?"

I didn't know, but despairing of my current state of broken-hearted confusion, I was willing to try. Little by little, with the guidance of the psychologist, I began picking up the pieces of my damaged self and putting them back together into a functioning ego—fragile, but functioning. I stopped asking, "Where did I come from?" and started concentrating on where I wanted to go.

I still wanted to become a doctor, I decided. And I knew that in order to achieve that goal I had to rededicate myself to my studies. My decision to do that put me truly on the path to recovery, because the more absorbed I became in my schoolwork, the less time I spent mourning the loss of my heritage. Also, I discovered that I was still good at learning. When I worked hard on a paper or studied diligently for an exam, I got top marks, along with the praise of my professors and the admiration of my peers, none of whom seemed to give a damn whether I was a Trouste or a Fudd.

I began practically living on the Internet. Hunched in front of my computer, I would slog endlessly through obscure articles in even more obscure medical journals. When I was about to overdose on scientific technospeak, I'd escape to the biochem lab, where I'd spend uninterrupted hours observing the performance of chemically hyped mice on various miniature apparatuses designed to measure their athletic ability and stamina.

I even allowed Joey Markham, my would-be boyfriend, to occupy what little time I had left over in a given day. He'd take me to a rock concert in Portland or to dinner at my favorite Italian restaurant. I would let him kiss me and tell me how wonderful I was, and I would want to believe him.

The one thing I didn't do was talk to or correspond with the man I used to call Dad. I let all my ex-father's calls go to voice mail and didn't call him back. I deleted his e-mails and dumped his letters in the trash. It wasn't long before he stopped e-mailing, writing, and calling. And I didn't go home to Fir Valley on weekends or during school vacations. I tried to stop thinking of Fir Valley as my home, and began telling new acquaintances I'd been raised by foster parents.

The only link that remained between me and Russell Trouste was the school bills I continued sending him. I didn't know what he'd do with them. But he continued paying them—out of guilt or confusion or misguided love. I didn't know and didn't care. He owed me, I reasoned, for all the years of lies and deception.

In June, I graduated from Willamette University with honors and, after a summer spent mostly traveling in Canada with college friends, went off to medical school at Oregon Health Sciences University in Portland. Medical school was all-consuming. I had no time to fret about anything except making it to my next class, passing the next exam, staying awake during my rotations to the various clinical assignments. But with blind determination—and Russell Trouste still silently paying the bills—I made it through. At the end of the four-year course of study, I had the title "Dr." in front of my name and was newly engaged in my residency in Family Practice at Portland's Good Samaritan Hospital.

The evening of Vera's frantic call, I was working in Urgent Care with a patient who'd come in complaining of nonspecific abdominal pain. The patient, an unkempt white male in his fifties, was lying on his back on an exam table with the soft white flesh of his lower belly exposed. I was pressing with my gloved fingers on the area of complaint, feeling for any swollen organs and probing for tenderness, when a nurse came into the exam room and told me I had an emergency phone call that I could take at the nurse's station.

"Be right there," I said, abstracted, and continued with my exam.

"Lower," the man said.

I probed lower. "Any pain here?"

"Down lower," he said, jutting out his stubbled chin, pointing the way for me.

I worked my way down to just above the pubic region without any complaint on his part.

"Almost there," the man said.

I glanced down at his grizzled face, at his bloodshot eyes almost hidden by the heavy folds of skin around his eye sockets. "Really? That low?"

"Uh huh," he said.

I stripped off my gloves. "Looks like we're searching in the wrong place." I disposed of the gloves in a medical waste bin. "I need to take a phone call now. But when I come back, we'll do some extensive rectal probing. I'm sure we'll find something there." I bestowed upon him my professional smile and left the room, knowing that when I returned he'd be gone.

I strode down the hall to the nurse's station, where I was handed a phone and told which button to push. I brushed back my hair and pressed the receiver against my ear. "This is Dr. Trouste."

"You may not care, but your father is very ill. If you were half the person—" Vera's voice broke off bitterly.

I winced—not out of concern for Russell Trouste, but because of Vera's expression of her low assessment of me as a person. Although I'd had no further contact with her during my estrangement from my counterfeit dad, I still cared about her. Her opinions mattered. But at that moment, my need to safeguard my ego took precedence over her feelings. My back stiffened and my emotional defenses went up. "I'm sorry to hear that Russell isn't doing well," I said with as much equanimity as I could summon. "There are some fine doctors practicing in Douglas County. I suggest he see one."

A hollow silence lingered and then was finally broken by Vera's strained reply. "If you would get off your high horse for a minute, you would understand that it's not as simple as that. Your father refuses to see a doctor. He says it doesn't matter now whether he lives or dies. He's lost the one thing left in this world he cares about." A heavy sigh, like a howling wind, gushed through the phone line. "I think there's a problem with his heart again."

Evading the emotional shield I'd thrown up, the doctor in me took over. "Does he have a fever?"

"I suspect he does," Vera said. "But I don't know for sure. He won't let me near him with a thermometer. He's eaten very little in the last three days, and has hardly been out of bed in that time." Her voice took on an ominous tone. "I'm scared for him, Felicity."

I felt a surge of resentment as I listened to her. I didn't want to be sucked back into the whirlpool of emotion waiting to swallow me up if I spent too much time dwelling on the past. I still had unresolved issues with Russell Trouste, but for my own well-being, I'd stored them away in a locked compartment in my brain, to be opened and dealt with at a time of my choosing—and this was not the time.

But neither did I want to be derelict in my professional life. I was a doctor, after all. I had taken the Hippocratic Oath. As a physician, I was obligated to care. I pressed the heel of my hand against a place above my right eye that had begun to throb. "Okay," I said, my mind whirling as I tried to settle on a response. "If he has a fever, it means he probably has an infection. It could be nothing more than a cold, or—" I sighed, knowing what action my next words would inevitably give birth to. "It could mean a problem with his mechanical heart valve. If the tissue around the valve has become infected—"

Vera's voice pulsed with passion across the wire. "He needs you, Felicity."

"He needs a doctor."

"You're a doctor."

I braced myself against the counter. "Yes."

8   I WAS WORKING the nightshift at the hospital, a 6 PM to 6 AM grind that I could look forward to for the entire month of November. I arrived back at my Portland apartment about six-thirty in the morning, exhausted and cursing myself for what I was about to do. Grudgingly, I set my alarm for two hours later and collapsed into bed. I got up in a stupor and with the help of a tall French vanilla latte purchased at a nearby convenience store stayed awake long enough to complete the three-hour drive, in crisp clear weather, down the interstate to Fir Valley.

As I approached the outskirts of town, I began experiencing hot flashes. I'd worked hard to distance myself from my past life as the daughter of Russell Trouste, from memories that elicited more sorrow than sweetness because they were based on a lie. But places come attached with memories the way flesh is attached to bone, and I knew I couldn't go back to Trouste House without revisiting in my mind some of the joyful times I'd spent there in my youth, along with the terrible emptiness I'd felt upon learning that that part of my life had been nothing but a sham.

By the time I reached the entrance to the estate, I was having trouble breathing. My stomach had become an active volcano, spewing juices like molten lava, so that my esophagus was burning from acid reflux. There was a buzzing in my head that produced a sense of disorientation mingled with dread.

I pulled to a stop in the driveway, aware that I needed to get a grip. I closed my eyes, took several measured breaths as I tried to wipe clean the slate of my mind. *You can do this*, I told myself. You're a doctor going to see a patient. You're a twenty-six-year-old woman in charge of her life and in control of her feelings. Let the past be the past.

But a few minutes later, I was trembling inside, if not outwardly, while standing at the front door of Trouste House waiting for someone to respond to my ringing of the doorbell.

When Vera opened the door, we both stood there mute looking at one another, frozen in a moment that seemed misplaced in time, trying to peel back the years to reach that connection between us that had once been so strong. Finally Vera produced a smile, but one that barely crossed the line from sadness. "Thank you for coming."

"How is he?" I inquired. I stepped over the threshold, feeling dazed.

"I don't know. He's in his room. I knocked on his door this morning and told him you were coming."

I nodded, not wanting to say too much, afraid to start a conversation I wasn't prepared to finish. "I'll go check on him."

Upstairs, I tapped on Russell's bedroom door.

"Come in," he said in a stronger voice than I'd expected.

I entered the room, thinking to find him in bed under a pile of covers, fighting off the chills. Or huddled on his settee in his bathrobe and slippers, with an afghan tucked up under his chin. Instead, he was standing by his vanity dressed in black, pin-striped suit pants, a white shirt—collar turned up—and a cobalt-blue tie that he was in the process of wrapping around his neck.

I looked him over, checking for signs of illness in his coloring or his posture or the lack of steadiness in his hands. I could see that his hair was thinner, the lines on his face deeper, his eye sockets more hollowed than before. But he didn't appear to be a man with a failing heart.

He glanced at me while knotting his tie. "Word of his demise passed along the wires."

"What?"

"Oh, nothing. Just something I read in a book once about a famous king that stuck in my brain and seemed appropriate to the moment."

I scowled at him. "You knew Vera would call me if she thought you were ill enough to need a doctor but refused to see one."

His face took on a sober expression. "Yes, but I didn't know if you would come." His eyes brightened. "But now that you're here," he said, scrutinizing my attire, which consisted of running shoes, stone-washed jeans, and a faded gray sweatshirt, "you have just enough time to freshen up and change into something more suitable to the occasion."

I frowned. "What are you talking about?"

The sober look returned. "Felicity, I need you to go somewhere with me. It will take only a little while. It's important."

I couldn't believe what I was hearing. He'd lured me there with a ruse and now expected me to go along with him on some cockamamie adventure. "You can't be serious," I said, and, disgusted with myself for falling for his con, turned to leave.

"I haven't told you the whole truth about the day you were born," he said. "If you're going to hate me, then you should at least know the truth."

I stopped in my tracks. My hands balled into fists. I swung around to face him. "Are you capable of telling the truth?"

He looked at me with a steady gaze. "I love you, Felicity. I know I was wrong to have withheld things from you all these years. Please, let an old man repent of his sins."

"So, it's absolution you seek?"

He smiled grimly. "Only a chance to set the record straight."

I wanted to walk away. I wanted to refuse to allow this man to assault me with more "truth," only to suit his purpose. Hadn't he crushed my spirit enough with his soul-cleansing confessions? I glared at him with an intensity that made my eyes ache. "And you really believe the truth will set you free?"

"No," he said softly, "but it might you."

9　　VERA CLAIMED TO KNOW nothing of Russell's subterfuge, and I decided to believe her. It was easier to believe she too had fallen victim to his lies than to think she'd been part of an elaborate con. Also, I felt the need for an ally at the moment, and although time had deposited a layer of rust on our relationship, I knew Vera's heart was solid gold.

"Do you know where he wants to take me?" I asked, feeling my skin prickle.

I was sitting across from Vera at the little table in her kitchenette, nibbling distractedly on a piece of butter-lathered toast. She'd invited me to her modest living quarters to wait while Russell made final preparations for our outing. I was still trying to control my agitation at being tricked into making the trip to Fir Valley and was already regretting having agreed to Russell's request to accompany him "somewhere." I'd refused to change clothes—although my sweatshirt was dark under the arms from nervous perspiration—or to stay in the main part of the house one minute longer than necessary. Vera had always been able to read my moods and offer just the right amount of support.

"I can't imagine what he has in mind," she said. She eyed me with concern. "You sure I can't fix you something more substantial to eat?"

"Thanks," I said, "but I'd probably just throw up." Already my stomach was twitching.

But Vera's company, as always, had a calming effect on me, and I was beginning to feel some relief—that is, until Lydia stuck her head into Vera's apartment and said in a loud whisper, "A hearse just pulled up in the driveway." Vera and I exchanged troubled glances. "Also, Felicity, Mr. Trouste says he's ready to go."

IT WASN'T A HEARSE, really, although the long black limo that sat in the driveway of Trouste House gave off the aura of a funeral wagon.

It was straight up twelve o'clock when, feeling weak in the knees, I reluctantly allowed myself to be escorted down the front steps to the waiting vehicle. A man in a chauffeur's cap sat behind the wheel. A second man, dressed in a brown suit and burgundy tie, stood erect alongside the limo. He was tall and gaunt, and despite his dignified bearing, looked careworn, like a well-used Bible. He responded to our appearance by immediately opening the passenger's door.

"Mr. Renault," Russell said as we approached. "I'd like you to meet my—Felicity."

"Felicity," said Mr. Renault with a nod and a smile.

With my mind blunted from too little sleep and too much agitation, I barely managed to return the gestures.

"After you," Russell said, outstretching a hand toward the plush backseat of the limo.

I'd ridden in limousines before. To my senior prom with Derrick Olsen. On special occasions, such as weddings and benchmark birthday celebrations, during which the best way to be rid of the children for an hour or so was to send them off for a chauffeured joy ride. And, of course, I'd been shuttled in mortuary style to a few funerals, including my mom's. For some reason, this particular limo ride had the feel of a funeral run. And as we traveled in decaying silence, I began to feel a chill settle into my bones and shadows darken my thoughts.

We descended Pine Ridge Road, turned onto Mill Street, and entered downtown Fir Valley, headed east. The closer we got to our destination—for at some point it became clear to me what our destination was—the faster my heart beat inside my chest. I began sweating again, though the limo was climate controlled.

We cruised through downtown, and the residential streets beyond, to the eastern outskirts of town. It was here that Valley Memorial Gardens unfurled like a blotchy green carpet from the roadside, up a slope, toward the tree-lined ridge above. The limo slowed and veered into the drive leading into the cemetery. "This isn't fair!" I said.

We passed through the ornate archway at the entrance and proceeded up the cemetery's narrow center lane. I wasn't breathing now, I was panting, my eyes darting from gravestone to gravestone, many of which were quite familiar. As the oldest burial site in town, Valley Memorial Gardens was the final resting place for many of Fir Valley's early citizens and succeeding generations of their families, including the Troustes. It was also where, more recently, we had interred my dear mother. Memories of that day came flooding back to me now, and I moaned involuntarily, feeling as if I were being crushed under the weight of them.

Russell reached for my hand. I jerked it away and used it to swipe brusquely at the tears beginning to leak from my eyes. "Shame on you!" I said. "How could you be so cruel?"

It was somewhat of a paradox, one that was destined to become steeped in irony, that my mother had escaped the fusillades of anger I'd directed toward Russell Trouste for causing me the humiliation of having lived a lie for all those years. Mother was merely his puppet, I had reasoned. How could I blame her for her behavior when she was merely responding to his manipulation of the strings? He was strong-willed. She was nurturing, but weak. I loved her dearly growing up and continued to love her memory after her passing, despite the subsequent revelation regarding my true parentage. Russell, I surmised, was trying to use this fact to his advantage, hoping to wrangle back into my favor. But I was having none of it. "I won't leave this vehicle," I said, clamping my fisted hands across my lap like a lock-bar on a risky carnival ride.

He shook his head. "It's not what you think."

I was about to protest further when, to my bewilderment, we rolled past the Trouste family plots and moved up the lane to the cul-de-sac at its far end, finally coming to a stop near the entrance gate to the mausoleum that housed the cremated remains of many other departed Fir Valley citizens. I knew this to be the purpose of this lichen-covered stone edifice because, when I was a young girl, I'd witnessed the interment of Uncle Brandon in one of the numerous vaults contained therein. He wasn't really my uncle. We just called him that. He was a close friend of the family, a well-respected doctor in town, who, I'd learned at that very service, had been the attending physician at my birth.

Thoroughly confused, but still mistrusting Russell's intentions, I glowered at him. "Dare I ask?"

Mr. Renault was already out of the vehicle, standing ready to open a door for us. Russell made a move to reach toward me again, then apparently thinking better of it, pulled his hand away. "Another small measure of forbearance is all I ask," he said.

I sniffled, squared my shoulders. "Then that's all I'll give."

"Right this way," Mr. Renault said as we emerged from the limo. I noticed then the small black leather case he was carrying, and my mind immediately began to puzzle over the nature of its contents. Despite the chill in the air, I felt sweat trickle down between my breasts. I sensed a conspiracy in the works.

Mr. Renault pushed open the wrought-iron gate, and reluctantly I followed him and Russell into the garden compound that circumscribed the mausoleum. The garden was apparently being renovated. Many of its ancient rose standards had been uprooted, some having been replaced by younger, healthier plants. In other instances, where a dead or dying bush had been removed, there remained only the hole from which it had been extracted, sated with water from the autumn rains.

The garden path ended at the entrance to the mausoleum—a massive wooden door that our guide unlocked with what looked like an old jailer's key. He reached inside and flipped up several wall switches. Faint-hearted light probed the bowels of the old stone structure. "I'll be out here when you need me," Mr. Renault announced, and stepped aside.

"Thank you," Russell said.

He motioned for me to pass through the doorway, but my legs wouldn't comply. My feet seemed frozen in place. The rest of my body began to shiver, not from the cold but from an icy dread that had come over me. Mr. Renault removed his jacket and draped it over my shoulders.

Russell put a hand on my back and prompted me forward. I shuffled through the vestibule, past a statue of the Virgin Mary, and into the pillared inner chamber, where I was greeted by the echo of my own footsteps and air that seemed more frigid than the outside atmosphere. I pulled Mr. Renault's jacket tight around my neck.

The support pillars extended to either side of us, along the breadth of the building. We rounded a pillar, and I pulled up short, unnerved by the gravity of the moment.

Ahead of us was one of the long marble walls that fronted the stacked rows of inlaid committal vaults. Each vault was marked by a gold plate on which was etched the name of the individual whose ashes were interred within, and the dates of his birth and passing. Uncle Brandon was tucked away in a nook to our left, if I remembered correctly. I took a jagged breath. "I don't understand why you've brought me here."

Russell didn't say anything, just stood there solemnly staring up at the wall of vaults as if he'd made some silent connection with the voiceless lives memorialized herein. Finally, still without speaking, he stepped forward, reached up, and touched his fingers lightly to a nameplate that was just above eye level for me. I moved alongside him and read the inscription.

"Who is Baby Ames?" I asked. There were no specific dates recorded on the plate—just a year: *1979*. Even that was hard to read because the nameplate had been dulled by time and neglect.

Another prolonged silence tolled. Then Russell started to speak, but the first word came out of his mouth croaky and indecipherable. He cleared his throat and tried again. "Ames," he said, "was Tamara Adberry's maiden name."

I stopped breathing at the mention of Tamara Adberry. My pulse thudded in my ears. *I haven't told you the whole truth about the day you were born*, Russell had said.

It had been five years since my one and only encounter with Tamara Adberry. It had also been that long since I'd heard her name spoken. This was the woman who'd given me up for adoption at birth and then waited twenty-one years to pop back into my life like a fairy godmother, only to disappear again hours later. Only the puff of smoke had been missing. I hadn't seen or heard from her since that first meeting. During the intervening years, I'd wanted to hate her for abandoning me. I'd

wanted, at other times, to feel some familial bond between us. But in
the end, I'd merely come to pity her for the loss she'd suffered by not
having me for a daughter. After all, I'd had a mother who'd loved me
unconditionally despite the lack of a biological connection between us.
Could I have asked for anything more?

Even so, the mere mention of Tamara Adberry's name caused my
stomach to surge as if I'd taken that first steep plunge on a roller coaster
ride. At the same time, my mind was wrestling with the implications of
Russell's comment: *Ames was Tamara Adberry's maiden name.* I could
come up with only one plausible explanation, and my heart did a drum
roll in my chest as I pondered the implications. "You mean Tamara
had another child the same year I was born?" Did I have a twin sister
or brother who'd died in childbirth?

Again Russell struggled with his answer, hesitating for as long as
the moment allowed, then speaking deliberately, as if each word was
being surgically excised from his brain. "No. The child whose ashes
are interred here wasn't born to Tamara Ames. This child was born"—
his voice cracked—"to your mother and me. It was *our* child, born the
same night as you, stillborn."

A light went out in my brain, dimming my perception of what was
being said. "Then why the name *Ames* on the plate?"

Russell looked at me, and the expression on his face was that of a
man skidding toward the edge of disaster. "Because the doctor who
delivered Tamara's baby told her it was stillborn."

"But why—?"

Occasionally there's a moment when seemingly disconnected events
are revealed to us as an integrated whole, like when you suddenly get
a joke or see the face of Christ in an inkblot. For me, this was such
a moment. I now understood the relationship between many past
events which, to this point, hadn't seemed at all connected. I gasped
and covered my face, not wanting to accept the horrible reality confronting me.

Russell must have sensed my horror. But having arrived at his
moment of truth, he was like a man standing on the edge of a precipice
who has already decided to jump. One foot was in the air. He had no

choice but to follow with the other. "And the doctor who delivered Tamara's baby also delivered your mother's and mine."

"Uncle Brandon?" I murmured, revolted by what I was hearing.

"Then the babies were switched. A live one—you—for a dead one."

I staggered backwards, feeling faint. Tears burned my eyes. Russell caught my arm and kept me from collapsing. Mr. Renault's jacket fell from my shoulders onto the floor.

I pulled away, slumped against a pillar. I gawked at Russell Trouste in disbelief, the magnitude of such deceit beyond my comprehension. "And you knew this was done?"

Even in the dim light I could see Russell's face blanch. "I did," he whispered in a voice as dry as chalk dust.

My body shook as I clung to the pillar. "And Mom?"

Russell sighed. "She didn't know. At least, she never acknowledged knowing. What she truly believed in her heart, only she could have said."

I gazed back at the wall of vaults, feeling as if the whole, insubstantial world—the world that exists only because we create it in our minds—was crashing down on me. I screamed and pushed myself away from the pillar. I rushed toward the mausoleum entrance, my scudding steps filling the air with an abrasive dissonance.

Mr. Renault must have heard my cry. He had the bulky door open and was about to enter. When he saw me running toward him, he stepped back and held the door ajar. The light from outside glinted off something in his hand. I paused in the doorway, my thoughts flashing on the leather case he'd been carrying earlier. What was in the case?

As if sensing my curiosity, Mr. Renault brought his hand up and displayed its contents: a shiny nameplate that read, *In Loving Memory, Baby Trouste, 1979.*

A wave of despair washed over me, sweeping me out the door. I reeled away from the mausoleum and fell to my knees in the soggy soil near a hole waiting for a new rose bush. Mr. Renault scrambled over and helped me up, then backed away as if from a rabid dog.

I stood there crouched over, unsteady on my feet, feeling buffeted by a mighty wind. Then, without connecting thought to action, I stumbled down the garden path, exited the mausoleum compound, and—skirting the black limousine—broke into a sprint in the direction of my mother's grave.

10   I DON'T REMEMBER the drive back to Portland that afternoon. I vaguely recall being pulled away from Mother's gravestone by insistent hands and deposited in the limousine. As soon as we arrived back at Trouste House, I bailed out of the limo and rushed to my car. I remember the sensation of crusted mud on my hands when I gripped the steering wheel. And I recall driving away from the estate, feeling a pervasive numbness inside me, as if a critical neural pathway had blown a fuse. But the trip home is a blank.

Back at my apartment, I sat hunched over on the edge of my bed, my mind scrambled beyond thought, until it was time for me to get ready for work. When I took off my clothes before getting into the shower, I wondered where all the caked dirt had come from. I went to work and must have done my job with rote efficiency, because no one told me later that I'd killed someone or left any open wounds unsutured.

I lived for a time after that in a feverish state of bewilderment. I didn't know who to love, who to hate, who deserved my forgiveness, who my pity. I felt like the victim of a great wrong, but wasn't sure who'd done the victimizing—or if, in fact, my hurt was self-inflicted.

For so long I'd assumed that Tamara Ames had given me up willingly. But, in reality, was she the real victim? Was Russell Trouste not merely negligent in failing to inform me of my true parentage, but the worst kind of miscreant imaginable—a baby stealer? The perpetrator of a scheme so diabolical I couldn't imagine it originating with someone whose breast contained a human heart?

But if all this was true, then what about the years since Tamara Ames Adberry had learned of my existence? Why hadn't she contacted me since our one and only meeting at Trouste House when I was twenty-one? She must have known then that I was her daughter. Why hadn't she tried to reclaim that relationship? Was she simply willing to let history dictate the future? Willing to let Russell Trouste have it his way after all?

I marched zombie-like through my daily routine—work, eat, sleep—with these questions swarming through my mind like angry bees stinging me without provocation. And at night as I lay in bed pleading with my mind to power down, the biggest question of all parked itself on my chest with the crushing weight of uncertainty: How would I ever know for sure how to feel about the two people in this world whose decisions had had the most influence on my life?

As usual, it was Vera who came to my rescue. Shortly after my disastrous visit home, she began calling me once a week at my apartment. "Just to check on you," she'd said. Then she whispered, "Mr. Trouste doesn't know."

"Good," I said, manipulating the phone cord with my fingers like worry beads.

We chatted that first day about innocuous things—the weather, my work, her thoughts of future retirement and travel. After that, our conversations remained light, with little or no delving into things personal. Then one afternoon while on the phone with her, without provocation, I burst into tears. "I just don't understand!" I cried.

"Understand what?" Vera said.

"Anything that's ever happened to me. My life is nothing but a string of unanswered questions."

Vera let me cry in her ear for a time. Then she stated the solution to my predicament as if solving a mathematical problem as simple as two plus two. "Talk to Tamara. I can give you a phone number."

The answer seemed so obvious, and yet I balked. "What if she doesn't want to talk to me?"

"Then you'll at least have an answer to one of your questions."

I didn't immediately follow Vera's advice, but rather like a smoker ignoring the warnings about the deadliness of her habit, I put off taking action until something other than logic swayed me. And so, on a day when I happened to examine more closely the inside of the container of leftover chili I'd been eating out of for days and discovered that the unusual flavor I'd been tasting wasn't from some exotic ingredient but from the mold spores flourishing there as if it were a Petri dish, I felt compelled to pick up the telephone and dial Tamara's number.

"Felicity," she said, when I'd identified myself, "I was hoping you would call."

For five years, she'd been hoping? Yet her voice resonated with a gladness that rang true.

"I'd like to see you," I said, my heart fluttering in my chest like a bird frantic to be free of its cage.

"I'd like that too," Tamara said.

So we set a time and place to meet. I had thought the meeting should be on neutral ground, but when Tamara suggested I come to her home, I agreed, reasoning that this was a chance for me to learn who this woman was, how she lived, and why she'd neglected contacting me during the last five years.

11   ON A SPRING MORNING that threatened rain but delivered sunshine mixed with clouds, I shunned the freeway and drove instead down the coast highway to the mouth of Coos Bay, a route that added time to my trip but also lent serenity to it in the form of scenic beauty. The rugged coastal cliffs. The immeasurable, undulating plain that was the Pacific. The breakers crashing frothy white against the rocky shore. The historic lighthouses with their life-saving mission. Filling my mind with these sights helped to loosen the tension on the rope of nerves I'd become.

Following Tamara's directions, I ventured inland on East Bay Drive and followed its winding path through the wooded hills that overlooked Coos Bay from the north. All during the morning's drive, I'd worked with some success to keep my emotions in check. But now, upon approaching the end of my journey, I found them scattering like a startled flock of geese.

I was excited, anxious, hopeful, fearful. I was about to meet with my birth mother for the first time since learning of my true parentage, and the prospect of that encounter had my head spinning and my heart beating in staccato. I wanted to become acquainted with the woman who'd given birth to me, to hear her side of a story I was only beginning to wrap my mind around. But "Truth," I'd learned from being on the receiving end of Russell Trouste's confessions, was like a so-called miracle drug. It had, potentially, the power to heal, but the side effects could kill you. And so, as I searched the roadside for an announcement of my destination, I couldn't help but wonder if I'd chosen the right course of treatment for what ailed me.

Along the road here and there mailboxes on wooden posts stood at the end of gravel drives that disappeared like rabbit holes into the dense shelter of evergreens blanketing the hills. Coming out of a curve, I saw the number I was looking for on a silver mailbox and, braking hard, was able to make the turn into the adjacent lane. I followed the driveway as it climbed steeply for a hundred feet or so and then leveled off before making a slight jog to the right.

At the end of the driveway, nestled in the trees, was a modest ranch-style home, painted gray with white trim. A late-model pickup truck was parked in front of an attached two-car garage. I pulled alongside the truck and got out of my car. A dog appeared from around the side of the house, barking and wagging its tail. It looked part Beagle and part something else. It trotted over to me. I bent down and ruffled its ears. Satisfied that I wasn't a threat, it ambled back in the direction from which it had come.

Tamara Adberry opened the front door of the house. She came out onto the stoop and stood there with her hands clasped at her waist. It had been over five years since our one and only meeting, and although the image of her I'd carried around in my head during that time had tarnished, she didn't seem to have changed much—some wrinkling at the corners of her eyes and a few threads of gray in her shoulder-length brown hair.

I'd wanted to approach this encounter with a semblance of scientific detachment. Observe. Gather the facts. Record the data. Draw a conclusion. But as soon as I glimpsed Tamara standing there in that self-conscious way, I experienced a surge of emotion that swept away all possibility of objectivity. This day was going to be all about feelings.

I had to swallow the brick in my throat before I could speak. "It's lovely here," I said, glancing about. Through an opening in the trees, I could see a shimmering patch of water in the distance and, beyond that, the hazy skyline of the city of Coos Bay.

"We get our share of cold wind and fog," Tamara said with a smile that twitched at the edges.

She continued standing there, smiling awkwardly, and I realized that she must have been as nervous as I was, her emotions just as topsy-turvy, and it made me want to reach out to her. But there was also within me a resistance to such an action, a feeling akin to self-preservation that told me to keep this woman at arm's length. So we remained poised at a safe distance from each other, neither of us sure of the other, or of our own feelings. And it seemed that perhaps that cold and fog to which Tamara had referred still lingered thereabouts in an emotional sense if not in reality.

It was the high-pitched bleat of a chainsaw engine revving nearby that finally cut through our emotional stalemate.

"My husband is out back," Tamara said with a nod in that direction. "Why don't we go let him know you're here."

I followed her inside the house, the interior of which reflected the modesty without. It had a cozy feel about it, looked lived-in but neat. Family portraits hung along one wall of a living room dominated by a stone fireplace and a few pieces of bulky furniture.

We went through the house to a back door off the kitchen and proceeded out onto a covered brick patio. We could see her husband a little ways into the trees, beyond a small fenced backyard. He was bent over a chainsaw in his grasp that was making sawdust fly as it ripped through a big log lying on the ground.

"A large cedar tree came down during a storm last week," Tamara said. "One of the hazards of living in the forest. Fortunately it missed the power lines—and the house."

We watched her husband make a few more cuts before shutting off his saw.

"Kurt, we have company!" Tamara hollered out to him. He looked over and waved. He set his saw down on the considerable remains of the log, along with his hard hat and gloves, and started walking toward the house.

I'd already learned from Vera that Kurt was not my biological father. She'd declined to tell me more, figuring it wasn't her place, and I respected that. But I did appreciate knowing in advance that I had no prior relationship with Tamara's husband, because that knowledge made our meeting one less thing for me to obsess about.

"Can I get you something to drink?" Tamara asked. "I've just made some iced tea."

"Iced tea would be nice," I said.

Kurt entered the backyard through a small gate in the fence. Before stepping onto the patio, he scraped mud off his boots and brushed sawdust from the front of his jeans and plaid flannel shirt.

Tamara introduced us. Kurt's hand was warm when I shook it, as was his smile. His cheeks were red from exertion, his hair limp with perspiration.

"There's iced tea, dear," Tamara said to him.

"I think I will," he said.

Tamara gestured toward some patio chairs situated around a glass-topped table. "You two sit down. I'll get the tea."

Kurt and I headed for the table, and I felt myself relaxing in his presence. There was an easiness about his movements that suggested he was comfortable in his own skin, and a lack of posturing that indicated he was equally as ready to allow me to be comfortable in mine.

"That handsome basketball player I saw in a photo hanging in your living room—is that your son?" I was referring to an eight-by-ten glossy of a young man in a green and gold uniform, hanging in midair with a basketball rising from his outstretched arm.

"Yep. That's Brent," Kurt said with a twinkle in his eyes. He pulled a chair out for me at the table. "He got a lot of playing time for the Ducks this past season as a sophomore," he added as we sat down.

"You must be very proud."

"We are." He was grinning unabashedly now. "We pretty much burn up the road between here and Eugene attending the games."

Tamara reappeared bearing a tray that supported a pitcher of tea and three glasses containing ice. She'd obviously caught the tail end of our conversation. "Don't get him started talking about Brent and basketball," she said. She set the tray down on the table. "You'll be listening to his stories until your ears fall off."

"I'm not that bad," Kurt said. "Besides, you yell louder at the games than anyone."

Tamara's face reddened. "Maybe I do," she said. And that ended the talk about their son and basketball.

Tamara filled the glasses, served them, and sat down at the table with us.

"Thank you," I said, and took a drink of tea. It could have used a tad more sugar for my taste.

"That hits the spot," Kurt said, bringing a half-empty glass away from his lips.

Tamara fingered the outside of her glass, smudging the film of moisture on it. She glanced in my direction. "How's your father?" she said. "I didn't get a chance to ask you on the phone."

I felt something coil tightly inside me like a depressed spring. I knew the rules of civil conversation. They were a Trouste legacy no amount of distance from the family could divest me of. But I didn't know how much contact Tamara had had with Russell Trouste in the last five years. Was this a guileless question or a blatant probe of my current feelings for him? "I doubt he's changed much since you saw him last," I said, and sipped from my glass again.

Tamara's eyelids fluttered as if she didn't know what to make of my response. But apparently willing to set aside for the moment the issue of Russell Trouste's current circumstances, she deftly followed up so as not to let me totally off the hook. "But you've changed a lot since then, Dr. Trouste," she said. "So, tell us about your recent adventures."

I looked at her, feigning a pained expression. "Are you sure you want to get *me* started?"

We all laughed then and the laughter was like a cool breeze on our heated emotions.

"By all means," Tamara said. She flapped a hand at her husband. "We've heard each other's stories a hundred times."

Kurt rolled his eyes. "At least."

"It will be a treat to listen to a few of yours."

I shrugged. "If you insist."

Briefly—and without revealing anything I considered personal—I filled them in on my dull exploits over the past five years, culminating in my medical residency in Portland.

"It sounds anything but dull," Tamara commented when I'd come to the end of my tale.

"Being a doctor is great," I said. "Becoming a doctor is sheer drudgery."

"Cuts into your social life, eh?" Kurt said with a wink.

"You got that right," I said, and we all laughed again.

We passed another half hour or so talking about this and that—again dodging all issues of a private sort. And I'll admit to having felt welcome in this home, and with these people, who seemed to want nothing more from me than what I was willing to give. Nevertheless, a certain tension remained between me and Tamara, and questions drifted just below the surface of our banter, lacking the buoyancy to rise above the waterline.

And so it went. We had lunch on the back patio—a main course of club sandwiches and coleslaw—while around us a gentle breeze stirred the trees. A mob of birds, mostly finches and sparrows, flitted about, twittering their displeasure at one another. The earthy smell of sawdust blended in my nostrils with the fragrance of jasmine to form a heady spring bouquet. The dog I'd encountered earlier appeared. He trotted to the edge of the patio, sniffed the air, then lay down on a lawn stippled with sunlight.

Dessert was a generous portion of hot apple pie. "This is delicious," I said, between bites.

"Tamara used to make pies for a restaurant where she worked," Kurt said, dipping into his own à la mode delight.

"They weren't very good at first," Tamara confessed. She crinkled her face as if swallowing something rancid. "As a matter of fact, they were awful. But I got better at it as time went on."

"That's obvious," I said, and relished another bite.

A telephone rang and Tamara got up and went into the house to answer it. I could hear her talking but couldn't make out what she was saying. She came out a few minutes later and sat back down at the table, but the lightness of the moment had dissipated, and it was obvious from the clouded expression on her face that something weightier was on her mind.

"I have to go somewhere for a little while," she said. She looked at me. "Would you like to come along? I think you might find it interesting."

I didn't know what to make of the offer. Our visit so far hadn't gone as I'd expected, although I wasn't sure what I'd expected. All I knew was that I'd just spent nearly two hours in polite conversation with the woman who'd given birth to me, the only person who could answer the questions that were keeping me awake at night, and to this point not a single reference had been made to our relationship. Was this intentional on her part? Was this the answer to one of my questions—a vital one? Did she not want to acknowledge me as her daughter?

"I'd probably just be in the way," I said. "I should be getting home."

But Tamara persisted. "It will only take an hour or so. And you wouldn't be in the way at all. Really, I'd like it if you came along."

"I'll clean up the dishes," Kurt said.

"Now you can't refuse," Tamara said with mock gravity.

So I agreed to go, telling myself that I needed to allow this day to play out to some satisfactory conclusion, not realizing what an unexpected turn it was about to take.

12   I OFFERED TO DRIVE and Tamara gladly accepted. So we left Kurt behind to deal with the aftermath of lunch.

"Beautiful car," she said as we got into my Lincoln Navigator. "It smells new."

"Thanks," I said. "Got it just last weekend."

I turned around in the driveway and drove down the gravel lane to the paved road.

"Go right," Tamara said.

I was curious about our destination but was reluctant to ask, figuring it best not to press Tamara on something she apparently felt no need to divulge. I sensed, nevertheless, a purpose at work here, and more than that, a kind of providence, as if somehow the two of us being together at this moment in time was part of a plan. Whose plan I wasn't sure.

We backtracked on my prior path around the bay, combating all awkward silences with barrages of small talk. At intervals we could view through the trees the shiny oval of water that was Coos Bay. Other times, the trees towered so close on both sides of the road that all we could see of the sky was a thin blue line above, mirroring the course of the snaking roadway.

Emerging from the hills, we passed through the bedroom community of Glasgow, which overlooked the entrance to Coos Bay. The throat of the bay was dotted with boats entering and leaving the harbor, all giving wide berth to a cargo ship steaming toward port.

We connected with Highway 101 South and, after crossing the bay via a majestic, steel-framed drawbridge, continued through North Bend into the city of Coos Bay. Keeping to the main drag, we moved past the massive timber pillars of the Mill Casino and along motel row to the south side of town. From there, we ventured onto a side street and followed it a mile or so west into an older residential neighborhood. At the end of a twenty-minute drive, we pulled up in front of a large, but otherwise nondescript, two-story, wood-framed house. I parked in the driveway as Tamara instructed, and we got out of the Navigator shaking our listless legs in unison.

Tamara led the way to the front door of the house. "It's a shelter for teen moms," she said. "I volunteer here."

I didn't say anything in response to this disclosure, which had been tossed out as casually as if she'd said, "Tuesday is laundry day." But my feelings became tangled again, and my insides knotted.

We entered the house without knocking, stepping into a front room that appeared to be a communal living area. The room was crowded with mismatched furniture—a leather sofa, a wicker loveseat, over-stuffed chairs with contrasting fabric, side tables of differing finishes and dimensions, lamps as varied as body types. Stuffed animals and toddler-age toys littered the scarce walking space.

From a side doorway emerged a thirty-something brunette. She was stick thin, had a porcelain complexion and big brown eyes that lit up when she smiled. She and Tamara hugged. I was introduced by name only. The skinny brunette was introduced as Dana, the manager of the house.

A teenage girl appeared from a hallway carrying a baby—two or three months of age, I guessed. She rushed up to Tamara and hugged her neck with her free arm. Tamara took the child from her and cradled it lovingly, cooing all the while.

"Felicity, I'd like you to meet Toni," Tamara said, nodding at the teenager. Toni, I found out later, was sixteen. She lived at the shelter while attending a local high school that had a children's daycare on site. She worked part time at a discount store after school. She planned to go to college after she graduated.

"And this precious bundle is Mandi," Tamara said, kissing the baby's plump cheek profusely.

"I have to show you," Toni squealed, and began dragging Tamara, still holding the baby, down the hall.

"Toni got some new clothes for the baby," Dana informed me. "She's pretty jazzed."

"I can tell."

The house manager looked at me and displayed a nervous smile. "Would you like the grand tour?"

I told her I would.

"This area speaks for itself," she said, spreading her palms wide as if to bless the hodgepodge of furniture inhabiting the room. She nodded toward the side door she'd just come out of. "My office is in there, buried in clutter."

I peeked inside the indicated niche and caught sight of a sign on the wall that said DANGER! SLIDE AREA.

"The kitchen is over here," Dana said.

She skirted a bulky armchair, squeezed between the sofa and the loveseat, and with me on her heels, passed through a doorway into a room with industrial-looking fixtures and appliances and an abundance of storage cabinets. Someone had obviously invested a good deal of money remodeling the kitchen.

Dana pointed to a handwritten menu attached to the face of a double-door refrigerator with a magnet. "The girls do their own shopping, cook their own meals, clean up their own messes." She sniggered. "I insist on that last part, because I'm not into cleaning."

Adjacent to the kitchen was a dining area. A rectangular wooden table, nicked from wear, was surrounded by an odd assortment of chairs—wooden, metal, plastic—including several highchairs with trays.

"How many girls do you have?" I asked, wanting to sound interested.

"It varies," the house manager said. "We have six bedrooms and three bathrooms. Right now we have four girls living here full time, and several more that come and go. We've been known to double up on the bedrooms, but we don't like to." She dipped her head to the side. "On the other hand, neither do we like to turn anyone away. Each girl's stay is meant to be temporary, and we tell the girls that up front. They get training in parenting, tutoring with their schoolwork if they need it, and help taking care of their babies. We have a nurse who volunteers, as well as a dietician from the local hospital who helps plan the meals."

"That's great," I said.

Dana drifted back toward the front room. "Yeah, the girls get a lot of support here. But they also know that the ultimate goal is for them to become self-reliant. For some that's more realistic than for others. It all depends on the kind of support network they have, which often is very minimal."

I followed her back into the furniture menagerie, all the while thinking that, even with all the volunteers, running an operation like this took plenty of money. "Where does your funding come from?"

Dana looked at me oddly, as if I'd asked a question to which I should already know the answer. But she proceeded to supply an explanation anyway. "Private charities mostly. We get some government funding, but mostly we survive on private donations—some of which are anonymous." She shook her head disconsolately. "Believe it or not, even in this day and age, programs for girls who get pregnant are controversial. Some people feel that helping pregnant teens and teenage moms perpetuates the problem. It's not unlike the debate that surrounds welfare or shelters for the homeless." She shrugged. "We all see things differently, I guess, depending on our circumstances."

I was wondering about my own feelings on the matter. "I suppose so," I said.

Dana regarded me now with a look of unreserved perplexity. "Did I hear your last name correctly when we were introduced? You're a Trouste?"

I stiffened, sensing that I'd walked into a trap. "You know the name?"

"Why, yes," she said, responding as automatically as if I'd said, Do cows eat grass? "A good deal of our funding comes from the Trouste Foundation, as did the original grant that funded the startup. I thought that was why you were here, to—well—" Her face flushed. "I just thought you knew."

My mind had sputtered at the mention of the Trouste Foundation. "Does Tamara know?" I asked naively.

Dana laughed. "Of course. She's on the board of the directors for the home. She was here when the shelter was founded. I understand she almost single-handedly got it going with the help of that initial grant."

"Really?" I said, shocked at the implications of what I was hearing. Tamara had had dealings with the Trouste Foundation *after* her baby had been stolen by Russell Trouste? What did that say about her supposed role as victim? And what did that reveal about my mother? It was my mother—not Russell—who'd represented the family on the board of trustees of the Trouste Foundation. Had she and Tamara become acquainted? How much did my mother really know about the day I was born?

"Are you all right?" Dana asked. "You look pale all of a sudden."

"I do feel a bit lightheaded," I confessed.

Dana had me sit down on one of the mismatched sofas. "I'll get you some water."

I sipped the water and tried to compose myself. But for the next few minutes, I continued to be rocked by a series of disturbing mental aftershocks, each one accompanied by a new question regarding what I'd just learned.

When Tamara rejoined us, I could tell from a flicker of illumination in her eyes that she sensed something had changed in me. I felt the change also. I was suddenly unsure of myself. I'd become unnerved, like a young child on a playground who's lost sight of her parents. I had an unqualified need to know about my past—about my conception and birth, about the father I never knew, about the biological mother I was just getting to know.

This change in my attitude must have been something Tamara had been waiting for, because she immediately took my hand and led me out to the car.

"It's time we talked—really talked," she said. "I know just the place."

13   SHE HAD ME DRIVE farther south on Highway 101 to Bandon, where we transitioned onto Beach Loop Drive and continued along its shoreline course until we came to a place called Face Rock Wayside. I parked along the curb in front of a small green. A flagstone path led across the green to an overlook on the high ground

above the Pacific Ocean. As we walked without speaking toward the overlook, my body tingled with the nervous anticipation of an early explorer.

The pathway brought us to a stone parapet that ran along the rim of a sheer cliff. A moist breeze swirled up the face of the cliff and gushed over the parapet, billowing our blouses and fluffing our hair.

"This is one of my favorite places," Tamara said, and filled her lungs with the crisp ocean air.

I gazed out over the water toward the far horizon where dense, gray clouds gathered, looking like newly formed mountains as they pressed hard against the sea. The late afternoon sun, filtered by a thickening mist, hung over the vast expanse like a ripe orange dangling from a low limb, its reflection off the water a broken trail of golden flames leading to the sandy shore. Beyond the shoreline a string of jagged rock outcroppings jutted up from the sea—dark, broken megaliths thrust up from the seafloor by some ancient upheaval.

Tamara pointed at one of the larger outcroppings, a massive mound of stone whose profile was etched against the backdrop of the shifting sea. "See how she looks to the sky for consolation," she said softly. Then she turned and looked at me, displaying her own vulnerability in the tenderness of her gaze.

I stared at the indicated rock feature for a time, confused by Tamara's remark. And then I saw it: the somber face of stone, looking toward the heavens with mournful hope.

"I was barely sixteen when I came to Fir Valley," Tamara said. She took my hand and pulled me down with her so that we sat together on the parapet, our backs to the breeze.

For the next half hour or so, Tamara talked almost nonstop about the events following her arrival in Fir Valley. When she spoke about the night I was born, tears spilled from her eyes. She swept them away with the back of her hand and continued with her story. And that's when I finally learned about Jimmy Stark, about his murder, and about the subsequent death of Tamara's stepbrother, Gary Neaves. That's when I learned about the sheriff's investigation into their deaths and about my own kidnapping at Tamara's hands, and the plea bargaining that took place after she and her friends had been apprehended and I'd been returned to the Troustes. The whole story flowed out of Tamara's mouth like the plot to a mystery novel—or a soap opera.

I listened in silence, trying to take it all in, wave after wave of emotion assaulting my senses. As Tamara recounted the days following the supposed stillbirth of her child, I found myself holding my breath one moment and puffing for air the next. I bit my lip and shed my own tears as she talked about being taken to the mausoleum for a private interment service.

"I can't begin to express my feelings when I realized you were alive," she said. "I guess I went a little crazy."

By the time Tamara finished speaking, I was shaking uncontrollably. "Those bastards," I said through clenched teeth, lumping together Gary Neaves, Dr. Castle, and Russell Trouste.

Tamara smiled sadly. "It's not exactly as you might think."

"Don't tell me you're prepared to defend their actions?" I said, bristling with righteous indignation.

"No," she said. "But before you condemn your father for everything that's happened, there's something else you should know." She let go of my hand as if anticipating a breach between us.

I squinted at her, thinking, What else do I need to know? Russell Trouste and his accomplices stole me away from my birth mother! But at the same time, I knew that the road leading to this moment had taken so many surprising twists and turns there had to be something else. What else, I couldn't imagine.

Tamara sat quietly for a time, staring into the distance, her hair swirling around her face in splayed ringlets. Then: "My attorney had a cousin who was a newspaper reporter," she said. And she went on to tell me about her attorney's very public campaign to have maternity testing performed to determine my true parentage. She paused, lips parted.

It was one of those moments when you want to say, "Stop right there; say no more. I can live without knowing what's coming next." But you never do. Because you think that that's the coward's way out, and you're no coward.

"I refused to be tested," Tamara said.

"You *refused*—" I shook my head, trying to understand what she was telling me, because to my analytical mind the logic wasn't there. Her action—based on what had gone before—was irrational, was a behavioral non sequitur. "Are you saying that you could have gotten me back simply by agreeing to a maternity test, but you refused to be tested?"

Tamara looked at me with a graveside expression on her face. "Nothing was simple back then. But, yes, I might have been able to get you back. But in the process, Russell's reputation would have been ruined. And he probably would have gone to jail, along with Dr. Castle."

"But—but—" A terrible sadness welled up in me, dark and horrifying, like a pestilence sweeping the land. I stared at her, still not understanding. I didn't care about what might have happened to Russell Trouste or Brandon Castle. I cared about only one thing. "You—willingly gave me up?"

The wind gusted, lashing Tamara's hair against her cheeks, besotting it with the tears that now flowed unchecked from her eyes. She nodded silently.

I could think of only one thing to say in response to her acknowledgement of this astonishing fact, and I couldn't stop shaking my head as I said it. "Why?"

"Because I loved you," Tamara said in a tremulous voice. She brushed back her hair and looked at me through liquid eyes. "I loved you more than anything and wanted what was best for you. And I knew that the Troustes could provide for you the way I couldn't." She held out her palms as if presenting me to the world. "Look at you, Felicity. Look at the woman you've become because you grew up as a Trouste. You think you'd be a doctor now if I'd raised you?"

"That's not the point."

She sighed. "Maybe not. But I was sixteen years old then, on my own, with no means of support. I was facing nine months in juvenile detention and an uncertain future. I had no idea things would work out for me and Kurt the way they did." She reached over and clutched my hand. "I loved you, Felicity. But I knew that I could never give you the kind of life the Troustes could give you. The kind of life you deserved."

I pulled my hand away, feeling as if all my internal organs had been removed and I was nothing but a hollow core.

We drove back to Tamara's house in the woods in silence, because I refused to say anything else or listen to anything else Tamara had to say. Nothing she could have added would have helped me understand why she'd given me up. And no words of mine could have adequately expressed the anguish I felt knowing that my birth mother had abandoned me after all.

I left the car running as we pulled to a stop in Tamara's driveway. I clenched the wheel and stared straight ahead.

Tamara pushed the passenger door open. "I don't expect you to understand," she said softly. "I'm not sure I understand myself. All I know is that I did what I thought was best for you, and I've been living with that decision ever since."

She got out of the car. "One other thing," she said before closing the door. "Whatever your father's sins, lack of love for you is not one of them."

She turned and walked up the path to her front door.

14

I DROVE HOME with a crushing ache in my breast that had me periodically clutching my heart and gasping for air. I carried the ache around with me for weeks after that, thinking that it might never go away, that one day I would simply keel over from acute arrhythmia. During this time, I tried to put Tamara Ames Adberry out of my mind, wanting to relegate her to the past the way I'd done Russell Trouste. But in my mind's eye, I kept seeing her holding that baby at the shelter for teen moms, showering it with affection, and the excited look on its sixteen-year-old mother's face as she dragged Tamara to her room. What if Tamara had had that kind of support when she was in Toni's situation? Would she have been so willing to give me up?

I'd never know the answer to that question or a hundred others that still haunted me, for it seemed the more I learned about my past the less I understood about the events that had shaped my life. So I did the only thing I knew to do. I continued going to work each day at the hospital, putting in my time mending others, and hoping that the passage of time would eventually soothe my aching heart.

I spoke over the phone with Vera now and then. "I went to see Tamara," I told her one day with forced nonchalance.

"Good," she said.

I worked to remain detached from what I was saying. "She could have gotten me back, you know."

"Maybe."

Then my brain short-circuited, bypassed my pretended apathy, and—unbidden—all the emotion of my visit with Tamara came flooding into my consciousness. I rocked back and forth on the sofa hugging myself. "She let me go because she loved me, she said."

There was silence in the line for a time. Then Vera said, "Love is not an exact science."

WHEN VERA CALLED a few weeks later to tell me that Russell Trouste was in Sacred Heart Hospital in Eugene, suffering from complications from his heart valve replacement, I surprised her and myself by agreeing to go see him. I didn't know what motivated me to do so. I only knew that something had changed in me since my meeting with Tamara.

The next day, having arranged for my twelve-hour shift to be covered by a co-worker who owed me a favor, I drove down to Eugene. By the time I arrived at the hospital, Russell had undergone emergency surgery to repair a leak in the tissue around his mechanical heart valve. I met Vera in the waiting area outside the surgical recovery ward.

I threw my arms around her and hugged her, not wanting to let go.

"Your father has been asking for you," she said softly.

My feelings were as muddled as life itself as I entered Russell's room. But when I saw him lying there hooked up to a heart monitor, with an oxygen tube up his nose and a half-full urine bag dangling from the side of his bed, I couldn't help but experience an upwelling of concern. I rushed to his side and took hold of his hand. Only then did he open his eyes.

"Hi," I said. "How are you doing?"

He looked up at me and smiled timidly, like a man who knows he's just been given a second chance at life and isn't sure he's earned it. "Still ticking," he said.

And in the hush that followed, I thought I could hear the whooshing sound his metal heart valve made as it opened and closed inside his chest.

I squeezed his hand. "That's good."

An awkward moment ensued, with both of us averting our eyes. Finally, Russell freed his hand from my grasp. He reached up, cupped my chin, and gently turned my head until our eyes met. "I will always love you as a daughter. Nothing can change that."

I wasn't sure I believed him. "Then why did you bring Tamara back into the picture? Why jeopardize what we had?"

Before he could answer, a nurse wearing a purple smock and a compassionate expression came into the room. I moved aside for her.

"This will take just a minute," she said. She checked Russell's vitals, verified the calibration on his oxygen flow, inspected his IV connections and his urine bag.

"We need to get a little blood," she said, and went about preparing a phlebotomy syringe. She secured a rubber tourniquet on Russell's arm. "A little stick," she said, and hit a vein the first time. I watched the dark fluid begin to flow into the vial.

When the nurse left, I resumed my position alongside Russell's bed. The hands-on care he'd received seemed to have buoyed his spirits. Then again, maybe he was merely lightheaded from having surrendered more of his blood. Whatever the reason, he lay there now with a dreamy look on his face.

"Are you okay?" I asked.

"You wanted to know why I brought Tamara into our lives."

"Yes."

He regarded me with keen eyes. This was obviously something he was eager to explain. "Because of the surgery I was facing at the time.

I thought, What if I died on the operating table? You would have been left parentless."

I reflected on that possibility. Heart valve replacements, as common as they had become, were still not a sure thing. That's why he'd put the doctors off for so long. He thought the surgery might kill him. And if he died, he would be taking the secret of my true lineage with him to the grave. He didn't want that to happen. He didn't want to leave me orphaned, as it were. So he had risked losing me in order to assure that I wasn't left alone in this world.

I looked at him with renewed admiration for the caring man he was. "Dad—" I said. But nothing more would come out of my clogged throat.

It was enough of a pronouncement for him. His face gave off light and his smile was oceans wide.

15

THAT EVENING, I paced the living room in my apartment as furiously as a hamster on a treadmill. I was relieved to have made peace with myself regarding my feelings for my dad, but still my emotions churned because of issues unresolved. Finally, having worked myself into a sweaty state of agitation, I picked up the phone and dialed Tamara Adberry's home number. When she answered, I told her in a gush of speech about my father's latest surgery. "I thought you'd want to know," I said, pausing only then to catch my breath.

"Yes," she said, "thank you. We'll keep him in our prayers."

We both fell silent then, and the longer the silence lasted, the more desperate I became to reach out to this woman. I clutched the phone in my hand like a child holding fast to her mother's skirt for fear of losing her in a crowd. In time, I found my voice again. "Basketball season will be starting in a few months."

"Yes."

"I suppose you'll be attending as many Ducks games as you can." There was unmistakable pride in her tone as she responded. "Brent hopes to be a starter this year."

I took a deep breath and held it so long I began to feel faint. "Would you mind if I came to some of the games?"

It seemed like forever before Tamara gave her reply. "I hope you will."

I LAY IN BED in the dark, staring up at an array of shimmering lights. A previous tenant had pasted tiny glow stickers on the bedroom ceiling, so that glimpsing up at night, one had the distinct impression of lying outdoors under a starry sky. I gazed up at the faux heavens and thought about my other mother, Margaret Trouste. How much did she really know about the night I was born and presented to her as *her* child? I considered the possibility of pursuing an answer to that question. I could research the history of donations made by the Trouste Foundation to find out how and when the original grant to the home for teen moms in Coos Bay had come about. I could question former Foundation board members about my mother's role in the matter. I could shake down Lance McKinney for what he knew. Not one penny of the company's money was spent without his knowledge. Or—I could simply ask Tamara. I was sure she knew.

In the end, I decided to do none of these things. I decided simply to let the matter go. It was, I concluded, a relic of the past I was better off leaving buried. Mother may have known much more about the night I was born than she'd ever let on. And for that she may have felt the need to seek atonement.

But how could any of that matter now? In our own way, we all must face up to our past. What was important to me now was how I faced up to mine. And I was happy to say that, for the first time in years, I had a good feeling about that. After all, I had the one thing I'd ever really wanted—the love and support of family.

I let my eyes wander among the pretend stars and soon fell into a deep and dreamless sleep. ❧

About the Author

B K MAYO LIVES in an area of southwestern Oregon known as the Hundred Valleys of the Umpqua.